Congressional Elections

CONGRESSIONAL ELECTIONS

Campaigning at Home and in Washington

Fifth Edition

Paul S. Herrnson
UNIVERSITY OF MARYLAND

CQ PRESS

A Division of Congressional Quarterly Inc.
Washington, D.C.

CQ Press
1255 22nd Street, NW, Suite 400
Washington, DC 20037

Phone: 202-729-1900; toll-free, 1-866-4CQ-PRESS (1-866-427-7737)

Web: www.cqpress.com

Cover design: Mike Grove, MG Design
Composition: Auburn Associates, Inc.

∞ The paper used in this publication exceeds the requirements of the American National Standard for Information Sciences—Permanence of Paper for Printed Library Materials, ANSI Z39.48-1992.

Printed and bound in the United States of America

11 10 09 08 07   1 2 3 4 5

Library of Congress Cataloging-in-Publication Data

Herrnson, Paul S.
    Congressional elections : campaigning at home and in Washington / Paul S. Herrnson. — 5th ed.
        p. cm.
    Includes bibliographical references and index.
    ISBN 978-0-87289-338-2 (alk. paper)
    1. United States. Congress—Elections. 2. Political campaigns—United States. 3. Campaign funds—United States. 4. Political action committees—United States. I. Title.

    JK1976.H47 2008
    324.973′0931—dc22

                                                          2007039007

In Memory of
Harry Perlman

Contents

Tables and Figures

Figures

Preface

The 2006 congressional elections bore witness to a number of exciting developments in campaign politics. In the technological arena, the use of the Internet became more widespread, as virtually every general election House and Senate campaign launched its own web site. In the realm of political strategy, members of the Democratic Party turned tradition on its head by using party money and campaign assistance to broaden the field of competition over the course of the election season, rather than focus resources on fewer and fewer contests. And, in terms of results, Democratic candidates succeeded in defeating enough incumbents and winning enough open seats to take control of both the House and the Senate.

Each congressional election cycle unveils continuities and changes in the way congressional campaigns are conducted, and the 2006 cycle was no different. Writing this new edition of *Congressional Elections* gave me the opportunity not only to analyze in depth the 2006 House and Senate campaigns and election outcomes but also to gauge the far-reaching changes that have taken place in recent years. It has been my challenge in this edition to show how changes in congressional campaigns and the context in which they are waged are helping to shape an enduring but imperfect election system.

One of these changes involves the growth of independent, parallel, and coordinated campaigns. These party- and interest group–sponsored campaigns comprise massive efforts in election agenda setting, television and radio advertising, direct mail and phone banks, and grassroots mobilization, some of which are financed with soft money. Their importance in competitive House and Senate races cannot be overstated.

The increasing complexity of interest group participation constitutes a second area of transformation. Groups have created a veritable alphabet soup of legal entities for the purpose of carrying out a variety of political functions designed to influence elections. Political action committees, 501(c) organizations, and 527 committees—defined by different provisions of federal law—offer different organizational advantages, such as the ability to contribute directly to congressional campaigns, to collect tax-deductible donations, to claim tax-exempt status, or to raise and spend soft money.

The coming-of-age of Internet campaigning builds on a trend begun only a short time ago. Nevertheless, by 2006 most major-party congressional candidates used the Internet to raise money, introduce themselves to voters, communicate their messages, and recruit volunteers. Some campaign web sites featured online chat rooms that supporters could use to voice their opinions, plan "meet-ups," and encourage the "viral" campaigning first introduced by Democratic National Committee chair Howard Dean during his 2004 presidential nomination campaign.

A final development I discuss in this edition involves the impact of the Bipartisan Campaign Reform Act of 2002, which was designed to close many of the loopholes commonly exploited in the campaign system. Its ban on party soft money, restrictions on issue advocacy advertising, and increased contribution limits promised to have a major impact on the ways in which campaigns were financed and waged. Although the law had profound effects on some aspects of campaign finance, it did not signal the death knell of political parties nor did it result in interest groups coming to dominate congressional campaigns, as some had predicted. Rather, campaigns remain candidate centered, and incumbents' advantages in fundraising persist. This is likely to remain the case, even though following the 2006 election the U.S. Supreme Court overturned some aspects of the law concerned with interest group issue advocacy advertising.

My focus on these developments characterizes this revision, but the fifth edition of *Congressional Elections* remains a comprehensive text about congressional elections and their implications for Congress and, more generally, for American government. Most congressional elections are contests between candidates who have vastly unequal chances of victory. Incumbents generally win not only because of their own efforts but also because of the catch-22 situation in which many challengers find themselves. Without name recognition, challengers have trouble raising funds, and without funds they cannot enhance their name recognition or attract enough support to run a competitive race. This conundrum hints at a fundamental truth of congressional elections: candidates wage two campaigns—one for votes and another for money and other resources. The former takes place in the candidate's district or state. The latter is conducted primarily in Washington, D.C.—where many political consultants; PACs; interest groups; and the parties' national, senatorial, and congressional campaign committees are located. The timing of the two campaigns overlaps considerably, but candidates and their organizations must conceptualize them as separate and plot a different strategy for each.

Although congressional election campaigns are the main focus of this book, voters, candidates, party committees, and interest groups receive considerable attention. The influence of these individuals and groups on election outcomes also receives substantial coverage. I conclude that the norms and expectations associated with congressional campaigns affect who runs, the kinds of organizations the candidates assemble, how much money they raise, the types of party and interest group support they attract, the strategies and communication techniques they use, and, ultimately, whether they win or lose. Incumbents are the major beneficiaries of the congressional election system, but the system constrains their reelection campaigns, as it does the efforts of challengers and candidates for open seats.

The need to campaign for votes and resources affects how members of Congress carry out their legislative responsibilities and the types of reforms they are willing to consider. These observations may seem intuitive, but they are rarely discussed in studies of voting behavior and are usually overlooked in research that focuses on the role of money in politics. Given their importance, it is unfortunate that congressional campaigns have not received more attention in the scholarly literature.

Throughout this book, I systematically analyze empirical evidence collected from candidates, consultants, parties, and interest groups that have participated in congressional elections since the early 1990s. The analysis in this edition is based primarily on interviews with and questionnaires from hundreds of House and Senate candidates and other political insiders who participated in the elections. It also relies on campaign finance data furnished by the Federal Election Commission, the Center for Responsive Politics, and Political Money Line; public opinion data collected in the American National Election Study and the Cooperative Congressional Election Study; and data about Internet web sites collected by Team E-Voter at the University of Maryland. Memoranda and interviews provided by campaign organizations, party committees, PACs, and other interest groups further contributed to the study. Generalizations derived from the analysis are supported with concrete—and what I hope are lively—examples from case studies of individual campaigns.

The analysis also draws insights from my own participation in congressional campaigns and from the questionnaires and interviews provided by the more than twelve hundred candidates and campaign aides who have contributed information and data for past editions. I hope the evidence presented convinces readers that the campaigns candidates wage at home for votes, and in Washington for money and campaign assistance, significantly affect the outcomes of congressional elections. My analysis of these sources also leads to the conclusion that the activities of party committees, interest groups, campaign volunteers, and journalists also are important.

This book gives students of politics a powerful tool to help them think about campaigns, elections, and their own political involvement. Professors using the book as a classroom text might be interested in reviewing the questionnaires I used to collect information from congressional campaigns. Students in my seminars found them valuable in guiding their field research on campaigns. The questionnaires, my syllabus, class assignments and other course materials, links to Internet resources, and methodological background information are all available on the book's companion web site (http://herrnson.cqpress.com) and on my personal web site (www.bsos.umd.edu/gvpt/herrnson/congels.html).

ACKNOWLEDGMENTS

The publication of *Congressional Elections* would not have been possible without the cooperation of many individuals and institutions. I am indebted to the hundreds of people who consented to be interviewed, completed questionnaires, or shared election targeting lists and other campaign materials with me. Their participation in this project was essential to its success.

The Center for American Politics and Citizenship at the University of Maryland provided a stimulating and productive environment in which to work. Virtually every member of the center participated in some aspect of the project. The data collection, data entry, statistical analysis, case study research, and writing proceeded smoothly because of the efforts of Elizabeth Bentley-Smith, Dawn Bowe, Kenneth Coriale, James Curry, Ozan Kalkan, Danielle Kogut, Amanda Lee, and Kelly Zavala. Chris Bailey, William Bianco, Robert Biersack, James Gimpel, John Green, Thomas Kazee, Sandy Maisel, Kelly Patterson, Stephen Salmore, Frank Sorauf, James Thurber, Ric Uslaner, and Clyde Wilcox made helpful comments on earlier editions of the book. Anthony Corrado, Colby College; Rogan Kersh, New York University; Jonathan Krasno, Binghamton University; and Antoine Yoshinaka, University of California–Riverside; made valuable suggestions for this edition. At CQ Press Dwain Smith and Erin Snow played vital roles in preparing the manuscript and cover copy, as did editors Nancy Geltman, Kerry Kern, and Mary Marik. I am delighted to have the opportunity to express my deepest appreciation to all of them. I am especially pleased to put into writing my gratitude to my wife for her love and support.

Finally, a few words are in order about the person to whom this book is dedicated. My uncle, Harry Perlman, did not live to see the completion of this book, but his contributions to it were critical. The construction jobs he gave me were the most important form of financial aid I received while pursuing my college education. His ideas about politics and philosophy helped me to appreciate the virtues of democratically held elections and to recognize the inferiority of other means of conferring political power. His unwavering belief that people can be taught to value what is good about their political system and to recognize its shortcomings was a source of inspiration that helped me complete the first edition of this book, and it continues to inspire me today.

Introduction

Elections are the centerpiece of democracy. They are the means Americans use to choose their political leaders, and they give those who have been elected the authority to rule. Elections also furnish the American people with a vehicle for expressing their views about the directions they think this rule ought to take. In theory, elections are the principal mechanism for ensuring "government of the people, by the people, for the people."[1]

An examination of the different aspects of the electoral process provides insights into the operations of the U.S. political system. Separate balloting for congressional, state, and local candidates results in legislators who represent parochial interests, sometimes to the detriment of the formation of national policy. Private financing of congressional campaigns, which is consistent with Americans' belief in capitalism, favors incumbents and increases the political access of wealthy and well-organized segments of society. Participatory primaries and caucuses, which require congressional aspirants to assemble an organization in order to campaign for the nomination, lead candidates to rely on political consultants rather than on party committees for assistance in winning their party's nomination and the general election. These factors encourage congressional candidates and members of Congress to act more independently of party leaders than do their counterparts in other democracies.

Congressional elections are affected by perceptions of the performance of government. Americans' satisfaction with the state of the economy, the nation's foreign policy and security, as well as their own standard of living provides a backdrop for elections and a means for assessing whether presidents, individual representatives, and Congress as an institution have performed their jobs adequately. Issues related to the internal operations of Congress—such as the perquisites enjoyed by members—can affect congressional elections.

Conversely, congressional elections can greatly affect the internal operations of Congress, the performance of government, and the direction of domestic and foreign policy. Major political reforms and policy reversals generally follow elections in which substantial turnover has occurred.

One of the major themes developed in this book is that campaigns matter a great deal to the outcome of congressional elections. National conditions are significant, but their impact on elections is secondary to the decisions and actions of candidates, campaign organizations, party committees, organized interests, and other individuals and groups. This comes as no surprise to those who toil in campaigns, but it is in direct contrast to what many scholars would argue.

To win a congressional election or even to be remotely competitive, candidates must compete in two campaigns: one for votes and one for resources. The campaign for votes is the campaign that generally comes to mind when people think about elections. It requires a candidate to assemble an organization and to use that organization to target key groups of voters, select a message they will find compelling, communicate that message, and convince supporters to go to the polls on election day.

The other campaign, which is based largely in Washington, D.C., requires candidates to convince the party operatives, interest group officials, political consultants, and journalists who play leading roles in the nation's political community that their races will be competitive and worthy of support. Gaining the backing of these various individuals is a critical step in attracting the money and campaign services that are available in the nation's capital and in other wealthy urban centers. These resources enable the candidate to run a credible campaign back home. Without them, most congressional candidates would lose their bids for election.

In this book I present a systematic assessment of congressional election campaigns that draws on information from a wide variety of sources. Background information on the roughly 20,000 major-party contestants who ran between 1978 and 2006 furnished insights into the types of individuals who try to win a seat in Congress and the conditions under which they run. Personal interviews and survey data provided by about 1,200 candidates and campaign aides who were involved in the House or Senate elections held between 1992 and 2006 permitted analysis of the organization, strategies, tactics, issues, and communications techniques used in congressional campaigns. They also provided insights into the roles that political parties, political action committees (PACs), and other groups play in those contests.

Case studies of campaigns conducted in the 2006 elections are interwoven throughout the book to illustrate with concrete examples the generalizations drawn from the larger sample. These include some typical elections, such as

Republican representative Wally Herger's 33-percentage-point victory over A. J. Sekhon in California's 2nd congressional district. They also include a few unusual contests, such as Democratic challenger Heath Shuler's victory over eight-term GOP representative Charles Taylor in North Carolina's 11th district; Democratic open-seat candidate Ed Perlmutter's win over Republican Rick O'Donnell in the GOP-held 7th district in Colorado; and the Senate contest in Ohio in which Democratic House member Sherrod Brown defeated two-term Republican incumbent Mike DeWine. The latter three contests are noteworthy because of the focus that the political parties and many interest groups placed on them. These races also highlight the importance of money and assembling a professional campaign organization in congressional elections.

Some races are included because they illustrate the role of scandal or negative campaigning. Four-term incumbent Don Sherwood, Republican of Pennsylvania, lost his 10th district general election contest to Democratic challenger Christopher Carney largely as a result of a scandal in which Sherwood allegedly physically assaulted his mistress. Mudslinging and personal attacks by the candidates, parties, and interest groups were a prominent feature of the donnybrook in Tennessee, where Republican Chattanooga mayor Bob Corker defeated Democratic representative Harold Ford Jr. in an open-seat race for the Senate. Other elections, such as Katherine Harris's bid for a Senate seat in Florida, demonstrate the limits of party influence in candidate recruitment and the impact organizational disarray can have on a campaign.

Most of the discussion focuses on House candidates and campaigns because they are easier to generalize about than Senate contests. Differences in the sizes, populations, and political traditions of the fifty states and the fact that only about one-third of all Senate seats are filled in a given election year make campaigns for the upper chamber more difficult to discuss in general terms. Larger, more diverse Senate constituencies also make Senate elections less predictable than House contests. Nevertheless, insights can be gained into campaigns for the upper chamber by contrasting them with those waged for the House.

Interviews with party officials, conducted over the course of the 1992 through 2006 elections, give insights into the strategies used by the Democratic and Republican national, congressional, and senatorial campaign committees. Similar information provided by a representative group of interest group leaders is used to learn about the strategies that PACs use to guide their contributions and independent expenditures and that advocacy organizations use to determine their endorsements, issue advocacy, and grassroots mobilization efforts. Campaign contribution and spending data furnished by the Federal Election Commission (FEC), the Center for Responsive Politics, and

Political Money Line are used to examine the role of money in politics. Web sites, newspapers, media releases, and advertising materials distributed by candidates, parties, and interest groups furnish examples of the communications that campaigns disseminate. Public opinion surveys provide insights into voters' priorities and the roles of issues. Surveys of individual campaign contributors furnish similar insights into their opinions and motives. Collectively these sources of information, along with scholarly accounts published in the political science literature and insights drawn from my own participation in congressional and campaign politics, have permitted a comprehensive portrayal of contemporary congressional election campaigns.

In the first five chapters I examine the strategic context in which congressional election campaigns are waged and the major actors that participate in those contests. Chapter 1 provides an overview of the institutions, laws, party rules, and customs that constitute the framework for congressional elections. The framework has a significant impact on who decides to run for Congress; the resources that candidates, parties, and interest groups bring to bear on the campaign; the strategies they use; and who ultimately wins a seat in Congress. The chapter also focuses on the setting for the congressional elections held since the 1990s, with special emphasis on 2006.

Chapter 2 contains a discussion of candidates and nominations. I examine the influence of incumbency, redistricting, national conditions, and the personal and career situations of potential candidates on the decision to run for Congress. I also assess the separate contributions that the decision to run, the nomination process, and the general election make toward producing a Congress that is overwhelmingly white, male, middle-aged, and drawn from the legal, business, and public service professions.

The organizations that congressional candidates assemble to wage their election campaigns are the subject of Chapter 3. Salaried staff and political consultants form the core of most competitive candidates' campaign teams. These professionals play a critical role in formulating strategy, gauging public opinion, fundraising, designing communications, and mobilizing voters.

Political parties and interest groups—the major organizations that help finance elections and provide candidates with important campaign resources—are the subjects of the next two chapters. Chapter 4 includes an analysis of the goals, decision-making processes, and election activities of party committees. I discuss many recent innovations, including party "independent," "parallel," and "coordinated" campaigns. In Chapter 5 I concentrate on the goals, strategies, and election efforts of PACs and other interest group organizations. Among the innovations covered are business- and union-sponsored issue advocacy ads and the political activity of groups that enjoy tax-exempt status.

In Chapter 6 I examine the fundraising process from the candidate's point of view. The campaign for resources requires a candidate to formulate strategies for raising money from individuals and groups in the candidate's own state, in Washington, D.C., and in the nation's other major political and economic centers. It is clear from Chapters 4, 5, and 6 that Washington-based elites have a disproportionate effect on the conduct of congressional elections.

In Chapters 7 through 9 I concentrate on the campaign for votes. A discussion of voters, campaign targeting, issues, and other elements of strategy makes up Chapter 7. Campaign communications, including television, radio, the Internet, direct mail, and field work, are the focus of Chapter 8. The subject of winners and losers is taken up in Chapter 9, in which I analyze what does and does not work in congressional campaigns.

In Chapter 10 I address the effects of elections on the activities of individual legislators and on Congress as an institution, including the collective impact that individual elections have on the policy-making process and substantive policy outcomes. Finally, Chapter 11 examines the highly charged topic of campaign reform. In it, I recommend specific reforms and discuss the obstacles that had to be overcome in order to pass the Bipartisan Campaign Reform Act of 2002 (BCRA; also referred to as the McCain-Feingold Act, after its Senate sponsors) and the challenges—legal and otherwise—that threatened to undermine its implementation.

CHAPTER ONE

The Strategic Context

Congressional elections, and elections in the United States in general, are centered more on the candidates than are elections in other modern industrialized democracies. Why is this the case, and how does it affect the conduct of congressional elections? In this chapter I discuss the candidate-centered U.S. election system and explain how the Constitution, election laws, and the political parties form the system's institutional framework. I also explain how the nation's political culture and recent developments in technology have helped this system flourish.

Also covered is the influence of the political setting in a given election year on electoral competition and turnover in Congress. The political setting includes some predictable factors such as the decennial redrawing of House districts; some highly likely occurrences such as the wide-scale reelection of incumbents; and transient, less predictable phenomena such as congressional scandals and catastrophic acts of nature or terrorism. These features of the political setting affect the expectations and behavior of potential congressional candidates, the individuals who actually run for Congress, political contributors, and voters.

THE CANDIDATE-CENTERED CAMPAIGN

Candidates, not political parties, are the major focus of congressional campaigns, and candidates, not parties, bear the ultimate responsibility for election outcomes. These characteristics of congressional elections are striking when viewed from a comparative perspective. In most democracies, political parties are the principal contestants in elections, and campaigns focus on national issues, ideology, and party programs and accomplishments. In the United States, parties do not run congressional campaigns nor do they become the major focus of elections. Instead, candidates run their own campaigns, and parties contribute money or election services to some of them. Parties also may advertise or mobilize voters on behalf of candidates. A comparison of the terminology commonly used to describe elections in the United States with that used in Great Britain more than hints at the differences. In the United States, candidates are said to *run* for Congress, and they do so with or without party help. In Britain, by contrast, candidates are said to *stand* for election to Parliament, and their party runs most of the campaign. The difference in terminology only slightly oversimplifies reality.

Unlike candidates for national legislatures in most other democracies, U.S. congressional candidates are self-selected rather than recruited by party organizations.[1] Candidates must win the right to run under their party's label through a participatory primary, caucus, or convention, or by scaring off all opposition. Only after they have secured their party's nomination are major-party candidates assured a place on the general election ballot. Until then, few candidates receive significant party assistance. Independent and minor-party candidates can get on the ballot in other ways, usually by paying a registration fee or collecting several thousand signatures from district residents.

The nomination process in most other countries, alternatively, begins with a small group of party activists pursuing the nomination through a "closed" process that allows only formal, dues-paying party members to select the candidate.[2] Whereas the American system amplifies the input of primary voters, and in a few states caucus participants, these other systems respond more to the input of local party members and place more emphasis on peer review.

The need to win a party nomination forces congressional candidates to assemble their own campaign organizations, formulate their own election strategies, and conduct their own campaigns. The images and issues they convey to voters in trying to win the nomination carry over to the general election. The efforts of individual candidates and their campaign organizations typically have a larger impact on election outcomes than do the activities of party organizations and other groups.

The candidate-centered nature of congressional elections has evolved in recent years as political parties and interest groups, including many based in Washington, D.C., have used independent expenditures, so-called issue advocacy advertisements, and sophisticated voter targeting and outreach efforts to communicate with and mobilize voters in competitive races. However, the basic structure of the system remains intact. That structure has a major impact on virtually every aspect of campaigning, including who decides to run, the types of election strategies the candidates employ, and the resources available to them. It affects the decisions and activities of party organizations, political action committees, other interest groups, and journalists. It also has a major influence on how citizens make their voting decisions and on the activities that successful candidates carry out once they are elected to Congress. Finally, the candidate-centered nature of the congressional election system affects the election reforms that those in power are willing to consider.

THE INSTITUTIONAL FRAMEWORK

In designing a government to prevent the majority from depriving the minority of its rights, the framers of the Constitution created a system of checks and balances to prevent any one official or element of society from amassing too much power. Three key features of the framers' blueprint have profoundly influenced congressional elections: the separation of powers, bicameralism, and federalism. These aspects of the Constitution require that candidates for the House of Representatives, Senate, and presidency be chosen by different methods and constituencies. House members were and continue to be elected directly by the people. Senators were originally chosen by their state legislatures but have been selected in statewide elections since the passage of the Seventeenth Amendment in 1913. Presidents have always been selected through the electoral college. The means for filling state and local offices were omitted from the Constitution, but candidates for these positions were and continue to be elected independently of members of Congress.

Holding elections for individual offices separates the political fortunes of members of Congress from one another and from other officials. A candidate for the House can win during an election year in which his or her party suffers a landslide defeat in the race for the presidency; experiences severe losses in the House or Senate; or finds itself surrendering its hold over neighboring congressional districts, the state legislature, the governor's mansion, and various local offices. The system encourages House, Senate, state, and local candidates to communicate issues and themes that they perceive to be popular in their districts even when these messages differ from those advocated by their party's leader. The system does little to encourage teamwork in campaigning or governance. In 2006 a considerable number of Republican candidates distanced themselves from the Republican president, George W. Bush, whose popularity and job approval ratings had reached historic lows for both his presidency and U.S. presidents in general. Several vehemently opposed the president's proposals to privatize part of the Social Security system, allow illegal immigrants to get temporary work permits, and ban funding for stem cell research. Such opposition would be considered unacceptable under a parliamentary system of government with its party-focused elections, but it is entirely consistent with the expectations of the Constitution's framers. As James Madison wrote in *Federalist* no. 46,

> A local spirit will infallibly prevail . . . in the members of Congress. . . .
> Measures will too often be decided according to their probable effect, not on
> the national prosperity and happiness, but on the prejudices, interests, and
> pursuits of the governments and people of the individual States.

When congressional candidates differ from their party's presidential nominee or national platform on major issues, they seek political cover not only from the Constitution but also from state party platforms, local election manifestos, or fellow party members who have taken similar positions.

Of course, congressional candidates usually adopt issue positions held by other party candidates for the House, Senate, or presidency. In 1932 most Democrats embraced Franklin D. Roosevelt's call for an activist government to battle the Great Depression. In 2002, many Republican candidates followed the advice of White House senior adviser Karl Rove and made the war on terrorism and national security key components of their campaigns. Democratic candidates were encouraged by their party's leadership to run locally oriented campaigns that did not focus on the war. The Republicans added the war in Iraq to their list of issues in 2004. By the elections of 2006, public sentiment had shifted on the Iraq War, and a new set of issues, less favorable to the GOP, took center stage on the political agenda; these included the administration's failure to respond effectively to the aftermath of Hurricane Katrina, a stalled immigration policy, rising energy prices, and a range of scandals involving Republican politicians. Thus, the Democrats were presented with an opportunity to campaign on national issues and the Republicans had strong incentives to focus on local matters.

Federal and state laws further contribute to the candidate-centered nature of congressional elections. Originally, federal law regulated few aspects of congressional elections, designating only the number of representatives a state was entitled to elect. States held congressional elections at different times, used different methods of election, and set different qualifications for voters. Some states used multimember at-large districts, a practice that awarded each party a share of congressional seats proportional to its share of the statewide popular vote; others elected their House members in odd years, which minimized the ability of presidential candidates to pull House candidates of their own party into office on their coattails. The financing of congressional campaigns also went virtually unregulated for most of the nation's history.

Over the years, Congress and the states passed legislation governing the election of House members that further reinforced the candidate-centered nature of congressional elections at the expense of parties. The creation of geographically defined, single-member, winner-take-all congressional districts was particularly important in this regard. These districts, which were mandated by the Apportionment Act of 1842, encouraged individual candidates to build locally based coalitions. Such districts gave no rewards to candidates who came in second, even if their party performed well throughout the state or in neighboring districts.[3] Thus, candidates of the same party had little incentive to work together or to run a party-focused campaign. Under the multimember district or general ticket systems that existed in some states prior to the act—and that continue to be used in most European nations—members of parties that finish lower than first place may receive seats in the legislature. Candidates have strong incentives to run cooperative, party-focused campaigns under these systems because their electoral fortunes are bound together.

The timing of congressional elections also helps to produce a candidate-centered system. Because the dates are fixed, with House elections scheduled biennially and roughly one-third of the Senate up for election every two years, many elections are held when there is no burning issue on the national agenda. Without a salient national issue to capture the voters' attention, House and Senate candidates base their campaigns on local issues or on their personal qualifications for holding office. On one hand, incumbents stress their experience, the services they provide to constituents, or their seniority. Challengers, on the other hand, attack their opponents for casting congressional roll-call votes that are out of sync with the views of local voters, for pandering to special interests, or for "being part of the problem in Washington." Open-seat races focus mainly on local issues, the candidates' political experience, or character issues.

In contrast, systems that do not have fixed election dates, including most of those in western Europe, tend to hold elections that are more national in focus and centered on political parties. The rules regulating national elections in those systems require that elections be held within a set time frame, but the exact date is left open. Elections may be called by the party in power at a time of relative prosperity, when it is confident that it can maintain or enlarge its parliamentary majority. Elections also may be called when a burning issue divides the nation and the party in power is forced to call a snap election because its members in parliament are unable to agree on a policy for dealing with the crisis. In contrast to congressional elections, which are often referenda on the performance of individual officeholders and their abilities to meet local concerns, these elections focus on national conditions and the performance of the party in power.

Because the boundaries of congressional districts rarely match those for statewide or local offices and because terms for the House, the Senate, and many state and local offices differ from one another, a party's candidates often lack incentives to work together. House candidates consider the performance of their party's candidates statewide or in neighboring districts to be a secondary concern, just as the election of House candidates is usually not of primary importance to candidates for state or local office. Differences in election boundaries and timing also encourage a sense of parochialism in party officials similar to that of their candidates. Cooperation among party organizations can be achieved only by persuading local, state, and national party leaders that it is in their mutual best interest. Cooperation is often heightened during presidential election years, when elections for many offices occur and the presidential contest dominates the political agenda and boosts voter turnout. Elections that precede or follow the decennial taking of the census also are characterized by increased cooperation because politicians at many levels of government focus on the imminent redrawing of election districts or on preserving or wresting control of new districts or those that have been significantly altered.

Although the seeds for candidate-centered congressional election campaigns were sown by the Constitution and election laws, not until the middle of the twentieth century did the candidate-centered system firmly take root. Prior to the emergence of this system, during a period often called the "golden age" of political parties, party organizations played a major role in most election campaigns, including many campaigns for Congress. Local party organizations, often referred to as old-fashioned political machines, had control over the nomination process, possessed a near monopoly over the resources needed to organize the electorate, and provided the symbolic cues that informed the electoral decisions of most voters.[4] The key to their success was their ability to command the loyalties of large numbers of individuals, many of whom were able to persuade friends and neighbors to support their party's candidates. Not until the demise of the old-fashioned machine and the emergence of new campaign technology did the modern candidate-centered system finally blossom.

Reforms intended to weaken political machines played a major role in the development of the candidate-centered system. One such reform was the adoption of the Australian ballot by roughly three-quarters of the states between 1888 and 1896.[5] This government-printed ballot listed every candidate for each office and allowed individuals to cast their votes in secret, away from the prying eyes of party officials. The Australian ballot replaced a system of voting in which each party supplied supporters with its own easily identifiable ballot that included only the names of the party's candidates. The Australian ballot, by ensuring secrecy and simplifying split-ticket voting, made it easy for citizens to focus on candidates rather than parties when voting. This type of ballot remains in use today.

State-regulated primary nominating contests, which were widely adopted during the Progressive movement of the early 1900s, deprived party leaders of the power to handpick congressional nominees and gave that power to voters who participated in their party's nominating election.[6] The merit-based civil service system, another progressive reform, deprived the parties of patronage. No longer able to distribute government jobs or contracts, the parties had difficulty maintaining large corps of campaign workers.[7] Issues, friendships, the excitement of politics, and other noneconomic incentives could motivate small numbers of people to become active in party politics, but they could not motivate enough people to support a party-focused system of congressional elections.

Congressional candidates also lacked the patronage or government contracts needed to attract large numbers of volunteer workers or to persuade other candidates to help them with their campaigns. By the mid-twentieth century the "isolation" of congressional candidates from one another and from their party organizations was so complete that a major report on the state of political parties characterized congressional candidates as the "orphans of the political system." The report, published by the American Political Science Association's Committee on Political Parties, went on to point out that congressional candidates "had no truly adequate party mechanism available for the conduct of their campaigns ... enjoy[ed] remarkably little national or local support, [and] have mostly been left to cope with the political hazards of their occupation on their own."[8]

Voter registration and get-out-the-vote drives and redistricting were about the only areas of election politics in which there was, and remains, extensive cooperation among groups of candidates and party committees. But even here the integration of different party committees and candidate organizations—and especially those involved in congressional elections—was and continues to be short of that exhibited in other democracies.

The Bipartisan Campaign Reform Act of 2002, the Federal Election Campaign Act that preceded it, and the regulatory rulings and court verdicts that have shaped federal campaign finance law have further reinforced the pattern of candidate-centered congressional elections.[9] The BCRA places strict limits on the amount of money parties can contribute to or spend in coordination with their congressional candidates' campaigns (see Tables 1-1 and 1-2). The law does allow parties to make unlimited issue advocacy expenditures ninety days prior to a primary or the general election and unlimited independent expenditures at any time, but both types of expenditures are strictly regulated: issue advocacy expenditures *cannot explicitly* call for a candidate's

TABLE 1-1
Federal Contribution Limits to Congressional Candidates and Political Parties

Donors or spenders	House candidates	Senate candidates	National party committees	State party committees' federal accounts	Federal PACs
Individuals	$2,000	$2,000	$25,000 per year	$10,000 per year	$5,000 per year
National party committees	$15,000	$35,000	Unlimited transfers to other party committees	Unlimited transfers to other party committees	$5,000 per year
State party committees' federal accounts	$5,000	$5,000	Unlimited transfers to other party committees	Unlimited transfers to other party committees	$5,000 per year
Federal PACs	$5,000	$5,000 per year	$15,000 per year	$5,000 per year	$5,000 per year
Corporations and unions	Prohibited	Prohibited	Prohibited	Prohibited	Prohibited
Section 527 committees	Prohibited	Prohibited	Prohibited	Prohibited	Prohibited
501(c)(4), 501(c)(6) and nonprofit social welfare organizations	Prohibited	Prohibited	Prohibited	Prohibited	Prohibited

Sources: Adapted from "Contribution Limits," Federal Election Commission, www.fec.gov; and "The Campaign Finance Guide," Campaign Legal Center, Washington, D.C., 2004, www.campaignfinanceguide.org/guide-29.html.

Notes: Individuals may contribute $2,000 in each phase of the election (primary, general, and runoff). They are limited to biennial contributions of $95,000 ($37,500 to all federal candidates and $57,500 to all party committees and PACs). The limits for individual contributions to candidates and national party committees, the biennial individual limit, and the national party committee limit for contributions to Senate candidates are indexed for inflation. In the event the millionaire's amendment is triggered, the limits for individual contributions increase. The parties' national, congressional, and senatorial campaign committees are considered separate committees for the purpose of making contributions to House candidates, so each contributor can contribute up to $5,000 to each committee, for a total of $15,000.

election or defeat, and independent expenditures must be made without the knowledge or consent of the candidate or anyone involved with the candidate's campaign, including consultants or party staff assisting the candidate. Further provisions of the law that limit the parties' involvement in congressional elections place ceilings on contributions from individuals to national party committees and an outright ban on parties accepting contributions from corporation, union, and trade association treasuries.[10] Moreover, the BCRA provides no subsidies for party research or other activities, including generic, party-focused campaign efforts. The two exceptions to this rule are the meager federal subsidies the parties receive to help finance their presidential nominating conventions and their eligibility for discount bulk postage—a subsidy available to all nonprofit organizations.

The law's provisions for political parties stand in marked contrast to the treatment given to parties in other democracies. Most of these countries provide subsidies to parties for campaign and interelection activities.[11] The United States is the only democracy in which parties are not given free television and radio time.[12] The support that other democracies give to parties is consistent with the central role they play in elections, government, and society, just as the lack of assistance afforded to American parties is consistent with the candidate-centered system that has developed in the United States.

Lacking independent sources of revenue, local party organizations are unable to play a dominant role in the modern cash-based system of congressional campaign politics.[13] The national and state party committees that survived the reform movements and changes in federal election laws lack sufficient funds or staff to dominate campaign politics. Perhaps even more important, party leaders have little desire to do so in most cases. For the most part, they believe a party should bolster its candidates' campaigns, not replace them with a campaign of its own.[14]

The availability of campaign support from interest groups also has limited the electoral influence of American political parties relative to their counterparts in other democracies and helped to foster candidate-centered congressional elections. Federally registered PACs, which numbered about 4,600 during the 2006 elections, provide candidates with sources of financial support other than political parties. Labor unions, trade associations, and nonprofit groups also have stepped up their efforts to influence congressional and other elections. Some of these groups, classified as 501(c) organizations, and 527 committees in the federal tax code, do not pay taxes because they purportedly exist for charitable, educational, or other civic purposes rather than to earn profits. In recent years, some tax-exempt groups have boosted their influence by spending millions of dollars in "soft money," which technically

TABLE 1-2
Federal Spending Limits in Congressional Elections

| | Coordinated expenditures on behalf of candidates | | Independent expenditures | Other expenditures | |
	House candidates	Senate candidates		Electioneering communications	Levin funds
Individuals	Considered a contribution	Considered a contribution	Unlimited	Unlimited	Whatever state law permits, up to $10,000
National party committees	$10,000	$20,000 or $.02 times a state's voting age population, whichever is greater	Unlimited	Unlimited	Prohibited
State party committees' federal accounts	$10,000	$20,000 or $.02 times a state's voting age population, whichever is greater	Unlimited	Unlimited	Prohibited
Federal PACs	Considered a contribution	Considered a contribution	Unlimited	Unlimited	Whatever state law permits, up to $10,000

(Table continues)

TABLE 1-2 (continued)

	Coordinated expenditures on behalf of candidates		Other expenditures		
	House candidates	Senate candidates	Independent expenditures	Electioneering communications	Levin funds
Corporations and unions	Prohibited	Prohibited	Prohibited	Prohibited	Whatever state law permits, up to $10,000
Section 527 committees	Prohibited	Prohibited	Prohibited if committee is incorporated	Prohibited if committee is incorporated. If not incorporated, unlimited	Whatever state law permits, up to $10,000
501(c)(4), 501(c)(6), and nonprofit social welfare organizations	Prohibited	Prohibited	Prohibited except for qualifying 501(c)(4) and nonprofit social welfare organizations	Prohibited except for qualifying 501(c)(4) and nonprofit social welfare organizations	$10,000 if permitted by state law

Sources: Adapted from "Contribution Limits," Federal Election Commission, www.fec.gov/; and "The Campaign Finance Guide," Campaign Legal Center, Washington, D.C., 2004, www.campaignfinanceguide.org/guide-29.html.

Notes: The limits for party coordinated expenditures in House and Senate elections are indexed for inflation. The limit for House elections in 2006 was $39,600 each for all national party committees and for state party committees, except for states with only one representative, in which case the limit was $79,200. The limit for Senate elections in 2006 ranged from $79,200 for all national party committees and for state party committees for the smallest states to $2,093,800 for all national party committees and for state party committees in California. If the millionaires' provision is triggered, the limits for coordinated expenditures in both House and Senate elections increase.

is raised and spent outside of the federal campaign finance system to finance activities intended to influence federal elections. Among the groups that spend soft money are the Club for Growth, an anti-tax group that supports Republican candidates who favor free-market economics; the League of Conservation Voters (LCV), an environmental group that supports mainly Democrats; and the Seniors Coalition, which is funded largely by U.S. pharmaceutical companies.[15] Although some of these organizations are allied with one party or the other, they all have their own goals, strategies, and independent decision-making processes. Because candidates can turn to so many interest group organizations for support, they do not need to depend heavily on any one of them nor do they need to turn exclusively to their political party for support.

The evolution of campaign finance law has created an environment that includes huge numbers of organizations and individual donors, but it has not fully ushered political parties to the periphery of congressional campaigns. Rather, party committees based in Washington, D.C., have adapted to the contemporary national economy of campaign finance. The individuals, PACs, and other organizations that are suppliers of campaign funds in this economy are primarily located in Washington, New York City, Los Angeles, and the nation's other wealthy population centers. The funds' recipients are candidates contesting House and Senate seats located across the country. They include both powerful incumbents and the small group of nonincumbents who are involved in close races in a typical election season. As will be discussed in Chapter 4, the parties have responded to the nationalization of the campaign finance system by becoming the major brokers or mediators between the financiers of congressional elections and the candidates who compete in them.

POLITICAL CULTURE

Historically, U.S. political culture has supported a system of candidate-centered congressional elections in many ways, but its major influence stems from its lack of foundation for a party-focused alternative. Americans have traditionally held a jaundiced view of political parties. *Federalist* no. 10 and President George Washington's farewell address are evidence that the framers of the Constitution and the first president thought a multitude of overlapping, wide-ranging interests preferable to class-based divisions represented by ideological parties. The founders designed the political system to encourage pragmatism and compromise in politics and thus to mitigate the harmful effects of factions. Although neither the pluralist system championed by the framers nor the nonpartisan system advocated by Washington has been fully realized, both visions of democracy have found expression in candidate-centered campaigns.

Congressional elections test candidates' abilities to build coalitions of voters and elites from diverse individuals. The multiplicity of overlapping interests, lack of a feudal legacy, and relatively fluid social and economic structure in the United States discourage the formation of class-based parties like those that have developed in most other democracies.[16] The consensus among Americans for liberty, equality, and property rights and their near-universal support for the political system further undermine the development of parties aimed at promoting major political, social, or economic change.[17]

Americans' traditional ambivalence about political parties has found expression during reform periods. The Populist movement of the 1890s, the Progressive movement that came shortly after it, and the rise of the New Left in the 1960s all resulted in political change that weakened the parties. Reformers at the turn of the twentieth century championed the Australian ballot, the direct primary, and civil service laws for the explicit purpose of taking power away from party bosses.[18] Similarly, the reform movement that took hold of the Democratic Party during the 1960s and 1970s opened party conventions, meetings, and leadership positions to the increased participation of previously underrepresented groups. The reforms, many of which were adopted by Republican as well as Democratic state party organizations, made both parties more permeable and responsive to pressures from grassroots activists. They weakened what little influence party leaders had over the awarding of nominations, thereby giving candidates, their supporters, and issue activists more influence over party affairs.[19]

Post–World War II social and cultural transformations undermined the parties even further. Declining immigration and increased geographic mobility eroded the working-class ethnic neighborhoods that were an important source of party loyalists. Increased educational levels encouraged citizens to rely more on their own judgment and less on party cues in political matters. The development of the mass media gave voters less-biased sources of information than the partisan press. The rise of interest groups, including PACs, and other forms of functional and ideological representation, created new arenas for political participation and new sources of political cues.[20] The aging of the parties, generational replacement, and the emergence of new issues that cut across existing fault lines led to the decline of party affiliation among voters and to more issue-oriented voting.[21] These developments encouraged voters to rely less on local party officials and opinion leaders for political information.[22] Cultural transformations created a void in electoral politics that individual candidates and their organizations came to fill.

Current attitudes toward the parties reflect the nation's historical experience. Survey research shows that most citizens believe that parties "do more to confuse the issues than to provide a clear choice on the issues," and "create conflict where none exists." Half of the population believes that parties make the political system less efficient and that "it would be better if, in all elections, we put no party labels on the ballot."[23]

Negative attitudes toward the parties are often learned at an early age. Many schoolchildren are routinely instructed to "vote for the best candidate, not the party." This lesson appears to stay with some of them into adulthood. Typically less than 10 percent of all registered voters maintain that the candidate's political party is the biggest factor in their vote decision. Candidates and issues rank higher.[24]

Although American history and culture extol the virtues of political independence and candidate-oriented voting, the electoral behavior of citizens provides an element of partisanship in congressional elections. Approximately two-thirds of all voters were willing to state that they identified with either the Democratic or the Republican Party in 2006, which is typical of the preceding two decades. About four-fifths of all self-identified independents indicate they lean toward a major party, holding attitudes and exhibiting political behaviors similar to those of self-identified partisans. Although few registered voters state that they cast their votes chiefly on a partisan basis, 72 percent of them cast their congressional ballots along party lines in 2006.[25] Such high levels of partisan voting are common in modern American politics, and party identification is among the best predictors of voting behavior in congressional elections, ranking second only to incumbency. The fact that roughly nine out of ten members of the voting population perceive, retain, and respond to political information in a partisan manner means that elections are not entirely candidate centered.[26] Yet the degree of partisanship that exists in the contemporary United States is still not strong enough to encourage a return to straight-ticket voting or to foster the development of a party-focused election system.

CAMPAIGN TECHNOLOGY

Political campaigns are designed to communicate ideas and images that will motivate voters to cast their ballots for particular candidates. Some voters are well informed; have strong opinions about candidates, issues, and parties; and will vote without ever coming into contact with a political campaign. Others will never bother to vote, regardless of politicians' efforts. Many voters need to be introduced to the candidates and made aware of the issues to become excited enough to vote in a congressional election. The communication of information is central to democratic elections, and those who are able to control the flow of information have tremendous power. Candidates, campaign organizations, parties, and other groups use a variety of technologies to affect the flow of campaign information and win votes.

Person-to-person contact is one of the oldest and most effective approaches to winning votes. Nothing was or is more effective than a candidate, or a candidate's supporters, directly asking citizens for their votes. During the golden age of parties, local party volunteers assessed the needs of voters in their neighborhoods and delivered the message that, if elected, their party's candidates would help voters achieve their goals.[27] Once these organizations lost their control over the flow of political information, they became less important, and candidate-assembled campaign organizations became more relevant players in elections.

The dawning of the television age and the development of modern campaign technology helped solidify the system of candidate-centered congressional elections.[28] Television and radio studios, printing presses, public opinion polls, personal computers, and sophisticated targeting techniques are well suited to candidate-centered campaign organizations because they, and the services of the political consultants who know how to use them, are readily available for hire. Congressional candidates can assemble organizations that meet their specific needs without having to turn to party organizations for assistance, although many candidates request their party's help.

New technology has encouraged a major change in the focus of most congressional election campaigns. It has enabled campaigns to communicate more information about candidates' personalities, issue positions, and qualifications for office. As a result, less campaign activity is now devoted to party-based appeals. Radio and television were especially important in bringing about this change because they are effective at conveying images and less useful in providing information about abstract concepts, such as partisan ideologies.[29] The Internet has reinforced the focus on candidate-centered appeals. Internet web sites enable candidates to post as many pictures, streaming video or radio ads, or other information as they wish. Web sites allow voters to access this information whenever they want and make it easy for voters to contact the campaign. Because this medium allows for direct candidate-to-voter and voter-to-candidate communication, its overall effect, like that of the electronic mass media more generally, is to direct attention away from parties and toward candidates.

The increased focus on candidate imagery that is associated with the "new style" of campaigning encourages congressional candidates to hire professional technicians to help them convey their political personas to voters.[30] Press secretaries, pollsters, issue and opposition researchers, media and direct-mail experts, and web site designers are involved in most congressional campaigns. Local party activists became less important in congressional elections as the importance of political consultants grew and the contributions of semiskilled and unskilled volunteers diminished. Skyrocketing campaign costs; the emergence of a national economy of campaign finance; and the rise of a cadre of fundraising specialists with the skills, contacts, and technology to raise money from individuals and PACs further increased the candidate-centered character of election campaigns because they provided politicians with the means for raising the contributions needed to purchase the services of political consultants.

Changes in technology transformed most congressional campaigns from labor-intensive grassroots undertakings, at which local party committees excelled, to money-driven, merchandised activities requiring the services of skilled experts. Most local party committees were unable to adapt to the new style of campaign politics.[31] Initially, party committees in Washington, D.C., and in many states also were unprepared to play a significant role in congressional elections. However, the parties' national, congressional, and senatorial campaign committees and several state party organizations proved more adept at making the transition to the new-style politics. They began to play meaningful roles in congressional election campaigns during the late 1970s and early 1980s and continued to do so in the twenty-first century.[32]

THE POLITICAL SETTING

Candidates, campaign managers, party officials, PAC managers, and others who are active in congressional elections consider more than the institutional framework, the culturally and historically conditioned expectations of voters, and the available technology when planning and executing electoral strategies. Individuals connected to the campaign also assess the political setting, including the circumstances in their district, their state, or the nation as a whole. At the local level, important considerations include the party affiliation, tenure, and intentions of the incumbent or other potential candidates, and the partisan history of the seat. Relevant national-level factors include whether it is a presidential or midterm election year, the state of the economy, the president's popularity, international affairs, and the public's attitude toward the government. Hostile sentiments directed at congressional Democrats and President Bill Clinton led to the Republican takeover of Congress in 1994. Disapproval of the performance of President Bush, congressional Republicans, and the war in Iraq helped the Democrats reclaim control of the House and Senate twelve years later.

Of course, one's perspective on the limits and possibilities of the political setting depends largely on one's vantage point. Although they talk about the competition and are, indeed, wary of it, congressional incumbents, particularly House members, operate in a political setting that works largely to their benefit. As explained in later chapters, incumbents enjoy significant levels of name recognition and voter support, are able to assemble superior campaign organizations, and can draw on their experience in office to speak knowledgeably about issues and claim credit for the federally financed programs and improvements in their state or district. Incumbents also tend to get favorable treatment from the media. Moreover, most can rely on loyal followers from previous campaigns for continued backing: supporters at home tend to vote repeatedly for incumbents, and supporters in Washington and the nation's other wealthy cities routinely provide incumbents with campaign money.

Things look different from the typical challenger's vantage point. Most challengers, particularly those with some political experience, recognize that most of the cards are stacked against an individual who sets out to take on an incumbent. Little in the setting in which most congressional campaigns take place favors the challenger. Most challengers lack the public visibility, money, and campaign experience to wage a strong campaign. Moreover, because those who work in and help finance campaigns recognize the strong odds against challengers, they usually see little benefit in helping them. As a result, high incumbent success rates have become a self-fulfilling prophecy. House incumbents enjoyed an overall reelection rate of better than 93 percent between 1950 and 2006; Senate reelection rates averaged more than 81 percent during this period. Even during the tidal wave elections of 1994 and 2006, more than 90 percent of all House members and 85 percent of all senators who sought to remain in office were able to do so, despite the defeat of thirty-eight House and two Senate Democratic incumbents in 1994 and losses by twenty-four House and six Senate Republican incumbents in 2006. Given their limited prospects for success in contesting a congressional seat, most experienced politicians wait until an incumbent retires, runs for another office, or dies before running for office. Indeed, substantial numbers of incumbents, especially in the House, are reelected without opposition or with weak opposition at best.

Most elections for open seats are highly competitive. They attract extremely qualified candidates who put together strong campaign organizations, raise huge amounts of money, and mount lively campaigns. Even House candidates of one party campaigning for seats that have been held by the other party for decades can often attract substantial resources, media attention, and votes.

Many explanations exist for the relative lack of competition in House elections. Some districts are so dominated by one party that few individuals of the other party are willing to commit their time, energy, or money to running for office. In many cases, the tradition of one-party dominance is so strong that virtually all the talented, politically ambitious individuals living in the area join the dominant party. When an incumbent in these districts faces a strong challenge, it usually takes place in the primary, and the winner is all but guaranteed success in the general election.[33]

Uncompetitive House districts are often the product of a highly political redistricting process. In states where one party controls both the governorship and the state legislature, partisan gerrymandering is often used to maximize the number of House seats the dominant party can win. In states where each party controls at least some portion of the state government, compromises are frequently made to design districts that protect congressional incumbents. Party officials and political consultants armed with computers, election returns, and demographic statistics can "pack" and "crack" voting blocs in order to promote either of these goals.[34] The result is that large numbers of congressional districts are designed to be uncompetitive. California exemplifies this. The 2002 elections, the first following redistricting, were notable for the fact that three of California's fifty-three House elections were decided by a margin of less than twenty points. The relatively few states that use nonpartisan commissions for redistricting tend to produce more competitive House races because the commissions generally place less emphasis on partisanship and incumbency. In contrast to the situation in California, four of Iowa's five House seats were decided by less than fifteen points in 2002.

Regardless of the method of redistricting used, elections that immediately follow redistricting traditionally have been marked by a temporary increase in competition. The creation of many new House seats and the redrawing of others usually results in increased numbers of incumbent defeats in both the primaries and the general election. The pitting of incumbents against each other almost always accounts for some of these losses, as does the fact that the prospect of newly drawn seats often encourages a surge in congressional retirements and more candidates than usual to challenge sitting House members. As a result, the decennial reapportionment and redistricting of House seats has historically produced a ten-year, five-election cycle of political competition. However, as will be noted later, the 2002 elections proved to be an exception to this rule.[35]

Another cyclical element of the national political climate that can influence congressional elections is the presence or absence of a presidential race. Presidential elections have higher levels of voter turnout than midterm elections, and they have the potential for coattail effects. A presidential candidate's popularity can become infectious and lead to increased support for the party's congressional contestants. A party that enjoys much success in electing congressional candidates during a presidential election year is, of course, likely to lose some of those seats in the midterm election that follows.[36] An unpopular president can further drag down a party's congressional contestants.[37] Presidential election politics had a strong impact on the election of 1932, in which the Democrats gained ninety seats in the House and thirteen seats in the Senate. The Democratic congressional landslide was a sign of widespread support for the Democratic presidential candidate, Franklin D. Roosevelt, as well as a repudiation of the incumbent president, Herbert Hoover, and his policies for dealing with the Great Depression.[38] Presidential coattail effects have declined since the 1930s, and Bill Clinton's and George W. Bush's presidential elections were conspicuous for their lack of them.[39] Democrats lost ten House seats and broke even in the Senate in 1992, and they gained only ten seats in the House and lost two seats in the Senate in 1996. Republicans lost two seats in the House and four seats in the Senate in 2000, and they picked up a mere three and four seats in these respective chambers in 2004. Of course, one cannot expect a presidential candidate's coattails to be long when the victory comes in at less than 50 percent of the popular vote as was the case with Clinton in 1992 and 1996 and Bush in 2000.

Congressional candidates who belong to the same party as an unpopular president also run the risk during midterm elections of being blamed for the failures of their party's chief executive.[40] The Republicans' forty-nine-seat House and four-seat Senate losses in 1974 grew out of a sense of disgust about the role of President Richard Nixon and members of his administration in the Watergate break-in at Democratic Party headquarters during the 1972 presidential campaign and the decision of his successor, President Gerald Ford, to pardon Nixon.[41] The Democrats' loss of fifty-two seats in the House and eight seats in the Senate in 1994 was caused largely by voter animosity toward Clinton, dissatisfaction with his party's failure to enact health care reform or a middle-class tax cut, and the Republicans' successful portrayal of the White House and the Democratic-controlled Congress as corrupt and out of step with the views of most voters. The Republicans' thirty-seat House and six-seat Senate losses in 2006 grew out of public discontent with the policies, performance, and scandals associated with the GOP-controlled federal government. Of course, some elections buck the normal trend, as when the Democrats gained five House seats in 1998.

The economy, foreign affairs, homeland security, and other national issues can affect congressional elections. The president's party has historically lost congressional seats in midterm elections when economic trends are unfavorable, although the relationship between economic performance and congressional turnover has weakened in recent years.[42] Foreign affairs also may be important. The Vietnam War contributed to the Democrats' congressional losses in 1972, and the wars on terrorism and in Afghanistan may have cost Democrats seats in 2002 and 2004. The war in Iraq certainly contributed to the defeats of some Republicans in 2006. Americans, however, tend to be less concerned with "guns" than with "butter," and so international events generally have less of an effect on elections than domestic conditions.

Other national issues that can affect congressional elections are civil rights, social issues, and the attitudes of voters toward political institutions. The civil rights revolution, the women's movement, urban decay, the emergence of the hippie counterculture, and the protests they spawned influenced voting behavior during the 1960s and 1970s.[43] Political scandal, and the widespread distrust of government that usually follows, can lead to the defeat of politicians accused of committing ethical transgressions, but as the 1974, 1994, and 2006 elections demonstrate, individual members of Congress who are not directly implicated in scandal can also suffer because of it.

National issues are likely to have the greatest effect on congressional elections when candidates take unambiguous stands on them.[44] Presidential politics are likely to have the most influence on congressional elections when voters closely identify congressional candidates with a party's presidential nominee or an incumbent president. House and Senate candidates generally respond strategically to national politics in order to improve their electoral fortunes. When their party selects a popular presidential candidate or has a popular incumbent in the White House, congressional candidates ally themselves with that individual to take advantage of the party cue and their opponents' focus on other matters, such as local issues. When their party selects an unpopular nominee or is saddled with an unpopular president, congressional candidates seek to protect themselves from the effects of partisanship by distancing themselves from the comings and goings of the executive branch. Naturally, their opponents try to prevent them from succeeding. The partisan campaigns that Democratic congressional candidates ran during the New Deal era and in 1992 and the campaigns that Republicans mounted in 2002 and 2004 exemplify the strategy of alliance with a popular executive. The independent, nonpartisan campaigns that many congressional Republicans conducted in 1992 and 2006 and that Democrats carried out in 1998, 2002, and 2004 are representative of the strategy of distancing.

The desire of incumbents to retain their seats has changed Congress in ways that help discourage electoral competition and can help insulate incumbents against national political tides. Most of those who are elected to Congress quickly understand that they will probably never hold a higher office because there are too few of such offices to go around. Like most people, they do everything in their power to hold onto their jobs. Congress has adapted to the career aspirations of its members by providing them with resources that can be used to increase their odds of reelection. Free mailings, unlimited long-distance telephone calls, Internet web sites, district offices, and subsidized travel help members gain visibility among their constituents. Federal pork-barrel projects also help incumbents win the support of voters.[45] Congressional aides help members write speeches, respond to constituent mail, resolve problems that constituents have with executive branch agencies, and follow the comings and goings in their bosses' districts.[46] Congressional hearings provide incumbents with forums in which to address issues of concern to their constituents. These perquisites of office give incumbents tremendous advantages over challengers. They also discourage experienced politicians who could put forth a competitive challenge from taking on an entrenched incumbent.

The dynamics of campaign finance have similar effects. Incumbents have tremendous fundraising advantages over challengers, especially among PACs and wealthy individual donors. Many incumbents build up large war chests to discourage potential challengers from running against them. With the exception of millionaires and celebrities, challengers who decide to contest a race against a member of the House or Senate typically find they are unable to raise the funds needed to mount a viable campaign.

Because the cards tend to be stacked so heavily in favor of congressional incumbents, most electoral competition takes place in open seats. Open-seat contests draw a larger-than-usual number of primary contestants. They also attract significantly more money and election assistance from party committees, individuals, PACs, and other groups than do challenger campaigns.[47] Special elections, which are called when a seat becomes vacant because of an incumbent's resignation or death, are open-seat contests that tend to be particularly competitive and unpredictable. They bring out even larger numbers of primary contenders than normal open-seat elections, especially when the seat that has become vacant was formerly held by a longtime incumbent.

RECENT CONGRESSIONAL ELECTIONS

The political settings that have shaped the opportunities presented to politicians, parties, interest groups, and ultimately voters since the early 1990s have had some important similarities. All but the 1994, 2004, and 2006 elections elections took place during a period of divided control, which made it difficult to credit or blame only one party for the government's performance or the nation's affairs. Most of the elections also took place under the shadow of a weak economy and were haunted by the specter of huge budget deficits. The 1998 and 2000 elections were important exceptions, occurring as the two parties debated how to spend projected budget surpluses.

Civil rights and racial and gender discrimination were issues in many campaigns during this period as a result of the highly publicized studies of the unequal salaries and advancement prospects for women and African Americans. Women's issues also were recently highlighted as a court case over the constitutionality of the ban on what opponents call "partial birth" abortion wended its way through the federal judiciary to the Supreme Court. Gay rights found its place on the agenda as the nation debated the military's "don't ask, don't tell" policy regarding homosexuals serving in the military and several states put initiatives on the ballot concerning same-sex marriages or civil unions.

A final arena in which civil rights issues were fought was redistricting. In 1986 the Supreme Court ruled that any gerrymandering of a congressional district that purposely diluted minority strength was illegal under the 1982 Voting Rights Act.[48] Most states interpreted the ruling cautiously, redrawing many of the districts after the 1990 census with the explicit purpose of giving one or more minority group members better-than-even chances of being elected to the House. Several opposition groups successfully sued in more than a half dozen states, including North Carolina, where redistricting battles continued to be fought well into the 1998 congressional election season. Several of the redistricting plans drawn prior to the 2002 elections also were subject to court challenges. Indeed, only twenty-nine plans went unchallenged before the election, and Mississippi's redistricting plan continued to be challenged after the election.[49] The latest twist in partisan battles over redistricting occurred in 2003, when Rep. Tom DeLay, the Republican House majority leader at the time, engineered the redrawing of congressional seats in his home state of Texas just two years after they had been redrawn. Although this unprecedented mid-decade gerrymandering increased the number of Republican-held seats in Texas by six, the Supreme Court in *League of United Latin American Citizens v. Perry, Governor of Texas* declared part of the redrawn map unconstitutional because the new boundaries failed to protect the voting rights of Hispanics.

Dissatisfaction with the political establishment in Washington also occupied a prominent position on the political agenda at the onset of the twenty-first century. Problems associated with immigration, the environment, rising energy and health care costs, the performance of the nation's schools, the deficit, and myriad other seemingly intractable issues resulted in voter frustration with national politicians. Much of this hostility was directed toward Congress, and many incumbents responded with a strategy that had served them well in the past—running for reelection by campaigning against Congress itself.[50]

Political scandal and the anti-Washington mood gave open-seat and challenger candidates for Congress many powerful issues to use in campaigns during the elections held in the early 1990s and mid 2000s. Support for the national legislature plummeted to a modern day record prior to the 1994 elections, when an estimated three-fourths of all Americans disapproved of Congress's performance, although that record was tied during the 2006 election season.[51]

Conditions were ripe in 1994 for the Republicans to pick up a significant number of congressional seats. Public hostility toward the Democratic Party–controlled executive and legislative branches of the national government and Clinton's early missteps on health care reform, gays in the military, and tax cuts combined with allegations of ethical misconduct by the president and his administration energized Republicans and demoralized Democrats. Under Newt Gingrich's leadership, the Republicans capitalized on these circumstances by running an anti-Washington campaign that was national in scope and that drew on the Contract with America.[52]

Following the Republican takeover of Congress in 1994, House Republicans passed most of the popular elements of their contract, but the public objected to GOP plans to provide tax cuts to the very rich while reducing spending on Medicare, Medicaid, and education. Political stalemate led to two federal government shutdowns, which were largely blamed on the Republican Congress. Many voters also objected to what they viewed as overreaching by House Republicans. Democrats sought to capitalize on Republicans' difficulties in 1996 by campaigning against what they labeled "the extremist Republican Congress" and offering policy proposals designed to appeal to middle-income and blue-collar families.

The settings for the 1998 and 2000 elections were more promising for incumbents of both parties. Most Americans benefited from a strong economy marked by rising incomes, low inflation, a high employment rate, a booming stock market, and the first federal budget surplus in three decades.[53] The elections took place in an environment that favored the status quo, gave neither party a strong advantage, and benefited incumbents in general, few of whom were defeated.

At their outset, the 2002 elections also were shaping up to favor incumbents across the board. In the House, this outlook was in part the result of an exceptional round of redistricting that bucked previous precedents by increasing the number of secure incumbent-held seats and reducing the number of competitive contests. One reason for this result was an increase in the number of divided state governments, which gave both Democrats and Republicans influence in the redrawing of congressional boundaries in many states. Another was that improved technology enabled district mapmakers to estimate with tremendous precision the numbers of Democratic, Republican, and independent voters. Still another was that House incumbents and their allies participating in redistricting were unusually risk averse, preferring to carve out extremely safe seats for themselves instead of sacrificing a little political security to improve the chances of increasing their party's House membership. Moreover, public approval of Congress was relatively high, which had the potential to advantage incumbents in both the House and the Senate.

The attacks of September 11, 2001, greatly altered the political agenda in ways that would benefit the Republican Party. National security and the war on terrorism, which previously had barely registered among the public, rose to prominence in national opinion polls. The president's approval ratings skyrocketed, as has historically occurred when the United States has become involved in an international crisis. This worked to the advantage of Republican congressional candidates, who were able to bask in the rays of Bush's high ratings. The president, drawing on his increased popularity and role as commander in chief, sought to capitalize on the situation in 2002 and 2004 to help Republican congressional candidates raise money and attract public support.[54]

The environment for the 2006 elections was considerably less favorable to Republican congressional candidates as much of the public had become critical of the Bush administration and the performance of the federal government under unified GOP control. Growing numbers of U.S. fatalities in Iraq, the failure to capture al-Qaida leader Osama bin Laden, and the limited military and political progress made in Iraq and Afghanistan were sources of voter dissatisfaction. Others were the inadequacy of the government's response to Hurricane Katrina, its failure to enact an immigration policy, and the complexities and out-of-pocket expenses associated with GOP-sponsored prescription drug reform. Voter discontent also stemmed from the economic insecurity felt by many voters in response to rising energy costs, a decline in desirable high-quality jobs, an exploding federal deficit, and a sense that future generations of Americans would no longer enjoy an improved standard of living.

Adding to these international and domestic woes were some major political scandals. First among these scandals were some proven and some alleged acts of corruption involving convicted lobbyist Jack Abramoff and several high-ranking congressional Republicans, including Majority Leader Tom DeLay of Texas, Rep. Randy "Duke" Cunningham of California, and Rep. Bob Ney of Ohio—all of whom resigned their seats before the November 2006 election.

A second set of scandals, which broke about five weeks before election day, involved sexually suggestive e-mails and instant messages that Rep. Mark Foley, R-Fla., had sent to former House pages and the failure of Republican House leaders to properly address the matter by reporting it to the House Ethics Committee or to the bipartisan board that oversees the page program. The Foley scandal caused public outrage and weakened the GOP's ability to proclaim itself as the defender of traditional moral values.

Unlike the previous few elections, Republican congressional candidates also would have to contend with negative public evaluations of Congress and the president. President Bush's job approval ratings never rose above 43 percent during the fifteen months preceding the election and had dropped to about 38 percent by election day.[55] Public evaluations of Congress also were abysmally low, with more than 60 percent consistently disapproving of Congress's performance beginning in April.[56] When asked about their voting preferences, most voters said they would vote for a Democrat for the House rather than a Republican, all other things being equal.[57] Rather than campaign with the president and Republican congressional leaders, many GOP House and Senate candidates avoided the joint appearances they had so assiduously sought in the prior two elections. Republican Party officials and consultants encouraged their standard-bearers to focus on themselves and local issues rather than on the national political agenda.

The Democrats, by contrast, sought to benefit from the political environment by nationalizing the election. They offered voters two powerful appeals for change. The first was encapsulated in a positive message that focused on health care affordability, energy independence, jobs and wages, and other domestic issues of importance to working- and middle-class Americans. The second appeal was based on the performance of the Republican-controlled national government, which Democrats criticized as pursuing a failed Iraq War policy and plagued by a "culture of corruption" and "government incompetence." Most Democratic candidates embraced much, if not all, of their party's message.

Given the public mood and strongly pro-Democratic issue agenda in 2006, a major challenge for the Democratic Party was to find a way to win more House seats on a political map that appeared to have few competitive seats as a result of redistricting. The Democrats and their interest group allies approached this dilemma by recruiting and backing strong candidates in seats held by Republicans. In contrast with previous election years when both parties focused and repeatedly refocused their resources in the closest elections and, in the process, caused the numbers of such seats to diminish, the House Democrats' Red to Blue Program took the unusual step of using party resources to expand the field of competition. The result was a Democratic sweep in which the party regained control of Congress with a net gain of thirty-one seats in the House and six seats in the Senate. (The figure for the House includes the seat formerly occupied by Independent Bernard Sanders of Vermont; the figure for the Senate includes the seat occupied by Joseph I. Lieberman of Connecticut who, although technically an Independent, caucuses with the Democrats.)

The 2006 elections, like several other recent contests, demonstrate that despite the inherent advantages of incumbency, the political setting in a given year can pose obstacles for some lawmakers and result in significant numbers losing their seats. Nineteen House incumbents lost their primaries in 1992— a post–World War II record; and another thirty-four lost in the general election two years later—the most since the post-Watergate housecleaning of 1974 (see Table 1-3). The results of the four congressional elections from 1998 through 2004 deviated significantly from the moderate-to-high levels of incumbent losses recorded in 1992, 1994, and 1996. In 2006, there was a significant uptick in incumbent losses, with two House members losing their primaries and another twenty—all Republicans—losing in the general election.

The increase in competition in 2006 is also evident when candidates are divided into categories on the basis of the closeness of their elections. During that election, 33 percent of the House candidates in major-party contested races ran

TABLE 1-3

Number of Unchallenged and Defeated House Incumbents, 1986–2006

	1986	1988	1990	1992	1994	1996	1998	2000	2002	2004	2006
Incumbents unchallenged by major-party opposition in general election	71	81	76	25	54	20	94	63	78	64	55
Incumbents defeated											
In primary	3	1	1	19	4	2	1	3	8	2	2
In general election	6	6	15	24	34	20	6	6	8	7	20

Sources: Compiled from various editions of *CQ Weekly* and *Congressional Roll Call* (Washington, D.C.: CQ Press). The primary and general election results are from Norman J. Ornstein, Thomas E. Mann, and Michael J. Malbin, *Vital Statistics on Congress, 2001–2002* (Washington, D.C.: AEI Press, 2002), 69; and author's data.

Notes: The 1992, 2002, and 2004 figures include incumbent-versus-incumbent races. Also, Rep. Henry Bonilla, R-Texas, was defeated in a runoff in 2006 and is included among incumbents defeated in the general elections. Shelley Sekula-Gibbs, R-Texas, who ran as a write-in candidate for the seat of Tom DeLay, is included in the incumbent category because she replaced Tom DeLay after his resignation.

in marginal districts compared with 22 percent in 2004. Included in this group are the 14 percent of the candidates classified as "incumbents in jeopardy" on the basis of their having lost the general election or having won by a margin of 20 percent or less of the two-party vote; the 14 percent of the candidates who opposed them—labeled "hopeful challengers"; and the 5 percent of the candidates—classified as open-seat "prospects"—who ran in contests decided by 20 percent or less of the two-party vote (see Table 1-4). The remainder of the candidates, who were involved in uncompetitive races, are referred to as "incumbent shoo-ins," "likely-loser challengers," and "mismatched" open-seat candidates.[58]

Similarly, the mood surrounding the 2006 elections led to heightened competition in the Senate. Senator Joseph Lieberman of Connecticut lost his Democratic primary to challenger antiwar candidate Ned Lamont, only to reclaim his seat as a self-proclaimed "Independent Democrat" in the general election. Six other incumbents, all Republicans, lost in the general election (see Table

TABLE 1-4

Competition in House Elections, 1986–2006

	1986	1988	1990	1992	1994	1996	1998	2000	2002	2004	2006
Incumbents											
In jeopardy	9%	8%	15%	14%	17%	15%	14%	11%	8%	9%	14%
Shoo-ins	35	39	32	25	27	29	31	35	35	37	32
Challengers											
Hopefuls	9	8	15	14	17	15	14	11	8	9	14
Likely losers	35	39	32	25	27	29	31	35	35	37	32
Open-seat candidates											
Prospects	7	5	5	13	9	8	7	6	8	4	5
Mismatched	4	3	1	9	5	4	3	3	5	4	4
N	720	712	696	794	766	812	680	746	694	732	754

Source: Compiled from Federal Election Commission data.

Notes: Figures are for major-party candidates in contested general elections, excluding incumbent-versus-incumbent races (which occasionally follow redistricting), runoff elections, and contests won by independents. Incumbents in jeopardy are defined as those who lost or who won by 20 percent or less of the two-party vote. Shoo-ins are incumbents who won by more than 20 percent of the two-party vote. Hopeful challengers are those who won or who lost by 20 percent or less of the two-party vote. Likely-loser challengers are those who lost by more than 20 percent of the two-party vote. Open-seat prospects are those whose election was decided by 20 percent or less of the two-party vote. Mismatched open-seat candidates are those whose election was decided by more than 20 percent of the two-party vote. Some columns do not add to 100 percent because of rounding.

TABLE 1-5

Number of Unchallenged and Defeated Senate Incumbents, 1986–2006

	1986	1988	1990	1992	1994	1996	1998	2000	2002	2004	2006
Incumbents unchallenged by major-party opposition in general election	0	0	5	1	0	0	0	1	4	0	1
Incumbents defeated											
In primary	0	0	0	1	0	1	0	0	1	0	1
In general election	7	4	1	4	2	1	3	6	3	1	6

Sources: Compiled from various issues of *CQ Weekly* and *Congressional Roll Call* (Washington, D.C.: CQ Press). The primary and general election results are from Norman J. Ornstein, Thomas E. Mann, and Michael J. Malbin, *Vital Statistics on Congress, 2001–2002* (Washington, D.C.: AEI Press, 2002), 70; and author's data.

Note: Sen. Joseph I. Lieberman, I-Conn., was defeated in the 2006 Democratic primary in Connecticut and then ran in the general election as an independent candidate. He is included here as a primary candidate, but he is excluded from the general election data because of his independent status.

1-5). When the classification scheme used for House candidates is applied to the Senate (Table 1-6) it becomes clear that the number of competitive incumbent-challenger contests increased substantially compared with 2004. Collectively, the results for 2004 provide further evidence that the political setting in a given election year can have an impact on incumbents' prospects for reelection.

The competitiveness of congressional elections influences the number of new faces in Congress. As a group, those serving in the 110th Congress are more diverse than those who served a decade ago. The House opened its first session of the 110th Congress with twenty more women, three more African Americans, and five more Hispanics than had served in the 105th Congress. It also featured the nation's first female House Speaker, its first Muslim, and its first two Buddhist House members. Change generally comes more slowly to the upper chamber. Sixteen female senators serve in the 110th Congress, seven more than had served in the 105th. The Senate currently has one African American, Barack Obama, D-Ill., and only three Hispanics.

Despite this increased diversity, the vast majority of newcomers had at least one thing in common with one another and with their more senior colleagues: they came to Congress with significant political experience under their belts. Thirty-three of the fifty-four freshmen House members in the 110th Congress had previously held another public office; twelve had served as party officials, worked as political aides or consultants, or run for Congress at least once before

TABLE 1-6

Competition in Senate Elections, 1986–2006

	1986	1988	1990	1992	1994	1996	1998	2000	2002	2004	2006
Incumbents											
In jeopardy	20%	17%	20%	22%	23%	21%	15%	17%	18%	12%	22%
Shoo-ins	20	24	25	16	14	9	28	26	20	27	23
Challengers											
Hopefuls	20	17	20	22	23	21	15	17	18	12	22
Likely losers	20	24	25	16	14	9	28	26	20	27	23
Open-seat candidates											
Prospects	12	12	3	21	14	35	9	15	24	22	7
Mismatched	6	6	7	3	11	6	6	0	0	0	3
N	*68*	*66*	*60*	*68*	*70*	*68*	*68*	*66*	*60*	*64*	*60*

Source: Compiled from Federal Election Commission data.

Notes: Figures are for major-party candidates in contested general elections. Incumbents in jeopardy are defined as those who lost or who won by 20 percent or less of the two-party vote. Shoo-ins are incumbents who won by more than 20 percent of the two-party vote. Hopeful challengers are those who won or who lost by 20 percent or less of the two-party vote. Likely-loser challengers are those who lost by more than 20 percent of the two-party vote. Open-seat prospects are those whose election was decided by 20 percent or less of the two-party vote. Mismatched open-seat candidates are those whose election was decided by more than 20 percent of the two-party vote. Some columns do not add to 100 percent because of rounding.

getting elected; and only nine were political amateurs. Of the nine candidates elected to the Senate for the first time in 2006, only one, Sen. Jim Webb, D-Va., had not previously held at least one elective office. Senator Webb did have extensive nonelective political experience, however; he had worked as a congressional aide and had served as secretary of the navy during the Reagan administration.

SUMMARY

The Constitution, election laws, campaign finance regulations, and participatory nominations provide the institutional foundations for the candidate-centered congressional election system. The United States's history and individualistic political culture, which inform Americans' traditional ambivalence toward political parties, shore up that system. Candidates who can afford to hire political consultants to learn about and contact voters have benefited from technological advancements, which have allowed the system to assume its con-temporary pro-incumbent, professionally oriented, money-fueled form.

How campaigns are conducted in the future will be influenced by changes currently under way in the strategic environment in which congressional seats are contested. Recent changes in campaign finance law, for example, especially those concerning soft money and issue advocacy ads, will affect the abilities of political parties and interest groups to influence the tenor and outcomes of congressional elections.

CHAPTER TWO

Candidates and Nominations

Can I win? Is this the right time for me to run? Who is my competition likely to be? These are the types of questions that have always gone through the minds of prospective candidates. During the golden age of political parties, party bosses helped individuals decide whether to run for Congress. In many places the bosses' control over the party apparatus was so complete that, when in agreement, they could guarantee the nomination to the person they wanted to run. Moreover, receiving the nomination usually was tantamount to winning the election because strong political machines typically were located in one-party areas. After the golden age, party leaders had less control over the nomination process and less ability to ensure that the individuals they recruited would, in fact, win the nomination.[1]

Political parties are no longer the primary recruiters of congressional candidates. Party leaders encourage some individuals to run for office and discourage others, but local and national party committees serve more as vehicles that self-recruited candidates use to advance their careers than as organizations that can make or break those careers. Party recruitment has been largely replaced by a process referred to as candidate emergence.[2]

In this chapter I examine who decides to run for Congress, how potential candidates reach their decisions, and the influence of different individuals and groups on these decisions. I also examine the impact of candidate emergence and political experience on an individual's prospects of winning the nomination and the general election and the implications of these contests on the representativeness of the national legislature.

STRATEGIC AMBITION

The Constitution, state laws, and the political parties pose few formal barriers to running for Congress, enabling virtually anyone to become a candidate.

Members of the House are required to be at least twenty-five years of age, to have been U.S. citizens for at least seven years, and to reside in the state they represent. The requirements for the Senate are only slightly more stringent. In addition to residing in the state they represent, senators must be at least thirty years old and have been U.S. citizens for at least nine years. Some states bar prison inmates or individuals who have been declared insane from running for office, and most states require candidates to pay a small filing fee or to collect anywhere from a few hundred to several thousand signatures before having their names placed on the ballot. As is typical for election to public offices in many democracies, a dearth of formal requirements allows almost anyone to run for Congress. More than sixteen hundred people declare themselves candidates in most election years.

Although the formal requirements are minimal, other factors, related to the candidate-centered nature of the electoral system, favor individuals with certain personal characteristics. Strategic ambition—which is the combination of a desire to get elected, a realistic understanding of what it takes to win, and an ability to assess the opportunities presented by a given political context—is one such characteristic that distinguishes most successful candidates for Congress from the general public. Most successful candidates also must be self-starters because the electoral system lacks a tightly controlled party-recruitment process or a well-defined career path to the national legislature. In addition, because the electoral system is candidate-centered, the desire, skills, and resources that candidates bring to the electoral arena are the most important criteria separating serious candidates from those who have little chance of getting elected. Ambitious candidates, sometimes referred to as "strategic," "rational," or "quality" candidates, are political entrepreneurs who make rational calculations about when to run. Rather than plunge right in, they assess the political context in which they would have to wage their campaigns, consider the effects that a bid for office could have on their professional careers and families, and carefully weigh their prospects for success.[3]

Strategic politicians examine many institutional, structural, and subjective factors when considering a bid for Congress.[4] The institutional factors include filing deadlines, campaign finance laws, nomination processes that allow or prohibit pre-primary endorsements, and other election statutes and party rules. The structural factors include the social, economic, and partisan composition of the district; its geographic compactness; the media markets that serve it; the degree of overlap between the district and lower-level electoral constituencies; and the possibilities for election to some alternative office. One structural factor that greatly affects the strategic calculations of nonincumbents and is prone to fluctuate more often than others is whether an incumbent plans to run for reelection.

Potential candidates also assess the political climate in deciding whether to run. Strategic politicians focus mainly on local circumstances, particularly whether a seat will be vacant or whether the results of the previous election suggest that an incumbent is vulnerable.[5] National forces, such as a public mood that favors Democrats or Republicans or challengers or incumbents, are usually of secondary importance. The convergence of local and national forces can have a strong impact on the decisions of potential candidates. The widespread hostility the public directed at Congress and its members played a major role in influencing who ran in the 1994 and 2006 primaries and general elections. These forces motivated many would-be House members to believe that a seat in Congress was within their reach. In 1998, 2000, 2002, and 2004 the nation's overall prosperity and the public's positive feelings toward incumbents had the opposite effect.

Incumbents

For House incumbents the decision to run for reelection is usually an easy one. Congress offers its members many reasons to want to stay, including the ability to affect issues they care about, a challenging work environment, political power, and public recognition. It is also an ideal platform for pursuing a governorship, cabinet post, or even a seat in the Oval Office. Name recognition and the advantages inherent in incumbency—such as paid staff and the franking privilege (which have an estimated worth approaching $2 million per member per year)—are two factors that discourage strong opposition from arising. Furthermore, House members recognize that the "home styles" they use to present themselves to constituents create bonds of trust that have important electoral implications.[6]

Incumbents undertake a number of additional preelection activities to build support and ward off opposition.[7] Most raise large war chests early in the election cycle to intimidate potential opponents.[8] Many keep a skeletal campaign organization intact between elections and use it to send their supporters campaign newsletters and other political communications. Some even shower their constituents with greeting cards, flowers, and other gifts.[9] Incumbents' activities in office and preelection efforts, as well as the fact that they have been elected to Congress at least once before, make most incumbents fairly certain that they will be reelected.

In some circumstances, however, incumbents recognize that it may be more difficult than usual to hold on to their seats. Redistricting, for example, can change the partisan composition of a House member's district or it can force two incumbents to compete for one seat.[10] A highly publicized ethical transgression usually weakens an incumbent's reelection prospects. A poor economy, an unpopular president or presidential candidate of the same party, or a wave of antigovernment hostility also can undermine legislators who represent marginal districts. These factors can influence incumbents' expectations about the quality of the opposition they are likely to face, the kinds of reelection campaigns they will need to wage, the toll those campaigns could take on themselves and their families, and their desire to stay in Congress.

When the demands of campaigning outweigh the benefits of getting reelected, strategic incumbents retire. Elections that immediately follow redistricting are often preceded by a jump in the number of incumbents who retire, as was the case in 1952, 1972, 1982, and 1992 (see Figure 2-1). The number of retirees jumped slightly in 2002 relative to the previous two elections, but fewer House members retired that year in comparison with most previous post-redistricting elections. This is most likely because of the pro-incumbent orientation of the redistricting that preceded the 2002 elections.

Elections held during periods of voter frustration, congressional scandal, or incivility within Congress itself also are preceded by high numbers of retire-

FIGURE 2-1

Number of Retirements by House Incumbents, 1950–2006

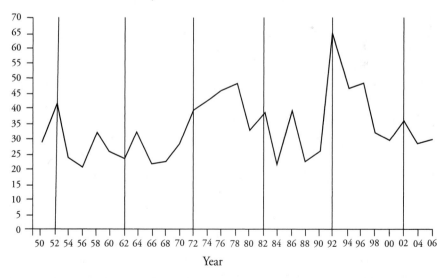

Year

Sources: Compiled from various issues of *CQ Weekly, Congressional Roll Call* (Washington, D.C.: CQ Press), and Norman J. Ornstein, Thomas E. Mann, and Michael J. Malbin, *Vital Statistics on Congress, 2001–2002* (Washington, D.C.: AEI Press, 2002), 71.

ments.[11] A combination of redistricting, anti-incumbent sentiments, and a decline in comity in the House led 15 percent of all House members to retire in 1992—a post–World War II record. Whereas the numerous hard-fought elections that took place in 1994 inspired many congressional retirements in 1996, the number of members deciding not to run for reelection declined between 1998 and 2004. The relatively high appraisals of Congress that preceded those elections helped reduce the number of retirements. The efforts of party leaders, who wanted to minimize the number of open seats they had to defend so they could compete more effectively for control of the chamber, also helped to avert many retirements in those years. Similar efforts, mainly on the part of Republican leaders, helped to minimize the number of retirements in 2006 despite growing public hostility toward Congress.[12] In 2006 only thirty House incumbents decided not to run for reelection.

Elections that occur following upheaval within Congress itself also are marked by large numbers of congressional retirements. The political reforms passed during the mid-1970s, which redistributed power from conservative senior House members to more liberal junior ones, encouraged many senior members to retire from the House.[13] The Republican takeover of the House in 1994 also encouraged large numbers of Democrats, and some Republicans, to retire. For the Democrats, retirement was preferable to waging a reelection campaign that, if successful, would result in their continuing to suffer the powerlessness associated with being in the minority. For the Republicans, it was preferable to enduring the indignity of being passed over for a committee chairmanship or some other leadership post.

The individuals most likely to retire from Congress are senior members who decide they would rather enjoy the fruits of old age than gear up for an election campaign, members who are implicated in some type of scandal, or members who anticipate losing influence or tire of having little political clout in the first place.[14] The retirements that took place before the 2006 elections occurred for the usual reasons. Rep. Lane Evans, D-Ill., who has Parkinson's disease, and Rep. Henry Hyde, R-Ill., aged eighty-two, retired for health and age-related reasons. Rep. Major Owens, D-N.Y., aged seventy, who won his primary with only 45 percent of the vote, was believed to have decided to retire because of considerations of age and his weakening grip over his district. Rep. Bill Thomas, R-Cal., left the House because of an impending loss of personal political power. GOP House rules that limited committee chairs to a maximum of three terms required Thomas to relinquish his chairmanship of the powerful House Ways and Means Committee at the end of the 109th Congress regardless of which party controlled the House in 2006. Thomas, who had chaired the House Committee on Administration for the previous three terms, would have been left without a committee chairmanship for the first time in twelve years.

Scandal certainly cut short the careers of a number who left the House prior to the 2006 elections. As noted in Chapter 1, these include Tom DeLay, who departed under a cloud of indictments concerning conspiracy, money laundering, and violations of campaign finance laws; Duke Cunningham, who resigned after pleading guilty to federal charges of conspiracy to commit bribery, mail and wire fraud, and tax evasion; Bob Ney, who resigned after admitting to making false statements in relation to the Native American lobbying scandal involving convicted lobbyist Jack Abramoff; and Mark Foley, who left the House after a highly publicized scandal involving inappropriate communications to former House pages.

Finally, some legislators give at least some thought to influencing future politics in their districts as they consider retirement. Representative Thomas, for example, endorsed a former aide, Kevin McCarthy, before retiring in 2006. Two years earlier, Rep. William Lipinski, D-Ill., announced his retirement from the House after easily winning renomination and laying the groundwork for his son Dan to replace him on the ballot. Lipinski senior's attempt at legacy politics is not unusual. Retiring members often try to create or continue family dynasties in Congress.[15]

Nonincumbents

The conditions that affect the calculations of strategic incumbents also influence the decision making of nonincumbents who plan their political careers strategically.[16] Redistricting has a significant impact on these individuals. More individuals with previous experience holding an elective office run for the House in election cycles that follow redistricting than in other years (see Figure 2-2).[17] Many of these candidates anticipate the opportunities that arise from the creation of new seats, the redrawing of old ones, or the retirements that often accompany elections after redistricting. The "pulling effects" of redistricting at the congressional level are sometimes accompanied by "pushing effects." The redistricting of state legislatures, county councils, and other offices may encourage current officeholders to seek a seat in the House. Term limits for state legislators, which were on the books in fifteen states in 2006, can have the same impact.[18] The combined effects of redistricting, term limits, and other aspects of the political environment encouraged almost 300 major-party candidates who had experience holding an elective office to run in 2002. The conditions in the 2004 and 2006 elections led another 248 and 257 elected officials to throw their hats into the ring.

FIGURE 2-2

Number of House Primary Candidates by Political Experience, 1978–2006

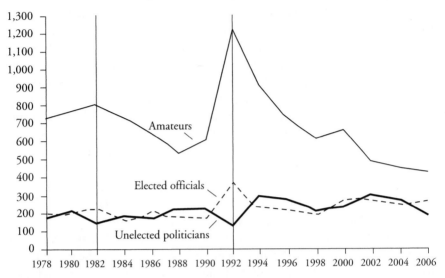

Sources: Compiled from various issues of *CQ Weekly* and candidates' web sites.

Note: Includes nonincumbent candidates for major-party nominations only.

Candidates who have significant campaign and political experience but who have never held elective office also respond to the opportunities that emerge in specific election years. These "unelected politicians" comprise legislative and executive branch aides, political appointees, state and local party officials, political consultants, and individuals who previously ran for Congress. Most of these politicians think strategically. Prior to deciding to run, they monitor voter sentiment, assess the willingness of political activists and contributors to support their campaigns, and keep close tabs on who is likely to oppose them for the nomination or in the general election.

Unelected politicians differ somewhat from elected officials and former officeholders in their perceptions of what constitutes a good time to run because elected officials weigh heavily in the strategic calculations of the unelected politicians. Unelected politicians appreciate that most elected officials possess more name recognition and fundraising advantages than they do. Unelected politicians typically balk at the opportunity to contest a primary against an elected official, even when other circumstances appear favorable. However, if a candidate with elective experience does not come forward, individuals with other significant forms of political experience will usually run. Relatively few unelected politicians viewed the 1982 and 1992 post-redistricting election cycle as promising for their causes. The pro-incumbent political environment discouraged unelected politicians from running. However, in 2002 and 2004 similar numbers of unelected politicians ran as did politicians with office-holding experience. In 2006 the number of unelected politicians dropped off by about one hundred.

Political amateurs are an extremely diverse group, and it is difficult to generalize about their political decision making. Only a small subgroup of amateurs, referred to as "ambitious amateurs," behave strategically, responding to the same opportunities and incentives that influence the decisions of more experienced politicians. Most amateurs do not spend much time assessing these factors. "Policy amateurs," comprising another subgroup, are driven by issues, whereas "experience-seeking" or "hopeless amateurs" run out of a sense of civic duty or for the thrill of running itself.[19]

The large number of amateurs who ran in the 1992 elections set a record that is likely to stand for some time. A few of these candidates were ambitious challengers, who, after weighing the costs of campaigning and the probability of winning, declared their candidacies. Many policy-oriented and experience-seeking amateurs also were compelled to run in the early and middle 1990s. These elections provided political landscapes that were ideal for running advocacy-oriented or anti-incumbency campaigns. The National Organization for Women, EMILY's List, and other pro-choice and women's groups recruited women to run for Congress and mobilized women voters and donors. Calls for change and relentless government-bashing in the media provided reform-minded candidates from both parties with ready-made platforms. Republican recruitment efforts and the Contract with America helped inspire more GOP than Democratic candidates to run in 1994 for the first time in decades. Reflecting the unusual pro-incumbent redistricting prior to 2002 and the relatively few open seats created by post-redistricting retirements, an unusually small number of amateurs ran in the election that immediately followed.[20] Many ambitious amateurs undoubtedly realized that their odds of victory were virtually nil, and many policy-oriented amateurs understood that they would have little ability to attract media attention to either their candidacies or priority issues in a lopsided race. Moreover, the number of amateurs of all types who run for Congress appears to be declining since the 1992 elections. Some observers attribute this trend to politics having become generally less appealing to Americans, leading some potential candidates to seek fulfillment from volunteering in other civic enterprises.[21]

What appears to be a year of opportunity for strategic politicians of one party is often viewed as a bad year by their counterparts in the other party. Democrats with experience in lower office considered 1978 and 1982 to be good years to run for the House; Republicans with comparable levels of experience did not (see Figure 2-3). Republicans, in contrast, judged 1980 and 1990 to be good years, but many similarly qualified Democrats were discouraged from running in those years. The 1992 election was somewhat unusual in that elected officials from both parties judged the effects of redistricting, a weak economy, congressional scandal, and voter antipathy to hold tremendous possibilities.

The Republican takeover of Congress had a significant effect on candidate emergence in the 1996 elections. The number of Republican candidates with elective or significant nonelective experience decreased slightly after 1994 because many individuals in the GOP's candidate pool undoubtedly believed that their party had captured virtually every vulnerable Democrat-held seat in the tidal wave of that year. Demoralized by their party's low standing in the polls, President Bill Clinton's unpopularity, the House Republicans' initial legislative success, and the risk of political defeat, many Democratic elected officials also opted not to run in 1996, even against

FIGURE 2-3

House Primary Candidacies of Politicians by Party and Experience, 1978–2006

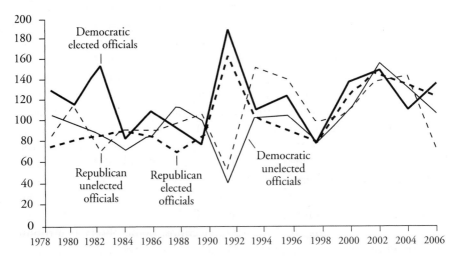

Sources: Compiled from various issues of *CQ Weekly* and candidates' web sites.

Note: Includes candidates for major-party nominations only.

some GOP freshmen who were vulnerable to a strong challenge. Democratic unelected politicians filled the void in some of these districts; political amateurs did likewise in others.

Riding on the wave of President George W. Bush's popularity and widespread support for the Iraq War and the war on terrorism, more Republican than Democratic elected officials and unelected politicians ran for the House in 2004. This pattern reversed in 2006, as the president's poll numbers declined, support for continuation of the conflict in the Middle East waned, political scandals increased, and the perceived poor performance of the federal government created electoral incentives for Democrats, but not Republicans.

Typically, most of the best-qualified office seekers wait until a seat opens, through either the retirement or the death of the incumbent, before throwing their hats into the ring.[22] Once a seat becomes vacant, it acts like a magnet, drawing the attention and candidacies of many individuals. Usually several strategic politicians will express interest in an open seat. Open-seat races, defined as contests in which there is no incumbent at the beginning of the election season, accounted for roughly 7 percent of the 2006 House elections. About one-third of the Democratic elected officials who ran for the House that year, and half of their Republican counterparts, competed in open-seat races (see Table 2-1).

TABLE 2-1

Effect of Seat Status on Nonincumbent Candidates for House Nominations in 2006

	Democrats			Republicans		
	Elected officials	Unelected politicians	Political amateurs	Elected officials	Unelected politicians	Political amateurs
Open seat	34%	19%	14%	50%	23%	19%
Democratic incumbent seeking reelection	11	12	10	35	68	67
Republican incumbent seeking reelection	55	69	76	16	8	14
N	*136*	*104*	*239*	*121*	*70*	*171*

Sources: Compiled from candidates' web sites.

Note: Some columns do not add to 100 percent because of rounding.

Incumbency discourages competition in primary elections, especially within the incumbent's party. Only 11 percent of the Democratic elected officials who ran for the House in 2006 were willing to challenge one of their party's incumbents for the nomination. Another 55 percent were willing to run in an incumbent-opposing primary; that is, in a primary that had the potential to earn them the right to oppose a Republican incumbent in the general election.[23] Given voter uneasiness with the GOP leading up to the election and the scandals plaguing their party, it is not surprising that Republican politicians were somewhat less gun shy about attempting to commit political fratricide: 16 percent were willing to challenge a GOP House member in the primary. Another 35 percent ran in incumbent-opposing primaries to challenge a sitting House Democrat.

The candidacies of unelected politicians and amateur candidates contrast with those of elected officials: unelected politicians are more likely than elected officials to run for a seat held by an incumbent of their own or the opposing party, and amateurs are more likely than unelected officials to run in these same contests. Compared with elected officials, these other candidates have fewer political costs to weigh when considering whether to enter a congressional primary. Prospective candidates who do not hold an elective office do not have to give up a current office to run for Congress, as do most officeholders whose positions are coterminous with congressional elections.[24] They also do not have to be as concerned about the effect a defeat could have on an established political career.

Others Involved in the Decision to Run

The drive to hold elective office may be rooted in an individual's personality and tempered by the larger political environment, but potential candidates rarely reach a decision about running for Congress without touching base with a variety of people.[25] Nearly all candidates single out their family and friends as being highly influential in their decision to enter a race.[26] More than one young, talented, experienced, and well-connected local politician who wanted a seat in Congress has remarked only half in jest that family members would probably shoot them if they decided to run. Family concerns, financial considerations, and career aspirations have kept many ambitious and highly regarded local politicians from running for Congress.

Political parties, labor unions, other organized groups, and political activists and consultants also can affect a prospective candidate's decision, but they have much less impact than the people directly involved in an individual's daily life. Potential candidates usually discuss their plans with these groups only after mulling over the idea of running. Sometimes would-be candidates approach local party leaders; fellow party members in the House or the Senate; or officials from their party's state, national, congressional, or senatorial campaign committees to learn about the forms of assistance that would be available should they decide to run. On other occasions the party initiates the contact, seeking to nurture the interest of good prospects.

Barred from simply handing out the nomination, party leaders can influence a prospective candidate's decision to run in a variety of ways. They can help size up the potential competition and try to encourage some and discourage others from contesting the nomination.[27] In some states party leaders can help a candidate secure a pre-primary endorsement, but this does not guarantee nomination.

Members of Congress and the staffs of the Democratic and Republican congressional and senatorial campaign committees often encourage prospective candidates to run. Armed with favorable polling figures and the promise of party assistance in the general election, they search out local talent. Party leaders crisscross the country looking to sound out the best possible candidates for competitive districts. Sometimes they have a profile in mind, such as candidates who can afford to self-finance most of their own election campaigns. In 2006 both parties sought out war veterans to run for Congress. These candidates enjoyed considerable success as almost three-fourths of them won their primaries.

Once the parties have identified promising individuals, they take steps to entice them to run. This can be a major challenge in districts or states where a congressional seat has been occupied by a member of the opposite party and may not look winnable at first glance, as appeared to be the case with many seats that the Democrats ultimately won in 2006. To help convince individuals to contest those seats, party leaders invite them to meet with members of Congress and other leaders in Washington and to attend campaign seminars. They also give them lists of PACs and political consultants who possess some of the resources and skills needed to conduct a congressional campaign.[28] Some potential candidates are promised fundraising and campaign assistance by members of Congress and other politicians. Presidents, vice presidents, cabinet officials, high-ranking White House aides, or individuals who have previously held those posts also are often asked to try to entice prospective candidates to enter the race. In 2006 President Bush, Vice President Richard B. Cheney, presidential adviser Karl Rove, and other GOP leaders were among those involved in recruiting potential Republican candidates. For the Democrats, former president Clinton; former first lady, Sen. Hillary Rodham Clinton; and a host of other party leaders were heavily involved in trying to field a strong team of Democratic House and Senate contenders.

When more than one candidate signs up to run for a nomination, the national parties usually remain neutral unless a primary challenger seriously threatens an incumbent. On rare occasions, however, the parties' congressional and senatorial campaign committees will provide their preferred candidate with assistance in winning the primary. In addition, incumbent members of Congress are free to support primary candidates of their choosing. Many do, including Hill committee chairs and members, viewing a pre-primary contribution as an opportunity to help elect a candidate who has a strong chance of winning or similar policy stances or who is likely to support their own advancement up the ranks of the congressional leadership.

Party recruitment is especially important and difficult when local or national forces favor the opposing party. Just as a strong economy or popular president can encourage members of the president's party to run, it can discourage members of the opposition party from declaring their candidacies, most notably when an incumbent of the opposing party is seeking to remain in the seat. Sometimes the promise of party support can encourage a wavering politician to run under what at the outset appear to be less than optimal conditions.

Recruiting candidates to run for traditionally uncompetitive seats is not a major priority, but party committees work to prevent those seats from going uncontested. According to staffers from both parties' congressional and senatorial campaign committees, convincing candidates to run for these seats is an important part of building for the future. These candidacies can strengthen state and local party committees by giving them a campaign on which to focus and deepening the farm team from which candidates emerge. They also help prepare a party for opportunities that might arise when an incumbent retires, House districts are redrawn, or a scandal or some other event changes the partisan dynamics in the district.

The 2006 race in North Carolina's 11th House district illustrates the degree to which national parties can be influential in candidate recruitment. The seat had been held by Republican representative Charles Taylor for sixteen years. After his initial victory in 1980, Taylor won his ensuing elections with between 55 and 60 percent of the vote. Following the 2004 election, however, the Democrats thought Taylor might be vulnerable. Controversies involving an overdue tax bill on timberland he owned, his purchase of a Russian bank, his association with lobbyist Jack Abramoff, and his opposition to a memorial to the people who died when Flight 93 crashed in Pennsylvania on September 11, 2001, raised questions about Taylor's prospects for reelection. His failure to vote against the Central American Free Trade Agreement, passed by a 217–215 vote in the House, made the incumbent even more vulnerable because it was widely believed that the agreement would result in the export of jobs from the 11th district.[29]

Democratic Congressional Campaign Committee (DCCC) chair Rep. Rahm Emanuel, of Illinois, sought to capitalize on Taylor's vulnerability by recruiting a strong candidate whose profile was well-suited to the district. Emanuel quickly identified Heath Shuler, former star quarterback at the University of Tennessee and retired Washington Redskin. Shuler was raised in North Carolina, and his conservative issue positions match those of most 11th district residents. To help Shuler decide to run, Emanuel personally sought to address the candidate's concern that serving in Congress would reduce the time he had to spend with his children. During a two-week period, Emanuel peppered Shuler with dozens of telephone calls to report the time he was spending with his own children. As recounted by Shuler, "He [Emanuel] calls one Monday morning: 'Heath, I'm taking my kids to school,' then he just hangs up.... At 11:30, he calls and says, 'I'm leaving my office to eat lunch with my kids.' Then, 'Heath, it's 3:30, and I'm walking into school.'"[30] Emanuel's very public recruitment of Shuler, the candidate's celebrity status, and other potential Democratic candidates' perceptions of their inability to defeat Taylor, resulted in Shuler facing only weak opposition in the primary.[31] This enabled Shuler to win the nomination unscathed and eventually led to his eight-percentage-point victory over Taylor.

Just as the Democrats' successful outreach to Shuler demonstrates the possibilities of party success in candidate recruitment, the attempts by the National Republican Senatorial Committee (NRSC) to discourage Rep. Katherine Harris from running for the GOP nomination in Florida demonstrate the limits of persuasion. According to the committee's executive director, Mark Stephens, he and other Republican leaders considered Democratic senator Bill Nelson vulnerable in 2006 because of partisan divisions among Florida voters. Florida elected Nelson in 2000 with 51 percent of the vote, but the voters then chose Republican Jeb Bush as governor in 2002, elected Republican Mel Martinez senator in 2004, and provided President George W. Bush with 52 percent of the popular vote in that same year. Republicans took polls early in the election season to help them recruit the best possible candidate to challenge Nelson, but they ran into a major hurdle when Harris declared she would contest the seat and refused to exit the race. Stephens's description of the poll results demonstrates the GOP's predicament:

> The results showed Harris was unassailable in the Republican primary and without hope in the general election. The Republican base loved her, the Democratic base hated her because of what she did in the 2000 presidential election, and independent and cross-over voters had a negative opinion of her, in part because the media portrayed her as "odd." There was no hope of

pulling together enough groups of voters to win. Her name recognition was at 100 percent. A majority had firm opinions in favor or against her. She was totally defined.[32]

First, Stephens asked Harris in private not to run; then, also in private conversations, NRSC chair Sen. Elizabeth Dole, Governor Bush, White House adviser Rove, and President Bush repeated their party's request. When she refused to withdraw, Dole, both Bushes, and several others declared their lack of support for her publicly and sought to recruit other prominent Republicans to run. However, every potential candidate interpreted Harris's support among 80 percent of expected Republican primary voters as evidence she could defeat them, and they declined to compete.[33] As a result, Harris faced no major opposition in the primary and handily dispatched immigration lawyer William McBride, but she was defeated by Nelson by twenty-two percentage points in the general election.

Labor unions, PACs, and other organized groups typically play more limited roles in candidate recruitment, compared with parties. A few labor PACs and some trade association committees, such as the Committee on Political Education (COPE) of the American Federation of Labor–Congress of Industrial Organizations (AFL-CIO) and the American Medical Association's AMPAC, take polls to encourage experienced politicians to run.[34] Others, such as the National Federation of Independent Business's PAC, sponsor campaign training seminars to encourage individuals who support the group's position to run for the House. Some PACs, such as the pro-women EMILY's List, WISH List, and Women's Campaign Fund, search out members of specific demographic groups and offer them financial and organizational support.[35] Stimulated by the war in Iraq, a number of veterans groups were active in recruiting congressional candidates and helping to finance their campaigns in 2006. Among them were the two bipartisan PACs—the VFW PAC (sponsored by the Veterans of Foreign Wars) and VetPAC—as well as Iraq Veterans for Progress, which supported only Democrats, and Veterans for Victory PAC, which supported only Republicans. Labor unions focus most of their candidate-recruitment efforts, and campaign activities in general, on Democrats. Ideological PACs are among the most aggressive in searching out candidates, and many offer primary assistance to those who share their views. Few corporate PACs become involved in recruiting candidates because they fear offending incumbents.

Finally, political consultants can become involved in a potential candidate's decision making. In addition to taking polls and participating in candidate-training seminars, consultants can use their knowledge of a state or district to assist a would-be candidate in assessing political conditions and sizing up the potential competition. Politicians who have had long-term relationships with consultants usually seek their advice before running for Congress.

PASSING THE PRIMARY TEST

There are two ways to win a major-party nomination for Congress: in an un-contested nominating race or by defeating an opponent. It is not unusual for incumbents to receive their party's nomination without a challenge. Even in the 1992 elections, which were marked by a record number of nonincumbent candidacies, 52 percent of all representatives and 42 percent of all senators who sought reelection were awarded their party's nomination without having to defeat an opponent. In 2006 a mere 19 percent of all representatives and only 48 percent of all senators seeking reelection faced no primary opponent.

Incumbent Victories in Uncontested Primaries

Victories by default occur mainly when an incumbent is perceived to be invul-nerable. The same advantages of incumbency and preelection activities that make incumbents confident of reelection make them seem invincible to those contemplating a primary challenge. Good constituent relations, policy repre-sentation, and other job-related activities are sources of incumbent strength. A hefty campaign account is another.

The loyalties of political activists and organized groups also discourage party members from challenging their representatives for the nomination. While in office, members of Congress work to advance the interests of those who sup-ported their previous election, and in return they routinely receive the support of these individuals and groups. With this support comes the promise of en-dorsements, campaign contributions, volunteer campaign workers, and votes. Would-be primary challengers often recognize that the groups whose support they would need to win the nomination are often among the incumbent's staunchest supporters.[36]

Senior incumbents benefit from the clout—real and perceived—that comes with climbing the ranks of congressional leadership. Rep. Wally Herger, R-Cal., who sought reelection for an eleventh term in 2006, is typical of most senior incumbents who are routinely awarded their party's nomination with-out a fight. One of the major reasons that in 2006 no one was willing to chal-lenge Herger was his good fit for California's 2nd district. Growing up on a cattle ranch and holding conservative positions on the issues, Herger shares the views of those in his rural agricultural district. He opposes government handouts, prefers workfare programs over welfare, and is against environmental regulations that would prevent loggers, ranchers, and other landowners from fully utilizing their property.[37] However, ideology does not keep him from advancing his district's interests, including winning federal funding improvements in irrigation to boost crop production.[38]

Herger also enjoys widespread support because he excels at other aspects of his job: he maintains two district offices to provide constituent services, returns to the district regularly, and votes in accordance with his constituents' views. As a long-time member of the Ways and Means Committee and as chairman of its Human Resources subcommittee in the 109th Congress, he has prioritized legislation to strengthen and preserve the traditional family. Prospective GOP challengers, and the Republican activists whose support they would need to defeat Herger in a primary, recognize the district's interests would suffer should he leave Congress. Moreover, as a Ways and Means Committee member, Herger is in a position to raise large sums of campaign money. Despite winning with more than 60 percent in his last eight elections, Herger raised almost $700,000 for his 2006 contest. His fundraising prowess has probably helped scare off primary opposition.[39]

Finally, Herger has the support of many interest groups and is covered like a hero in the local press. The endorsement that a local paper, *The Paradise Post,* gave Herger a week before the 2006 election is typical of the media coverage he receives:

> While Herger may not be the most eloquent of speakers … [h]e's always accessible to his district…. The *Post* believes that because Herger understands his district and is an experienced legislator he deserves another term. Sekhon is the most credible opposition he has yet faced, but as far as we're concerned, it's still no contest.[40]

The support Herger has received from the local press and advocacy groups deprives would-be primary challengers of much of the organizational and financial support and media coverage needed to defeat him. Not surprisingly, none of the Republican politicians who would normally be included on a list of Herger's rivals or potential successors has challenged him for the nomination.

Junior incumbents rarely have the same kind of clout in Washington or as broad a base of support as senior legislators, but because junior members tend to devote a great deal of time to expanding their bases of support they too typically discourage inside challenges.[41] Junior members also may receive special attention from national, state, and local party organizations. Both the DCCC and the National Republican Congressional Committee (NRCC) hold seminars immediately after each election to instruct junior members on how to use franked mail, town meetings, and the local press to build voter support. Prior to the start of the campaign season, these party committees advise junior members on how to defend their congressional roll-call votes, raise money, and discourage opposition.[42]

State party leaders also give junior members of Congress advice and assistance. During the redistricting process, many of these legislators receive what is perhaps the most important form of help state party leaders can bestow on a candidate: a supportive district. Party leaders in statehouses add areas with high concentrations of party voters who are predisposed to support the candidate. As a result, these candidates usually face little or no primary opposition and weak opposition in the general election.

Considerations of teamwork rarely protect House members who are vulnerable because of scandal. These incumbents face stronger challenges from within their own party than do others. Experienced politicians often are willing to take on an incumbent who is toiling under the cloud of scandal.

Contested Primaries with an Incumbent

When incumbents do face challenges for their party's nomination, they almost always win. Of the seventy-five House members who were challenged for their party's nomination in 2006, only two lost: Cynthia McKinney, D-Ga., who was defeated largely as result of what many considered an objectionable public persona and her involvement in a scandal, and Joe Schwarz, R-Mich., who was subjected to a wave of interest group attack ads that portrayed him as too liberal for his party's primary voters. With the exception of House members who are forced to run against each other after redistricting, typically only those members of Congress who have allegedly committed an ethical transgression, lost touch with their districts, or suffer from failing health run a significant risk of falling to a primary challenger.

What kinds of challengers succeed in knocking off an incumbent for the nomination? The answer is: candidates who have had significant political experience. Only 29 percent of the Democratic and 39 percent of the Republican challengers who sought to defeat an incumbent in a 2006 House primary had been elected to lower-level office. Yet, these elected officials accounted for the two primary challengers who managed to wrest a party nomination away from an incumbent that year (see Table 2-2). This is typical, although unelected politicians also are occasionally successful. Experienced candidates typically succeed where others fail because they are able to take advantage of previous contacts to gain the support of the political and financial elites who contribute to or volunteer in political campaigns. Elected officials can make the case that they have represented some of the voters in the district and know

TABLE 2-2

Political Experience and Major-Party Nominations for the House in 2006

	Primary challenges to an incumbent		Primary contests to challenge an incumbent		Primary contests for an open seat	
	Demo-crats	Repub-licans	Demo-crats	Repub-licans	Demo-crats	Repub-licans
Level of experience						
Elected officials	29%	39%	23%	20%	46%	56%
Unelected politicians	23	12	22	23	20	15
Political amateurs	48	48	55	57	35	29
N	*52*	*49*	*333*	*203*	*97*	*106*
Primary winners						
Elected officials	100%	100%	23%	23%	56%	72%
Unelected politicians	0	0	24	20	15	17
Political amateurs	0	0	53	57	30	10
N	*1*	*1*	*200*	*145*	*27*	*29*
Primary success rates						
Elected officials	7%	5%	60%	80%	33%	35%
Unelected politicians	0%	0%	66%	60%	20%	31%
Political amateurs	5%	0%	58%	72%	23%	9%

Sources: Compiled from candidates' web sites.

Notes: Figures are for nonincumbents only. Some columns do not add to 100 percent because of rounding.

what it takes to get elected. Some of these candidates consciously use a lower-level office as a steppingstone to Congress.[43]

Hank Johnson's victory over McKinney in Georgia's 4th district primary highlights some of the factors that are usually present when a challenger knocks off an incumbent in a nomination contest. McKinney, who was first elected to Congress in 1992 and then defeated in 2002 by county judge Denise Majette, was reelected in 2004 when Majette abandoned the seat to run for the Senate. McKinney was a controversial figure for most of her five terms in Congress. A strong advocate for liberal causes, she ferociously attacked policies she perceived as harming minorities, the poor, unions, or the cause of international human rights. Her confrontational style alienated many of her constituents and made her politically vulnerable. Her remarks on a radio talk show implying that the Bush administration may have had advance knowledge of the terrorist attacks of September 11, 2001, are widely believed to have been critical to her primary defeat in 2002.[44]

Other intemperate actions contributed to her primary 2006 defeat. At a hearing on Hurricane Katrina, she implied that Secretary Michael Chertoff was guilty of negligent homicide because of the poor performance for his leadership of the Department of Homeland Security. When an officer of the U.S. Capitol Police failed to recognize her as a member of Congress and sought to stop her when she walked past a security checkpoint, she allegedly punched him in the chest, leading to a media feeding frenzy. The situation further escalated when her security officer shoved a newspaper reporter who was trying to interview the representative about the incident.

Johnson was a formidable challenger to McKinney in the 2006 primary election. Serving as DeKalb County commissioner, he presented himself as a reasonable, can-do politician—a sharp contrast to McKinney. In declaring his candidacy, he stated:

> The Fourth District faces serious problems of traffic and transportation, public
> safety, health care and education. I'm a nuts-and-bolts public servant. My
> record speaks for itself. I am committed to getting results for those that made
> me their County Commissioner. I will bring that same approach to represent-
> ing the District in the 110th Congress.[45]

Although Johnson and McKinney dominated the race, the presence of a third candidate, John Coyne, an architect, prevented either front-runner from winning an outright majority of the vote in the district's July 18th primary. As a result, the nomination had to be decided in a runoff. The runoff was well-funded and negative in tone, with each candidate attacking the other over the sources of campaign contributions.[46] Johnson raised more money than McKinney, and according to most commentators, he outperformed her when they debated.[47] Perhaps his biggest advantage was one of political style. Many 4th district voters were displeased with McKinney's leadership style, enabling Johnson to present himself as the "un-Cynthia McKinney."[48] After winning the primary runoff with 59 percent of the vote, Johnson went on to trounce Republican candidate Catherine Davis by amassing 76 percent of the vote. As is often the case when a member of Congress losses a nomination contest, the challenger in this case had significant political experience and the incumbent was embroiled in scandal.

Open Primaries

In opposing-incumbent primaries, contestants seek the nomination of one party when an incumbent of the opposing party has decided to seek reelection.

Another type of open nomination, called an open-seat primary, occurs in districts in which no incumbent is seeking reelection. Both types of primaries attract more candidates than do contests in which a nonincumbent must defeat an incumbent to win the nomination, but opposing-incumbent primaries are usually the less hotly contested of the two.

In opposing-incumbent primaries, political experience is usually a determining factor. Elected officials and unelected politicians do well in such primaries. In 2006 elected officials made up 23 percent of the Democratic candidates and 23 percent of the winners in these races. They enjoyed a nomination rate of 60 percent. Similar percentages of their Republican counterparts ran in and won incumbent-opposing primaries, but the GOP candidates had a success rate of 80 percent. Unelected politicians also did well in opposing-incumbent primaries in 2006. Among the Democrats, they included about one-fifth of the candidates and almost one-quarter of the winners, and they enjoyed a success rate of 66 percent. In the case of the Republicans, a similar number of unelected politicians ran in opposing-incumbent primaries, but substantially fewer won and they had a somewhat lower success rate. Political amateurs typically outnumber politically experienced candidates, and as a consequence they win more primaries. The 2006 contests were no exception, but they were unusual in that Republican amateurs enjoyed a very high success rate.[49]

Open-seat primaries are the most competitive of all nominating contests. They typically attract many highly qualified candidates, especially individuals who have experience holding elective office. These candidates make up the largest share of primary winners and have the highest success rates. As can be expected, the success rates of political amateurs are substantially lower, which was especially true among Republicans in 2006.

The Democratic primary in Maryland's 3rd congressional district, like most open-seat primaries, was a hard-fought contest. The seat opened up when the Democratic incumbent, Rep. Benjamin L. Cardin, decided to run for the Senate seat being given up by Sen. Paul S. Sarbanes, D-Md., who was retiring. Eleven Democrats originally ran for the House seat (one later dropped out). The field of candidates included three elected officials (two state legislators and a county council member), five unelected politicians (a state commissioner, city commissioner, mayoral aide, state party treasurer, and county government relations director), and two amateurs (a well-known television newscaster and a dentist). The ultimate winner of the primary (and the general election) was John Sarbanes, a lawyer and the son of soon-to-retire Senator Sarbanes who had held the district before he became a senator; the younger Sarbanes was an unelected politician who had clerked in both a state and a federal court. The Republican field was made up of eight candidates. All were political amateurs, which is not surprising given the Democrats' dominance of the state. Marketing executive John White won the nomination, only to lose to Sarbanes by a vote margin of almost 2 to 1.

The electoral process—which transforms private citizen to candidate to major-party nominee to House member—greatly influences the makeup of the national legislature. Those parts of the process leading up to the general election, especially the decision to run, play an important role in producing a Congress that is not demographically representative of the U.S. population. The willingness of women and minorities to run for Congress during the past few decades and of voters to support them has helped make the national legislature somewhat more representative in regard to gender and race. Still, in many respects Congress does not mirror U.S. society.

Occupation

Occupation has a tremendous effect on the pool of House candidates and on their prospects for success. Individuals (many of whom have legal training) who claim law, politics, or public service as their professions are a minuscule portion of the general population, but in the 2006 elections they made up 33 percent of all nomination candidates and 40 percent of all general election candidates. In the 110th Congress they comprised 52 percent of all House members (see Table 2-3). The analytical, verbal, and organizational skills required to succeed in the legal profession or in public service help these individuals undertake a successful bid for Congress. The high salaries that members of these professions earn give them the wherewithal to take a leave of absence from work so that they can campaign full time. These highly paid professionals also can afford to make the initial investment needed to get a campaign off the ground. Moreover, their professions place many attorneys and public servants in places where they can rub elbows with political activists and contributors whose support can be crucial to winning a House primary or general election.

Business professionals and bankers are not as overrepresented among nomination candidates, major-party nominees, or House members as are public servants and lawyers, but persons in business tend to be successful in congressional elections. Many possess money, skills, and contacts that are useful in politics. Educators (particularly college professors) and other white-collar professionals also enjoy a modicum of success in congressional elections. Of these, educators

TABLE 2-3

Occupational Representativeness of 2006 House Candidates and Members of the 110th Congress

Occupation	General population	Nomination candidates	General election candidates	House members
Agricultural or blue-collar workers	30%	4%	4%	2%
Business or banking	4	23	25	22
Clergy or social work	1	2	2	1
Education	4	10	10	9
Entertainer, actor, writer, or artist	1	1	1	1
Law	1	14	16	27
Medicine	3	4	4	9
Military	—	4	4	9
Politics or public service	3	19	24	25
Other white-collar professionals	20	4	5	5
Outside work force	33	—	—	—
Unidentified, not politics	—	15	5	—
N	*281,400,000*	*1,331*	*781*	*435*

Sources: General population figures are from U.S. Department of Commerce, Bureau of the Census, *Statistical Abstract of the United States* (Washington, D.C.: U.S. Government Printing Office, 2001), 380–384; candidate occupation data are from Project E-Voter, University of Maryland.

Notes: Figures include all 2006 major-party House candidates and all House members of the 110th Congress, including Rep. Bernard Sanders, I-Vt. The figures for the general population are from 2001. — = less than 0.5 percent. Some columns do not add to 100 percent because of rounding.

are the most successful group of candidates. They rarely possess the wealth of lawyers and business professionals, but educators frequently have the verbal, analytical, and organizational skills needed to get elected. Although both parties have taken to recruiting veterans in recent years and 101 House members serving in the 110th Congress have done some form of military service, very few members of Congress are typically drawn from the ranks of the career military.

Just as some professions are overrepresented in Congress, others are underrepresented. Disproportionately few persons employed in agriculture or blue-collar professions either run for Congress or are elected. Even fewer students, homemakers, and others who are considered outside the workforce attempt to win a congressional seat.

Closely related to the issue of occupation is wealth. Personal wealth is a significant advantage in an election system that places a premium on a candidate's ability to spend money. Roughly 7 percent of House members have assets worth in excess of $4.67 million, a much larger percentage than the proportion of the general population who enjoy similar wealth.[50]

Gender

A record seventy-four women were elected to the House in 2006—just more than one-sixth of the number of men. The major reason for the underrepresentation of women in the legislative branch is that fewer women than men run for Congress (see Figure 2-4). Only 17 percent of all contestants for

FIGURE 2-4

Gender Representativeness of 2006 House Candidates and Members of the 110th Congress

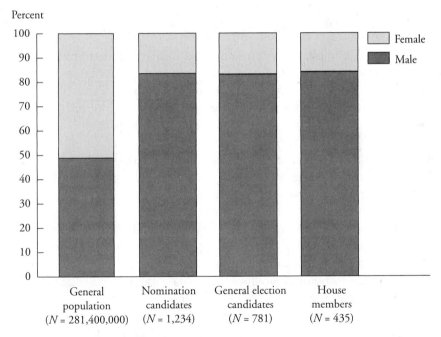

Sources: General population figures are from U.S. Department of Commerce, Bureau of the Census, *Statistical Abstract of the United States* (Washington, D.C.: U.S. Government Printing Office, 2001), 13; candidate gender data are from Project E-Voter, University of Maryland.

Notes: Figures include all 2006 major-party House candidates and House members of the 110th Congress. The figures for the general population are from 2001.

major-party nominations in 2006 were female. Women are underrepresented among congressional candidates for many reasons. Active campaigning demands greater time and flexibility than most people, particularly women, can afford. Women continue to assume primary parenting responsibilities in most families, a role that is difficult to combine with long hours of campaigning. Only since the 1980s have significant numbers of women entered the legal and business professions, which often serve as training grounds for elected officials and political activists. Women also continue to be underrepresented in state legislatures and other elective offices, which commonly serve as steppingstones to Congress.[51]

Once women decide to run, gender does not affect their election prospects.[52] Women are just about as likely as men to advance from primary candidate to nominee to House member.[53] As more women come to occupy lower-level offices or to hold positions in the professions from which congressional candidates usually emerge, one can expect that the number of women who consider a bid for Congress, run, and get elected to increase.[54]

Age

Congressional candidates also are somewhat older than the general population, and this is due only partly to the age requirements imposed by the Constitution. The typical candidate for nomination is more than three times as likely to be forty to fifty-four years of age as twenty-five to thirty-nine (see Figure 2-5). Moreover, successful nomination candidates tend to be slightly older than those whom they defeat. The selection bias in favor of those who are forty to seventy-four continues into the general election; as a result, Congress is made up largely of persons who are middle-aged or older.

The underrepresentation of young people is due to an electoral process that allows older individuals to benefit from their greater life experiences. People who have reached middle age typically have greater financial resources, more political experience, and a wider network of political and professional associates to help them with their campaigns. Moreover, a formidable group of people who are forty to seventy-four years old—current representatives—also benefit from considerable incumbency advantages.

Religion

Religion has an impact on candidate emergence, sometimes providing politicians with a policy concern, such as abortion or human rights, that gives them the motivation to run. Jews and mainline Protestants are overrepresented in

FIGURE 2-5

Age Representativeness of 2006 House Candidates and Members of the 110th Congress

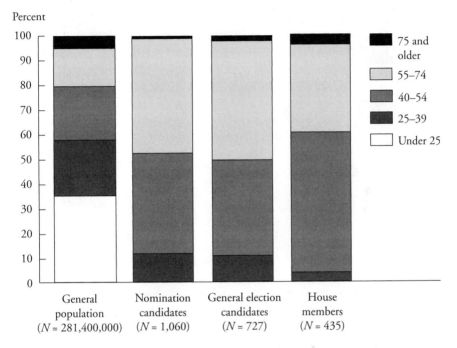

Sources: General population figures are from U.S. Department of Commerce, Bureau of the Census, *Statistical Abstract of the United States* (Washington, D.C.: U.S. Government Printing Office, 2001), 13; candidate age data are from Project E-Voter, University of Maryland.

Notes: Figures include all 2006 major-party House candidates and House members of the 110th Congress. The figures for the general population are from 2001.

the candidate pool (see Figure 2-6). Evangelical Christians, those belonging to other religions—including Congress's first two Buddhists and first Muslim—and individuals who profess to have no religious affiliation are underrepresented. Yet, once individuals enter the pool, religion has little effect on how they do.

Individuals who claim no religious identification make up the most underrepresented "belief" group in Congress for a few reasons. People who do not participate in church activities typically have fewer political and civic skills compared with those who do, which may discourage them from running for Congress.[55] Atheists and agnostics also may believe that it would be impossible for them to get elected given the large role that organized religion plays in

FIGURE 2-6

Religious Representativeness of 2006 House Candidates and Members
of the 110th Congress

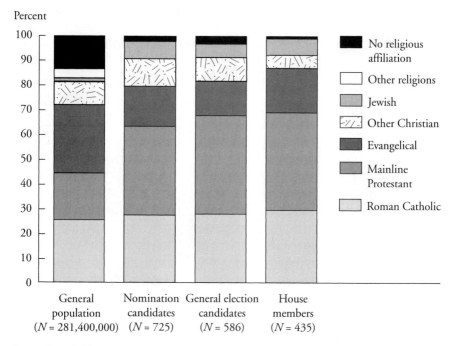

Percent

	No religious affiliation
	Other religions
	Jewish
	Other Christian
	Evangelical
	Mainline Protestant
	Roman Catholic

General population (*N* = 281,400,000) Nomination candidates (*N* = 725) General election candidates (*N* = 586) House members (*N* = 435)

Sources: Compiled from Barry A. Kosmin and Egon Mayer, *American Religions Identification Survey,* Graduate Center, City University of New York, November 2002; candidate religion data are from Project E-Voter, University of Maryland.

Notes: Figures include all 2006 major-party House candidates and House members of the 110th Congress.

politics in many parts of the country. As a result, they have little presence in politics or national government.

Race and Ethnicity

Race and ethnicity, like religion and gender, have a greater effect on candidate emergence than on electoral success.[56] Whites are heavily overrepresented in the pool of nomination candidates, whereas persons of other races are underrepresented (see Figure 2-7). This situation reflects the disproportionately small numbers of minorities who have entered the legal or business professions or who occupy state or local offices.

FIGURE 2-7

Racial and Ethnic Representativeness of 2006 House Candidates and Members of the 110th Congress

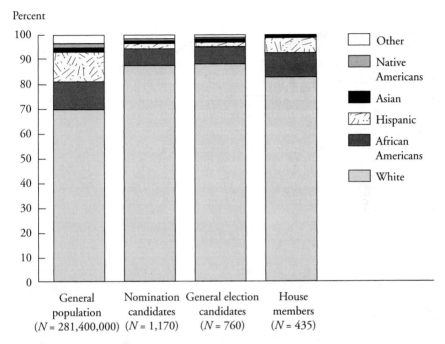

Percent

| General population (N = 281,400,000) | Nomination candidates (N = 1,170) | General election candidates (N = 760) | House members (N = 435) |

Legend:
- Other
- Native Americans
- Asian
- Hispanic
- African Americans
- White

Sources: General population figures are from U.S. Department of Commerce, Bureau of the Census, *Statistical Abstract of the United States* (Washington, D.C.: U.S. Government Printing Office, 2001), 19; candidate race data are from Project E-Voter, University of Maryland.

Notes: Figures include all 2006 major-party House candidates and House members of the 110th Congress. The figures for the general population are from 2001.

Once minority politicians declare their candidacies, they have fairly good odds of winning their party's nomination and getting elected. The recent successes of minority House candidates are largely due to redistricting processes intended to promote minority representation.[57] A few House members, such as J. C. Watts, an African American elected in 1994 who retired in 2003, won seats that were not specifically carved to promote minority representation in Congress. Still, most minority candidates are elected in districts that have large numbers of voters belonging to their racial or ethnic group, and once they win these seats they tend to hold onto them. Only one such incumbent, Representative McKinney in Georgia, was defeated in 2006, and she lost the primary runoff to a candidate of her own race. The success of the minority members of Congress can be attributed to their ability to build multiracial coalitions and the advantages that incumbency confers on them.[58]

Party Differences

Public servants and members of the legal profession make up a large portion of each party's candidate pool, but more Republican candidates come from the business world and more Democratic candidates are lawyers and public servants (see Table 2-4). The GOP's overrepresentation of business professionals continues through each stage of the election and in the House, as does the Democrats' overrepresentation of lawyers and career politicians. Attorneys and career public servants from both parties do well in elections, but they are more strongly represented in the Democratic than the Republican Party. Business executives, in contrast, have a bigger presence in the ranks of Republican legislators. Even though Republicans have historically been viewed as the defenders of the rich, members of both parties are found among Congress's wealthiest legislators.[59]

More women run for Democratic than Republican nominations for Congress. This gender gap reflects the greater number of women who identify with the Democratic Party and that party's greater acceptance of female candidates. Democratic women also are more successful in winning the nomination and getting elected to the House than are their GOP counterparts.[60]

Democratic primary candidates tend to be somewhat older than their Republican counterparts, reflecting the different orientations of the individuals in the parties' candidate pools. Democratic primary candidates are more likely to come from the ranks of politicians and to consider a congressional election as a somewhat risky opportunity to take a step up the career ladder. Members of the Republican candidate pool are more apt to have careers in the private sector. Many run for Congress before they have taken major strides in their profession, recognizing that if they wait too long they may have advanced too far professionally to want to sacrifice their career in order to run.[61] The initial age difference between Democratic and Republican candidates lays the foundation for an uneven trend toward a middle-aged Congress. The age difference between the parties gets smaller as the candidates progress through the primaries and the general election.

The parties also draw candidates from different religious, racial, and ethnic groups. Republican primary contestants are mainly Protestant and white, as are the GOP's nominees and House members. The Democratic Party attracts candidates from a wider array of groups, including significant numbers of Catholics, Jews, and African Americans. These patterns reflect the parties' electoral coalitions.

TABLE 2-4

2006 Major-Party Nomination and General Election Candidates and
House Members of the 110th Congress

	Nomination candidates		General election candidates		House members	
	Demo-crats	Repub-licans	Demo-crats	Repub-licans	Demo-crats	Repub-licans
Occupation						
Agricultural or blue-collar workers	4%	6%	3%	5%	2%	1%
Business or banking	19	31	18	32	13	35
Clergy or social work	2	1	1	1	1	1
Education	14	6	14	6	12	7
Entertainer, actor, writer, or artist	1	1	1	1	1	1
Law	18	13	19	14	32	23
Medicine	5	4	4	4	4	4
Military	4	4	5	3	—	1
Politics or public service	21	21	25	25	28	23
Other white-collar professionals	5	5	4	5	6	4
Unidentified, not politics	7	8	5	5	—	—
N	*662*	*528*	*418*	*363*	*233*	*202*
Gender						
Male	79%	88%	78%	88%	79%	90%
Female	21	12	22	12	21	10
N	*678*	*556*	*418*	*363*	*233*	*202*
Age						
25–39	13%	13%	10%	12%	6%	6%
40–54	38	44	36	41	33	40
55–74	46	41	52	44	57	51
75 and older	3	2	3	3	4	3
N	*577*	*483*	*388*	*339*	*233*	*202*

(Table continues)

TABLE 2-4 *(continued)*

	Nomination candidates		General election candidates		House members	
	Demo-crats	Repub-licans	Demo-crats	Repub-licans	Demo-crats	Repub-licans
Religion						
Roman Catholic	32%	23%	33%	22%	38%	20%
Mainline Protestant	30	45	30	50	29	52
Evangelical	12	17	12	16	13	20
Jewish	7	4	7	4	12	—
Other Christian	14	9	12	7	4	8
Other	1	—	1	—	1	—
No religious affiliation	3	7	4	—	3	—
N	*370*	*355*	*296*	*290*	*233*	*202*
Race and Ethnicity						
White	81%	92%	84%	93%	72%	98%
African American	11	3	9	2	17	—
Hispanic	5	3	5	3	9	2
Other	3	2	3	2	2	—
N	*636*	*534*	*405*	*355*	*233*	*202*

Sources: Compiled from data from Project E-Voter, University of Maryland.

Notes: Figures are for all major-party nomination candidates, all major-party general election candidates, and all major-party members of the 110th Congress. — = less than 0.5 percent. Some columns do not add to 100 percent because of rounding. Candidates under twenty-five years of age are omitted from the table because none ran in 2006.

THE SENATE

The Senate historically has been less demographically representative than the House. The election of more women and minorities during the past few decades has resulted in a slow move toward more accurately mirroring the U.S. population. However, descriptions of the Senate as a bastion for white, wealthy, middle-aged, professional men are very close to the mark.

Part of the reason that the Senate has been slower to change than the House is that Senate terms are six years, and only one-third of the upper chamber is up for election at a time. Other reasons have to do with the heightened demands of Senate campaigns. As statewide races, Senate primary and general election campaigns require larger amounts of money, more extensive organizations, and more complex strategies than do House campaigns. Successful Senate candidates generally possess more skill, political connections, and campaign experience than do their House counterparts. The fact that so many members of the Senate had extensive political experience prior to their election suggests that the dearth of women and minorities in lower-level offices may help to explain why the upper chamber is changing more slowly than the lower. To gain seats in the Senate, members of traditionally underrepresented groups have had first to place citizens in positions that serve as steppingstones to that body. As more women, African Americans, and members of other underrepresented groups are elected or appointed to local, state, and federal offices, their numbers in the Senate will probably increase.

Nevertheless, a single election can have a great effect on the Senate's makeup. After the polls closed in 1992, the number of women was set to increase from two to six, including the Senate's first African American woman, Illinois Democrat Carol Moseley-Braun. In addition, the Senate prepared to swear in its first Native American, Coloradan Ben Nighthorse Campbell. Few ensuing elections had as big an impact on the demographic makeup of the Senate as that of 1992. Following the 2006 election, the number of women grew to sixteen, the number of African Americans remained at one, and the number of Hispanics reached three.

Even though traditionally underrepresented groups have increased their numbers in the Senate, this does not mean that the upper chamber has become a place of employment for individuals with a diverse array of backgrounds. Fifty-eight of the senators in the 110th Congress were drawn from the legal profession, including several who also worked in other fields. About a dozen or so had careers in public service. Twenty-seven had worked in business or banking. Fourteen had been involved in education. Six had worked in agriculture and another four had been journalists. Two had worked as veterinarians, one was a butcher, and another was a social worker. The average age for a senator was sixty-two when the 110th Congress was sworn in.[62]

Most senators had significant political experience prior to getting elected, often having held more than one office. Forty-eight of the senators in the 110th Congress had previously served in the U.S. House of Representatives, seven had been governors of their states, fifteen had held some other statewide office, and nineteen had been elected to a state legislature or local office.[63] Eleven senators, including Mel Martinez, R-Fl., Herb Kohl, D-Wis., and Hillary Rodham Clinton, D-N.Y., were first elected to the Senate after holding a significant unelected political position. Martinez had been secretary of housing and urban development, Kohl was chair of the Wisconsin Democratic Party, and, of course, Clinton had been first lady.

Although senators are more likely than representatives to have to defend their nominations, Senate primaries tend to be less competitive than those for the House. Between 1982 and 2004, only three senators were defeated in their bids for renomination. Joseph I. Lieberman of Connecticut was added to the group in 2006, when he was defeated by Ned Lamont, an antiwar candidate and former town selectman from Greenwich, whom Lieberman went on to defeat when running as an independent in the general election. The relative ease with which members of the Senate retain their party's nomination can be attributed to a number of factors besides the tremendous demands that Senate primary contests make on challengers. For one thing, senators and Senate candidates are highly strategic. Like their counterparts in the House, members of the Senate use their office to help their state receive its share of federal projects, to garner positive coverage in the press, and to build support among voters. Senators, like representatives, also build huge campaign treasuries to discourage potential opponents. In addition, most members of the Senate are shrewd enough to recognize when it is time to step down. In 2006 four senators opted for voluntary retirement from politics: Paul S. Sarbanes, D-Md., James Jeffords, I-Vt., Bill Frist, R-Tenn., and Mark Dayton, D-Minn. Age undoubtedly influenced the decisions of Sarbanes and Jeffords, each of whom was over seventy years old and had served several terms in the Senate. Frist, who had begun to lay the groundwork for a 2008 presidential candidacy and later changed his mind, honored an earlier pledge to serve only two terms. Dayton's retirement was probably the only one influenced by political calculations, as many thought the one-term senator had done little to shore up his hold on the seat and was vulnerable.[64]

The effect of scandal, aging, infirmity, declining public support, and strategic ambition on Senate turnover tends to be felt more through members' retirements than primary defeats. Moreover, the most qualified opponent a senator is likely to face in a primary is a current House member or some other elected official. Because these individuals are also highly strategic, only a few are willing to risk their current positions by picking a primary fight. Most prefer to wait until a seat becomes open.

When an incumbent does announce an upcoming retirement, or a member of the opposite party appears vulnerable, political parties and interest groups help to shape the field of Senate candidates by encouraging potential candidates to declare their candidacies. These organizations promise the same types of support, under the same kinds of circumstances, to potential Senate candidates as they offer to House candidates.

The Democratic Senatorial Campaign Committee (DSCC), for example, played a significant role in encouraging State Auditor Claire McCaskill, who two years earlier had defeated an incumbent governor in the Democratic primary, to challenge Republican James Talent for his Senate seat from Missouri. To help convince McCaskill to run, DSCC chairman Sen. Charles E. Schumer, D-N.Y., made an early commitment of party money, fundraising assistance, and other campaign services. Sen. Harry Reid, D-Nev., the Senate minority leader at the time, and former Democratic House leader Richard Gephardt of her home state of Missouri personally weighed in to encourage her to run.[65] It is not surprising that McCaskill joined the race, given the large amount of support she was promised and that she had done so well in her previous statewide election.

Party organizations have not traditionally become involved in contested Senate primaries even though they may promise a candidate from hundreds of thousands to millions of dollars in campaign support upon winning the nomination. In 2006, however, the senatorial campaign committees of both parties were actively involved in a number of primaries. In addition to McCaskill's race, the Democrats provided pre-primary support to Bob Casey of Pennsylvania, Amy Klobuchar of Minnesota, and Jim Webb of Virginia, all of whom went on to win the nomination and general election.[66] The Republicans were involved in recruiting candidates for several races, including Michael McGavick of Washington State and Thomas Kean Jr. of New Jersey. However, the GOP senatorial campaign leadership did not have as strong a recruitment year as did the Democrats, reflecting the constraints imposed by a political environment that was unfavorable to them. Their attempts to recruit House members Shelley Moore Capito of West Virginia and Tom Osborne of Nebraska to run for the Senate were unsuccessful. Perhaps their greatest disappointment was a failure to recruit a stronger candidate than Katherine Harris to run against Senator Bill Nelson in Florida.[67]

Whether successful or not in specific cases, the senatorial campaign committees are singled out by candidates as the most influential organizations involved in the candidate-recruitment process. They are not as important as family and friends, issues, or a desire to improve government or become a national leader, but they are more influential in the decisions of candidates than are other political organizations.[68] In this sense, candidate emergence in Senate elections is similar to that for the House.

SUMMARY

Virtually anyone can run for Congress because there are few legal requirements for serving, and neither party committees nor interest groups have the power to simply hand out a congressional nomination. Strategic politicians, mainly individuals who have held office or have some other significant nonelective experience, carefully assess political conditions before deciding to run. Most incumbents—who are the most strategic of all politicians—choose to run again, but personal considerations, a loss of political clout in Congress, redistricting, scandal, or a wave of voter hostility toward the federal government or their party can encourage incumbents to retire. These factors also have an impact on the candidacy decisions of strategic nonincumbents, but the opening of a congressional seat is even more important than other political conditions in spurring on their candidacies. Amateur politicians tend to be less discriminating and are less likely to win their party's nomination.

Candidate emergence, nomination, and election processes have a major impact on who serves in Congress. Most members of the contemporary House and Senate are white, middle- or upper-class males. Most are middle-aged or older and belong to a mainstream religion. The vast majority also have had significant political experience prior to getting elected. The number of national legislators who belong to underrepresented groups has increased in recent years, but change comes slowly to Congress, especially in the Senate.

CHAPTER THREE

The Anatomy of a Campaign

What types of organizations do candidates assemble to wage their campaigns? How do they budget their resources? This chapter addresses these two questions. During the parties' golden age, the answers were simple: most House and Senate candidates relied on state and local party committees to wage their campaigns and to determine how much to spend on different election activities. An individual candidate's "organization" was often little more than a loyal following within the party. But by the mid-1950s, few congressional candidates could count on party organizations to obtain their nominations and wage their campaigns. Senate campaigns became significantly more professional during the 1950s and 1960s; House campaigns followed suit during the 1970s.[1] The decline of the political machine and the legal and systemic changes that fostered that decline led to the development of the modern campaign organization.[2]

Most contemporary congressional campaigns are waged by specialized, professional organizations. Few campaign organizations are fully self-sufficient. Most employ paid staff and volunteers to carry out some of the tasks associated with running for Congress and hire political consultants to perform skilled campaign activities such as taking polls and producing campaign ads. But consultants do more than carry out isolated campaign tasks. Political consulting has become a profession, replete with its own standards, trade association, newsletters, and magazine. Consultants help budding politicians learn what to expect and what will be expected of them during the campaign. Consultants' opinions of what is strategically and tactically advisable and ethical have a major impact on candidate conduct.[3] In this chapter I describe campaign organizations, focusing on the political consultants and other personnel who work in them and on how campaigns spend their money.

CAMPAIGN ORGANIZATIONS

Candidates need to achieve several interrelated objectives to compete success-fully in an election, including raising money, formulating a strategy, and com-municating with and mobilizing voters. Specialized skills and training are re-quired to meet many of these objectives. Senate campaigns, which are larger and must typically reach out to more voters, employ more paid staff and con-sultants than do their House counterparts.

The biggest factor in House campaigns is incumbency. Assembling a cam-paign organization is an easy task for incumbents. Most reassemble the person-nel who worked on their previous campaign. A substantial number of incum-bents keep elements of their organizations intact between elections. Some of these organizations consist only of a part-time political aide or fundraiser. Others are quite substantial, possessing the characteristics of a permanent busi-ness. They own a building and have a large professional staff; a fundraising ap-paratus; an investment portfolio; a campaign car; an entertainment budget; and a team of lawyers, accountants, and consultants on retainer. House incum-bents typically spend hundreds of thousands of dollars on organizational maintenance during the two years leading up to an election. Some congres-sional leaders put together "Cadillac" campaigns. In 2006 Speaker of the House Dennis Hastert, R-Ill., spent more than $2.7 million on staff, rent, of-fice equipment, supplies, and other resources used solely for organizational maintenance.[4]

Few House challengers or open-seat candidates possess even a temporary or-ganization capable of contesting a congressional election until just before their declaration of candidacy. Nonincumbents who have held an elective post usu-ally have advantages in assembling a campaign organization over those who have not. Some have steering committees, "Friends of 'Candidate *X*'" clubs, or working relationships with political consultants from previous campaigns. Candidates who have never held an elective office but have been active in pol-itics usually have advantages over political amateurs in building an organiza-tion. Previous political involvement gives party committee chairs, political aides, and individuals who have previously run for office some knowledge of how to wage a campaign and ties to others who can help them. The organiza-tional advantages that incumbents possess over challengers are usually greater than the advantages that experienced nonincumbents have over political amateurs.[5]

Almost nine out of ten House members' campaign organizations are man-aged by a paid staffer or some combination of a paid staffer and outside consultant (see Table 3-1). Often the campaign manager is the administrative

TABLE 3-1

Staffing Activities in House Elections

	All	Incumbents In jeopardy	Incumbents Shoo-ins	Challengers Hope-fuls	Challengers Likely losers	Open-seat candidates Pros-pects	Open-seat candidates Mis-matched
Campaign management							
Paid staff	62%	79%	82%	81%	35%	77%	65%
Consultant	6	4	6	12	2	11	12
Party/interest groups	2	—	1	—	3	—	—
Volunteer	9	3	4	3	17	3	6
Candidate	22	10	10	12	41	6	18
Not used	4	3	5	—	6	3	—
Press relations							
Paid staff	66%	86%	84%	84%	37%	89%	71%
Consultant	5	—	5	12	5	3	12
Party/interest groups	1	—	—	—	1	3	—
Volunteer	10	3	4	3	20	3	—
Candidate	19	10	7	3	38	3	18
Not used	4	—	4	—	7	—	—
Issue and opposition research							
Paid staff	40%	38%	57%	62%	28%	23%	35%
Consultant	21	38	21	22	8	43	35
Party/interest groups	10	17	4	16	6	29	12
Volunteer	11	—	2	3	22	6	12
Candidate	14	3	1	3	29	3	24
Not used	10	7	17	—	12	3	—
Fundraising							
Paid staff	52%	83%	75%	59%	25%	63%	53%
Consultant	14	14	20	16	6	23	24
Party/interest groups	5	—	4	6	3	14	6
Volunteer	9	3	5	6	15	3	6
Candidate	28	7	10	25	50	11	24
Not used	4	—	—	—	10	—	—
Polling							
Paid staff	7%	3%	10%	3%	6%	14%	6%
Consultant	49	86	56	81	17	74	71
Party/interest groups	6	7	5	3	6	9	6
Volunteer	4	—	1	—	6	6	—
Candidate	4	—	3	3	6	—	—
Not used	32	3	26	12	58	—	18

(Table continues)

TABLE 3-1   *(continued)*

	All	Incumbents		Challengers		Open-seat candidates	
		In jeopardy	Shoo-ins	Hope-fuls	Likely losers	Pros-pects	Mis-matched
Media advertising							
Paid staff	27%	17%	40%	28%	22%	17%	41%
Consultant	46	72	51	69	20	80	53
Party/interest groups	3	3	—	6	4	3	—
Volunteer	6	—	2	3	11	3	6
Candidate	15	7	5	—	35	—	—
Not used	9	—	10	9	13	—	6
Direct mail							
Paid staff	27%	31%	41%	31%	16%	23%	24%
Consultant	34	52	42	44	10	60	65
Party/interest groups	6	—	2	12	6	11	12
Volunteer	12	7	6	12	20	6	—
Candidate	7	3	4	—	15	3	—
Not used	21	10	14	9	39	3	—
Internet web site							
Paid staff	41%	69%	41%	59%	27%	46%	41%
Consultant	17	21	21	22	7	29	35
Party/interest groups	6	3	4	12	6	6	6
Volunteer	18	—	14	6	30	20	6
Candidate	10	—	1	3	24	—	6
Not used	10	7	22	—	7	3	6
Mass phone calls							
Paid staff	15%	10%	21%	16%	13%	11%	6%
Consultant	25	31	25	34	11	46	59
Party/interest groups	12	14	7	9	11	23	18
Volunteer	24	24	21	28	23	34	18
Candidate	3	—	1	3	6	3	—
Not used	29	24	34	9	43	3	—
Get-out-the-vote							
Paid staff	30%	38%	31%	50%	14%	54%	47%
Consultant	4	—	9	6	2	6	6
Party/interest groups	33	28	30	28	34	46	29
Volunteer	31	28	29	22	37	23	35
Candidate	6	3	4	—	10	3	6
Not used	11	3	10	3	19	6	6

(Table continues)

TABLE 3-1 *(continued)*

	All	Incumbents		Challengers		Open-seat candidates	
		In jeopardy	Shoo-ins	Hope-fuls	Likely losers	Pros-pects	Mis-matched
Legal advice							
Paid staff	15%	10%	15%	19%	11%	23%	18%
Consultant	20	21	27	19	11	26	29
Party/interest groups	13	24	9	34	4	26	6
Volunteer	13	14	10	9	15	11	18
Candidate	9	—	3	9	17	—	6
Not used	35	35	38	19	42	14	41
Accounting							
Paid staff	51%	62%	64%	56%	31%	71%	59%
Consultant	11	14	17	12	6	14	12
Party/interest groups	3	10	1	12	—	6	—
Volunteer	19	7	12	16	30	9	18
Candidate	10	—	2	—	24	3	—
Not used	7	7	5	3	11	—	12
Average number of activities performed by paid staff or consultants	6.7	8.8	8.4	8.8	3.6	9	8.6

Source: "2002 Congressional Campaign Study," Center for American Politics and Citizenship, University of Maryland.

Notes: Figures are for general election candidates in major-party contested races, excluding those in incumbent-versus-incumbent races. The categories are the same as those in Table 1-4. Figures for interest groups include labor unions. Dashes = less than 0.5 percent. Some columns do not add to 100 percent because some activities were performed by more than one person or because of rounding. $N = 316$.

assistant or chief of staff in the House member's congressional office. Administrative assistants and other congressional staffers routinely take leaves of absence from their jobs to work for their boss's reelection, sometimes as volunteers who consider as compensation enough the bonuses or high salaries they receive as congressional aides when they are not on leave. Shoo-in incumbents (those who were reelected by more than 20 percent of the two-party vote) are just about as likely as incumbents in jeopardy (those who lost or won by less than 20 percent of the two-party vote) to hire a paid staffer to handle day-to-day management and a general consultant to assist with campaign strategy. Most hopeful challengers (those who eventually won or lost by 20 points or less) have professionally managed campaigns, but only 37 percent of all likely-loser challengers (those who eventually lost by more than 20 percent of the vote) have campaigns managed by a paid staffer or general consultant. Many of these campaigns rely on volunteer managers, but some have no managers at all, relying on the candidates themselves to run their own campaigns.

Open-seat campaigns are similar to those waged by incumbents. All but 12 percent of the open-seat prospects (whose races were eventually decided by margins of 20 percent or less) rely on a paid staffer or general consultant to manage their campaigns. Many open-seat candidates who are considered mismatched (whose election was decided by more than 20 percent of the vote) also have professional managers, but a substantial portion of them rely on the candidate or volunteers for campaign management. Few campaigns are managed by personnel provided by a political party or interest group, regardless of their competitiveness.

Professional staffs carry out press relations in most campaigns. More than 85 percent of all incumbents in close races rely on a paid staffer, frequently a congressional press secretary who is on a leave of absence, to handle their relations with the media. A small number of incumbents also hire campaign consultants to issue press releases and handle calls from journalists. Challengers and open-seat candidates in close races are just as likely as incumbents to rely on paid staff to handle media relations. A somewhat larger number hire political consultants for this purpose. Slightly fewer open-seat candidates in one-sided contests rely on paid staff. Only 42 percent of all challengers in uncompetitive races are able to turn to campaign professionals to help them work the press, relying on volunteers and their own efforts instead.

Issue and opposition research is often carried out by a combination of professional staff, outside consultants, party committees, interest groups, and volunteers. Incumbents, challengers, and open-seat candidates in one-sided races are more likely to rely on volunteers or the candidate to conduct research, or not even bother with it, than are candidates in close races. Some shoo-in incumbents turn to memos that congressional staff write about the major issues facing the nation and the district. These memos are usually drafted to help House members represent their constituents, but the political payoffs from them are significant. Most likely-loser challengers, who could benefit from the research, are unable to afford it.

Although most incumbents in jeopardy, hopeful challengers, and open-seat prospects depend on paid professionals for research, some also benefit from research packages assembled by party organizations and a few interest groups. Since at least the mid-1980s the National Republican Congressional Committee has furnished more candidates with opposition and issue research than its Democratic counterpart has.[6] However, the Democrats came close to reaching parity in 2006. Some labor unions, trade associations, advocacy groups, and other organizations also provide candidates with campaign research.

Fundraising is a campaign activity that requires skill and connections with individuals and groups that are able and willing to make political contributions. Some campaigns use a mix of a paid campaign staffer, a professional finance director, and volunteers to raise money. Incumbent campaigns rely heavily on professional paid staff and professional consultants, regardless of the competitiveness of their races. Some keep fundraising experts, including those who specialize in direct mail or in organizing fundraising events, on the payroll to collect contributions between elections. Apparently a few reduce the costs of keeping their fundraising operations in place by putting fundraising experts on the payrolls of their PACs or charitable foundations.[7] Direct mail is typically used to collect modest contributions, and events are known for raking in sums of all sizes, including large contributions from individuals and PACs.[8] Fewer nonincumbents, particularly those in one-sided contests, hire professional staff and consultants to help with fundraising. Their campaigns depend more heavily on the candidate, volunteers, party committees, and interest groups to raise money.

Polling, mass media advertising, and direct mail are three specialized aspects of campaigning that are handled primarily by political consultants hired on a contractual basis. Most candidates running for marginal seats hire an outside consultant to conduct polls. Substantial numbers of incumbents who are shoo-ins and mismatched open-seat candidates do not feel the need to take polls. But a much greater number of challengers in lopsided races, who could benefit from accurate public opinion information, do not take them as well. Most likely-loser challengers opt not to conduct surveys to save money for other campaign activities. Consultants typically consider this an ill-advised approach to campaigning. In the words of one pollster, "It's like flying without the benefit of radar."[9]

Incumbents are the most likely to have professionally produced campaign communications. The vast majority of incumbents hire a media consultant or use some combination of media consultant and campaign aide to produce television and radio commercials. Most challengers and open-seat candidates in closely contested races also hire professional media consultants. Challengers in one-sided contests, who face the biggest hurdles in developing name recognition among voters and conveying a message, are by far the least likely to employ the services of a media consultant.

Similarly, fewer likely-loser challengers hire professional staff or consultants for direct mail, one of the most effective means House campaigns can use to reach voters. Indeed, 39 percent said that they do not use direct mail at all. The vast majority of competitive challengers, open-seat candidates, and incumbents, by contrast, rely mainly on a combination of paid staff and consultants to write their direct-mail copy and compile address lists.

Although the Internet is a relatively new weapon in campaign arsenals, it can serve a number of purposes, including providing campaigns with an inexpensive and reliable means to communicate with and organize voters, raise money, disseminate press releases, and showcase their television and radio ads. Internet web sites also furnish voters and journalists with a place to turn for unmediated information about a candidate's professional qualifications, personal achievements, and issue positions.[10] Virtually all general election candidates create Internet web sites. Most employ professional staff or consultants to develop and maintain them. The exception is likely-loser challengers who rely more heavily on volunteers or themselves to create and maintain their Internet presence.[11]

Mass telephone calls can be made live at phone banks or can be automated and prerecorded. Although such calls are not used as routinely as mass media advertising or direct mail, roughly 70 percent of all House campaigns use telephone calls to identify and mobilize supporters. Most of the campaigns that use mass telephone calls rely on a combination of consultants and volunteers, although some candidates turn to paid campaign aides, parties, or interest groups for help with writing their scripts and making calls.

Field work involves voter identification, registration, literature drops, and get-out-the-vote (GOTV) drives. Campaign staff, parties, interest groups, and volunteers figure prominently in the GOTV activities of virtually all campaigns. Incumbents depend almost as much on these sources of help as do challenger and open-seat candidates. Where these campaigns differ is that incumbents rely somewhat less on paid staff for field work than do open-seat candidates and competitive challengers. Democratic House candidates also receive significantly more help with mobilizing voters from unions, reflecting their party's historical ties with the labor movement.

Because of the intricacies of campaign finance laws, the rules governing the use of the mass media, and requirements for getting on the ballot, almost two-thirds of all House candidates need legal expertise at some point in the campaign. House campaigns call on paid staff, volunteers, or lawyers they keep on retainer, or they get help from one of the high-powered attorneys employed by a party committee or an interest group when they need legal assistance. As is the case with most other aspects of campaigning, challengers running in lopsided races are the most likely to rely on volunteers or the candidate or to forgo the use of legal counsel.

Finally, accounting has become an important aspect of contemporary cash-driven congressional election campaigns. Most candidates hire staff with accounting skills to file their Federal Election Commission reports and oversee the books. Fewer likely-loser challenger campaigns have a salaried employee or professional consultant in charge of accounting. As is the case in some other areas of electioneering, these campaigns often turn to volunteers or the candidate to perform this function.

The overall professionalism of contemporary House campaigns is reflected in the fact that the average campaign uses paid staff or political consultants to carry out roughly seven of the preceding twelve activities (see the bottom of Table 3-1); this is three times the number of activities conducted by campaign professionals in a typical 1984 House race.[12] The average incumbent in jeopardy, hopeful challenger, or open-seat prospect uses skilled professionals to carry out nine of these activities. Incumbents and open-seat candidates in uncompetitive elections also assemble very professional campaigns. Only challengers in one-sided contests are substantially less reliant on professional help. Nonincumbents who are officeholders and unelected politicians assemble campaign organizations that are more professional than political amateurs do.[13]

The organization Rep. Wally Herger assembled to conduct his 2006 reelection campaign in California's 2nd congressional district is typical of those put together by most shoo-in incumbents. Given the representative's eighteen-year dominance of the district, lack of primary opposition, and perception he would face weak opposition in the general election, it is not surprising that Herger mounted a low-key campaign. He relied on Gilliard Blanning Wysocki & Associates, Inc., a general consulting firm based in Sacramento, California, to provide strategic advice, media advertising, and assistance with fundraising. The Hammond Group, specializing in PAC fundraising and located in Alexandria, Virginia, organized the campaign's Washington area fundraising events. Light Graphics of Sacramento designed his web site, and the KAL Group was responsible for accounting.[14] The campaign also was assisted by numerous volunteers, including many who had worked on Herger's previous campaigns. Volunteers helped to staff the office, organize events, stuff envelopes, telephone or knock on the doors of supporters, and do other activities associated with grassroots politicking and field work. Had Herger perceived the race to be more competitive, he probably would have put together a larger team and campaigned more aggressively.

The campaign team Arjinderpal "A. J." Sekhon put together to challenge Herger was underfunded and understaffed, as is typical of most campaigns waged by likely-loser challengers. Sekhon—a medical doctor, lawyer, Gulf War veteran, and colonel in the U.S. Army Reserve—relied on a largely volunteer campaign team. Perhaps the campaign's most important volunteer was Stephanie Ford, a colleague of Sekhon's who managed the campaign and served as its principal strategic adviser. In addition to management, her responsibilities included media relations, communications, scheduling, and overseeing outreach activities. Sekhon's wife, Daljit, had an important role in developing the candidate's one television ad and provided accounting services. The Sekhons' daughter, Ashu, a New York attorney, provided legal advice. This inner circle was complemented by two paid staffers, Peter Baruccini and Manny Chauha, who managed the office and were responsible for mailing its 80,000 hand-signed letters. Their campaign was assisted by volunteers from nearby high schools and members of the Student Democratic Club at California State University, Chico. The volunteers made telephone calls and campaigned door-to-door to persuade voters to support Sekhon and remind them to go to the polls on election day. The campaign's web site was created by Sarah's Graphic Design. The campaign did not enjoy the services of a direct-mail expert, telephone contact firm, fundraiser, pollster, issue or opposition researcher, or other professional consultants employed in many other campaigns because Sekhon could not afford them. By fielding a largely amateur campaign organization, the candidate was able to minimize the expenses associated with overhead and marshal his scarce resources to communicate to voters.[15]

The 2006 campaign waged in North Carolina's 11th district by Democratic challenger Heath Shuler contrasts sharply with those of Sekhon and Herger, but it is typical of the House campaigns of hopeful challengers. Shuler entered the race with little political experience, but he had widespread name recognition for his successes on the football field and the support of Democratic Congressional Campaign Committee chair Rahm Emanuel. With the assistance of the DCCC, Shuler assembled a professional organization, drawing from former DCCC alumni and other political talent from the Washington area. The campaign manager was Drew Lieberman, a nationally known Democratic operative who had worked for three years at the DCCC. He was assisted by Andrew Whalen, the campaign's communications director and deputy campaign manager. Peter Cari, a former DCCC aide, produced the campaign's television advertisements. Stones' Phones, headed by Marty Stone, a former DCCC PAC director, conducted the campaign's persuasion and get-out-the-vote calls. Fenn Communications Group of Washington, D.C., provided general consulting, and the Mack|Crounse Group of Alexandria, Virginia, handled the candidate's direct mail. Hamilton, Beattie & Staff of Washington, D.C., and Fernandina Beach, Florida, did the candidate's polling. Liberty Concepts of Boston was responsible for the candidate's web site, blast e-mails, and blog monitoring. An army of volunteers drawn from the ranks of Democratic activists, environmentalists, and labor union workers helped the campaign carry out its voter education and mobilization efforts.[16]

Shuler's campaign also drew assistance from a variety of groups, including party organizations and interest groups. The DCCC provided opposition research and was in touch with the campaign virtually every day. It also hosted fundraisers for the campaign and worked in other ways to direct contributions to it under the guise of its Red to Blue Program. The DCCC, the Democratic National Committee (DNC), and the North Carolina Democratic Central Committee helped the campaign recruit volunteers and communicate with voters as part of a coordinated voter mobilization campaign. Defenders of Wildlife, the League of Conservation Voters, MoveOn.org, several unions, and other groups provided volunteers to help with voter registration, education, and mobilization.[17]

Charles Taylor, the Republican incumbent in the 11th district, approached the 2006 election with a campaign organization that was somewhat modest for an incumbent in jeopardy. Perhaps he did not fully recognize that controversies concerning his personal finances, his association with convicted lobbyist Jack Abramoff, and some unpopular positions he took during the 109th Congress put him at risk. Taylor assembled a staff that was similar to the one he had used in previous elections. Trish Smothers served as his campaign manager, chief fundraiser, and event coordinator—roles similar to those she had played in 2004. Sean Dalton, chief of staff in Taylor's congressional office, took a leave of absence to provide strategic advice and help run the campaign's day-to-day operations. Aaron Latham, a press aide to Republican Rep. Patrick T. McHenry in North Carolina's neighboring 10th district, also took a leave of absence from Congress, to assist with campaign communications. The campaign hired Arena Communications of Salt Lake City, Utah, to carry out its direct-mail advertising. Creative Communications of Greenville, South Carolina, handled the campaign's media buys. The Republican National Committee (RNC) and the North Carolina Republican Party provided volunteers and assistance with voter targeting, education, and mobilization. The NRCC provided only limited monetary support because Taylor could rely on his tremendous personal wealth to finance his reelection, and his campaign was not receptive to the suggestions of committee staff. The local chamber of commerce and local business leaders provided volunteers and incidental support.[18]

The campaigns by Democrat Ed Perlmutter and Republican Rick O'Donnell in Colorado's 7th congressional district are representative of those undertaken by most open-seat prospects. Both campaigns employed a full coterie of professional staff, political consultants, and volunteers. Each was led by a manager who had extensive political experience and strong party ties. Perlmutter's manager, Danielle Radovich Piper, had been the chief of staff for the Democratic leadership in the Colorado state senate and a senior associate at IKON, a Washington- and Denver-based strategic lobbying, consulting, and communications firm.[19] O'Donnell's manager, K. C. Jones, had worked for the RNC and President Bush's 2004 reelection campaign. She also had played a significant role in former representative Bob Beauprez's victory in the 7th district in 2002. Each campaign hired some of the top general consultants, pollsters, media consultants, direct-mail experts, and fundraisers available from around the country. To this core of professional political operatives, each campaign added a substantial army of volunteers who assisted with organizing events, staffing the office, carrying out literature drops, reaching out to voters via telephone calls and door-to-door visits to voters, and various other grassroots campaign activities.

Both the Perlmutter and O'Donnell campaigns also received substantial party and interest group assistance, which is typical of a campaign that appears on the national radar for competitive elections. The DCCC provided the Perlmutter campaign with strategic and tactical advice and fundraising assistance. The DCCC, the DNC, and the Colorado Democratic State Central Committee also put together a coordinated campaign effort under the guise of Colorado Victory 2006, which worked to register, persuade, and mobilize pro-Democratic voters.[20] The AFL-CIO and several other labor unions provided volunteers; hosted fundraising events; and organized voter identification, education, and mobilization programs. Candidate O'Donnell benefited from opposition research carried out by the NRCC. The RNC used its data files to develop a list of voters for microtargeting and took the lead in running the campaign's voter mobilization effort. The Colorado Republican Party, the U.S. Chamber of Commerce, various other business groups, and Focus on the Family, which champions family values, also sought to turn out the vote for O'Donnell.

Although the above campaigns varied in their degrees of professionalism and the levels of party and interest group support they received, they all were similar in that they were smooth-running operations that worked to advance their candidate's cause. Not all campaigns work that way. Severe organizational problems, some allegedly stemming from the candidate herself, hampered the bid of Rep. Katherine Harris, R-Fla., for a Senate seat. During the months between November 2005 and September 2006, the Harris campaign repeatedly hemorrhaged top-level campaign aides and consultants. The turnover included no fewer than three campaign managers, one pollster, one media consultant, four fundraising experts, and five individuals involved in coordinating field activities. Not surprisingly, the campaign was unable to formulate a viable strategy, disseminate a coherent message, or raise sufficient funds. Its repeated implosions received widespread media coverage and distracted from the candidate's ability to present herself effectively to voters. Few campaigns leave behind on the tarmac as many aides and consultants as this one, but Harris's bid for the Senate strongly demonstrates the importance of building a strong, coherent campaign team.

CAMPAIGN BUDGETS

The professionalism of contemporary congressional campaigns is reflected in how they budget their money. House candidates spend 56 percent of their campaign funds on communicating with voters and 40 percent on fundraising, staff salaries, travel, and other miscellaneous expenses (see Figure 3-1). Polling and other research account for about 4 percent of campaign costs. The substantial amounts budgeted for electronic media demonstrate the important role played by modern communication techniques in most House campaigns and their rising costs. The typical House campaign spent approximately 22 percent of its budget on television and 12 percent on radio. Of course, the precise amount that a campaign spends on TV depends largely on how closely the boundaries of the district match the area of the broadcast coverage of the television and radio stations that create the media market. The next-largest expenses are for direct mail and campaign literature, each of which accounted for 8 percent of total costs. The remaining 5 percent was spent largely on voter registration and GOTV drives; newspaper ads; Internet web sites; and billboards, yard signs, and other campaign paraphernalia.

One of the most interesting facts about congressional elections is that the different types of candidates differ little in their approaches to budgeting. Among the largest differences, nonincumbents commit about 65 percent of their budgets to campaign communications, whereas incumbents apportion only 48 percent. The nonincumbents compensate by scrimping on overhead, especially fundraising and the salaries and fees that incumbents incur when conducting various campaign-related activities between elections. Candidates in contests decided by 20 percent or less of the two-party vote dedicate 46 percent of their budgets to television and radio, more than twice the amount allocated by candidates in one-sided races. The amounts that Democratic and Republican House candidates budget for various campaign activities are virtually the same.

The Taylor, Shuler, Herger, and Sekhon campaigns illustrate how incumbency, competitiveness, finances, and the costs of airing a television ad in the

FIGURE 3-1

Budget of a Typical House Campaign

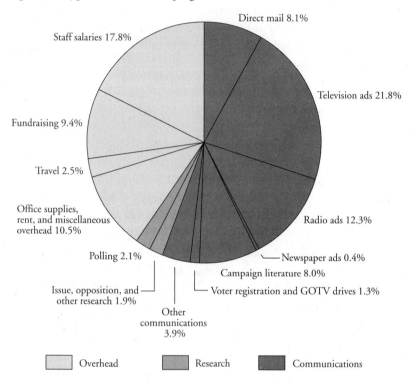

Staff salaries 17.8%

Direct mail 8.1%

Television ads 21.8%

Fundraising 9.4%

Travel 2.5%

Office supplies,
rent, and miscellaneous
overhead 10.5%

Radio ads 12.3%

Polling 2.1%

Newspaper ads 0.4%

Campaign literature 8.0%

Issue, opposition, and
other research 1.9%

Voter registration and GOTV drives 1.3%

Other
communications
3.9%

Overhead   Research   Communications

Source: Compiled from data provided by Political Money Line (http://www.tray.com).

Notes: Staff salaries include some miscellaneous consulting fees. Figures are for major-party candidates in contested general elections. *N* = 694.

campaign's media market (or markets) can influence certain aspects of spending. The Taylor campaign allocated $2.8 million (about 73 percent of its budget) for television ads compared with the $837,000 (47 percent) the Shuler campaign spent. The Herger and Sekhon campaigns invested little in broadcast TV—about $57,000 (12 percent) and $41,000 (27 percent), respectively—because of the inefficiency of advertising in the three media markets that cover the district, the one-sided nature of the race, and in Sekhon's case a very small campaign budget.[21]

The overall similarity in campaign budgets is remarkable given the different sums that incumbent, open-seat, and challenger campaigns spend. The widespread availability of campaign technology; the tremendous growth of the political consulting industry; and the extensive dissemination of information through the American Association of Political Consultants, *Campaigns & Elections* magazine, and campaign seminars sponsored by organizations, political parties, and interest groups have fostered a set of shared expectations about how a campaign should spend its funds. These expectations are reinforced when campaign personnel negotiate their salaries and draw up budgets, when political consulting firms set their rates, and when party officials and PAC managers scrutinize campaign budgets before making contributions.

SENATE CAMPAIGNS

Senate campaigns are more expensive, are run by more professional organizations, and attract more party and interest group attention than do House campaigns. Because campaigns for the upper chamber must reach out to more voters, senators possess more political clout than their House counterparts, and senators run only once every six years, candidates for the Senate typically raise and spend more money.[22] They also rely primarily on paid staffs and nationally known political consultants to develop their strategies and carry out their campaigns. Most Senate incumbents keep a substantial organization intact between elections, often spending millions of dollars on overhead and fundraising between elections.

Senate campaigns often have combinations of individuals sharing responsibilities for various aspects of the campaign. Virtually every campaign assigns a paid aide to work with a mass media advertising firm to develop the candidate's communications. Opposition research is typically conducted by a campaign aide, often in conjunction with a private consultant or party official. Campaign staff, consultants, volunteers, party committees, and interest group representatives make substantial contributions to Senate candidates' fundraising efforts. Most Senate campaigns also hire one or more field managers to participate in coordinated voter mobilization efforts that draw on the resources of national, state, and local party committees. Democratic Senate candidates also coordinate their field work with labor unions, and most Senate candidates of both parties rely on volunteers to help with their voter registration and GOTV efforts.

The major difference in spending between Senate and House contests is in the allocation of media expenditures. Senate campaigns spend about one-third of their money on television advertising, as opposed to the one-fifth spent by House campaigns. Senate campaigns also allocate far smaller portions of their budgets to radio advertising, campaign literature, newspaper ads, billboards, and yard signs than do House contestants. The differences in communications expenditures reflect both the greater practicality and the necessity of using television advertising in statewide races.

SUMMARY

Contemporary congressional elections are waged primarily by candidate-centered organizations that draw on the expertise of political consultants for polling, mass media advertising, and other specialized functions. Few candidates depend on parties and interest groups to carry out many campaign activities; the important exception is voter mobilization. Incumbents and open-seat candidates in competitive races wage the most professional campaigns; challengers in lopsided contests rely the most on amateur organizations. Despite these variations in organizations and tremendous disparities in funding, campaigns are more alike than different in how they budget their resources. The match between district boundaries and media markets and the preferences of individual candidates and their campaign aides affect campaigns' budgetary allocations more than incumbency or the closeness of the race.

CHAPTER FOUR

The Parties Campaign

Political parties in the United States have one overriding goal: to elect their candidates to public office. Policy goals are secondary to winning control of the government. Nevertheless, the parties' electoral influence has waxed and waned as the result of legal, demographic, and technological changes in U.S. society and reforms instituted by the parties themselves. During the golden age of political parties, local party organizations dominated elections in many parts of the country. They picked the candidates, gauged public opinion, raised money, disseminated campaign communications, and mobilized voters, most of whom had strong partisan allegiances. "The parties were, in short, the medium through which the campaign was waged."[1]

By the 1950s most state and local party organizations had been ushered to the periphery of the candidate-centered system. Party organizations at the national level had not yet developed into repositories of money and campaign services for congressional candidates. Most contenders for the House and Senate were largely self-recruited and relied on campaign organizations that they themselves had assembled to wage their bids for office. Professional consultants helped fill the void left by deteriorating party organizations, providing advice about fundraising, media, polling, and campaign management to clients willing to pay for it.[2]

During the late 1970s and early 1980s, first Republican and then Democratic national party organizations in Washington, D.C., began to adapt to the contemporary candidate-centered system. This system emphasizes campaign activities requiring technical expertise, in-depth research, and money. Many candidates, especially nonincumbents running for the House, lack the funds or professional know-how needed to conduct a modern congressional campaign. Candidates' needs created the opportunity for party organizations to assume a more important role in congressional elections.[3] The national parties responded to these needs, not by doing away with the candidate-centered election system but by assuming a more important role in it.[4]

In the late 1990s the national parties expanded their activities to include issue advocacy advertisements financed with soft money. Both major parties, and numerous interest groups, began conducting "independent," "parallel," and "coordinated" campaigns comprising millions of dollars of spending on television, radio, direct mail, mass telephone calls, and other communications and voter mobilization efforts. Following enactment of the Bipartisan Campaign Reform Act of 2002, with its ban on national party soft money, the parties adapted by raising more hard money and pumping it into competitive elections using independent expenditures and issue advocacy ads when allowable under the law. By carefully tailoring these activities to meet the circumstances in a small number of competitive congressional elections, parties have greatly increased their influence in those contests, thereby assuming an even greater role in the candidate-centered system.

In this chapter I discuss the roles of party organizations in congressional elections, including their influence on the agendas around which campaigns are fought, the types of assistance they give to House and Senate candidates, the strategies that inform their giving, how they select candidates for support, and the effects of their assistance on candidates' campaigns. Special attention is given to four Hill committees in recognition of their impact on congressional campaigns.

NATIONAL AGENDA SETTING

Contemporary House elections are usually fought on local issues, and Senate elections typically focus on statewide concerns. The factors that contribute to the candidate-centered nature of congressional elections, discussed in Chapter 1, are primarily responsible for this situation. During periods of divided government, it is especially difficult for one party to take credit or cast blame for the state of national affairs. However, this does not prevent Democratic or Republican leaders from working to set a national agenda that favors their own party. Indeed, party leaders seek to focus on issues that voters associate positively with their party or negatively with the opposition, and congressional candidates who discuss those issues typically emphasize their local implications.[5] Since the early 1980s, Democratic and Republican congressional leaders have produced lengthy issues handbooks, white papers, or "talking points" for congressional candidates that focus on national issues and include instructions on how to use party rhetoric and statistics compiled in Washington to address local concerns.[6] Many candidates found these materials useful, but the materials were not intended to produce nationalized campaigns and did not do so.

Nevertheless, congressional elections are not always dominated by local issues. In 1932 the Great Depression dominated the national political agenda and the outcomes of many House and Senate races. In 1974, Democrats nationalized the elections on the issues of Watergate, the Nixon administration's ethical lapses, and reform. During the 1994 elections, House Republicans focused on the ethical and policy failures of the Clinton administration and congressional Democrats, the "special interest" culture that Republicans asserted had developed in the House under forty years of Democratic control, and Newt Gingrich's Contract with America.[7] As a result of the terrorist attacks of September 11, 2001, the GOP concentrated on national security in the 2002 and 2004 elections. President George W. Bush and other GOP leaders crisscrossed the country to make the case that Republican candidates were better equipped to work with the president to protect U.S. national security than their Democratic opponents.[8]

The 2006 elections were fought in an environment that was more favorable to Democratic candidates than to Republicans. President Bush's and Congress's low job approval ratings and widespread voter concerns about the direction of U.S. domestic and foreign policy combined to provide the Democrats with an opportunity to set the national political agenda. Both parties' national, congressional, and senatorial campaign committees tried to influence that agenda by airing television commercials, hosting media events, issuing press releases, posting information on their web sites, and mailing and e-mailing millions of Americans. However, it was the Democrats who largely succeeded. Issues raised by Democrats played a role in more individuals' congressional voting decisions than did the issues emphasized by Republicans. Just over 31 percent of all congressional voters considered the war in Iraq as their most important voting issue, and another 20 percent ranked it second (see Figure 4-1). Corruption in government came next, with terrorism and national security, immigration, moral values, and jobs and the economy following close behind.[9] Health care–related concerns, taxes, and Social Security were considerably less prominent on the national agenda. Energy and gas prices, the environment, and education were substantially less important voting issues in 2006.

Democratic congressional candidates clearly benefited from the political agenda. Of the 51 percent of all voters stating that the war in Iraq—the Democrats' top election issue—was their first or second most important vot-

FIGURE 4-1

Most Important Issues in Congressional Voting Decisions in 2006

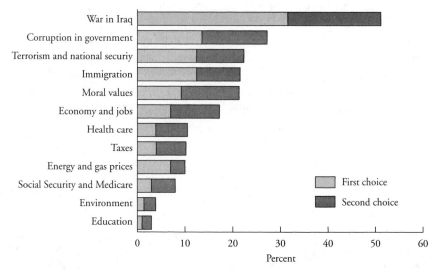

Source: "2006 Congressional Campaign Study," Center for American Politics and Citizenship, University of Maryland and Brigham Young University modules.

ing concern, 61 percent voted for a Democratic congressional candidate and 22 percent voted for a Republican (see Figure 4-2). This gave Democratic candidates a thirty-nine-point voting advantage on the issue. The Democrats reaped even larger benefits from the number two issue on the national agenda—corruption in government—where they enjoyed a fifty-one-point voting advantage. Democrats also enjoyed significant benefits from the economy and jobs and several lower-priority issues. Although the Republicans enjoyed a partisan advantage of more than sixty percentage points on terrorism and national security and substantial advantages on tax policy, immigration, and moral concerns, these issues were not high enough on the political agenda to offset the Democrats' advantages, particularly on the top two voting issues.

THE NATIONAL, CONGRESSIONAL,

AND SENATORIAL CAMPAIGN COMMITTEES

Party organizations in the nation's capital have developed into major sources of campaign money, services, and advice for congressional candidates. The Democratic National Committee and the Republican National Committee

FIGURE 4-2

Partisan Advantage in Congressional Voting Decisions in 2006

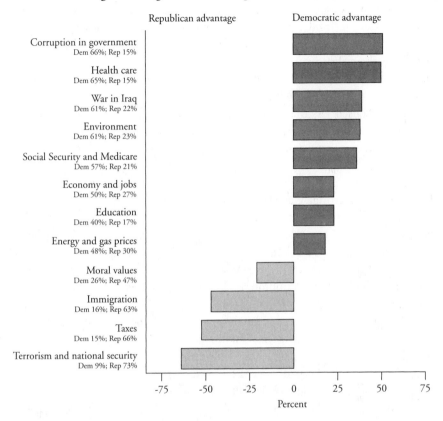

Source: "2006 Congressional Campaign Study," Center for American Politics and Citizenship, University of Maryland and Brigham Young University modules.

focus most of their efforts on presidential elections but also become involved in some gubernatorial and statehouse elections and in a small number of mayoral elections. They also seek to set the national campaign agenda and strengthen state and local party organizations. The national committees' involvement in House and Senate elections tends to be relatively limited. It includes conducting candidate training seminars; furnishing candidates with party platforms, campaign manifestos, and talking points; and coordinating with congressional, senatorial, state, and local party campaign committees to mobilize partisan voters. Congressional candidates in search of money, election services, or assistance in running their campaigns rarely turn to their national committee for help. Any assistance the national committee offers is usually channeled through a congressional or senatorial campaign committee or distributed in coordination with one of those organizations.[10]

The parties' congressional and senatorial campaign committees, sometimes referred to as the "Hill committees," have developed into major support centers for House and Senate candidates.[11] The congressional campaign committees focus their efforts on House races, and the two senatorial campaign committees focus on Senate contests. Three of the four Hill committees set fundraising records in 2006; only the National Republican Congressional Committee raised less than it had in the previous year. The parties' national, state, and local organizations also set fundraising records for a midterm election. The Democratic Congressional Campaign Committee raised $139.9 million, substantially less than its Republican rival, the NRCC, which collected more than $179.5 million. The two senatorial committees—the Democratic Senatorial Campaign Committee and the National Republican Senatorial Committee—raised approximately $121.4 million and $88.8 million, respectively. Despite the DSCC's fundraising advantage over its Republican counterpart, GOP committees, including the RNC and Republican state and local party organizations, out-fundraised their Democratic counterparts $602.3 million to $483.1 million.[12] The Republican committees have enjoyed fundraising advantages in virtually every election in the past three decades, but the Democrats have been closing the gap. A surge in modest contributions from individuals, including many who contributed over the Internet, has worked to the Democrats' advantage in recent years.

The Republicans' control over the House, George W. Bush's occupancy of the White House, the close division between the parties in the Senate, and the mobilization of GOP-leaning donors helped the Republicans rake in record funds in 2006. President Bush's fundraising efforts were especially important in this regard. Although out of favor with most Democratic and independent voters, he capitalized on his popularity among those who comprise the Republican Party's donor pool by traveling around the country to raise hundreds of millions of dollars for GOP candidates. He also raised tens of millions of dollars for Republican party committees, including $27 million for the RNC, NRCC, and NRSC at just one event, fittingly named "The President's Dinner."[13] In addition, Vice President Dick Cheney, presidential adviser Karl Rove, and other White House staff, cabinet officials, and Republican leaders raked in tens of millions for Republican candidates.

The chairs, vice chairs, and members of the Hill committees are members of Congress who are selected by their colleagues in the House or Senate. For the most part the members of each committee act like a board of directors, setting priorities and giving the committee staff the support it needs to participate in campaigns. In one area, however, members play an essential role: fundraising. Congressional and senatorial campaign committee chairs, vice chairs, and other party leaders have always raised money from individuals, political action committees, and other interest groups, but in recent years they have tapped into a another source—their colleagues in the House and Senate.

Congressional leaders of both parties in both chambers have established quotas—sometimes referred to as dues—for incumbents. In 2006, House Republicans asked rank-and-file members to contribute $70,000; chairs of the most powerful committees, such as Ways and Means, Appropriations, Energy and Commerce, and Rules, were asked to contribute $500,000. GOP leaders were expected to give even more: Speaker of the House Dennis Hastert, R-Ill., gave $700,000 and House Majority Whip Roy Blunt, R-Mo., contributed $550,000. Some members tackled the chore with relish. For example, John Boehner, R-Ohio, who chaired the House Education and Workforce Committee in 2006, contributed almost $1.2 million from his leadership PAC, the Freedom Project, and his campaign account to the NRCC, another $26,000 to various state and local Republican party committees in Ohio, and $15,000 to the RNC. Two other Republicans, Rep. Jim McCrery of Louisiana and Sen. Mitch McConnell of Kentucky—who was then the majority whip— contributed more than $1 million each to Republican Party organizations. Others grumbled about being dunned for contributions, but the competition for control over both the House and the Senate has given Hill committee chairs persuasive arguments to employ in their fundraising efforts. The final tally showed that Republican leaders had raised roughly $26.7 million for the NRCC, $5.8 million for the NRSC, $529,000 for the RNC, and $4.4 million for state and local GOP organizations from Republican members of the House and Senate, congressional retirees, and GOP politicians' leadership PACs.[14]

Democratic leaders also set dues for their members, with the highest level set to $600,000 for the party's top two House leaders and the lowest— $100,000—for rank-and-file members. Other House party leaders were expected to contribute $400,000 or more, ranking members or chairs on exclusive committees were supposed to pay $300,000, and lesser amounts were set for others holding various committee assignments. The Democrats enjoyed greater success than their GOP rivals, collecting $51.1 million from Democratic members of Congress, congressional retirees, and other politicians. These individuals transferred from their election accounts and the leadership PACs they sponsor roughly $30.2 million to the DCCC, $11.2 million to the DSCC, $1.1 million to the DNC, and $8.7 million to state and local Democratic Party committees. Six Democrats contributed more than $1 million each from their leadership PACs or campaign accounts to various Democratic committees. First among them was New York senator and presidential candidate, Hillary Rodham Clinton, who contributed almost $2.8 million. She was followed by Massachusetts senator and former presidential candidate, John Kerry; Kerry's Massachusetts colleague, Sen. Edward M. "Ted" Kennedy; and Rep. Steny H. Hoyer, of Maryland, who was Democratic whip at the time. Kerry, Kennedy, and Hoyer contributed roughly $2.2 million, $1.9 million, and $1.5 million, respectively.[15] On top of these funds, Democratic House leaders coaxed their colleagues into contributing or raising $24.7 million for the party's Red to Blue Program, which was designed to provide financial and other assistance to promising Democratic challengers who succeeded in meeting various organizational, fundraising, and strategic benchmarks.[16]

Member contributions to party committees involve massive redistributions of money from the powerful politicians who can raise it to the candidates who need it. They demonstrate that Hill committee leaders can get locally elected legislators to look beyond their own campaigns to consider their party's national goals. A sense of enlightened self-interest, particularly as it relates to control over the House and Senate, encourages members to raise money for national, state, and local party organizations. Once involving only a few party leaders and senior members, in 2006 this redistribution of wealth involved hundreds of lawmakers and candidates, including some first-term legislators who aspire to leadership posts. The Democrats may have contributed substantially more to party committees than did Republicans because they responded to the opportunity to take control of Congress provided by the 2006 elections, and they believed that Democratic Party committees were the best vehicle for effecting this change. The greater confidence that many Democratic incumbents had in their own reelections also may have been important.

Regardless of partisan affiliation or ideological leanings, the politicians who contribute to their party's campaign committees share an understanding that such contributions are an effective way to build political alliances that can be used to advance their careers and legislative goals. Representative Hoyer's contributions to the DCCC, Democratic candidates, and other party causes helped him get elected House majority leader after his party won control of the House in 2006. Boehner's support for the NRCC was instrumental in his being elected House Republican leader, McCrery's contributions to the Committee on Ways and Means helped him get selected to be the ranking Republican member of that committee, and McConnell's support for the NRSC helped him get selected Republican leader of the Senate at the opening of the 110th Congress.

Some members of Congress provide fundraising assistance to party campaign committees in addition to any direct contributions they make. One popular method is to create "joint fundraising committees." These financial accounts enable party committees and candidates to raise money through one or more political events and divide the funds so that all involved receive a predetermined portion of the spoils. Joint fundraising committees involving candidates and party committees usually distribute first the legal maximum amount an individual or PAC can contribute to participating candidates. The remainder is then distributed to one or more party committees. Joint fundraising committees enable participating candidates and party committees to raise large contributions from individuals who, although they are in their party's donor network, may have had little or no prior contact with the party's national apparatus or may have been unfamiliar with the participating candidates.[17]

The parties' congressional and senatorial campaign committees comprise many highly skilled political professionals in addition to the members of both houses of Congress. During the 2006 elections the DCCC and DSCC employed 106 and 56 full-time staff, and their Republican counterparts had 74 and 57 full-time employees. The staffs oversee the committees' daily operations, influence the formulation of party strategies, and play a major role in the implementation of those strategies. The staffs are divided along functional lines: different divisions are responsible for administration, fundraising, research, communications, and campaign activities. Staffers working in these divisions draw expertise from the constellation of consultants that services their party's candidates, including many individuals who formerly worked for a party committee. Pollsters, media experts, and other campaign professionals also are hired to provide Hill committees and selected candidates with campaign services.[18]

In addition, because federal law requires that independent expenditures be made without the knowledge or consent of the candidate, campaign aides, and others involved in a particular campaign and because party staff routinely communicate with the campaigns of their candidates in close races, the party committees set up separate organizations for the purposes of making independent expenditures. These so-called independent expenditure groups, routinely referred to as "IE groups," are prohibited from receiving any information from their parent party committee other than communications about the funds the party is transferring to their bank accounts. They also are prohibited from providing their parent committee with information about their electioneering efforts. Regular party staff remark that they learn about their IE group's undertakings only after they have occurred and from the mass media and other public sources.[19]

As major centers of political expertise and campaign support, the Hill committees are expensive to operate. They typically spend between 45 percent and 55 percent of their budgets on voter lists, computers, salaries, consulting fees, fundraising, loan repayments, and other overhead. The GOP committees have traditionally invested more than their Democratic rivals in maintaining and updating their Washington operations, but both parties have made major investments in improving their databases, targeting capabilities, and physical infrastructures in recent years.

STRATEGY, DECISION MAKING, AND TARGETING

The Hill committees have a common overriding goal of maximizing the number of seats their parties hold in Congress.[20] They become heavily involved in some elections, giving selected candidates large contributions and making substantial expenditures on their behalf, including expenditures on issue advocacy ads and voter mobilization efforts. They also give these candidates strategic, research, technical, and transactional assistance. The latter form of help enables candidates to raise the money and other resources needed to conduct a congressional campaign. Finally, the Hill committees participate with the national committees and state and local party organizations in generic, party-focused election activities designed to help candidates for Congress and other offices get elected.

The campaign committees try to focus most of their efforts on competitive House and Senate contests. Protecting incumbents in jeopardy is a major priority. Pressures from nervous incumbents can skew the distribution of committee resources from competitive challenger and open-seat candidates toward members of Congress who hold safe seats. The funds available to a committee also can affect the way it distributes its resources. Other institutional forces that affect committee decision making are the aspirations of its chair and other members. The two individuals who had the most significant roles in modernizing the NRCC and DCCC, former representatives Guy Vander Jagt and Tony Coelho, sought to use their chairmanships as vehicles for advancement in the ranks of the House leadership. The same is true of most of their successors, including Rep. Thomas M. Davis III, R-Va., who became chair of the House Government Reform Committee in the 108th Congress following his term as NRCC chair, and DCCC chair, Rep. Rahm Emanuel, D-Ill., who took over as chair of the House Democratic Caucus in the 110th Congress after helping his party gain a majority of House seats in 2006.[21] Similarly, Tennessee senator Bill Frist's meteoric rise to Senate majority leader in 2002, after having served only eight years in Congress, can be attributed at least partially to his successful chairmanship of the NRSC during the 107th Congress.

National political and economic conditions are additional factors that influence which candidates get campaign resources. When the president is popular or the economy is strong, the campaign committees of the president's party usually invest more resources in challenger and open-seat races. Conversely, the out-party committees use more of their resources to support incumbents. When national conditions do not favor the president's party, the patterns are reversed: the in-party committees take a defensive posture that favors incumbents, and the out-party committees go on the offensive, using more of their resources to help nonincumbents.[22] The unpredictable nature of national political conditions and economic trends and of events that take place in states and congressional districts means that committee decision making and targeting are necessarily imperfect. As a result, some safe incumbents and uncompetitive nonincumbents inevitably receive committee assistance, whereas some competitive nonincumbents get little or no help.

The conditions surrounding the elections held in recent decades have made strategic decision making and targeting difficult, especially for the two House campaign committees.[23] Redistricting, always fraught with ambiguities, became more complicated by issues involving race, which led to some districts being challenged in the courts and redrawn. Reconfigured districts or newly created seats are only two of several factors that complicate the committees' tasks. The president's popularity often shifts up and down, making it difficult for the committees to decide whether to pursue an offensive or a defensive strategy. Congressional scandals and voter frustration with Congress result in some incumbents unexpectedly finding themselves in jeopardy. These circumstances give some challengers a correspondingly unexpected boost. The late retirements of some House members and the primary defeats of others further complicate the committees' efforts.

Because of the uncertainty surrounding post-redistricting elections, the NRCC and DCCC in the early 1990s drew up huge "watch" lists of so-called "opportunity," or competitive, races. During the 1992 elections, each committee's watch list initially included approximately 300 elections. The committees shortened the lists over the course of the campaign season, but going into the last week of the election each list still had more than 150 opportunity races—more than three times the number included at that point in the 1990 election. During the elections held between 1994 and 2000, the committees initially focused on about 150 seats before they pared down their lists to about 75 races midway in the campaign season, and further reduced them later.[24] As discussed in Chapter 1, 2002 was very different from previous election years in that the redistricting had reduced the number of marginal House seats. This had a major impact on party strategy in House elections, as the DCCC and NRCC initially concentrated on about 90 races each before honing in on around 45 competitive contests midway through the election season, and about 20 during the last two weeks or so.[25] Among the lingering effects of redistricting was that the 2004 elections also were characterized by a concentration of competition in only a very few districts. Prior to the 2006 elections, the Democrats recognized that to have any chance at all of retaking the House they would need to expand the number of competitive districts beyond the small number that had been in play in the previous two elections. This was the major objective of the House Democrats' Red to Blue Program.

Individual candidates are selected for placement on the committees' watch lists on the basis of several criteria. The competitiveness of the district and incumbency are the first two considerations. Candidates running in districts that were decided by close margins in the most recent election or who are competing for open seats are likely to be placed on a committee's watch list. The strength of the candidate is another consideration in the case of nonincumbents. Those who have had political experience or have celebrity status are likely to be targeted for assistance. Challengers and open-seat contestants who demonstrate an ability to raise money and do well in the polls also are likely to receive support, as are those who field a professional campaign organization. Having an organization comprising talented campaign staff assures the committee that its resources will not go to waste. In some cases the Hill committees insist that certain personnel be hired as a precondition for receiving their assistance.

A variety of idiosyncratic factors also come into play when the committees select the candidates who will be given the most support initially. An incumbent who is accused of committing an ethical transgression, perceived to be out of touch with people in the district, in poor health, or in trouble for some other reason is a likely candidate for extra committee help. These difficulties often provoke a response by the other party's campaign committee, resulting in the incumbent's opponent also benefiting from extra party money and campaign services. Although party leaders work aggressively to recruit women and minorities to run for Congress, neither party uses gender or race as a criterion for determining who gets campaign assistance. Ideology also is not used to select candidates for support. Women, minorities, liberals, and conservatives are assisted only to the degree that their races are expected to be competitive.[26] Rep. Chris Van Hollen, D-Md., cochair of the Democrats' Red to Blue Program in 2006 and DCCC chair in the 110th Congress, explains: "We have a big-tent approach, not an ideological purity test. We have two questions: does the candidate want to help build our majority in Congress in order to implement our agenda for change, and can he or she win?"[27]

The committees' lists of competitive elections are revised throughout the election season. Regional coordinators who monitor congressional races within designated parts of the country advise their colleagues in Washington about the latest developments in individual elections. As a result, some candidates drop in priority or are cut off from party help, and others gain more committee attention and support. The 2006 elections were notable for the number of unpredictable events that resulted in the parties changing their initial resource allocations. The growing number of revelations about scandals involving GOP members of Congress led Republican Party committees to repeatedly reallocate their resources to defend the growing number of endangered Republican incumbents and led their Democratic counterparts to refocus their efforts in support of the Democratic candidates challenging them. Other unanticipated events led the parties to reevaluate their commitments to specific races. Both parties increased their involvement in the Senate race in Virginia, for example, when Republican senator George Allen's campaign imploded after he called a U.S. citizen of Indian descent who was volunteering for his opponent a *macaca* (a Francophone epithet for North Africans) and allegations surfaced about Allen using other racial slurs, flying the Confederate flag, and concealing his Jewish ancestry. As a result of an increasingly poisonous environment for GOP candidates, the Republican Party was forced to reallocate money and television advertising, which it had previously reserved to compete for Democratic-held seats, to defend its incumbents, including Allen and even NRCC chair Thomas M. Reynolds of New York.[28]

Because of the uncertainty surrounding recent congressional elections, the Democratic and Republican congressional and senatorial campaign committees distribute their resources incrementally. Rather than drop a large quantity of money or extensive election services in a candidate's lap early in the campaign season, the committees distribute them piecemeal in response to the candidate's ability to meet a series of discrete fundraising, organizational, and publicity goals. Incumbents usually meet these goals quickly and, ironically, may receive party support in response to campaign failures rather than successes. However, the committee goals pose more formidable hurdles for challengers and open-seat candidates. Nonincumbents who meet their goals in a timely fashion are usually within reach of victory at the end of the election season and receive substantial party support. Those who do not reach the goals find themselves cut off. Of course, a party committee's ability to support its candidates is limited by the availability of funds.

CAMPAIGN CONTRIBUTIONS AND COORDINATED EXPENDITURES

Party contributions to candidates in the congressional elections are restricted by federal law. The national and congressional party campaign committees were able to give a total of $15,000 to a House candidate at each stage of the election process (primary, runoff, and general election), and state party committees could give $5,000 (see Table 1-1).[29] The parties' national and senatorial campaign committees were able to give a combined total of $35,000 in an election cycle to a candidate for the Senate. State committees could contribute an additional $5,000 to Senate candidates.

Parties also can spend larger sums to expressly help individual candidates. These outlays, referred to as "coordinated expenditures" because they can be made in direct coordination with a candidate's campaign, typically are for campaign services that a Hill committee or some other party organization gives to a candidate or purchases from a political consultant on the candidate's behalf. Coordinated expenditures often take the form of polls, TV commercials, radio ads, fundraising events, direct-mail solicitations, issue research, or voter targeting assistance. They differ from campaign contributions in that both the party and the candidate share control over them, giving the party the ability to influence some aspects of how the campaign is run. Originally set at $10,000 for all national party organizations, the limits for coordinated expenditures on behalf of House candidates are adjusted for inflation and reached $39,600 in 2006.[30] The limits for national party coordinated expenditures in Senate elections vary by state population and are indexed to inflation. In 2006 they ranged from $79,200 per committee in the smallest states to $2,093,800 in California.

If a House candidate contributes or lends more than $350,000 to his or her own campaign (and other conditions are met) the "millionaires' provision" of the BCRA (sometimes referred to as the millionaires' amendment) allows an opponent's national and state party committees to make unlimited coordinated expenditures and allows the opponent to accept contributions of three times the usual amount from individuals. For Senate candidates, the threshold amount that triggers the millionaires' provision is based largely on a state's voting-age population. The consequences of triggering the provision in a Senate election are staggered in three levels, and the more a self-financing candidate contributes, the more an opponent can accept from an individual donor. Once the highest level of candidate self-funding is reached, the opponent's party can make unlimited coordinated expenditures.[31] Although the millionaires' provision is not relevant in many elections, it was triggered in some recent contests, allowing the parties to increase their coordinated expenditures and channel large individual contributions from members of their donor pool to candidates competing in these elections.

State party committees are authorized to spend the same amounts in coordinated expenditures in House and Senate races as are the parties' national organizations, but some state party committees do not have the funds to do so. In races in which a state party lacks resources and a party's congressional or senatorial campaign committee deems it important for the party to spend as much money as possible, the state and national party organizations form "agency agreements" that transfer the state party's quota for coordinated expenditures to the national party.[32] Such agreements enable the parties to concentrate funds raised from across the nation into Senate and House races taking place in a small number of states and districts. By controlling the money flow, agency agreements are among the methods Washington-based party organizations have used to coordinate national spending strategies in congressional elections.

From the mid-1970s through the early 1990s, most party activity in congressional elections took the form of cash contributions or coordinated expenditures on polling, fundraising, research, and other campaign services. The 1996 contests were the first in which the parties were permitted to make independent expenditures with hard money and to spend soft money on issue advocacy ads. Most of the national party spending that ensued involved issue advocacy ads because soft money was easier to collect than hard money. Following the BCRA's prohibition against national party soft money, the parties committed more resources to contributions, coordinated expenditures, and independent expenditures. The Democrats distributed more than $606,000 in contributions and $8.8 million in coordinated expenditures in the 2006 House races; the Republicans distributed roughly $975,000 and $4.7 million in these contests (see Table 4-1). The 2006 elections are a significant departure from previous contests in that the Democrats distributed more resources directly to candidates than did the Republicans.

Coordinated expenditures are an important aspect of party activity in congressional elections. Their higher limits, compared with those for cash contributions; the possibility for creating agency agreements; and the control they afford party committees in candidates' campaigns make coordinated expenditures an attractive avenue for party involvement. Coordinated spending also enables the parties to take advantage of economies of scale when purchasing and distributing campaign services. Because the parties purchase the services of political consultants in large quantities, they pay below-market rates, which enables them to provide candidates with services whose true market value exceeds the law's coordinated expenditure limits.

The four Hill committees determine the parties' congressional campaign spending strategies and are an important source of party funds spent in congressional elections. Some funds are distributed directly to candidates; others are first transferred to state or other party committees and then given to candidates. The Hill committees also direct most of the contributions of many other party organizations. The Democrats were very successful in deploying

TABLE 4-1

Party Contributions and Coordinated Expenditures in the 2006
Congressional Elections

	House		Senate	
	Contributions	Coordinated expenditures	Contributions	Coordinated expenditures
Democratic				
DNC	$2,000	$44,439	$200	$0
DCCC	215,103	2,183,233	0	0
DSCC	0	0	596,800	5,739,467
State and local	389,329	6,573,743	175,202	4,023,664
Total Democratic	$606,432	$8,801,415	$772,202	$9,763,131
Republican				
RNC	$378,080	$2,739,072	$40,000	$6,000
NRCC	371,860	1,611,474	196	0
NRSC	0	0	346,292	8,784,684
State and local	225,420	365,663	79,241	474,660
Total Republican	$975,360	$4,716,209	$465,729	$9,265,344

Source: Compiled from Federal Election Commission data.

Note: Figures include party spending in all congressional elections, including primaries, runoffs, and uncontested races.

resources through state and local party committees in 2006. Finally, the Hill committees deliver most of the parties' campaign services.

Party committees distribute most of their campaign support to candidates in close elections (see Table 4-2). The Democrats' allocation patterns for House candidates in 2006 indicate the party went on the offensive. The party directed 86 percent of its contributions to challengers and open-seat candidates. These funds include nearly $1.6 million in coordinated expenditures the DCCC made on behalf of challenger Heath Shuler when Republican incumbent Charles Taylor, a wealthy North Carolina businessman, triggered the millionaires' provision of the BCRA. The Democrats committed their remaining funds to incumbents, primarily those in jeopardy. The minority party usually takes a more aggressive posture than does the majority party, especially in a midterm election year in which a member of the opposing party occupies the White House. The 2006 elections were no exception. Given the public's low approval ratings of the president, Congress, and the Republican Party, the political landscape was more hostile to GOP House candidates. The DCCC's

TABLE 4-2

Allocation of Party Contributions and Coordinated Expenditures in the 2006 Congressional Elections

	House		Senate	
	Democrats	Republicans	Democrats	Republicans
Incumbents				
In jeopardy	9%	54%	21%	59%
Shoo-ins	4	4	10	—
Challengers				
Hopefuls	55	12	55	23
Likely losers	2	3	—	1
Open-seat candidates				
Prospects	28	25	7	15
Mismatched	1	1	6	—
Total ($, thousands)	$9,358	$5,523	$10,453	$9,633

Source: Compiled from Federal Election Commission data.

Notes: The categories of candidates are the same as those in Table 1-4. Figures include contributions and coordinated expenditures by all party committees to major-party general election candidates in contested races. They do not include soft money expenditures. — = less than 0.5 percent. Columns do not add to 100 percent because of rounding. $N = 754$ for the House; $N = 60$ for the Senate.

strategy in 2006 reflected the confidence the party had in its ability to pick up some Republican-held seats.

Democratic Party contributions and coordinated expenditures were extremely well targeted in 2006. The party delivered 55 percent of these resources to hopeful challengers, 28 percent to open-seat prospects, and 9 percent of its funds to incumbents in jeopardy. The party's ability to distribute 92 percent of its funds to candidates in elections decided by twenty or fewer percentage points was a substantial improvement over some years, including 2004 when it distributed 77 percent of its funds to candidates in close races, and 1992 when only 53 percent of its funds found their way into campaigns of similarly classified candidates.[33] The 2006 elections were remarkable for the Democrats' aggressive support of their competitive nonincumbent candidates.

In contrast to the Democrats' strategy, the plan adopted by the Republican Party in the 2006 House elections was extremely defensive. The Iraq War, unfolding scandals, and public dissatisfaction with Republican-led government in general encouraged the NRCC to focus on protecting endangered incumbents. Indeed, the NRCC's allocation of contributions and coordinated expenditures was almost the mirror image of the Democrats' allocation. While the Democrats spent just over half of their funds on hopeful challengers and less than one-tenth on incumbents in jeopardy, the GOP distributed 54 percent of its resources to incumbents locked in close races and a mere 12 percent on hopeful challengers trying to defeat Democratic incumbents. Only in House races featuring open-seat prospects did the two parties spend similar portions of their funds. The Republican Party organizations distributed their resources about as effectively as did the Democrats, as both parties delivered more than 90 percent of their funds to House candidates in competitive contests in 2006.

It is relatively easy for the parties to target their money in Senate elections. DSCC and NRSC officials typically have to assess their candidates' prospects in only thirty-three or thirty-four races per election season, and those races take place within borders that do not shift every ten years because of redistricting. Polling data also are available for all of the races. As a result, virtually all the parties' funds are spent in close elections. In 2006, the fact that there were only thirty major-party contested races meant that DSCC and NRSC strategists had fewer elections to monitor. The volatile political environment complicated their task, however, because many Senate elections did not become competitive until late in the election season. The Democrats distributed more than two-thirds of their funds to nonincumbents, and the Republicans disbursed 60 percent of their funds to incumbent senators seeking reelection, demonstrating that, as was the case in the House elections, the Democrats were in an aggressive posture and the Republicans in a defensive one. One crucial difference was that the Democrats committed 16 percent of their funds to several contests that ended up being one-sided, but the Republicans spent only 1 percent of their funds in these races.[34]

In addition to distributing campaign contributions and coordinated expenditures directly to candidates, the Hill committees encourage the flow of "party-connected" contributions from incumbents' leadership PACs and re-election accounts to needy candidates, such as nonincumbents and some new members. Leadership PACs have been involved in congressional elections since Rep. Henry Waxman, D-Calif., founded the first one in 1978, but they were few in number and distributed relatively little money before the late 1980s.[35] Their numbers had grown to 285 by 2006, when they distributed almost $41.8 million in contributions to congressional candidates. Although leadership PACs are technically political action committees, not party organizations, and although contributions from one candidate to another are not the same as those from the party, the candidates who make these contributions share several of the party's objectives, and many rely on party cues when making them. Their ties to the congressional parties, their reliance on them for information, and the fact that, with few exceptions, all of their contributions flow to members of their party warrant the labeling of these contributions as party connected.

During the 2006 elections, former and current members of Congress—mostly incumbents seeking reelection—and a small number of other prominent politicians contributed more than $53.6 million from their campaign accounts or leadership PACs to 876 primary and general election candidates (see Table 4-3). Republican politicians redistributed substantially more funds in the form of party-connected contributions to House and Senate candidates than did their Democratic opponents. Members of the GOP strongly preferred to make donations directly to each other while Democratic politicians were more likely to make their donations to party committees, allowing the committees an intermediary role in redistributing the wealth. The biggest contributors to other candidates were party leaders. Rep. Eric Cantor of Virginia, the Republicans' chief deputy whip, and Democratic whip Steny Hoyer of Maryland led their respective parties in contributions, giving almost $1.4 million and $1.2 million from their leadership PACs and campaign committees. Another twenty party leaders and policy entrepreneurs redistributed more than $500,000 to House and Senate candidates. Included among them were Democratic presidential hopefuls Sen. Barack Obama, D-Ill., and Mark Warner, former Democratic governor of Virginia, each of whom apparently recognized the benefits of using campaign funds to build political alliances both in and out of Congress.[36]

Party-connected contributions were distributed strategically, the vast majority of them to candidates in competitive contests (see Table 4-4). The major difference between party-connected contributions and money contributed by formal party organizations is that the distribution of party-connected funds is somewhat more favorable to incumbents, particularly those who are shoo-ins. This difference reflects the fact that the contributors of party-connected funds are, like party committees, concerned with maximizing the number of seats under their party's control, but they also want to do favors (on which they can later collect) for congressional colleagues, including those who occupy safe seats. Party-connected contributions, like politicians' donations to party committees, demonstrate that parties have become important vehicles for redistributing wealth among congressional candidates.

CAMPAIGN SERVICES

The parties' congressional and senatorial campaign committees provide selected candidates with assistance in specialized campaign activities such as

TABLE 4-3

Party-Connected Contributions in the 2006 Congressional Elections

	House		Senate	
	Democrats	Republicans	Democrats	Republicans
Leadership PAC contributions	$6,093,682	$20,280,301	$5,135,167	$8,113,632
Candidate contributions	7,700,572	4,962,736	61,917	89,003
Contributions from retirees and members not up for reelection	247,849	307,325	390,257	142,786
Contributions from nonfederal PACs	43,973	34,411	8,900	4,000
Total	$14,086,076	$25,584,773	$5,596,261	$8,349,221

Source: Compiled from data provided by the Center for Responsive Politics.

Note: Figures are for contributions from leadership PACs, congressional candidates, retired members, members of Congress not up for reelection in 2006, and PACs sponsored by nonfederal politicians to candidates in all congressional elections, including those in primaries, runoffs, and uncontested races.

management, gauging public opinion, issue and opposition research, and communications.[37] They also provide transactional assistance, acting as brokers between the candidates and the interest groups, the individual contributors, the political consultants, and the powerful incumbents who possess some of the money, political contacts, and campaign expertise that candidates need. The DCCC and NRCC typically become closely involved in the campaigns of candidates on their watch lists and have little involvement in others. The DSCC and NRSC focus most of their attention on Senate candidates in competitive contests, but with so few elections to monitor they are better able to structure their relationships in response to the specific needs of individual candidates. As former DSCC political director Andrew Grossman explains, "We love all of our campaigns as much as they need to be loved. Some campaigns need a huge amount of help; some need little help, but help of a specific kind. Some campaigns build relationships around one party service; some campaigns build relationships around several services. Our help is customer based."[38] Although it is difficult to estimate precisely the value of Hill committee assistance, candidates in close races often receive campaign services that would cost hundreds of thousands of dollars if purchased from a professional political consultant.

TABLE 4-4

Distribution of Party-Connected Contributions in the 2006 Congressional Elections

	House		Senate	
	Democrats	Republicans	Democrats	Republicans
Incumbents				
In jeopardy	15%	65%	12%	50%
Shoo-ins	12	9	30	7
Challengers				
Hopefuls	48	8	40	12
Likely losers	2	3	—	9
Open seats				
Prospects	18	13	12	13
Mismatched	4	3	6	8
Total ($, thousands)	$14,908	$25,983	$3,981	$6,812

Source: Compiled from data provided by the Center for Responsive Politics.

Notes: Figures are for contributions from leadership PACs, candidates, retired members, and members of Congress not up for reelection in 2006 to general election candidates in major-party contested races. Some columns do not add to 100 percent because of rounding. $N = 754$ for the House; $N = 60$ for the Senate.

Campaign Management

Candidates and their campaign organizations can get help from their Hill committees with hiring and training campaign staff, making strategic and tactical decisions, and other management-related activities. The committees maintain directories of campaign managers, fundraising specialists, media experts, pollsters, voting list vendors, and other political consultants whom candidates can use for free and from whom they can purchase campaign services. Committee officials sometimes recommend that candidates, particularly non-incumbents in targeted races, hire from a list of "trusted" consultants, many of whom have worked for the party or an interest group that routinely supports the party. In some cases, hiring from a Hill committee's list of recommended consultants is a requirement for receiving other forms of party assistance. The DSCC political director, Guy Cecil, recounts that his committee took things a step further in 2006 and required that a campaign's manager, communications director, finance director, and research director meet with its approval before the DSCC provided campaign assistance.[39]

The Hill committees' field representatives and political staffs in Washington also serve as important sources of strategic advice. In most close races, party aides or consultants the parties hire are assigned to work with individual campaigns. Because they have established "war rooms" to monitor elections nationwide and can draw on experiences from previous elections, the Hill committees are among the few organizations that have the information, knowledge, and institutional memory to advise candidates and their managers on how to deal with some of the dilemmas they encounter. The congressional and senatorial campaign committees' political staffs are usually most heavily involved in the planning and tactical decision making of open-seat and challenger candidates. In addition, they also provide a great deal of advice to first-term members and other legislators in close races. National party strategic advice is usually appreciated, but some candidates and campaign aides have complained that Hill committee staff can be heavy-handed.

The six Washington party organizations also introduce candidates—both incumbents and challengers—and their aides to the latest campaign techniques. At committee headquarters the DCCC and NRCC hold training seminars for incumbents that cover topics such as staying in touch with constituents, getting the most political mileage out of franked mail, defending unpopular votes, and PAC fundraising. Congressional campaign committee staff also work with the national committees to host seminars for challengers and open-seat candidates around the country. These seminars focus on more basic subjects, such as giving the stump speech, filing campaign finance reports with the Federal Election Commission, and building coalitions. Even long-term members of the House and Senate find the seminars beneficial as reminders of what they ought to be doing. Hill committee assistance is generally more important to hopeful challengers and open-seat prospects than to incumbents in jeopardy, reflecting the fact that incumbents' electoral difficulties are rarely the result of inexperience or a lack of knowledge about how to campaign.

In 2006 both the DNC and the RNC hosted campaign training seminars across the nation for political candidates and activists. The DCCC held five candidate training sessions and a dozen training sessions for campaign aides at its Washington headquarters.[40] These featured presentations by DCCC directors and deputy directors on how to outline a campaign budget and develop finance, field, and media plans.[41] The NRCC also held two training seminars in Washington and one in Chicago to advise challengers and open-seat candidates how to discuss homeland security, the war in Iraq, and other national issues.[42] DSCC and NRSC staff met one-on-one with nonincumbent candidates when they came to Washington and sent aides to help campaign staffs start writing the candidate's budget and campaign plan. The DSCC also provided training sessions for campaign staff and state party operatives involved in field activities such as voter registration and mobilization.[43] The RNC performed this function for the Republicans.[44] Both parties sought to help the candidates staff their campaigns properly so that they could do the bulk of the work on their own and call on their party for assistance only when needed.

Gauging Public Opinion

The national party committees possess expertise in assessing public opinion, and many candidates find the party's assistance in this area significant. The DNC and RNC disseminate the findings of nationwide polls via newsletters, memoranda, faxes, and e-mails to members of Congress, party activists, and congressional candidates. The parties' congressional and senatorial campaign committees commission hundreds of district and statewide polls and targeting studies in a given election season. Early in the campaign cycle, they use recruitment surveys to show potential candidates the possibilities of waging competitive races as well as benchmark polls to inform declared candidates of their levels of support and of public opinion on the major issues. They use tracking polls to assist a small group of candidates who are running neck and neck with their opponents at the end of the campaign season. Some of these surveys are paid for entirely by a Hill committee and reported to the FEC as in-kind contributions or coordinated expenditures. Most are jointly financed by a committee and the candidates who receive them.

Parties have significant advantages over individual candidates when it comes to purchasing polls. Parties are able to get polls at discount rates because they contract for so many of them. Parties also can use their extensive connections with polling firms to arrange to piggyback questions on polls taken for other clients. All six Washington party organizations commission polls to research issues they expect to influence the national agenda or public opinion in particular elections. In 2006, both parties spent millions of dollars on gauging public opinion through benchmark, trend, and tracking surveys. The DCCC allocated about $2.6 million on about 200 polls, and the NRSC spent about $1.9 million in connection with ten close Senate races.[45] While exact figures are not available for the NRCC or DSCC, these committees took surveys in most of the same races. Officials from the six national party organizations emphasize that polling is essential to waging an effective campaign.

Selected candidates also receive precinct-level targeting studies from party committees. Some studies are based on microtargeting, taken from the field of marketing research and pioneered in politics by the RNC. Microtargeting involves using voter files that overlay previous election results with individuals' voter turnout histories, contact information, and detailed demographic and consumer information that is correlated with political preferences.[46] Other candidates receive data files that combine district-level geodemographic data about voters' backgrounds with previous election results and current polling figures. Although these latter data are based on small geographic units rather than individuals, both can be used to guide the candidates' direct-mail programs, media purchases, voter mobilization drives, and other campaign efforts.

Issue and Opposition Research

During the 1980s, party organizations in Washington became major centers for political research. The DNC and RNC extended their research activities in several directions, most of which were and continue to be focused on the party rather than directed toward congressional candidates. The national committees routinely send materials on salient national issues to candidates for Congress, governorships, and state legislatures; to "allied" consultants and interest groups; and to activists at all levels. Typical party research includes statistics, tables, and charts drawn from major newspapers, the Associated Press wire service, the Internet, the LexisNexis computerized political database, national public opinion polls, and government publications. It weaves factual information with partisan themes and powerful anecdotes to underscore major campaign issues. Some individuals receive this information through the U.S. mail, but most get it by way of "blast" faxes and e-mails and web site postings that the committees transmit daily to hundreds of thousands during the campaign season. Many journalists and political commentators also are sent issue research—albeit with a partisan spin—by the national committees.

The congressional and senatorial campaign committees also disseminate massive amounts of issue-related materials by e-mail, web postings, and faxes to candidates, party activists, and partisan political consultants. During the past few Congresses, both parties' House and Senate leaderships distributed talking points, memoranda, pamphlets, or issue handbooks designed to help candidates develop issue positions, write speeches, and prepare for debates. In 2006 the Hill committees furnished their candidates with information on a host of domestic and international issues. For example, the DCCC gave its candidates research and talking points on the Iraq War, government corruption, and other areas where they found the performance of the Republican-controlled federal government was questionable. Republican research focused on homeland security, taxes, and other traditional GOP strengths.

More important than this generic research are the more detailed materials that the Hill committees distribute to individual candidates. Each committee routinely distributes information on the substance and political implications of congressional roll call votes. Many nonincumbents, who are unable to turn to congressional aides, the Library of Congress, or Washington-based interest groups for information on important issues, use this information to develop policy positions. Challengers also use it to plan attacks on incumbents.

The two House campaign committees assemble highly detailed issue research packages for some candidates involved in competitive races. These packages present hard facts about issues that are important to local voters and talking points that help candidates discuss these issues in a thematic and interesting manner. The committees also provide information pinpointing vulnerabilities in an opponent's issue positions, previous roll call votes, and professional and personal lives. A fairly new aspect of their research concerns the use of satellite technology to monitor campaign ads. This technology enables the committees to identify almost immediately the attacks their opponents use against their candidates, which greatly accelerates a campaign's ability to prepare a response.

During the 2006 elections the DCCC spent $400,000 on individualized research packages for forty candidates in targeted races. The packages presented detailed information on incumbent Republican House members' vulnerabilities, including their roll call votes and speeches on the Iraq War, health care, the environment, Social Security, and Medicare. They also projected how different groups of constituents would be likely to react to this information.[47] The NRCC produced similar detailed research packages for well over a hundred candidates, including fifty incumbents and every House challenger or open-seat candidate in a close contest. This research for incumbents and open-seat contests highlighted talking points and statistics on Republican-supported tax cuts, national security efforts, and other popular GOP proposals. The research for challengers also identified aspects of the opponent's candidacy that were vulnerable to attack.[48] The DSCC provided research assistance to some candidates, but most of its efforts in this area involved ensuring that its campaigns hired highly skilled research directors.[49] The NRSC provided issue and opposition research for all of its Senate candidates. Regardless of the specific nature of the assistance their committees provided, top aides in all four Hill committees emphasized its importance. In the words of NRSC executive director, Mark Stephens: "All campaigning starts with research, whether it is concerned with fundraising, television, radio, direct mail, speeches, or press conferences."[50]

Campaign Communications

The Hill committees assist selected candidates with campaign communications. During the 1980s and 1990s, the Hill committees owned television and radio production facilities, and they furnished large numbers of candidates with technical and editorial assistance in producing campaign ads. By 1998, technological developments made it possible for candidates and media consultants to gain access to high-quality, inexpensive recording and editing technology without visiting their party's Washington headquarters or renting an expensive editing suite. As a result, few congressional candidates used party television production facilities, and only a handful received a full-service media package wherein the committee developed the campaign's advertising themes, wrote its scripts, and arranged for its advertisements to be aired on local television stations. Some incumbents and a few nonincumbents used the center's satellite capabilities to appear "live" on television news shows, at fundraisers, and at events in their districts.

The committees continue to play an important role in advising their campaigns on the quality of their television, radio, and direct-mail advertisements. Using e-mail attachments and streaming video on the Internet, committee aides are able to receive these ads within minutes of when they were produced, review them seconds later, and discuss their recommendations with campaign representatives almost immediately.

In 2006, the Hill committees and a small number of candidates in close races entered into some relatively new agreements involving joint expenditures on campaign communications. Under these arrangements, a party committee and one or more candidates make an advertisement that mentions all of the involved parties, and they share in its costs. In practical terms, joint expenditures appear to be a vehicle that enables parties to directly provide a specific campaign with more resources than are permissible under the BCRA's contribution and coordinated expenditure limits. The practice is controversial and awaiting a ruling by the FEC.

The Hill committees also take on supporting roles in other aspects of campaign communications by doing work that candidates' campaign committees cannot. They plant stories with the national and local media. They release negative information about the opposing party's candidates. And, as is discussed later, their issue advocacy and independent expenditures can have a major impact on the tenor of a congressional campaign. Senatorial and congressional campaign committee research and communication efforts have clearly contributed to the nationalization of American politics.

Fundraising

In addition to providing contributions, coordinated expenditures, and campaign services directly to candidates and steering party-connected contributions to them, the Hill committees help candidates in competitive contests raise money from individuals and PACs. To this end, the committees give the candidates strategic advice and fundraising assistance, and they disseminate information about these candidates to their top donors. They also furnish PACs and individual donors with other forms of information they can use when formulating their contribution strategies and selecting individual candidates for support.

All six national party organizations give candidates tips on how to organize fundraising committees and events. The Hill committees even furnish some candidates with contributor lists, with the proviso that the candidates surrender their own lists to the committee after the election. They also have meeting rooms and dozens of telephone suites that offer incumbents a place to host events and make fundraising calls when they are in Washington; this is an important benefit because it is illegal to make these calls from the United States Capitol and other federal office buildings. Sometimes the parties host high-dollar events in Washington or make arrangements for party leaders to attend events held around the country either in person or via satellite television uplink. The Speaker of the House and other congressional leaders can draw lobbyists, PAC managers, and other big contributors to even the most obscure candidate's fundraising event. Of course, nothing can draw a crowd of big contributors like an appearance by the president, and in 2006 President Bush, members of his cabinet, and the White House staff participated actively in campaign fundraising.

The Hill committees also steer large contributions from wealthy individuals, PACs, or members of Congress to needy candidates. It is illegal for the parties to earmark checks they receive from individuals or PACs for specific candidates, but committee members and staff can suggest to contributors that they give to one of the candidates on the committee's watch list. Sometimes they reinforce this message by sending out fundraising letters on behalf of a candidate, sponsoring events that list congressional leaders as the event's hosts, or organizing joint fundraising events. A major component of the DCCC's Red to Blue Program involved bringing promising nonincumbents and members of Congress together with deep-pocketed Democratic supporters at events held across the nation. These introductions enabled candidates to raise contributions from several hundred individuals who otherwise may not have even heard of them. The program enabled some little-known Democratic nonincumbents to exploit a part of the Democratic donor pool that was inaccessible to their predecessors in previous elections.

The Hill committees give candidates the knowledge and tools they need to obtain money from PACs. The committees help candidates design "PAC kits" they can use to introduce themselves to members of the PAC community.[51] They also distribute lists of PACs that include the name of a contact person at each PAC and indicate how much cash the PAC has on hand, so that candidates will neither waste their time soliciting committees that have no money nor take no for an answer when a PAC manager claims poverty but still has funds. Candidates are coached on how to fill out the questionnaires that some PACs use to guide their contributions and how to build coalitions of local PAC contributors so that they can raise money from national PACs.

The committees also help candidates raise money from PACs and wealthy individuals by manipulating the informational environment in which donors make their contribution decisions. The committees' PAC directors work to channel the flow of PAC money toward their party's most competitive congressional contenders and away from their opponents. This is an especially difficult task to perform for House challengers and open-seat candidates, and even for some junior House members, because they are largely unknown to the PAC community.

The Hill committees use several methods to circulate information about House and Senate elections to PACs and other potential contributors. The committees publicize their targeting lists and contribution activities to draw the attention of PACs and wealthy individual contributors, sometimes through briefings or press releases but also by posting information about the candidates on the committees' web sites. The committees also host receptions—"meet and greets"—at their headquarters and national conventions to give candidates, especially nonincumbents, an opportunity to ask PAC managers and lobbyists for contributions. Every week during the peak of the election season, campaign updates are mailed, e-mailed, or faxed to about one thousand of the largest PACs to inform them of targeted candidates' electoral prospects, financial needs, poll results, endorsements, campaign highlights, and revelations about problems experienced by their opponents. Streams of communications also are sent to the editors of the *Cook Political Report,* the *Rothenberg Political Report,* and other political newsletters that handicap congressional races. A favorable write-up in one of these can help a nonincumbent raise more PAC money.

The Hill committees' PAC directors and party leaders spend a tremendous amount of time making telephone calls on behalf of their most competitive and financially needy candidates. Some of these calls are made to PAC managers who are recognized leaders of PAC networks. The DCCC and DSCC, for example, work closely with the National Committee for an Effective Congress (NCEC) and the AFL-CIO's COPE; their GOP counterparts work closely with the Business-Industry Political Action Committee (BIPAC). The committees encourage these "lead" PACs to endorse the party's top contestants and to communicate their support to other PACs and to individuals in their donor networks.

One of the more controversial ways that the Hill committees raise money for needy candidates is by leveraging it. Campaign committee staffs organize functions and clubs that promise PAC managers, lobbyists, and others access to congressional leaders in return for large contributions. Since the 1970s, Democratic and Republican leaders in the House and Senate have used their influence in their respective chambers to pressure PACs to support their candidates. The former Republican majority leader, Tom DeLay, for example, greeted lobbyists with a list that categorized the four hundred largest PACs as "friendly" or "unfriendly," depending on the proportion of their contributions that went to Republicans, in order to hammer home the message that groups that wanted access to GOP leaders would be expected to give most of their PAC money to Republican candidates and party committees in the future.[52] One can anticipate that as long as they remain in control of Congress, Democratic leaders will use similar tactics to increase their party's share of PAC contributions.

The Hill committees also use "buddy systems" to match financially needy but promising nonincumbents and freshmen with committee chairs and other powerful incumbents for fundraising purposes. These senior incumbents offer their partners contributions, provide advice on campaign-related topics, and use their influence to persuade PAC managers and individuals who have made large contributions to their campaigns to contribute to their "buddy."[53] The buddy system's impact on fundraising is hard to estimate, but during the 2006 elections Republican and Democratic House and Senate party leaders, committee chairs, and ranking members raised millions of dollars for colleagues who were in jeopardy or for competitive nonincumbents. As suggested by the number of incumbents who made contributions from their campaign accounts and leadership PACs to other House candidates, even more members of Congress were involved in redistributing the wealth in 2006 than in previous elections.

The Hill committees are important intermediaries in the fundraising process because they help needy challengers, open-seat candidates, and incumbents raise money from PACs, other candidates, and individuals who make large contributions. The committees have created symbiotic relationships with some PACs, resulting in parties' becoming important brokers between candidates and contributors. The relationships are based largely on honest and reliable exchanges of information about the prospects of individual candidates. Hill committee officials and PAC managers recognize that accurate information is the key to this relationship and to the ability of both groups to help candidates.

Party communications to PACs and wealthy individual donors are somewhat controversial because they can harm some individual candidates' fundraising prospects. Candidates who receive their Hill committee's endorsement derive significant fundraising advantages from such communications, but challengers and open-seat candidates who do not are usually unable to collect significant funds. Some groups and individuals who routinely make large contributions justify refusing a contribution request because a nonincumbent was not included on a Hill committee's watch list. Hill committee fundraising efforts can create both winners and losers in the campaign for money and, thus, have a major impact on many congressional elections.

Grassroots Activities

Not all of the campaign assistance that House and Senate candidates get from parties comes from Washington, and not all of it is given by the parties' congressional and senatorial campaign committees. Some state and local party committees give candidates assistance in a few of the aspects of campaigning discussed above, but these committees tend to be less influential than the Hill committees in areas requiring technical expertise; in-depth research; or connections with Washington PACs, other major contributors, and political consultants.[54] State and local party committees do, however, provide congressional candidates with substantial help in grassroots campaigning. Most state committees help fund and organize registration and get-out-the-vote drives, set up telephone banks, and circulate campaign literature to voters.[55] Many local parties conduct these same activities as well as organize house parties to introduce candidates to voters, canvass door-to-door, distribute posters and lawn signs, put up billboards, and engage in other types of campaign field work.[56] Some of this activity is organized and paid for by the state and local party committees themselves; however, a significant portion of it is planned and funded by party committees in Washington under the guise of the coordinated campaign—a cooperative party-building and voter mobilization program discussed below.

INDEPENDENT, PARALLEL, AND COORDINATED CAMPAIGNS

Party campaigning extends beyond the money and campaign services party organizations provide directly to candidates. The national parties' increased roles in setting the national political agenda and their provision of campaign funds and services to candidates and state and local party organizations constitute their earliest adaptations to the modern, federally regulated, campaign finance system. As the candidate-centered system and campaign finance law continued to evolve, political parties began to extend their roles in congressional elections by using new campaign communications and voter mobilization techniques. By the turn of the century the parties were using independent, parallel, and coordinated campaigns involving pollsters, issue and opposition researchers, voter targeting experts, communications consultants, and other strategists to influence congressional elections. The Hill committees were at the epicenter of these campaigns, but national, state, and local party committees also were involved in them. The same is true of numerous party-connected groups, mostly sponsored by current and former members of Congress, and allied interest groups.

The Independent Campaign

Independent party campaigns consist primarily of what the federal law classifies as independent expenditures—advertisements that *expressly* call for the election or defeat of a federal candidate. They are conducted almost exclusively in targeted races, and they are generally more aggressive than are candidate communications. The parties were first allowed to make these in 1996 after the Supreme Court's ruling in *Colorado Republican Federal Campaign Committee v. Federal Election Commission.* Independent expenditures must be made with federally regulated funds and without the candidate's knowledge or consent. They usually take the form of television, radio, direct mail, or mass telephone calls. To keep these expenditures legal, the parties' independent expenditure groups are located on different premises and directed to have no contact with candidates, campaign aides, or consultants involved in campaigns where the group is making independent expenditures. The same directive is given to the consultants the IE groups hire to help them design and implement their strategies.

Unlike candidate ads, independent expenditures that appear on television or radio do not qualify for lowest unit rate charges. This, and the cost of establishing a separate IE group to make the ads, makes them very expensive. Given that control over the House and Senate was at stake in 2006 and that the BCRA had banned party issue advertising funded by soft money, it is not surprising that the parties engaged in record-setting independent expenditures. Party committees—mainly the four Hill committees—spent almost $223.4 million in independent expenditures in connection with House and Senate races (see Figure 4-3). The Democrats spent almost $8.5 million advocating the election of their House candidates and another $53 million calling for the defeat of their Republican opponents. Most of this $61 million was spent on two hundred unique TV ads to influence fifty House races, although about 10

FIGURE 4-3

Party Independent Expenditures in the 2006 Elections

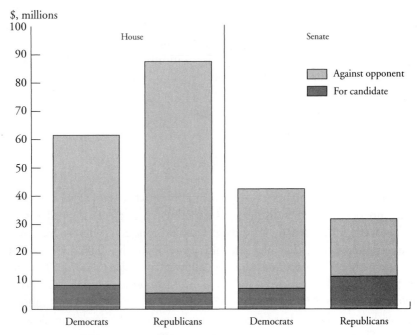

Source: Compiled from Federal Election Commission data.

percent was used to finance radio and direct mail.[57] The Republicans created 195 TV ads for 51 House races, but spent significantly more than the Democrats and for somewhat different purposes. The GOP devoted substantially fewer IE dollars to advocating on behalf of its House candidates and substantially more on criticizing its opponents.[58] Although both parties aired about fifty to sixty independent TV ads in ten Senate races, the spending patterns are reversed for those contests.[59] The Democrats outspent the Republicans, and the Republicans allocated more money to positive ads and the Democrats more to negative ones. Of course, the reason for the differences in total independent spending are rooted in the parties' abilities to raise funds, and 2006 was a challenging year for the NRSC. In fact, the RNC, not the NRSC, made almost 39 percent of all GOP independent expenditures in Senate elections.

The reason that most party independent spending is allocated to negative campaigning is that many candidates and political operatives believe that it is easier to tear down an opponent than build up their own candidate. Academic studies support this generalization. Negative campaign ads are more likely than positive ads to be perceived and remembered and to motivate voters to go to the polls.[60] Negative ads are especially harmful to nonincumbents who are not as well known to voters as are current officeholders.[61] Moreover, in recent years a de facto division of labor has developed between parties and candidates in close races, wherein candidates broadcast mostly positive ads and political parties (and interest groups) disseminate mainly negative or comparative ones.[62]

Virtually all party independent expenditures occur in close elections. Consistent with their aggressive strategy, the Democrats in 2006 spent 65 percent of their independent expenditures to influence elections being waged by hopeful challengers and 21 percent on Democratic hopefuls running for open seats. Only 6 percent of such ads were broadcast to influence races waged by Democratic incumbents in jeopardy, with the remaining 8 percent being spent in uncompetitive contests. Consistent with the distribution of Republican Party contributions and coordinated expenditures, GOP independent spending was in many ways the mirror image of what the Democrats did: the party made 65 percent of its independent expenditures to assist incumbents locked in close contests, 21 percent to help candidates for open seats, and the remainder to aid challengers and candidates in lopsided races. Party spending in Senate races was virtually identical.

Because most party advertising is negative, it has become highly controversial. One of the most notorious and effective independent television ads to air in recent years was run in 2006 by the RNC against Democrat Harold Ford Jr., an African American member of the House who was running against Chattanooga mayor Bob Corker in Tennessee's open-seat Senate contest. The ad opened with a woman remarking, "Harold Ford looks nice"; then it moves on to another woman who commented that "terrorists need their privacy," and a middle-aged man who stated that "when I die Ford will want me to pay taxes again." Several other individuals, apparently representing various other elements of society, made other outrageous and hilarious statements. The ad closed with a scantily clad white woman saying, "Harold, call me." The ad's use of humor and innuendo made it entertaining and memorable, and it had the effect of generating a great deal of free coverage in the media, which multiplied its effect. Its attacks on ethical issues were potent because Ford was running a campaign highlighting his values, and he was using television ads recorded in a church. Its closing scene probably evoked some racial prejudices that are still quite potent in parts of Tennessee. While not the sole cause of the outcome, the ad undoubtedly contributed to Ford's failed bid for the Senate.

Not all party independent expenditures are as effective as the anti-Ford ad, and some can do more harm than good. The prohibitions against coordination among the IE group making the ads, the candidate whose election they are attempting to influence, and the party organizations that are involved in the election mean the ads can sometimes backfire. An attack ad aired in 2006 by the NRCC to influence the open-seat contest between Democrat Michael Arcuri, a district attorney from upstate New York, and Republican New York state senator Ray Meier illustrates this. The ad claims that Arcuri used taxpayer dollars to pay for phone sex. The Arcuri campaign responded by pointing out that the incident cited in the ad occurred when an aide from the district attorney's office tried to call the state Division of Criminal Justice, which had a phone number nearly identical to the porn line. Although both Arcuri and Meier condemned the ad, it was heavily covered by the media, and Arcuri, the ultimate victor in the contest, was able to use it to capture the moral high ground by relating the ad to broader themes about dirty politics.

The Parallel Campaign

Party parallel campaigns consist mainly of so-called issue advocacy advertisements that are made on behalf of or against a congressional candidate. They involve many of the same efforts as independent expenditure campaigns, including polling, issue research, and campaign communications, and there are some similarities in how they are treated under federal campaign finance regulations. As is the case with virtually all federal campaign activities, party parallel campaign efforts must be financed with hard money, and they do not qualify for lowest unit rate charges. Federal regulations also treat parallel campaigns differently in some respects. First, parallel campaigns do not need to be independent of the campaign activities of candidates, party organizations, or other groups; coordination is permissible. Second, they can feature a candidate's name and picture, but they *cannot expressly* advocate the candidate's election or defeat. Third, party parallel campaigns can only be conducted up to ninety days prior to a primary or general election, at which point they must cease. Finally, the reporting requirements make it difficult to identify the specific candidates who are the beneficiaries of some party parallel campaign activities.

Among the earliest efforts at parallel campaigning were the RNC's televised ads "Vote Republican, For a Change," aired in 1980 and the Democrats' "It Isn't Fair, It's Republican," aired in 1982. Both of these ads were designed to set a broad national political agenda intended to benefit their candidates. More recent parallel campaigns have focused on individual contests. The congressional and senatorial campaign committees spearheaded and financed most of these efforts. Much of the party money used to finance the parallel campaign originates at the national level and is transferred to party committees in states hosting competitive elections, which in turn use the funds to hire political consultants who take primary responsibility for developing, recording, and airing issue advocacy ads.

Parties (and some interest groups) use parallel campaigns to set the political agenda or to praise or criticize specific federal candidates. All four Hill committees aired issue advocacy ads for these purposes in 2006, but most visible parallel campaigning consisted of negative advertising by the two senatorial campaign committees. The Senate race in Montana provides a telling example of parallel campaigning. Beginning in March 2006 the DSCC ran issue advocacy ads to set an agenda based on political corruption and to focus voter and media attention on Republican senator Conrad Burns's ties to the convicted lobbyist Jack Abramoff. The committee continued to air the issue ads until ninety days before the state's June 6 primary, at which point it switched over to independent expenditures. After Democratic challenger John Tester won the primary, the DSCC reverted to televising coordinated issue advocacy ads until ninety days before the general election, when it again switched over to independent expenditure ads.[63] The NRSC followed a similar tactic as it mounted a parallel campaign of issue advocacy that attacked Tester when it was legally permissible and then negative independent expenditures ninety days prior to the general election. The Democrats' parallel campaign was more successful: Burns was forced to campaign on an agenda focusing on political corruption and lost the election.

The Coordinated Campaign

The coordinated campaign entails traditional grassroots party campaigning enhanced by innovations in communications, database management, and voter mobilization. Important elements of the coordinated campaign involve voter identification, absentee ballot programs, and other voter turnout efforts. These activities are especially important in midterm congressional elections because the midterms are not as salient as presidential contests. Without extra grassroots efforts, many voters who have low or medium levels of political engagement will fail to show up at the polls.

Beginning in the 1960s, first the RNC and then the DNC assisted state party organizations with voter registration, voter-list development, targeting, GOTV drives, and other campaign efforts designed to benefit a party's entire ticket. The Republicans' coordinated campaign is directed by the RNC, which uses its Voter Vault data files, microtargeting techniques, and lists of volunteers to identify, educate, and turn out likely Republican voters. The key grassroots component of the Republicans' coordinated campaign is its 72-Hour Program. Modeled after the marketing operation created by Amway, the homecare products company, the 72-Hour Program uses paid organizers and layers of volunteers to recruit and train other volunteers who also help build the organization. Individuals located at the lower layers of the organization are primarily responsible for knocking on doors, registering voters, assisting with absentee ballot applications, making telephone calls, sending out e-mails, arranging rides, and other personalized forms of direct voter contact focused primarily on their neighbors. The program's reliance on targeted grassroots activities is so reminiscent of party campaigning at the dawn of the twentieth century that party officials have labeled it a "back to the future approach."[64]

The RNC's recent coordinated campaign efforts were supported by President Bush, Vice President Cheney, and other well-known GOP leaders who made appearances in states and districts for the purposes of motivating Republican campaign workers and volunteers. These visits also drew media attention to GOP candidates' campaigns, knocked the candidates' opponents out of the news, and helped the party capture extra votes in competitive contests.[65] They were most successful in 2002 and 2004, when the president and his administration enjoyed high ratings. However, given the administration's lack of popularity in many localities in 2006, the sites for these visits had to be selected carefully. The GOP's coordinated campaign appears to have succeeded in rounding up millions of voters who might not have voted otherwise. It is also likely that in 2006 the visits by high-level administration officials may have combined with Democratic efforts to propel the Democratic base and energize many swing voters to turn out in record numbers in support of Democratic candidates.

The Democrats did not begin to develop their own microtargeting operation or assemble their Data Mart voter file until after the 2004 election. Their efforts, involving the DNC, DCCC, DSCC, and a coalition of allied interest groups, have been more decentralized than Republican efforts. The Democrats also assisted candidates by using a more traditional approach that relies on geodemographics and information collected by field staff to target voters and local political activists who work to mobilize them.

Typical campaigns coordinated by the Democratic Party are less centralized than Republican campaigns. They usually involve national, senatorial, congressional, state, and local party organization staffs; aides from gubernatorial, senatorial, congressional, state, and local campaigns in overlapping districts; and labor union and other interest group members. Visits by Democratic leaders also are an important part of the Democrats' coordinated campaign. In 2006, Democratic congressional leaders Nancy Pelosi and Harry Reid, Democratic presidential aspirants Hillary Rodham Clinton and Barack Obama, and former President Bill Clinton, and many others traveled to many closely contested seats to mobilize Democratic activists and voters.[66]

Given the more hierarchical structure of the Republicans' voter mobilization program and party organization more generally, it is not surprising that the RNC carried out and funded the lion's share of the party's 72-Hour Program. In addition to providing most of the financing for the party's database, the RNC transferred $37.5 million to Republican state parties to help underwrite their infrastructure and coordinated campaign activities. The NRCC transferred approximately $474,000 and the NRSC provided close to $300,000. The combined efforts of the Republicans' national, state, and local party organizations resulted in the 72-Hour Program contacting a record 35 million voters with person-to-person telephone calls and 13 million home visits.[67]

Reflecting its more decentralized administration, the Democrats' coordinated campaign was financed by a variety of organizations. DNC, DCCC, and DSCC transfers of $26.5 million, $10.4 million, and $29.5 million paid for a significant portion of the coordination. One of the reasons the party's congressional and senatorial campaign committees invested so heavily in the coordinated campaign was that DNC chairman Howard Dean's 50-State Program directed substantial resources for party building to states that were not hosting competitive elections. Much to the chagrin of the DCCC chair, Rahm Emanuel, and the DSCC chair, Charles Schumer of New York, this meant that their committees would have to invest more in coordinated campaigns in targeted races.

Party-connected organizations sponsored by members of Congress, congressional candidates, congressional retirees, other party leaders, and allied interest groups also participate in independent, parallel, and coordinated campaigns. Some of these groups are classified as leadership PACs. However, some are 501(c) organizations or 527 committees, which were discussed in Chapter 1. This makes it difficult to determine the exact amounts some of these committees spend to influence congressional elections. Nevertheless, estimates for the 2006 congressional elections suggest that the top sixty 527 committees spent roughly $142.5 million.[68] Almost 64 percent of this amount was spent by a mere eight 527 committees. Much of this money was used to influence the outcomes of competitive congressional elections, but other sums were spent on candidate recruitment, training, and other election-related activities. Democratic candidates were the major beneficiaries of party-connected spending, as 62 percent of these expenditures were made by Democratic-oriented 527s.

Party and party-connected independent, parallel, and coordinated campaign activities can be a tremendous boon to a candidate, but they often cost a campaign some of its autonomy and may backfire. Pressure from Hill committee staff in Washington, D.C., can be frustrating and demoralizing to a campaign organization but not nearly as devastating as when a party commits a major blunder. Poor research or coordination between a party committee and a candidate's campaign organization can result in a candidate having to go "off message" to respond to an ad aired by the candidate's own party. Some party advertisements, such as the NRCC ad against New York's Arcuri, have to be taken off the air because they falsely accuse an opponent and harm a candidate.

THE IMPACT OF PARTY CAMPAIGNING

How valuable do House and Senate candidates find the campaign services they receive from party organizations? When asked to rate the importance of campaign assistance from local, state, and national party organizations and union, business, and advocacy groups and PACs in aspects of campaigning requiring professional expertise or in-depth research, candidates and campaign aides involved in House elections rank their party's Hill committee highly. Campaigners gave top evaluations to the Hill committees for campaign management, information about voters, issue and opposition research, mass media advertising, and development of the candidate's public image. Interest groups received somewhat higher evaluations for assistance in fundraising.

Recall that congressional campaign committee assistance is generally targeted to a small number of close contests.[69] For example, about one-half of all Republican House candidates in elections decided by 20 percent or less of the vote as well as 28 percent of their Democratic counterparts rated their party's congressional campaign committee as moderately, very, or extremely helpful in campaign management (see Table 4-5). More than half of each party's candidates in competitive races considered the fundraising and mass communications assistance they received from their party's congressional campaign committee to have been at least moderately important. Competitive Republicans gave even more favorable evaluations to Hill committee assistance in campaign management, public opinion assessment, and issue and opposition research than did their Democratic counterparts. With the exception of fundraising, for which more incumbents in jeopardy reported receiving the most congressional campaign committee assistance, open-seat prospects provided the most positive evaluations of Hill committee campaign services. In sum, the evaluations of House campaigners indicate the Hill committees are important campaign service providers, and most congressional campaign committee help is given to candidates in close races, consistent with the parties' goal of winning as many seats in Congress as possible.

TABLE 4-5
House Campaigners' Appraisals of the Assistance Provided by the Congressional Campaign Committees

	DCCC						NRCC					
	Incumbents		Challengers		Open-seat candidates		Incumbents		Challengers		Open-seat candidates	
	In jeopardy	Shoo-ins	Hopefuls	Likely losers	Prospects	Mismatched	In jeopardy	Shoo-ins	Hopefuls	Likely losers	Prospects	Mismatched
Campaign management	12%	9%	33%	3%	37%	13%	42%	3%	47%	9%	60%	10%
Fundraising	53	30	46	9	53	25	67	8	47	7	57	20
Media advertising	47	16	50	2	67	13	58	19	53	15	63	20
Information about voters	31	42	53	13	74	25	64	29	47	18	75	20
Issue and opposition research	25	15	57	9	53	38	46	14	71	30	80	40
Voter mobilization	18	18	43	6	21	13	25	9	25	9	47	10
Volunteer workers	—	2	36	3	42	25	42	—	12	—	40	10

Source: "2002 Congressional Campaign Study," Center for American Politics and Citizenship, University of Maryland.

Notes: Figures represent the percentage of House campaigners who evaluated their congressional campaign committee as moderately, very, or extremely helpful in each campaign activity. Figures are for general election candidates in major-party contested races, excluding those in incumbent-versus-incumbent races. — = less than 0.5 percent. *N* = 314.

Local party committees received the strongest evaluations for assistance with registering voters, GOTV drives, and providing campaign volunteers. Roughly half of all campaigners assessed their local party's contributions to have been moderately, very, or extremely important. State party committees were rated next highest for voter mobilization activities. Republicans reported their party's state committee played a substantial role in providing campaign workers. Many Democrats were somewhat less impressed with their state parties' performance in this regard; most maintained that labor unions provided them with more volunteer campaign workers. These evaluations demonstrate the vibrancy of state and local parties in some parts of the country. They also show the limited visibility of the congressional, senatorial, and national committees' involvement in grassroots campaigning, which frequently amounts to providing leadership and funding rather than directly recruiting armies of volunteers.

Colorado's 7th congressional district race in 2006 between Ed Perlmutter and Rick O'Donnell is an example of a House race in which both parties became heavily involved.[70] The Democratic Party provided the Perlmutter campaign with substantial direct support, including $3,500 in contributions and $55,000 in coordinated expenditures. Democratic members of Congress, retirees, and other federal politicians contributed an additional $96,000 from their campaign accounts and $108,000 from their leadership PACs. The total of these dollars accounted for approximately 9 percent of the campaign resources under Perlmutter's control. The DCCC also provided the campaign with daily briefings; weekly access to its consultants; and fundraising, research, and other forms of assistance. The efforts of the DCCC's PAC director and other personnel undoubtedly had a major impact on Perlmutter's ability to raise money from PACs and individuals tied into congressional donor networks.

The Democrats also carried out significant independent campaign activity. The DCCC spent more than $372,000 on independent expenditures in support of Perlmutter and almost $1.6 million attacking O'Donnell. Much of these funds were spent on four TV ads, and a small portion financed two direct-mail pieces. Each of these communications criticized O'Donnell on an important issue, such as Social Security or embryonic stem cell research, on the Democrats' national and local campaign agendas, and all of them linked O'Donnell to President Bush who was extremely unpopular in the district. The Colorado Democratic Party (CDP) broadcast two radio ads and sent out seven pieces of mail that focused on one of these issues, illegal immigration, or some controversial aspect of O'Donnell's professional career.

The Democrats' coordinated campaign was equally impressive. The DCCC and the DNC committed $385,000 and $602,000, respectively, to Colorado.

Some of these funds were given to Colorado Victory 2006 (CV06), an umbrella organization that spent almost $500,000 in the 7th district. CV06 drew support from party organizations, activists, labor unions, and women's groups. It initially had a staff of about twenty, but its numbers mushroomed later in the campaign season. CV06 conducted strong voter registration, absentee ballot, early voting, and election-day voter turnout programs that relied heavily on the CDP. These programs targeted Democratic voters who normally skip midterm elections, voters who had not declared a party affiliation on their voter registration forms, Latino and African American voters, and women. As part of its contribution to CV06, the CDP paid for targeted voters to receive three personal contacts from campaign volunteers and eighteen live or recorded telephone calls. The Democrats did not mount a parallel campaign in this race because they felt that issue advocacy ads were not necessary.

The Republican Party also committed significant resources to the campaign. It provided O'Donnell with $25,000 in direct contributions and $77,000 in coordinated expenditures. Republican members of Congress and other federal politicians contributed an additional $47,000 from their campaign committees and $220,000 from their leadership PACs. Party and party-connected dollars accounted for almost 13 percent of O'Donnell's resources. As was the case with the DCCC, the NRCC provided extensive strategic and tactical advice, including two polls and an opposition research package. As an NRCC targeted race, the O'Donnell campaign also received substantial fundraising assistance.[71]

The Republicans' independent campaign was not as well-funded as the Democrats'. Still, the GOP allocated $35,000 for ads advocating O'Donnell's election and $521,000 calling for Perlmutter's defeat. Most of these funds were spent on three television and two radio ads that labeled Perlmutter a hypocrite on renewable energy and attacked him for killing a plan to protect children from sex offenders. A portion of the independent expenditures was committed to sixteen pieces of direct mail, each of which was released on the heels of a new O'Donnell television ad so that it could reinforce the candidate's message. Five of these focused on immigration, four on Social Security and taxes, and three on crime and ethics. Several made derogatory references to Perlmutter as a bankruptcy lawyer.

As is typical in close contests, the RNC took primary responsibility for the coordinated campaign. It transferred more than $1 million to the Colorado Republican Party and paid three field directors and numerous field staff to work in the 7th district. These individuals helped establish a volunteer recruitment network and organized the field operations. Using lists of microtargeted voters drawn from the RNC's Voter Vault database, the field team initiated several types of direct voter contacts, including telephone calls, mail, and volunteers who knocked on doors. Special attention was given to senior citizens, women, and Hispanics. Voters having no registered party affiliation and who were believed to be concerned about specific issues such as immigration or the war on terrorism received between four and five contacts to discuss them.

Late in the election season, the RNC redeployed many of its field staff from Colorado's 7th district to its 4th district to shore up the prospects of Republican incumbent Marilyn Musgrave. Musgrave was locked in a head-to-head sprint with Democratic state representative Angie Paccione (Musgrave won by a mere 5,984 votes), and O'Donnell had failed to narrow Perlmutter's lead in the polls. Nevertheless, the GOP carried out a robust 96-Hour Program (the Colorado GOP's four-day version of the 72-Hour Program). During the final four days of the campaign, five hundred volunteers worked one thousand four-hour shifts to call every persuadable voter at least once and meet with many in person; included among these were approximately thirty-five hundred Hispanics who had face-to-face contact with a Hispanic volunteer. Although almost 104,000 voters were contacted during this period, O'Donnell's and the Republican Party's efforts were insufficient for the GOP to retain control over the seat.

Most Senate candidates and campaign aides give evaluations of Hill committee assistance that are as favorable as those given by House candidates. The senatorial campaign committees are rated above any other group in every area of campaigning, except providing information about voters, mobilizing voters, and recruiting volunteers. State and local party organizations and interest groups were ranked higher for these activities.[72]

Senate candidates in battleground races receive more campaign resources from their party than from any other group. The contest in Ohio between Republican incumbent Mike DeWine and the Democratic challenger, Rep. Sherrod Brown, demonstrates how important party activity can be in an election for the upper chamber.[73] The race turned out to be the most expensive in the state's history. It featured campaign visits by President Bush, former president Clinton, and several presidential hopefuls, including Sen. John McCain, R-Ariz., Sen. Joseph Biden, D-Del., Senator Clinton, and Senator Obama. The contest took place in the shadow of a number of statewide scandals involving Governor Robert Taft, a Republican, and several other high-ranking GOP officials. Coupled with voters' low evaluations of President Bush and Congress, the environment in the Buckeye state posed some high hurdles for Republican candidates to clear. An important factor that worked to DeWine's advantage was that Brown alienated some Democratic activists during the nomination season by declaring in the summer of 2005 that he would not run for the Senate and then reversing his decision in October. Brown's entry into the contest led party leaders to pressure declared candidate Paul Hackett to exit the race, and this created some hard feelings among Democratic supporters.

Once the general election season started, both parties began to provide substantial support to their candidates. The Democratic Party provided $39,000 in contributions and $1.4 million in coordinated expenditures—the legal maximum. Democratic senators and other politicians contributed $72,000 from their campaign committees and almost $194,000 from their leadership PACs. The DSCC also entered into a joint expenditure agreement with the Brown campaign that enabled the two organizations to spend more than $530,000 on television advertising featuring Brown. Combined, these contributions accounted for almost 19 percent of the resources under the candidate's control. In addition, the DSCC provided strategic and fundraising assistance, including organizing a joint fundraiser in California attended by big donors to Brown and to Senate hopeful Claire McCaskill of Missouri.

Brown also received help in the form of a parallel campaign mounted by the DSCC. His late entry into the race left him strapped for cash early in the general election season, which might have allowed DeWine to dominate the airwaves unanswered. The DSCC helped fill the void on the Democratic side by televising issue advocacy advertisements and creating a joint expenditure agreement to finance some ads. The DSCC continued to run the issue ads until ninety days before the election, when it began its independent spending campaign.[74]

The core of the Democrats' independent campaign was the more than $2 million in expenditures it made advocating Brown's election and the $4.2 million it spent calling for DeWine's ouster. Almost all of the DSCC's money was spent on television advertising; state and local Democratic parties in Ohio spent most of their funds on twenty-eight mailings and four e-mails; the DNC also provided a mailing and two e-mails. Most of the Democratic Party ads sought to link DeWine with several Republicans, including Rep. Bob Ney and Governor Taft, who were involved in scandals.

The Democrats also conducted an impressive coordinated campaign in Ohio. The DSCC took the lead in organizing the effort when it transferred more than $2.5 million to the Ohio Democratic Party. The DSCC appointed a coordinated campaign director, a field director, and a communications expert to lead the effort.[75] The committee used its investment to leverage resources from other party committees, labor unions, groups, and participating candidates. The DNC invested $1.4 million, and the DCCC provided about $961,000. The coordinated campaign was able to attract the involvement of many groups because, in addition to a hotly contested Senate election, Ohio hosted several competitive House, statewide, and local races. The Democratic Party's direct contributions and coordinated expenditures and its parallel, independent, and coordinated campaigns were instrumental in paving Brown's road to victory.

The Republicans also invested heavily in the Ohio Senate race. Although they made little in the way of direct contributions to DeWine, Republican party committees provided almost $1.3 million in coordinated expenditures, and GOP senators and politicians contributed $13,000 and $466,000, respectively, from their campaign committees and leadership PACs. The NRSC and the DeWine campaign also jointly funded about $131,000 in television ads. In total, the Republican Party contributed about 14 percent of the resources that were under the candidate's control. Like its Democratic counterpart, the NRSC also provided extensive strategic and fundraising assistance.

DeWine's overwhelming financial advantage over Brown early in the election season led the NRSC to decide not to run a parallel campaign in Ohio. As the outcome of the race became more uncertain, the Republicans decided to mount an extensive independent campaign despite the fact that DeWine was able to outspend Brown by almost $6.6 million. The NRSC and RNC spent a combined $39,000 praising DeWine and more than $4.2 million to attack Brown. Most of these funds were used to air ten TV ads, but some party funds were spent on direct mail. The Ohio Republican Party sent out at least thirteen separate mail pieces.

The closeness of the Senate contest and the many competitive U.S. House races and state elections in Ohio caused the Republicans to mount a considerable coordinated campaign in the state. As usual, the RNC took the lead in this endeavor. It transferred $3.9 million to the Ohio Republican Party. The NRCC contributed $53,000, but the cash-strapped NRSC made no financial contribution. Similar to Republican coordinated campaign efforts in other close races, the GOP used data generated from Voter Vault and a large volunteer database to mount an extensive voter identification, education, and GOTV operation that included four mass e-mails, seventeen rounds of telephone calls, and other direct voter contacts.

As in the House race in Colorado's 7th district, it is impossible to determine exactly what led to the election outcome in Ohio's 2006 Senate contest. Nevertheless, party activity was important. The parties spent a total of more than $23 million in the state, just 10 percent less than Brown's and DeWine's combined expenditures. In addition to these funds, the parties provided extensive campaign services. Given the Brown campaign's financial disadvantages, it is probably safe to assert that without the involvement of the DSCC and other Democratic Party organizations this contest would have been decided differently.

SUMMARY

Political parties, particularly party organizations in Washington, play important supporting roles in contemporary congressional elections. Their agenda-setting efforts encourage voters to focus on issues that traditionally work to the advantage of their candidates. The Hill committees distribute most of their contributions, coordinated expenditures, and campaign services to candidates in close races. They also provide transactional assistance to help these candidates attract funding and campaign resources from other politicians, their leadership PACs, other PACs and interest groups, and individual contributors. Local parties assist candidates in mobilizing voters in some parts of the country. National party organizations have substantially increased their influence in congressional elections, particularly those with unpredictable outcomes, by carrying out independent, parallel, and coordinated campaigns.

Republican Party organizations historically have been wealthier than their Democratic counterparts, and GOP party committees, particularly at the national level, have traditionally played a greater role than Democratic Party organizations in congressional elections. The Democrats closed that wealth gap considerably in 2006, however, and they have greatly increased their involvement in congressional campaigns. Although the Democrats raised about $120 million less than their GOP rivals during the 2006 election season, the analysis of their contributions, coordinated expenditures, joint expenditures, party-connected contributions, independent expenditures, and national party financial transfers to the states strongly suggests that the Democrats delivered more support to their congressional candidates.

CHAPTER FIVE

The Interests Campaign

Organized interests, pejoratively referred to as "special interests," have always been involved in American elections. During the earliest days of the Republic, leaders of agricultural and commercial groups influenced who was on the ballot, the coverage they received in the press, and the voting patterns that determined election outcomes. As the electorate grew and parties and candidates began to spend more money to reach voters, steel magnates, railroad barons, and other captains of industry increased their roles in political campaigns. Labor unions counterorganized with manpower and dollars.[1] Religious and ethnic groups also influenced elections, but their financial and organizational efforts paled next to those of business and labor.

Interest groups continue to flourish at the beginning of the twenty-first century, and several developments have significantly affected their roles in congressional elections. The growth in the number of organizations that located or hired representatives in Washington, D.C., resulted in the formation of a community of lobbyists that was, and continues to be, attuned to the rhythms of legislative and election politics. The enactment of the Federal Election Campaign Act (FECA) of 1974, one of the predecessors of the Bipartisan Campaign Reform Act of 2002, paved the way for the development of the modern political action committee—the form of organizational entity that most interest groups use to carry out the majority of their federal campaign activities. Court decisions and Federal Election Commission rulings handed down in recent years weakened the 1974 law, and the enactment of the BCRA made the world of interest groups more complex. The determinations of the courts and the FEC led some interest groups to augment their federal PAC activities with nonfederal dollars from their treasuries or from nonprofit tax-exempt organizations connected to their group, including 501(c) and 527 entities. Other groups pooled their resources to create new, mostly nonprofit, organizations for these same purposes. These for-profit and nonprofit organizations contribute to party committees or influence congressional elections through public relations campaigns, issue advocacy advertising, and voter mobilization activities financed with soft money.

This chapter covers the growth and development of the PAC community and the roles that PACs and other groups play in congressional elections. I analyze the motives that underlie PAC strategies and activities, the methods that PACs use to select candidates for support, and the distribution of PAC contributions and independent expenditures. I also examine other interest group activities, including politically motivated educational campaigns, issue advocacy ads, and voter mobilization efforts that comprise the independent, parallel, and coordinated campaigns that interest groups carry out to influence congressional elections.

THE RISE OF PACS AND
OTHER ELECTORALLY ACTIVE ORGANIZATIONS

Interest groups have been active in politics throughout U.S. history. Many attempts have been made to limit their election activities or, at the very least, disclose them to the public to allow for at least a modicum of accountability in the roles of groups in campaigns. A major by-product of these efforts has been the creation of different forms of interest group entities that have assumed different roles in campaign politics. Interest groups now form PACs, 501(c) organizations, 527 committees, and in some cases a myriad of interrelated groups to influence congressional elections.

Political Action Committees

The Committee on Political Education, the first forerunner to the modern political action committee, was founded in 1943 by the Congress of Industrial Organizations.[2] A PAC can be best understood as the electoral arm of an organized interest. Interest groups form PACs to give campaign contributions or services directly to federal or, in some cases, state or local candidates in the hope of influencing election outcomes, the formation of public policy, or both. Some PACs also make independent expenditures for or against federal candidates. Most PACs have a sponsoring, or parent, organization, such as a corporation, labor union, trade association, or other group. However, for "nonconnected" PACs, the PAC itself is the organizing group.

Federal campaign finance reform set the scene for the PAC explosion of the mid-1970s. One of the goals of federal campaign finance reform was to dilute the influence of moneyed interests on federal elections. As noted in Chapter 1, federal law limits the amount an individual can contribute to a specific federal candidate and places a ceiling on the total contributions an individual can make to federal candidates, parties, and PACs in a given election cycle. The law also bars corporations, labor unions, trade associations, cooperatives, and other organized groups from giving contributions directly from their treasuries to candidates for federal office. By limiting the total contributions a candidate can collect from any one source, the law encouraged, and continues to encourage, candidates to solicit smaller donations from a broader array of interests and individuals.

The law also encouraged many interest groups to establish PACs. Although neither the Bipartisan Campaign Reform Act nor its forerunner, the Federal Election Campaign Act, mentions the term *political action committee,* both laws allow for "a multicandidate committee" that raises money from at least fifty donors and spends it on at least five candidates for federal office to contribute a maximum of $5,000 per candidate at each stage of the election.[3] The ceilings that federal campaign finance statutes established for individual contributions to candidates and the $5,000-per-year limit it set for individual contributions to any one PAC have the combined effect of making PAC contributions a popular vehicle among wealthy individuals who wish to influence congressional elections.

In November 1975, in an advisory opinion written for Sun Oil Company, the FEC counseled the company that it could pay the overhead and solicitation costs of its PAC, thereby freeing the PAC to spend on federal elections all the funds it collected from donors. The Sun PAC decision clarified a gray area in the law and in the process made PACs a much more attractive vehicle for collecting and disbursing funds. The advisory ruling contributed to an explosion in the number of PACs that lasted from the mid-1970s to the mid-1980s.

The Supreme Court's ruling in *Buckley v. Valeo* allowed PACs to make unlimited independent expenditures (made without the knowledge or consent of a candidate or the candidate's campaign organization) in federal elections. Both the FEC advisory opinion and the Supreme Court decision created new opportunities for organized groups to participate in politics. The advisory opinion was especially important, encouraging a wide range of political leaders, business entrepreneurs, and others to form new PACs.

Between 1974 and the 2006 elections, the PAC community grew from more than 600 to 5,094 committees (see Figure 5-1). Most of the growth occurred in the business sector, with corporate PACs growing in number from

FIGURE 5-1

Growth in the Number of Registered PACs, 1974–2006

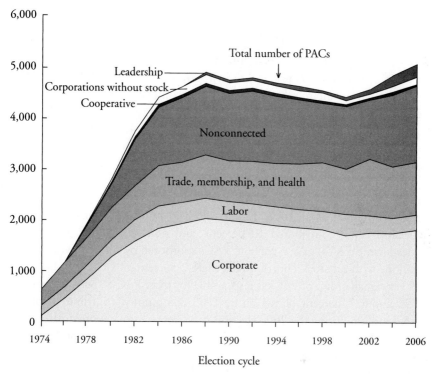

Sources: Joseph E. Cantor, *Political Action Committees: Their Evolution, Growth, and Implications for the Political System* (Washington, D.C.: Congressional Research Service of the Library of Congress, 1984), 88; Federal Election Commission; and Center for Responsive Politics.

Note: Leadership PACs are classified separately from nonconnected PACs.

89 in 1974 to 1,809 in 2006. Labor unions, many of which already had PACs in 1974, created the fewest new PACs, increasing the number from 201 to 315. The centralization of the labor movement into a relatively small number of unions greatly limited the growth of labor PACs. In addition, three new species of political action committee—the nonconnected PAC (mostly ideological and issue-oriented groups) and PACs whose sponsors are either cooperatives or corporations without stock—emerged on the scene in 1977. The nonconnected PACs are the most important of these. By 2006 their number had grown to 1,511; in contrast, the combined total for the two other types of PAC had reached only 155.[4]

Leadership PACs, covered briefly in Chapter 4, are the most recently formed type of PAC. Sponsored by politicians and closely tied to the parties, these PACs traditionally have been categorized as nonconnected PACs. They remained scarce until the late 1980s because few members of Congress could raise the money to form them. During the 1990s an increasing number of politicians, including some relatively junior members of the House, began to sponsor them. Their numbers reached 58 in 1994, 86 in 1996, and 285 in 2006.

The growth in the number of PACs was accompanied by a tremendous increase in their activity. PAC contributions to congressional candidates grew from $12.5 million in 1974 to approximately $348.5 million in 2006. Corporate and other business-related PACs accounted for most of that growth (see Figure 5-2). In 2006, corporate PACs accounted for roughly 35 percent of all PAC contributions to congressional candidates, followed by trade association PACs, which accounted for about 28 percent. Labor PACs gave just under 16 percent of all contributions received by congressional candidates, leadership PACs contributed 12 percent, and nonconnected PACs (excluding leadership PACs) gave 7 percent. PACs sponsored by cooperatives and corporations without stock contributed a mere 2 percent.

A very small group of PACs is responsible for most PAC activity. A mere 351 PACs, about 7 percent of the entire PAC community, contributed roughly $243.4 million during the 2006 election cycle, representing approximately two-thirds of all PAC money given in that period (see Table 5-1). Each of these committees, which are clearly the "all-stars" of the PAC community, gave over $250,000 to federal candidates. These include PACs sponsored by corporations, trade associations, and unions, such as United Parcel Service, the National Association of Realtors, and the American Federation of Labor–Congress of Industrial Organizations, as well as nonconnected PACs such as EMILY's List, which supports pro-choice Democratic women candidates.[5]

Another 9 percent of all PACs are "major players," each having contributed between $100,001 and $250,000 to candidates during the 2006 election cycle. These committees, which include the National Association of Mortgage Brokers PAC, the American Insurance Association PAC, the National Association of Postal Supervisors PAC, the League of Conservation Voters (LCV) PAC, and Washington PAC (WASHPAC, a pro-Israel group), accounted for 19 percent of all PAC contributions. The all-stars and major players are particularly influential because their wealth allows them to contribute to virtually every candidate whose election is of importance to them.

The "players" are PACs that have the resources to give a significant contribution to many but not all of the candidates they wish to support. Comprising 8 percent of all PACs, they include PACs representing the interests of the U.S. sub-

FIGURE 5-2

Growth of PAC Contributions in Congressional Elections, 1974–2006

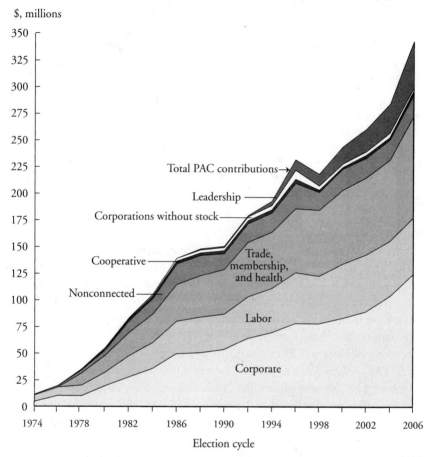

Sources: Joseph E. Cantor, *Political Action Committees: Their Evolution, Growth, and Implications for the Political System* (Washington, D.C.: Congressional Research Service of the Library of Congress, 1984), 88; Federal Election Commission; and Center for Responsive Politics.

Note: Leadership PAC contributions are separated from contributions made by nonconnected PACs.

sidiary of the Heineken Brewing Company, the American Gaming Association, the Association of Professional Flight Attendants, and the Marijuana Policy Project. Each of the players contributed between $50,001 and $100,000, accounting for roughly 7 percent of all PAC contributions.

The contributions of the next group of PACs, which might be labeled the "junior varsity," are clearly constrained by their size. These PACs each

TABLE 5-1

Concentration of PAC Contributions in the 2006 Election Cycle

	Total contributions by PACs					
	Over $250,000	$100,001– $250,000	$50,001– $100,000	$5,001– $50,000	$1– $5,000	$0
Percentage of all PACs	7	9	8	28	16	33
N	*351*	*451*	*394*	*1,409*	*798*	*1,691*
Percentage of all PAC contributions ($, millions)	65 $243.4	19 $70.6	7 $28.0	8 $28.4	— $1.7	0 $0

Source: Compiled from Federal Election Commission data.

Note: Includes contributions to candidates not up for election in 2006.

contributed between $5,001 and $50,000. They constitute 28 percent of the PAC community and gave 8 percent of all PAC contributions. Their donations tend to be significantly smaller than those of the larger PACs. The managers of most junior varsity PACs routinely have to answer requests for contributions by stating that they support the candidate and would like to give a contribution but do not have the money. Such PACs include those representing the Burger King Corporation, the American Sportfishing Association, and the International Association of Heat and Frost Insulators and Asbestos Workers PAC, as well as WILD PAC, which seeks to protect America's wilderness and national parks.

Members of the next group, the "little league," each gave between $1 and $5,000, accounting for less than 1 percent of all PAC contributions during the 2006 election cycle. They include the Unisource Energy Corporation PAC, the Concerned Friends for Tobacco PAC, and the Providence (Rhode Island) Fraternal Order of Police PAC. These committees, which make up about 16 percent of the PAC community, play a marginal role in the funding of congressional elections.

Finally, 1,691 PACs gave no money during the 2006 elections. Many of these are, for all practical purposes, defunct. Although they registered with the FEC, they spent no money to collect contributions, pay off debts, or cover the costs of committee administration during the 2006 election cycle.

Not-for-Profit and For-Profit Groups

Nonprofit interest group organizations have been in existence for a long time, but their conspicuous presence in congressional elections is only a recent phenomenon, resulting primarily from the exploitation of loopholes in federal campaign finance law. Some interest groups capitalized on changes in federal campaign finance regulations by using existing nonprofit entities that were part of their organizational structure or by creating new ones in order to raise and spend unregulated soft money and make issue advocacy expenditures intended to influence federal elections. Five types of legal entities became highly visible in congressional elections: 501(c)(3), 501(c)(4), 501(c)(5), 501(c)(6), and 527 committees. As defined in the U.S. Internal Revenue Code, 501(c)(3) organizations are tax-exempt groups organized for charitable purposes. They are prohibited from becoming directly involved in federal campaigns, including endorsing or contributing to candidates or organizing a PAC, but they can conduct research and educational activities, carry out nonpartisan voter registration drives and get-out-the-vote drives, and sponsor candidate forums. Donations made to a 501(c)(3) organization are tax deductible and are subject to some level of disclosure.

The revenue code defines 501(c)(4) organizations as nonprofit social welfare organizations. They are exempt from federal taxes and their financial activities are subject to minimal disclosure requirements. Donations made to them are not tax deductible. These groups can engage in partisan political activities as long as such activities are not the group's primary purpose. These groups are allowed to rate candidates, promote legislation, make independent expenditures, and engage in issue advocacy. Similar activities and tax benefits apply to labor groups that enjoy 501(c)(5) status and business groups that organize as 501(c)(6) organizations.[6]

Traditionally, federal candidate campaign committees and other political committees participating in federal elections were governed by section 527 of the tax code, which exempts "political organizations" from paying income taxes. This provision was originally designed to cover candidate campaigns, PACs, and party committees that disclosed their finances to the FEC, making it unnecessary for the IRS code to encompass these organizations in its contribution, expenditure, and disclosure provisions. However, some politicians and nonprofit interest groups created 527 committees solely to raise and spend soft money on voter mobilization and issue advocacy efforts intended to influence federal elections. Because these committees did not expressly advocate the election of federal candidates, they were not required to report their receipts and expenditures to the FEC and were thus able to evade contribution limits and disclosure rules. Congress reformed the tax code to require these organizations to disclose such transactions beginning in January 2001; however, this reform did not bar them from raising and spending soft money to affect congressional elections.

Indeed, 527 committees raised $164 million and spent $204.6 million with the goal of influencing the 2006 congressional elections. The top five spenders were the Service Employees International Union (SEIU), which spent $28.2 million, the Democratic-leaning America Votes ($14.1 million), the Republican-oriented Progress for America ($13 million), EMILY's List ($11.1 million), and the College Republican National Committee ($10.3 million). The Club for Growth (an anti-tax, pro-Republican group), rated seventh, spent $8.2 million. The top ten 527 committees accounted for 53 percent of all federally oriented 527 spending.[7] Approximately two-thirds of these groups spent most, if not all, of their money to help the Democrats.[8]

Corporations, trade associations, unions, and other groups play a major role in financing most 527 committees, but the same is true of some wealthy individuals. The top three donors to 527s in 2006 were Bob Perry, a Texas homebuilder; Jerry Perenchio, the founder of Univision (the largest Spanish television network in the U.S.); and George Soros, a financial speculator. Perry and Perenchio contributed roughly $9.8 million and $6 million, respectively, to Republican-oriented groups. Soros contributed $3.9 million to Democratic-oriented groups. These amounts contrast sharply with the $91,800, $39,900, and $95,400 in federally regulated funds these individuals contributed directly to congressional candidates, political parties, and PACs. When combined, the amounts that the top ten donors contributed to 527 committees accounted for 18 percent of these organizations' receipts.[9] Groups incorporated in section 527 of the tax code clearly have become a vehicle that some extremely wealthy individuals and groups use to influence congressional elections. Nevertheless, it is important to bear in mind that it is impossible to get a complete picture of the election activities of interest groups. Because of the lack of full disclosure of the financing of the political activities of some 501(c) organizations, it is impossible to know the full impact of wealthy interest groups and their backers.

Multifaceted Groups

The AFL-CIO is an example of an interest group with a complex interconnected organizational structure that enables it to participate aggressively in the political process without violating the federal campaign finance or tax statutes. The group uses its federal PAC to make contributions to congressional candidates and independent expenditures. Its 501(c)(5) organization finances research, educates, and mobilizes union members around major campaign themes. Its 501(c)(4) organization targets similar efforts to nonunion households.[10] The group's 527 account finances issue advocacy ads and other political activities. Soft money is also used to finance at least two important partnerships: the first is with the

Democracy Alliance, a taxable corporation that guides the contributions of member groups to 527 and 501(c) organizations that promote civic engagement, media, leadership, and policy development for liberal organizations; and the second is with Catalist, a private organization founded by former DNC chairman Harold Ickes to develop a database to microtarget and mobilize pro-Democratic voters.[11] The AFL-CIO also coordinates its activities with other progressive organizations, including the dozens of unions that affiliate with it.

The AFL-CIO's activities are designed to influence several audiences: the candidates who receive its contributions; other unions and progressive organizations and individuals that utilize its publications to help formulate their campaign strategies and contribution decisions; political activists who are guided by its endorsements and public relations efforts when selecting candidates for support; and union members and other ordinary voters who are influenced by its independent expenditures, issue advocacy ads, and other outreach efforts. Other pro-Democratic groups with interlocking structures that enable them to make campaign contributions and conduct independent, parallel, and coordinated campaigns include the SEIU, EMILY's List, America Coming Together (which conducts GOTV drives designed to help Democrats), and the League of Conservation Voters. Among the pro-Republican groups that have developed complex organizational structures for similar reasons are the Club for Growth, the Economic Freedom Fund (a pro-Republican, anti-tax group backed primarily by Bob Perry), and the WISH List (which supports pro-choice GOP women candidates).

STRATEGY, DECISION MAKING, AND TARGETING

Interest group goals and strategies are more diverse than are those of the two major parties, reflecting the fact that the parties are consumed with electing candidates and the groups have other goals, such as promoting issues and influencing the policy process. Some interest groups and their PACs follow "ideological" or "electoral" strategies designed to increase the number of legislators who share their broad political perspective or positions on specific, often emotionally charged issues such as abortion. These groups are similar to political parties in that they consider congressional elections as opportunities to alter the composition of Congress and view the electoral process as their primary vehicle for changing or reinforcing the direction of public policy.[12] Nonconnected PACs have traditionally been categorized as ideological committees.

Ideological PACs make most of their contributions to candidates in close elections, in which the PACs have the biggest chance of affecting an election outcome. The same is true for the independent, parallel, and coordinated campaign activities of ideologically oriented nonprofit and for-profit organizations that participate in elections. However, some groups become involved in uncompetitive contests in order to attract attention to themselves, their issues, or politicians who share their views. By gaining visibility for themselves and their causes, these organizations can more easily raise money and increase their political clout.

PACs following ideological strategies have traditionally not given much money to members of Congress for the sake of gaining access to the legislative process. The issues these PACs support are often linked to values so fundamental that legislators would not be expected to change their views in response to a contribution or visit by a lobbyist. Before giving a contribution, many of these PACs, and some others, require candidates to complete questionnaires that elicit their views on certain issues.

Other groups pursue "access" strategies designed to enable the group to gain at least an audience with members of Congress.[13] These groups, which include PACs sponsored by corporate and trade associations, view elections pragmatically. For such groups, an election is a prime opportunity to shore up relations with members of Congress who work on legislation that is of importance to their parent organization. Elections give these groups the opportunity to create goodwill with powerful legislators or at least to minimize the enmity of legislators who disagree with them. Because PAC contributions are often delivered by a group's lobbyist (who is usually a member of the PAC's board of directors), these contributions provide an opportunity for lobbyists and legislators to mingle with one another. Thus, interactions involving elections lay the groundwork for later lobbying efforts.

A group that follows an access strategy is likely to contribute most of its money to incumbents. Members of the House and Senate who chair committees or subcommittees, occupy party leadership positions, or are policy entrepreneurs with influence over legislation are likely to receive large contributions regardless of the competitiveness of their contests.[14] In fact, many access-oriented PACs make contributions to legislators who do not even have opponents. Of course, members of Congress who have supported a group's legislation and who are involved in contests with unpredictable outcomes are singled out for extra support, including large PAC contributions or assistance with fundraising. Supporting incumbents enables PACs and other organizations to accomplish their goal of ensuring access and helping legislative allies, while meeting organizational imperatives such as backing a large number of winners and contributing to candidates who represent districts that contain many of the group's supporters.

Access-oriented groups also give significant sums to candidates for open seats. Most of these candidates have good chances of winning but need large amounts of money to run competitive campaigns. Giving an open-seat prospect a large contribution is useful to an access-oriented PAC because it can help elect an ally to Congress and create goodwill, helping to create a foundation for productive relations with a future member of Congress.

Access-oriented groups tend to ignore challengers because most of them are likely to lose. Giving a challenger a contribution is often considered a waste of money and could lead to serious repercussions from an incumbent. Moreover, backing challengers has a high probability of reducing a group's win-loss record and could lead to criticism of the PAC's manager. The managers of access-oriented PACs that decide not to support challenger or open-seat candidates know that, should these candidates win, they could make amends later by helping them retire their campaign debts or contributing to them early in the next election cycle.

Groups that use access strategies rarely make independent expenditures or broadcast issue advocacy ads because of the publicity these activities can generate. Such efforts could harm a corporation if they anger congressional incumbents, upset some of the group's donors, or call undue attention to the candidate or the group. Such publicity could lead to charges that a group is trying to buy influence and could hinder the achievement of its goals. The corporations that choose to back such high-profile campaign efforts often minimize the visibility of their involvement by contributing to one or more 527 committees or 501(c) groups. Organizations such as the Republican Governors Association, the Republican State Leadership Committee, the Democratic Governors Association, or the Democratic Legislative Campaign Committee benefited from millions of dollars in contributions from the pharmaceutical and tobacco industries during the 2006 elections. Although this money was not always directly targeted to House or Senate elections, the advertisements, voter education, and voter mobilization drives these funds supported were undoubtedly influential in benefiting congressional candidates. By channeling much of their electoral participation through these organizations, corporations are likely to have a bigger impact on the vote than if they broadcast TV ads or carried out other activities identifying themselves as the ads' sponsors.

Many groups, including a large number of labor unions, practice "mixed" strategies. They support some candidates with contributions, independent expenditures, issue advocacy ads, or grassroots activities because those candidates share the group's views; they support others because they wish to improve their access to legislators who work on policies the group deems important. Campaign assistance motivated by the former reason is usually distributed to those candidates embroiled in competitive contests. Assistance informed by the latter motive is given to incumbents who are in a position to influence legislation important to the group.

In some cases the ideological and access motives clash, for example, when a highly qualified challenger who represents a group's views runs a competitive race against an incumbent in a position of power. In these situations, groups usually support the incumbent, but sometimes they contribute to both candidates. Groups that follow mixed strategies and groups that are motivated by ideology are more likely than access-oriented groups to make independent expenditures or issue advocacy ads.

Interest Group Strategy and the Political Environment

Interest groups, like most other groups and individuals involved in politics, are strategic actors that respond to their environment in ways that enable them to pursue their goals.[15] During the 1970s most PACs used ideological strategies that followed partisan lines. They backed candidates who supported the positions to which their organizational sponsors adhered. Business-oriented PACs, including corporate and trade committees, largely supported Republican candidates. Labor organizations, which were and continue to be the most consistently partisan of all PACs, regularly gave 90 percent of their contributions to Democrats. In time, many business-oriented committees shifted from ideological to access or mixed strategies. These PACs, with the encouragement of then–Democratic Congressional Campaign Committee chair Tony Coelho, redirected their support from Republican House challengers to incumbents, many of whom were Democrats, out of recognition of the Democratic Party's decades-long control of Congress.[16]

Perhaps the clearest strategic response by PACs takes place after partisan control of one or both chambers of Congress changes hands. When control of the Senate switched from the Democrats to the Republicans in 1981 and back to the Democrats in 1987, many access-oriented PACs switched their contributions to Senate incumbents who belonged to the new majority party. Similarly, after the 1995 GOP takeover of the House and Senate, these PACs gave most of their funds to Republicans, once again reversing their previous contribution patterns.[17] Following the Democrats' takeover of Congress in 2007, the flow of PAC contributions appears to have changed direction once again—this time in favor of the Democrats.

Because of their desire to influence the composition of Congress, ideologically oriented groups are the most likely to capitalize on the conditions peculiar to a specific election. A group that uses an access strategy, such as a corporate or trade PAC, is less affected by a particular electoral setting unless changing conditions are almost certain to influence the ability of its lobbyist (or team of lobbyists) to meet with key legislators and their staffs. The strategic changes in PAC behavior that occurred in the early 1980s were the result of PACs learning how to get the most legislative influence for their dollars and the increasing aggressiveness of incumbent fundraising.[18] Changes that occurred following the 1994 and 2006 elections were a response to the change in partisan control of Congress. More recent changes in interest group behavior, particularly the concentration of issue advocacy ads and grassroots efforts in a small number of extremely close races, represent group responses to the slim majorities determining partisan control of the House and Senate.

Making strategic adjustments in anticipation of political change is more difficult. The manager of an access-oriented PAC who believes that a member of Congress is likely to go from having little to major influence in a policy area, for instance, may have difficulty persuading the PAC's board of directors to raise the member's contribution from a token sum to a substantial donation. The manager's prospects of convincing the board that the organization should totally revamp its strategy because partisan control of Congress might change are slim. For example, prior to the Republican takeover of Congress in 1995 many corporate and trade groups, whose support of a pro-business agenda suggests they would want to support Republicans who have real prospects for victory, poured more money into Democratic campaigns than campaigns mounted by Republicans. And in 2006, many of these and other access-oriented groups were unable to divert funds from Republican to Democratic incumbents. Some of the managers of these PACs may have been attuned to the fact that a confluence of anti-Washington sentiments, strong challengers, and vulnerable incumbents enhanced the prospects for a switch in partisan control, but their organization's decision-making process made it impossible for them to change its contribution patterns in anticipation of it.

Interest Group Decision Making

The decision-making processes that an interest group uses to select candidates for support are affected by the group's overall strategy, wealth, organizational structure, and location.[19] Ideological groups spend more time searching for promising challengers to support than do groups that use access or mixed strategies. Ideological PACs also are more likely than other groups to support nonincumbents in congressional primaries. Wealthy groups tend to spend more time searching for promising nonincumbents simply because they can afford to fund more candidates.[20] Federated groups whose organizational affiliates are spread across the country typically have to respond to the wishes of these constituents when making contributions, independent expenditures, or issue advocacy ads.[21] Nonconnected PACs, leadership PACs, and groups sponsored by a single corporation or cooperative, in contrast, are less constrained by the need to please a diverse and far-flung constituency. Interest groups located in the nation's capital have more information available to them about the relative competitiveness of individual races because they can readily participate in more communications networks than can groups located in the hinterlands.[22]

The decision-making processes of PACs vary according to the PACs' organizational capacities. The Realtors PAC (RPAC), a large institutionalized committee with headquarters in Washington, D.C., was formed in 1969.[23] This federated PAC, which is sponsored by the National Association of Realtors (NAR), receives its money from PACs sponsored by the NAR's eighteen hundred local affiliates and state associations located in all fifty states plus the District of Columbia, Guam, Puerto Rico, and the Virgin Islands. Realtors give donations to RPAC and to these affiliated PACs, each of which passes 30 percent of its revenues to the national PAC. In 2006 RPAC distributed almost $3.8 million in contributions, more than any other political action committee.

The Realtors PAC employs a mixed strategy to advance the goals of the real estate industry. As do most other institutionalized PACs, it has explicit criteria for selecting candidates for support and uses a complex decision-making procedure. Party, incumbency, and electoral competitiveness have a major impact on RPAC contributions. Incumbents, who are typically given preference over challengers, are evaluated on a number of criteria to assess their policy proclivities, level of activism on behalf of real estate issues, and local realtor support. Members who cosponsor priority NAR legislation, give a speech on behalf of NAR legislation on the House or Senate floor, or write letters to their colleagues in support of such legislation are top priorities. The same is true of those who use their congressional authority to compel the president or independent regulatory agencies to respond to real estate industry concerns, vote for key NAR issues in committee or on the floor, or assist constituents with real estate–related matters. Leaders of both parties and members who belong to committees that deal with real estate issues are also targeted for contributions.

Nonincumbents who have previously held elective office, and thus have a record on real estate issues, are judged for contributions using similar criteria. Most also are interviewed by RPAC representatives, usually local or state NAR members, and asked to complete an RPAC questionnaire to help the PAC further discern the candidate's political philosophy, background, and campaign skills. Nonincumbents who have not previously held office must be interviewed by RPAC representatives and complete a questionnaire to be eligible for a contribution. Finally, when considering both incumbents and nonincumbents for contributions, the PAC considers the competitiveness of the race, the amount of cash in a candidate's campaign account, and the number and partisanship of realtors who live in the district.

RPAC's contribution decisions are made in several ways. The PAC's staff and trustees and the NAR's political representatives and lobbyists deliberate using the preceding criteria to make one centralized set of contribution decisions. The PAC's In-State Reception Program constitutes a second, decentralized decision-making process. Under the program, realtors who want to attend a fundraising event held by one of their state's incumbents can make an RPAC contribution of up to $1,000, so long as the donation is approved by the chair of RPAC's state affiliate. The process for contributions to open-seat candidates is similar, except that the candidate must be personally interviewed and approved by state RPAC officials. The In-State Reception Program has a similar but more stringent process for challenger contributions because most challengers have poor prospects of success and NAR officials are concerned about angering incumbents. The state PAC's request for a contribution must be formally approved or rejected by national RPAC trustees, and the contribution is limited to a maximum of $1,000.

Other programs allow RPAC to further increase realtors' contact with legislators and to concentrate its resources in close races. The Special Recognition Fund is used to make additional contributions to party leaders, candidates who serve on committees with jurisdiction over real estate–related matters, and staunch supporters of real estate interests who are involved in competitive contests. The Washington Reception Program Fund allows NAR lobbyists to attend fundraising events held in the nation's capital and RPAC to host receptions for congressional candidates.

Like many interest groups, RPAC's and the NAR's election activities extend beyond making campaign contributions. RPAC and its parent organization mobilize realtors to support their preferred candidates, distribute educational and advocacy mailings in close contests, use telephone banks to conduct voter identification and GOTV efforts, and occasionally send professional organizers to carry out grassroots activities designed to help their preferred candidates. These efforts are financed with soft money.

The decision-making process of the RPAC is similar to that of other institutionalized committees, such as AT&T's PAC, the American Medical Association's PAC (AMPAC), and LCV's PAC.[24] RPAC relies on a combination of factual information, local opinion, and national perspective to determine which candidates to support. The requirement that all recommendations receive formal approval also is typical, as is the ability to conduct research on individual elections in-house. The PAC's lack of participation as either a source or a user of the information available in Washington communications networks is unusual for a PAC located in the nation's capital, but its size, federated structure, and tremendous resources enable it to make decisions with information it has collected independently of other committees.

At the opposite end of the spectrum from the Realtors PAC are the noninstitutionalized PACs. WASHPAC is a nonconnected committee founded in 1980 by Morris J. Amitay, formerly the executive director of the American Israel Public Affairs Committee (AIPAC), to promote a secure Israel and strong American-Israeli relations.[25] WASHPAC spent $243,000 in congressional elections in 2006, contributing the vast majority of its money to incumbents.

WASHPAC and thousands of other noninstitutionalized committees are essentially one-person operations with one-person decision-making processes. Noninstitutionalized PACs rely primarily on personal contacts with candidates and other Washington insiders for the political information that guides their contribution decisions. Amitay, who started WASHPAC as a hobby, peruses candidates' speeches and press releases and incumbents' voting records and letters to constituents to gauge their support for Israel. He exchanges information about the competitiveness of different elections when meeting with other pro-Israel political activists. He is open to the suggestions of individuals who give donations to his committee but generally does not make contributions to candidates solely on the basis of donor suggestions. After all, most of WASHPAC's supporters donate to the PAC because this enables them to rely on Amitay's research and judgment rather than having to research individual candidates themselves. Moreover, those who support WASHPAC can use its list of targeted races to guide their individual candidate contributions.

Noninstitutionalized PACs and multitudes of other one-person organizations use informal decision-making processes. Their lack of formal rules and procedures allows their managers great flexibility in choosing candidates for support. Their limited staff resources force the PAC managers to turn to others for election-related information. These PACs are in a better position than more institutionalized committees to adjust their initial strategies in response to changing electoral conditions. Of course, in the case of very small committees, such as the Concerned Friends for Tobacco PAC, which contributed only $2,000 in 2006, this is true only as long as their money holds out.

Between the institutionalized PACs and the small, one-person organizations are semi-institutionalized committees that possess some of the characteristics of the PACs in the other two groups. These PACs include the Powell, Goldstein, Frazer, and Murphy ("POGO") PAC, sponsored by a law firm with offices in both Washington, D.C., and Atlanta, Georgia. Semi-institutionalized PACs usually have staffs of two to four people, which are large enough to allow for a functional division of labor and to require the adoption of decision rules but small enough to render them dependent on outside research when making contribution decisions. For instance, POGO PAC, which has consistently pursued a modified access strategy, has a legal counselor, a treasurer, a PAC administrator, and a moderately active board of directors.[26] It contributed $78,500 during the 2006 elections, an amount sufficient to give the PAC and its law firm a presence in national and Georgia politics.

PACs with semi-institutionalized organizations typically rely on their staffs to process requests for contributions, but they look to others for political intelligence. POGO PAC gets most of its information from its parent firm's partners, associates, and clients, some of whom speak to party officials, members of other law firms and PACs, and other politically active individuals in the Washington and Atlanta metropolitan areas. The firm's members submit a short proposal for each contribution they would like the PAC to make. Then, the PAC's board, consisting of a small group of partners in Washington and Atlanta, votes on the request. Like most other semi-institutionalized committees, POGO PAC gives its board a significant role in decision making, but neither the staff nor the board becomes involved in time-consuming strategic planning sessions or searches for potential recipients of contributions.[27] These PACs do not give their officers as much flexibility as do the managers of one-person committees, but these officials have more freedom than is accorded the officers of institutionalized PACs.

Lead PACs constitute a final group of committees. These PACs, which include the National Committee for an Effective Congress, the AFL-CIO's COPE, and the Business-Industry Political Action Committee, are as complex organizationally as the institutionalized PACs.[28] Like the LCV, they are often one part of a larger interlocking interest group structure. These groups are every bit as thorough in their research and decision making as are the institutionalized committees and are motivated by ideological or policy goals. They differ from other PACs in that they carry out research and select candidates for support with an eye toward influencing the decisions of other donors, including PACs and individuals. Much of the research conducted by groups that sponsor lead PACs is oriented toward assessing the electability of individual candidates. Like the Hill committees, these groups spend much time, money, and energy disseminating information about specific campaigns to other interest group organizations. They occupy central positions in the networks of PACs, lobbyists, and individual contributors in the interest group community.

TABLE 5-2

PAC Contributions in the 2006 Congressional Elections ($, thousands)

	House		Senate		
	Democrats	Republicans	Democrats	Republicans	Total
Corporate	$31,701	$64,380	$9,099	$17,070	$122,250
Trade, mem-					
bership,					
and health	30,291	49,257	5,956	9,807	95,311
Cooperative	1,373	1,387	271	186	3,217
Corporations					
without stock	1,365	2,132	385	494	4,376
Labor	42,088	5,522	5,819	489	53,918
Leadership	8,675	21,920	3,774	7,408	41,767
Nonconnected	9,489	10,154	3,324	2,042	25,009
All PACs	$124,982	$154,752	$28,628	$37,496	$345,848

Source: Compiled from Federal Election Commission and Center for Responsive Politics data.

Notes: Contributions by nonconnected PACs exclude contributions made by leadership PACs. Figures are for PAC contributions to all major-party candidates, including candidates in primaries, runoffs, and uncontested races.

PAC CONTRIBUTIONS

PACs contributed more than $345.8 million to major-party candidates in the 2006 congressional elections (see Table 5-2). Corporate PACs accounted for the most PAC contributions, followed by trade groups, labor committees, leadership PACs, and nonconnected PACs. Corporations without stock and cooperatives contributed the least, giving less than $7.6 million.

Incumbents have laid claim to the lion's share of PAC money since the PAC boom of the 1970s. Since the mid-1980s, business-related PACs have been among the most incumbent-oriented committees, adhering more closely to an access strategy than do labor, leadership, or ideological PACs. In 2006, corporate PACs made 95 percent of their House contributions to incumbents involved in major-party contested races (see Table 5-3), distributing 55 percent of them to shoo-ins. These committees donated virtually nothing to House challengers and made a mere 5 percent of their House contributions to open-seat candidates. Corporate PACs made only 43 percent of their House contributions to candidates in competitive races. Their contributions in previous years suggest that if fewer Republican incumbents had been in jeopardy cor-

TABLE 5-3

Allocation of PAC Contributions to House Candidates in the 2006 Elections

	Corporate	Trade, membership, and health	Labor	Leadership	Non-connected
Democrats					
Incumbents					
In jeopardy	3%	3%	6%	4%	5%
Shoo-ins	25	26	48	3	21
Challengers					
Hopefuls	—	2	20	14	13
Likely losers	—	—	3	1	2
Open-seat candidates					
Prospects	—	1	8	5	5
Mismatched	1	1	4	1	2
Republicans					
Incumbents					
In jeopardy	37%	34%	8%	47%	28%
Shoo-ins	30	26	5	7	17
Challengers					
Hopefuls	—	1	—	5	1
Likely losers	—	—	—	2	—
Open-seat candidates					
Prospects	3	4	—	9	5
Mismatched	1	1	—	3	1
Total House contributions ($, thousands)	$83,729	$69,024	$40,254	$28,891	$16,654

Source: Compiled from Federal Election Commission and Center for Responsive Politics data.

Notes: Figures are for general election candidates in major-party contested races. — = less than 0.5 percent. Some columns do not add to 100 percent because of rounding. $N = 754$.

porate PACs would have distributed even fewer resources to candidates in close races.[29] The overall patterns of corporate PAC contributions reflect their goal of maintaining good relations with current members, the pressures incumbents place on them for contributions, and their lack of concern with changing the composition of Congress.

Corporate PACs also pursue access-oriented goals when they contribute to Senate candidates. In 2006 they distributed 85 percent of their Senate contri-

TABLE 5-4

Allocation of PAC Contributions to Senate Candidates in the 2006 Elections

	Corporate	Trade, membership, and health	Labor	Leadership	Non-connected
Democrats					
Incumbents					
In jeopardy	5%	5%	10%	4%	8%
Shoo-ins	26	23	37	10	26
Challengers					
Hopefuls	2	5	32	14	14
Likely losers	—	—	1	—	—
Open-seat candidates					
Prospects	3	4	9	3	6
Mismatched	—	1	5	2	2
Republicans					
Incumbents					
In jeopardy	41%	37%	3%	33%	29%
Shoo-ins	13	13	3	5	8
Challengers					
Hopefuls	2	2	—	8	3
Likely losers	2	2	—	6	1
Open-seat candidates					
Prospects	4	4	—	9	2
Mismatched	2	3	—	5	—
Total Senate contributions ($, thousands)	$25,676	$15,445	$6,152	$9,908	$5,954

Source: Compiled from Federal Election Commission and Center for Responsive Politics data.

Notes: Figures are for general election candidates in major-party contested races. — = less than 0.5 percent. Some columns do not add to 100 percent because of rounding. $N = 60$.

butions to incumbents, 6 percent to challengers, and 9 percent to open-seat candidates (see Table 5-4). Similarly, trade association PACs were generous to House and Senate incumbents and dedicated few resources to challengers and open-seat contests.

Labor PACs have consistently pursued highly partisan, mixed strategies. They contribute the vast majority of their money to Democrats. In 2006, labor PACs favored Democratic incumbents with 54 percent of their contri-

butions to House candidates, including 48 percent to shoo-ins. Labor's contributions to challengers and open-seat candidates, on the other hand, were
tilted toward those in competitive races. Labor committees gave 47 percent of
their Senate contributions to Democratic incumbents, including 37 percent
to Democratic shoo-ins. The rest of its contributions strongly favored nonincumbents in close contests. Labor contributions to candidates in both chambers appear to have been motivated by both access-oriented and election-
oriented goals.

The flow of leadership PAC contributions follows roughly the same pattern as that of party-connected contributions, which include contributions by
candidates, members of Congress not up for reelection, and congressional retirees. As has been the case in previous elections, in 2006 most leadership
PAC contributions in House and Senate races were given by Republicans to
Republicans. Most of the leadership PAC money flowed to candidates in
close races. Republican incumbents raised more from leadership PACs than
did any other group of candidates, largely because many were in closely contested races, and those making the contribution decisions recognized that
most of the recipients of these contributions would likely be in a position to
help the donor with some political or legislative efforts in the future.
Democratic politicians, in contrast, distributed the vast majority of their
leadership PAC money to challengers and open-seat contestants, which was
consistent with the Democrats' aggressive bid to win control of Congress. As
a group, leadership PACs were among the most supportive of challengers and
open-seat candidates.

Nonconnected PACs, which have traditionally followed the ideological
strategy of spending most of their money in close races, largely continued this
pattern in 2006. They made 62 percent of their Senate contributions and 57
percent of their House donations to candidates in close races. Nevertheless,
the flows of nonconnected PAC money to Democratic and Republican candidates differed sharply. Nonconnected PACs gave just as much money to
Democratic candidates in uncompetitive races as competitive ones, and Democratic incumbents in both the House and Senate were the major beneficiaries of these PACs' largess. When contributing to Republicans, on the other
hand, nonconnected PACs targeted most of their resources to incumbents in
close contests.

Several factors influenced nonconnected PACs' giving patterns. The insta-
bility of the political environment in 2006—driven by the possibility of a
change in partisan control of both chambers of Congress—encouraged conservative PACs to deliver most of their resources to Republican incumbents. They
made most but not all of their contributions to incumbents in close contests.

However, liberal nonconnected PACs appear to have contributed for both ideological and access reasons. Some of these PACs contributed to competitive challengers and open-seat contestants to help bring about a change in the party controlling Congress. Others contributed to safe incumbents. Some of these contributions were probably motivated by the desire for political access. In more than a few cases, nonconnected PACs may have contributed in response to the requests of safe incumbents, having made the reasonable assumption that these candidates would redistribute some of the funds to their party's competitive candidates or a party committee.

CAMPAIGN SERVICES

Although most of the journalistic reporting on interest groups and PACs has focused on contributions, independent expenditures, and issue advocacy ads, many groups also carry out activities that have traditionally been conducted by political parties.[30] Some interest groups, mainly ideological organizations, including various groups on both sides of the abortion rights issue, recruit candidates to run for Congress.[31] Others provide candidates with in-kind contributions of polls, issue research, fundraising assistance, campaign ads, or strategic advice. AMPAC, RPAC, and COPE, for example, contribute polls to some candidates.[32] The National Federation of Independent Business's SAFE Trust PAC, whose name stands for Save American Free Enterprise, hosts campaign training schools and produces media advertisements for many of the candidates it supports.[33] The NCEC gives selected Democratic House and Senate candidates and party committees precinct-level demographic profiles, targeting assistance, and technical advice.[34] The LCV provides research, endorsements—some in the form of inclusion on its renowned Dirty Dozen and Environmental Champions lists—and other forms of assistance to help pro-environment candidates. These and other groups furnish campaign assistance in lieu of, or in addition to, cash contributions because they want to influence how candidates' campaigns are run or leave a more enduring impression than one can get from simply handing over a check.

One of the most important forms of assistance that a PAC can give to a candidate, particularly a nonincumbent, is help with fundraising. Lead PACs, such as BIPAC, COPE, and the NCEC, brief other PACs about the campaigns on their watch lists, using techniques similar to those used by the Hill committees. Even some smaller PACs help congressional candidates raise money by cosponsoring fundraising events or serving on candidates' fundraising committees. Most PACs and some other groups also assist candidates with collecting money from individuals. When groups solicit donors, they usually provide them with a list of the candidates they are backing and information about the candidates' issue positions and backgrounds. Some groups post contact information for preferred candidates in written correspondence and on web sites, and they urge their supporters to contribute to these candidates directly. Others get their members to buy tables at candidates' fundraising events or they "bundle" checks from individual donors and deliver them to the candidate. The maturation of the Washington interest group community has led to the development of several networks of PACs, individual donors, and other organizations, which often assist each other in selecting candidates for support and in raising money.[35]

EMILY's List, whose name stands for "Early Money Is Like Yeast" and whose motto is "It makes the dough rise," is an example of a PAC that gives candidates fundraising assistance. This nonconnected committee supports pro-choice Democratic women candidates, helping them raise money in the early, critical stages of the election, including in contested congressional primaries where campaign contributions typically have several times the impact they have in general elections.[36] EMILY's List requires its members to donate $100 to the PAC and to make minimum contributions of $100 to each of two candidates whom the PAC has designated for support. Members are instructed to write these checks to the candidates and then send them to the PAC, which in turn forwards the checks to the candidates with a letter explaining the PAC's role in collecting the money. Through bundling, the PAC acts as a clearinghouse for individual campaign contributions and is able to direct more money to candidates than it is legally allowed to contribute. Bundling works well with individuals who wish to have a candidate acknowledge both their and the group's political support. Groups that bundle, and EMILY's List in particular, have played a major role in persuading individuals who have not previously made congressional contributions to become regular donors.[37]

EMILY's list contributed more than $268,000 to thirty-four candidates in the 2006 congressional elections, including almost $104,000 in in-kind donations. This activity was important, but it pales next to the $11 million in contributions it bundled from more than 109,000 members to women Democratic candidates. The group's 527 committee raised another $34 million that was used for a variety of television, radio, direct-mail, candidate training, and other election activities. Under the guise of its "Women Vote!" project, EMILY's List spent more than $8.5 million on polling, message testing, and precinct-by-precinct field work in twenty-one battleground races.[38]

The Club for Growth is another PAC that bundles contributions, gets involved in congressional primaries, and makes issue advocacy ads.[39] Founded in

1999, the Club claims thirty-six thousand members who raised or donated over $10 million to the organization and its endorsed candidates during the 2006 election season. Although the Club directly contributed less than $12,000 to eight Republican congressional candidates, it made almost $2.8 million in independent expenditures in connection with twenty-seven House and seven Senate races, including some primary challengers to Republican incumbents. Its 527 organization spent millions of dollars on issue advocacy ads. As is the case with EMILY's List, the Club's endorsements, bundling activities, and televised issue ads far outweigh its contributions in importance.

Although many interest groups are not known for bundling, a significant number of them influence the contributions of individuals associated with their group. Individual donors who make significant contributions to congressional candidates—at least one contribution of $200 per election cycle—comprise a group that has many similarities to the interest group community. It is a small, fairly elite, and relatively stable group. Many donors are motivated by reasons of political access, ideology, or both, although some contribute because they enjoy the social aspects of giving, including attending fundraising events. Moreover, individuals who make significant contributions also tend be active in political networks, including those associated with a variety of interest groups. Many of these individuals rely on business, industry, trade, single-issue, or ideological groups for the information they use to make contribution decisions. This magnifies the impact of the groups with which these donors associate.[40]

The financial, insurance, and real estate industries compose a sector of the economy that makes its influence in congressional elections felt through PAC contributions, contributions to parties, and the contributions of individuals associated with it. Organizations and individuals connected to these industries coalesce to influence policies ranging from mortgage regulations to building safety codes to federal appropriations for specific construction projects, as well as to try to affect the outcomes of elections. They have been extremely active in recent elections. PACs associated with these interests contributed $62.9 million directly to congressional candidates and an additional $246.4 million to party committees during the 2006 election cycle. Individuals linked to these interests, including corporate executives and their families, donated another $183.9 million in contributions of $200 or more to congressional candidates and party committees. These figures amply demonstrate that this economic sector is capable of bringing substantial financial resources to bear on the electoral process. Republicans received 56 percent of this sector's largess, and Democrats collected the remainder.[41]

Lawyers and lobbyists make up an economic sector even more partisan in its giving. Firms identified with these trades contributed $16.5 million to candidates and $144.5 million to party committees during the 2006 elections. Contributions of $200 or more from individuals linked to them reached nearly $129.7 million. About two-thirds of every dollar contributed by individuals or groups connected to the legal and lobbying trades went to Democratic candidates and party committees, with Republicans receiving the rest.[42]

Other organized interests provide a range of assistance to candidates in congressional elections. Think tanks, such as the Heritage Foundation, provide issue research. Labor unions and church-based organizations in African American and ethnic communities have long histories of political activism and have made decisive contributions to Democratic candidates' field activities; they also have conducted their own voter registration and GOTV campaigns.

Business leaders have traditionally assisted Republicans. AIPAC provides information about candidates to PACs and individuals who support Israel. Even though it carries out activities similar to those of lead PACs and the Hill committees, AIPAC gives no cash contributions to congressional candidates and so does not qualify as a federally registered PAC. Environmental groups and the Christian Coalition are relative newcomers to electoral politics, but their voter guides and voter mobilization efforts have played important roles in recent congressional elections.

INDEPENDENT, PARALLEL, AND COORDINATED CAMPAIGNS

Interest groups, like political parties, developed independent, parallel, and coordinated campaigns as a way to move beyond direct contributions to candidates when seeking to influence elections. The interest groups that conduct these campaigns carry out activities similar to those used by the parties. Both types of organizations use polling, research, television, radio, direct mail, mass telephone calls, e-mails, and grassroots activities to influence the outcome of congressional elections. Of course, there are differences, most of which are discussed below.

Independent Campaigns

Interest group independent expenditures carried out by PACs, like those made by parties, usually comprise television, radio, and direct-mail advertisements, but some consist of mass telephone calls, push polls, and other forms of voter outreach. Like party independent expenditures, these activities must be financed with federally regulated funds that are contributed without a candidate's knowledge or consent, and they can expressly advocate a candidate's election or defeat. Another similarity is that, like party television expenditures, interest group television ads do not qualify for lowest unit rate charges (ads placed by candidates do).

PACs spent nearly $35.7 million on independent expenditures for candidates in 2006—a record sum for a midterm election. Most of these were made by labor, trade, and nonconnected PACs. Independent expenditures are consistent with many of these PACs' ideological or mixed strategies. Moreover, because nonconnected, labor, and trade PACs are established to advance the political views of organizations that frequently have tens of thousands of members, these committees rarely worry about the retribution of an angry member of Congress or the negative publicity that might result from an independent expenditure. Unlike corporate PACs, these PACs are relatively safe from either unwelcome outcome because they lack a single sponsor whose interests can be harmed directly.

Some interest group independent campaigns take place during congressional nominating contests, but the vast majority of such campaigning occurs in hotly contested general election races. In 2006 left-leaning PACs strongly took to the airwaves, the U.S. mails, and other venues on behalf of Democratic House candidates who benefited from $18 million in expenditures—$6.2 million supporting their candidacies and $11.8 million attacking their opponent—in contrast with Republican House contenders who benefited from less than $7.2 million in conservative PAC spending (see Figure 5-3). The picture is reversed in the Senate elections: GOP-oriented PACs clearly made independent campaigning in contests for the upper chamber a bigger priority than did their Democratic-leaning counterparts.

Parallel Campaigns

The passage of the BCRA created an important change in the way the law treats interest groups compared with its treatment of political parties. As originally passed, the BCRA allowed interest groups to include soft-money-financed issue advocacy ads as part of their parallel campaigns. The groups—but not political parties—could air these ads up to thirty days before a congressional primary and up to sixty days before a general election. Interest groups' legal spending advantages increased in 2007 when the Supreme Court struck down part of the BCRA. In *Federal Election Commission v. Wisconsin Right to Life, Inc.* and *McCain et al. v. Wisconsin Right to Life* (the cases were considered jointly) the court ruled that in future elections interest group soft-money-financed issue ads could be aired at any time. Thus, in the future, interest groups will have spending options that are even more flexible than they had in the 2004 and 2006 contests.

FIGURE 5-3
PAC Independent Expenditures in the 2006 Elections

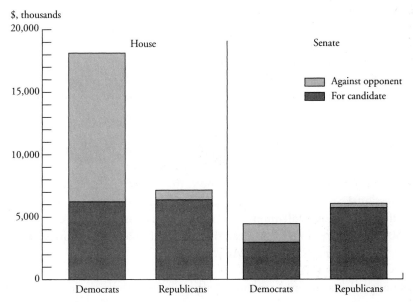

Source: Compiled from Federal Election Commission data.

Only a small portion of the funds interest groups spend on their parallel campaigns must be reported to the Federal Election Commission. Amounting to $14.2 million in 2006, most of it favoring the Democrats, these consist of newsletters, forums, or other internal communications that can be coordinated with a candidate's campaign. Few groups report spending much on internal communications because these expenditures can only be targeted to limited populations: employees, union members, or members of other groups.[43] An additional reason these sums are so small is that interest groups are required to report the costs of only the small portion of the communications that directly addresses an election, enabling them to underreport their communications' true value.

The remainder of interest group issue advocacy spending by 501(c) organizations, 527 committees, and other organizations is not subject to the same level of public disclosure as are federally regulated contributions, independent expenditures, or internal communications. This makes it impossible to learn precisely how much money interest groups spend on issue advocacy in a given election year and the sources of the funds that finance these ads. Nevertheless, most figures collected by various organizations suggest that the amounts spent by these groups to influence election politics are at least in the hundreds of millions of dollars.[44]

Most parallel and coordinated campaign efforts by interest groups are highly visible, but others fly largely below the radar. During the 2006 elections, 527 committees may well have spent millions on election-related activities (excluding fundraising, staff salaries, and other forms of overhead). These expenditures include $8.5 million on political consultants, $6.4 million on polling, and the $75.1 million spent directly on electoral communications and outreach.[45] These amounts do not include the $71.4 million these groups contributed to political parties, transferred to federal PACs, contributed to umbrella groups such as the pro-Democratic America Coming Together, transferred to state affiliates and other political organizations, or donated to state and local candidates—all of which potentially influenced the outcomes of fiercely contested congressional elections. Even though these sums do not provide a full accounting of interest group soft-money spending because they exclude expenditures by 501(c) organizations, it is clear that they overshadow the totals of independent expenditures made by PACs.

An analysis of several competitive House and Senate races suggests that various coalitions of labor unions, environmental protection organizations, and EMILY's List were among the top issue advocacy spenders for the Democrats. The Republicans' top spenders included Progress for America, Americans for Job Security (a pro-business group), and the U.S. Chamber of Commerce.[46] The Chamber of Commerce, alone, spent $10 million on TV ads and another $10 million on direct mail and phone calls to help Republican candidates across the nation.

A few other Democratic- and Republican-oriented interest groups also spent in excess of tens of millions of dollars on direct mail, but the Chamber was probably the leading single source of soft-money-financed direct mail. It sent 413 unique pieces of mail to 13.5 million Republican and swing voters. Not far behind it was the AFL-CIO and its auxiliary group, Working America, which used direct mail to contact 7.8 million union members, 4.6 million union families, and approximately a million nonunion workers.[47] Through their use of issue advocacy advertisements and direct mail, interest groups have been able to mount significant parallel campaigns. Some of these have influenced the national campaign agenda, and others have helped to set the issue agenda in a number of competitive House and Senate contests.

Coordinated Campaigns

Interest group coordinated campaigns also were impressive in 2006. Labor unions, America Votes, EMILY's List, and a raft of other left-leaning organizations spent hundreds of millions of dollars registering voters, making them aware of their state's laws governing early and absentee voting, and telephoning, e-mailing, and personally visiting targeted voters to make sure they cast their votes. One group, the Change to Win Coalition, made up of unions that broke away from the AFL-CIO following the 2004 elections, spent $40 million on voter registration efforts.[48] Several conservative groups, including the National Federation of Independent Business, the National Rifle Association, and the U.S. Chamber of Commerce, carried out similar activities. Although the work of the conservative groups was significant, their total expenditures and overall impact were, as usual, not as noteworthy as those made by the liberal organizations. The business sector took significant steps to narrow the gap in 2006, but the RNC's strong voter mobilization program indicated that the Republican-oriented interest groups were not as important to candidates as were the programs mounted by Democratic-leaning interest groups. As with interest group independent campaigns, interest groups' parallel and coordinated campaign activities were targeted primarily to very competitive races.

THE IMPACT OF INTEREST GROUP ACTIVITY

Congressional candidates and their campaign aides generally evaluate the help their campaigns get directly from labor, business, and advocacy groups and PACs less favorably than the assistance they get from party committees. The exception to this rule is fundraising, where as a function of their sheer numbers and the BCRA's contribution limits, political action committees as a group are in a position to contribute more money to a House campaign than are party organizations. The assessments of House campaigners indicate that interest groups play larger roles in the campaigns of Democrats than in those of Republicans. This is especially true for labor unions and labor PACs, which for decades have made large contributions in money and manpower to Democratic campaigns. The Republican candidates' relative lack of dependence on interest groups is also partially a result of their greater reliance on party committees for campaign services, as was noted in Chapter 4.[49] Senate candidates and campaign aides of both parties find PACs and other groups to be helpful in virtually every aspect of campaigning but not as helpful as the DSCC or NRSC.

Of course, interest group election efforts, like party efforts, are targeted to selected races. The information provided by both House and Senate campaigners indicates that interest group campaign assistance tends to be focused more heavily on competitive contests and to be more important to the election efforts of hopeful challengers and open-seat prospects than to those of incumbents. This is largely the result of incumbents beginning the election with high levels of name recognition and huge war chests, both of which nonincumbents lack.

Interest groups were active in many competitive 2006 House races, including the open-seat contest in Colorado's 7th district. Ed Perlmutter benefited from substantial direct support from interest groups, including the $809,000 he raised from PACs and the additional sums he raised from donors who are part of one or more interest group networks. Lawyer-lobbyist, labor, and liberal ideological groups were among Perlmutter's top backers. He raised $25,000 from PACs representing lawyers and lobbyists and another $414,000 in contributions of $200 or more from individuals working in these professions. Labor PACs accounted for $296,000 (union members donated a mere $300); and pro-choice, pro–human rights, and Democratic-leaning and liberal PACs and their networks of supporters accounted for another $306,000.[50]

Many groups also conducted independent, parallel, and coordinated campaign activities on behalf of Perlmutter. These included $48,000 in PAC independent spending and $14,000 in interest group internal communications advocating his election, and another $300 advocating Rick O'Donnell's defeat. Labor made extensive efforts to mobilize union workers and their families: the SEIU and a coalition of unions called Colorado Labor 2006 each sent out two waves of direct mail focusing on health care issues; the Alliance for Retired Americans, another labor-affiliated group, sent out two pieces of mail focusing on Social Security and prescription drugs; and the Colorado Fund for Children and Public Education, affiliated with the Colorado Education Association, sent out direct mail and made telephone calls advocating Perlmutter to supporters and swing voters. In addition, the Colorado AFL-CIO and several other unions drafted hundreds of volunteers to participate in Colorado Victory 2006, the Democrats' coordinated campaign. The volunteers registered voters, canvassed neighborhoods, put up yard signs, encouraged many voters to cast early or absentee ballots, and helped mobilize others on election day. The Sierra Club sent out a piece of mail supporting Perlmutter's positions on the environment. Too Extreme for Colorado, a Democratic-leaning 527 committee, spent $141,000 on a television ad attacking Perlmutter's opponent, Rick O'Donnell, as an extremist on Social Security issues. These activities helped frame the issue agenda in the race and were critical to mobilizing voters on behalf of Perlmutter.[51]

O'Donnell also was the beneficiary of significant interest group support. PACs contributed roughly $662,000 to his campaign, and PACs and other interest groups played a role in stimulating the contributions he raised from individual donors. In contrast to Perlmutter, O'Donnell raised no money from labor PACs but did very well with the business community. He raised $341,000 from corporate, cooperative, and trade association PACs.[52] The finance, insurance, and real estate industries were particularly supportive, viewing the pro-growth, anti-tax crusader as a natural ally. Political action committees and individuals associated with these groups contributed $418,000 to the O'Donnell campaign. Republican-leaning and conservative ideological groups also were obliging, contributing an additional $291,000.[53]

The O'Donnell campaign also benefited from interest group independent, parallel, and coordinated campaigning. PACs made $104,000 in independent expenditures advocating his election, and their parent organizations spent another $505 on internal communications to deliver that message directly to their members. The National Association of Homebuilders distributed two pieces of direct mail focusing on taxes. The U.S. Chamber of Commerce sent out a piece of mail endorsing O'Donnell and his positions on taxes, job creation, and the economy more generally. The Club for Growth, the National Right to Life PAC, the National Rifle Association's Political Victory Fund, and several other groups sent out direct mail, distributed e-mails, made phone calls, and undertook other methods to contact voters. Americans for Honesty on Issues, a 527 committee financed entirely by Bob Perry, spent $257,000 televising two issue advocacy ads, but it had to pull one of them off the air because of a lack of accuracy. Other mass media ads were broadcast by the Trust in Small Business PAC and the Trailhead Group, which is funded by the pharmaceutical industry. None of the PACs or other advocacy organizations backing O'Donnell made independent expenditures or internal communications against Perlmutter. Although not as successful as the coalition of interest groups supporting Perlmutter, groups on the right made important contributions to the O'Donnell campaign.

In Ohio, interest groups showed that they could play a significant role in Senate elections. Democratic challenger Sherrod Brown raised about $1.5 million from PACs, including $343,000, $139,000, and $288,000 from labor unions, corporations, and trade associations, respectively.[54] His best overall source of revenue was groups of lawyers and lobbyists, which furnished him with more than $68,000 in contributions from PACs and more than $1 million from individuals. PACs associated with finance, insurance, and real estate interests provided him with another $603,000. Labor provided Brown with another $360,000, almost all of it in PAC contributions.

In addition to this direct support, interest groups carried out a number of independent campaign activities on Brown's behalf.[55] Democratic-oriented PACs spent $337,000 expressly advocating Brown's election and another $26,000 calling for Senator Mike DeWine's defeat. Other pro-Democratic interest groups spent an additional $1.6 million on internal communications for these same purposes. Labor groups spent $77,000 on TV ads, with pro-Democratic 527 groups spending a total of about $600,000. In addition to the TV spots, labor organizations sent out about 45 pieces of direct mail, and labor and other volunteers made four waves of phone calls to more than 60,000 Brown supporters and persuadable voters. MoveOn.org, NARAL Pro-Choice America, America Votes, and a few other groups posted direct mail, bringing the total number of pieces to about sixty. Other forms of pro-Brown interest group activity consisted of about a dozen e-mails and six newspaper and magazine ads.

Interest groups provided DeWine with more campaign support than they did Brown. The incumbent collected more than $3.3 million in PAC contributions from a wide range of interests. The financial, insurance, and real estate industries provided him with $1.6 million in PAC and $2.1 million in individual contributions. Lawyers and lobbyists and their PACs provided another $1.2 million. Organized labor, which is generally not inclined to support Republicans, provided DeWine with less than $57,000.

Interest groups also mounted independent, parallel, and coordinated campaigns on DeWine's behalf. Federally regulated PACs spent about $280,000 on advocating DeWine's reelection, and other interest group organizations spent an additional $47,000 for this same purpose. The PACs spent relatively little attacking Brown, which is somewhat unusual. However, some other interest groups did choose to criticize the candidate. Perhaps the most hard-hitting and controversial pro-DeWine television ads aired during the campaign sought to focus voters' attention on terrorism. Progress for America spent more than $1.3 million on ads that featured the phrase, "these people want to kill us." The U.S. Chamber of Commerce, the National Right to Life Committee, Common Sense 2006 (a 527 group purportedly tied to leading Republican politicians in Ohio), and a few other conservative groups spent between $750,000 and $1 million on additional television ads.

It is impossible to tell whether interest group activities—or party efforts or the candidates' own campaigns—determined the outcomes of the Brown-DeWine race, the Perlmutter-O'Donnell match-up, or any other hotly contested 2006 congressional election. Nevertheless, these elections demonstrate that interest group independent, parallel, and coordinated campaigns can be important in setting the political agenda, touting the strengths and weaknesses of candidates, and mobilizing voters in competitive elections. The efforts of parties and groups have not done away with candidate-centered congressional elections, but the efforts of these organizations can prevent some candidates in very close races from dominating the campaign messages received by voters.

This is particularly true in elections where Washington-based interest groups and party committees outspend the candidates themselves.

SUMMARY

Interest groups, like parties, play important supporting roles in congressional elections. Most interest group activity takes the form of PAC contributions to candidates, but some PACs also distribute campaign services and make independent expenditures. In addition, some labor unions, business organizations, and issue-oriented and ideological groups provide congressional campaigns with volunteers; carry out voter mobilization drives; and use issue ads, direct mail, and a variety of other communications techniques to influence the political agenda or affect individual candidates' election prospects. Because some interest groups view elections as opportunities to lay the groundwork for lobbying members of Congress and as vehicles for changing the membership of the legislative branch, they distribute some resources to House and Senate members in safe seats and others to incumbents, challengers, and open-seat candidates in close elections. An abundance of business-oriented organizations, labor unions, and ideological groups from all sides of the political spectrum participate in congressional elections, making for a diverse, if not sometimes cacophonous, group of voices competing for voters' attention.

CHAPTER SIX

The Campaign for Resources

Vice President Hubert Humphrey described fundraising as a "disgusting, degrading, demeaning experience."[1] Few politicians would disagree with this sentiment. Yet spending money on political campaigns predates the Constitution. In 1757 George Washington purchased twenty-eight gallons of rum, fifty gallons of spiked punch, forty-six gallons of beer, thirty-four gallons of wine, and a couple of gallons of hard cider to help shore up his political base and pry loose the support of enough uncommitted voters to get elected to the Virginia House of Burgesses.[2] Population growth, technological advancements, suburbanization, and other changes associated with the emergence of a modern mass democracy in the United States have driven up the costs of campaigning since Washington launched his political career. Candidates, parties, and interest groups spent close to $3 billion on the 2006 elections.

Raising the funds needed to run for Congress has evolved into a campaign in and of itself. Part of this campaign takes place in the candidate's state or district, but many candidates are dependent on resources that come from party committees and PACs located in and around Washington, D.C., and from wealthy individuals who typically reside in major metropolitan areas.

The campaign for resources begins earlier than the campaign for votes. It requires a candidate to attract the support of sophisticated, goal-oriented groups and individuals who have strong preconceptions about what it takes to win a congressional election. Theoretically, all congressional candidates can turn to the same sources and use the same techniques to gather campaign funds and services. In fact, however, candidates begin and end on uneven playing fields. The level of success that candidates achieve with different contributors or fundraising techniques depends largely on whether they are incumbents, challengers, or candidates for open seats. It also depends on the candidates' party

166

affiliation and on whether they are running for the House or the Senate, among other factors. In this chapter I analyze the fundraising strategies and successes of different kinds of candidates.

Virtually every congressional election cycle sets a new record for campaign fundraising and spending. The 2006 elections were no exception. Candidates for the House set a fundraising record of about $871.5 million. Two hundred and forty-two candidates raised more than $1 million each, forty raised in excess of $3 million, and fifteen raised more than $4 million. Republican candidate Vern Buchanan, of Florida, collected the most of any House candidate—more than $8.1 million, with more than two-thirds of it coming from his personal bank account—in a successful bid to win an open-seat election in Florida's contested 13th district.

The Senate elections in 2006 also were record setting, as candidates raised a total of $557.7 million in those races. Fifty of these candidates each collected more than $3 million, including thirty-one who raised more than $6 million, nineteen who raised over $10 million, and seven who raised in excess of $15 million. The top Democratic fundraiser was Sen. Hillary Rodham Clinton of New York, who amassed a war chest of $39.8 million, of which a considerable portion was no doubt used to advance her presidential candidacy. The Republicans' top fundraiser was Sen. Rick Santorum of Pennsylvania, who collected $24.8 million in an unsuccessful attempt to defend his seat against a challenge by his state's treasurer, Bob Casey Jr. These candidates fell well short of the record set by former senator Jon Corzine, D-N.J., who raised almost $63.3 million—$60.2 million lent from his own bank account—to finance a successful open-seat race for the Senate in 2000.

INEQUALITIES IN RESOURCES

Significant inequalities exist in the resources, including money and party coordinated expenditures, that different types of candidates are able to raise. The typical House incumbent involved in a two-party contested race raised just under $1.4 million in cash and party coordinated expenditures in 2006, which is roughly three times more than the sum raised by the typical House challenger.[3] Open-seat candidates also gathered significant resources, raising an average of almost $1.6 million.

The resource discrepancies in competitive House races are great. Incumbents in jeopardy raised about 72 percent more in cash and party coordinated expenditures than did hopeful challengers during the 2006 elections (see Figure 6-1). Competitive open-seat contests were much more equal in regard to the amount raised. The resource discrepancies in uncompetitive House contests are even

FIGURE 6-1

Average Campaign Resources Raised in Competitive House Elections in 2006

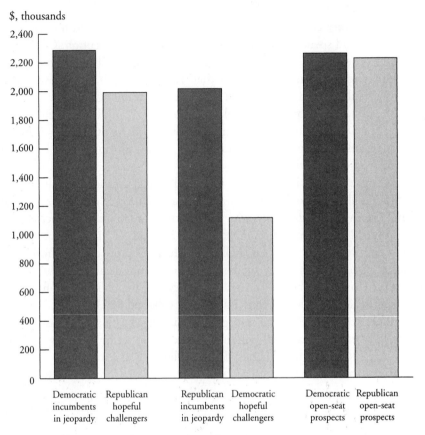

$, thousands

Source: Compiled from Federal Election Commission data.

Notes: Figures include receipts and party-coordinated expenditures for all two-party contests that were decided by margins of 20 percent of the vote or less. *N* = 244.

greater than are those in competitive ones. Incumbents, who begin raising funds early—often before they know whom they will face in the general election—collect much more money than do their opponents (see Figure 6-2). Incumbent shoo-ins raised approximately nine times more than likely-loser challengers in 2006. The spread among Democratic and Republican open-seat candidates in uncompetitive races is usually much smaller, averaging about $388,000.

The typical Senate incumbent raised about $4.4 million more than the typical challenger during the 2006 election (see Figure 6-3). Open-seat Senate

FIGURE 6-2

Average Campaign Resources Raised in Uncompetitive House Elections in 2006

$, thousands

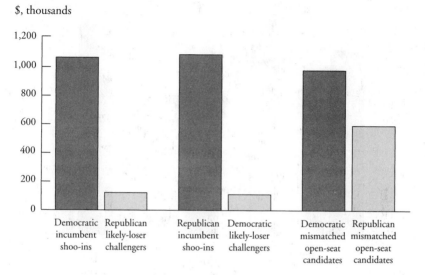

Source: Compiled from Federal Election Commission data.

Notes: Figures include receipts and party-coordinated expenditures for all two-party contests that were decided by margins greater than 20 percent of the vote. *N* = 510.

contests were fairly well funded, with contestants spending an average of $11.8 million. The differences in the amounts raised by Democratic and Republican candidates were fairly significant, favoring Democratic contenders by about $1.3 million or 18 percent. Finally, electoral competitiveness was important in attracting campaign resources. Senate candidates who defeated their opponents by 20 percent or less of the two-party vote raised twice as much as candidates involved in one-sided races.

HOUSE INCUMBENTS

Incumbents raise more money than challengers because they tend to be visible, popular, and willing to exploit the advantages of holding office. This is reflected both in how incumbents solicit contributions and in whom they turn to for cash. Incumbents rarely hesitate to remind a potential donor that they are in a position to influence public policy and will more than likely still be in that position when the next Congress convenes.

FIGURE 6-3

Average Campaign Resources Raised in the 2006 Senate Elections

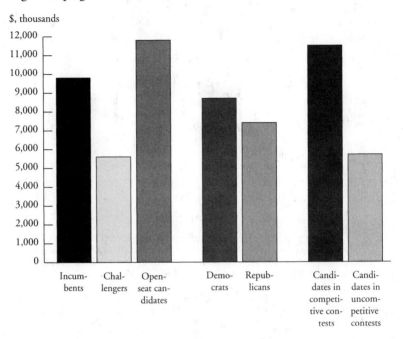

Source: Compiled from Federal Election Commission data.

Notes: Figures include receipts and party-coordinated expenditures for all two-party contested races. $N = 60$.

Sources of Funds

Individuals who make contributions of less than $200 are an important source of funds for House incumbents (see Figure 6-4). In 2006 they accounted for $110,000, or 8 percent, of the typical incumbent's campaign war chest.[4] These contributors are often viewed symbolically as an indicator of grassroots support. Individuals who contributed from $200 to $4,200 accounted for a bit more than $576,000, or 42 percent, of the typical incumbent's funds. These contributions are important for the obvious reason that a candidate needs to gather fewer of these larger contributions to raise a sum that would require many more small contributions. The doubling of the limits for individual contributions that came with the passage of the Bipartisan Campaign Reform Act of 2002 has resulted in House incumbents (and congressional candidates in general) becoming more dependent on large individual contributions.

FIGURE 6-4

Sources of House Incumbents' Campaign Receipts in the 2006 Elections

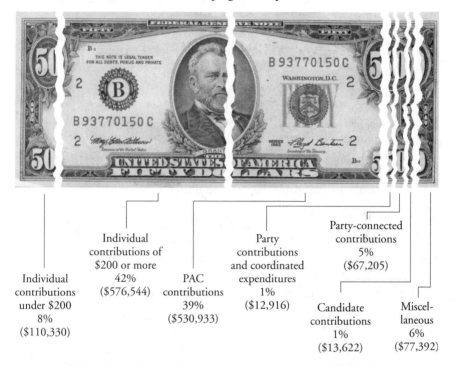

Individual contributions under $200
8%
($110,330)

Individual contributions of $200 or more
42%
($576,544)

PAC contributions
39%
($530,933)

Party contributions and coordinated expenditures
1%
($12,916)

Party-connected contributions
5%
($67,205)

Candidate contributions
1%
($13,622)

Miscellaneous
6%
($77,392)

Source: Compiled from Federal Election Commission and Center for Responsive Politics data.

Notes: The dollar values in parentheses are averages. Candidate contributions include loans candidates made to their own campaigns. PAC contributions exclude contributions by leadership PACs. Party-connected contributions are made up of contributions from leadership PACs, candidates, retired members, and members of Congress not up for reelection in 2006. Miscellaneous sources include interest from savings accounts and revenues from investments. Figures are for general election candidates in major-party contested races. Percentages may not add to 100 percent because of rounding. $N = 345$.

Many individuals made contributions to congressional incumbents (and some others) across district or state lines. Individuals living in the New York City metropolitan area alone donated $123 million to congressional candidates nationwide and to the party committees and PACs that supported their candidacies in 2006. These contributions, along with the millions distributed by Washington-based parties and PACs, have helped to form a national market for campaign contributions.[5] House incumbents from both parties rely heavily on this market, often fundraising in the same cities. The unequal distribution of wealth across the United States has made crisscrossing the country an important tactic in the campaign for resources. The unequal distribution of power between incumbents and other candidates has made contributing across geographic jurisdictions a prevalent tactic among access-oriented donors. That politicians go where the money is and that money flows to power speaks volumes about the campaign for resources. Because incumbents enjoy greater national recognition and influence, they are positioned to raise more money than challengers.

PACs provided approximately $531,000, or 39 percent, of a typical incumbent's campaign bankroll in 2006. Parties delivered much less, accounting for a mere 1 percent of the typical incumbent's total resources. Party-connected contri-butions from other members, leadership PACs, and congressional retirees accounted for an additional 5 percent. House members contributed even less of their own money to their campaigns. Finally, they raised about $77,000 from miscellaneous sources, including interest and revenues from investments.

Prior to the Republican takeover of Congress in 1995, Democratic House members collected a greater portion of their funds from PACs than did Republicans, who relied more heavily on individual contributors. The Democrats' procedural control of the House gave them greater influence over the substance and scheduling of legislation, which provided them with an over-whelming advantage in collecting PAC money. The 1996 elections represented a considerable change in this regard. Republican incumbents increased sub-stantially the money they raised from PACs, reaching parity with their Democratic counterparts. During the 2006 elections incumbents of both parties raised similar proportions of their funds from individuals and from PACs (see Table 6-1).

Fundraising Activities

Incumbents routinely complain about the time, effort, and indignities associated with raising funds. Their lack of enthusiasm for asking people for money figures prominently in how they raise campaign contributions. A fear of defeat and a disdain for fundraising have two principal effects: they encourage incumbents to raise large sums and to place the bulk of their fundraising in the hands of others, mainly professional consultants. Forty-six percent of all major-party House incumbents spend at least one-fourth of their personal campaign schedule raising funds. Seventeen percent spend more than half of their schedule asking others for money.[6] Of course, for their fundraising consultants the money chase is a full-time endeavor.

Most incumbents develop full-time fundraising operations. They hire direct-mail specialists and finance directors to write direct-mail appeals, update

TABLE 6-1

Sources of Support for House Incumbents in the 2006 Elections

	Democrats		Republicans	
	In jeopardy	Shoo-ins	In jeopardy	Shoo-ins
Individual contributions under $200	$168,323 (7%)	$101,786 (9%)	$152,150 (7%)	$77,955 (7%)
Individual contributions of $200 or more	$937,435 (39%)	$432,300 (40%)	$856,644 (42%)	$474,205 (43%)
PAC contributions	$798,782 (33%)	$461,630 (43%)	$674,051 (33%)	$465,041 (42%)
Party contributions and coordinated expenditures	$83,619 (3%)	$3,008 (—)	$31,637 (2%)	$1,976 (—)
Party-connected contributions	$221,453 (9%)	$13,699 (1%)	$176,913 (9%)	$22,049 (2%)
Candidate contributions	$5,200 (—)	$5,963 (1%)	$34,655 (2%)	$5,241 (—)
Miscellaneous	$193,234 (8%)	$55,222 (5%)	$125,508 (6%)	$51,330 (5%)

Source: Compiled from Federal Election Commission and Center for Responsive Politics data.

Notes: Figures are averages for general election candidates in major-party contested races. — = less than 0.5 percent. Candidate contributions include loans candidates made to their own campaigns. PAC contributions exclude contributions by leadership PACs. Party-connected contributions are made up of contributions from leadership PACs, candidates, retired members, and members of Congress not up for reelection in 2006. Miscellaneous sources include interest from savings accounts and revenues from investments. Some columns do not add to 100 percent because of rounding. $N = 345$.

contributor lists, identify and solicit potentially supportive PACs, script telephone solicitations, and organize fundraising events. These operations enable incumbents to limit their involvement to showing up at events and telephoning potential contributors who insist on having a direct conversation with them prior to making a large contribution.

Incumbents raise small contributions by making appeals through the mail, over the telephone, at fundraising events, and via the Internet. Direct mail can be a relatively reliable method of fundraising for an incumbent because solicitations are usually made from lists of previous donors that indicate which appeals garnered earlier contributions.[7] Most direct mail and telephone solicitations generate contributions of less than $100 and are targeted at the candidate's constituents. However, many prominent House members, beginning with the Speaker, have huge direct-mail lists that include hundreds of thousands of citizens who reside across the United States and even a few who live abroad. A significant portion of these individuals contribute large sums. In 2006 Speaker Dennis Hastert raised more than $848,000 and then–minority leader Nancy Pelosi raised almost $142,000 in individual contributions of $200 or more from outside their respective states (representing 36 percent and 27 percent, respectively, of these candidates' large individual contributions).[8]

The Internet emerged as an important fundraising tool during the 1998 congressional elections. By 2002, 57 percent of all House candidates in major-party contested races and virtually every Senate candidate used web sites or e-mail to solicit funds.[9] Their numbers increased by the 2006 election season. Some candidates' web sites enabled donors to contribute online using a credit card, and other sites provided instructions for making contributions via mail, phone, or fax.

Some candidates made solicitations using e-mail addresses purchased from Internet providers, other organizations, and individuals who visited their web sites. E-mail lists of individuals who share a candidate's issue concerns are a potential source of monetary and volunteer support, especially among computer-literate youth. The greatest advantage of e-mail and Internet fundraising is that the solicitation is delivered for free, compared with the $3 to $4 it costs to send out one first-class direct-mail solicitation. The trade-off for e-mail is that it is not always welcomed. Mass-distributed e-mails, often referred to as "spam," are frequently deleted without having been read, the electronic equivalent of tossing an unopened piece of direct mail into the trash or hanging up on a telemarketer. It is doubtful that most congressional candidates will be able to emulate the e-fundraising success of some presidential candidates, most notably 2004 Democratic presidential nomination candidate Howard Dean and 2008 presidential hopeful Barack Obama, but many high-profile House and Senate contestants are positioned to capitalize on the Internet for some of their fundraising needs.

Traditional fundraising events are another popular means for raising small contributions. Cocktail parties, barbecues, and picnics with admission costs ranging from $10 to $50 that are held in the candidate's district are useful ways to raise money. They also are helpful in generating favorable press coverage, energizing political activists, and building goodwill among voters.

Incumbents can ensure the success of local fundraising events by establishing finance committees that include business executives, labor officials, civic leaders, or political activists who live in their districts. These committees often begin with a dozen or so supporters who host "low-dollar" receptions (where individuals usually contribute from $20 to $100) in their homes and make telephone solicitations on the candidate's behalf. Guests at one event are encouraged to become the sponsors of others. In time, small finance committees can grow into large pyramid-like fundraising networks, consisting of dozens of finance committees, each of which makes a substantial contribution to the candidate's reelection efforts. Most House and Senate incumbents have fundraising networks that extend from their district or state to the nation's capital.

Large individual contributions and PAC money also are raised by finance committees, at fundraising events, and through networks of supporters. Events that feature the president, congressional leaders, sports heroes, or other celebrities help attract individuals and groups who are willing to contribute anywhere from a few hundred dollars to the legal maximum.[10] Some of these events are held in the candidate's state, but most are held in political, financial, and entertainment centers such as Washington, New York City, and Los Angeles. In 2006 the 23 Republican incumbents who were the beneficiaries of one or more visits by President Bush raised 159 percent more than did other GOP incumbents.

Traditional fundraising events can satisfy the goals of a variety of contributors. They give individuals who desire the social benefits of giving, including the proximity to power, the chance to speak with members of Congress and other celebrity politicians. Persons and groups that contribute for ideological reasons are able to voice their specific issue concerns. Individuals and organizations that are motivated by material gain, such as a tax break or federal funding for a project, often perceive these events as opportunities to build a relationship with members of Congress.[11]

In raising large individual contributions, House members have advantages over challengers that extend beyond the prestige and political clout that come with incumbency and an ability to rely on an existing group of supporters. Incumbents also benefit from the fact that many wealthy individuals have motives that favor them over challengers. About 25 percent of all individuals who contribute $200 or more to a congressional candidate—mainly incumbents—do so mainly because they wish to gain access to individuals who will be in a position to influence legislation once the election is over. Roughly 36 percent give contributions mainly for broad ideological reasons or because of their positions on specific, highly charged issues. These donors tend to rally around incumbents who champion their causes. Another 24 percent are motivated to contribute primarily because they enjoy attending fundraising events and mixing with incumbents and other elites who attend these functions. The final 15 percent are not strongly motivated by any one factor, whether it be access, ideology, or the social side of contributing. Though they contribute for idiosyncratic reasons, they, like other donors, primarily support incumbents.[12]

Moreover, information that parties and PACs mail to their big donors often focuses on incumbents' campaigns, further leading some wealthy individuals to contribute to incumbents in jeopardy rather than to hopeful challengers. The rise of national party organizations, PACs, and other organizations and individuals that provide potential donors with decision-making cues and the ceilings federal law places on campaign contributions have led to the replacement of one type of fat cat with another. Individuals and groups that gave candidates tens or hundreds of thousands of dollars directly have been replaced by new sets of elites who help candidates raise these sums rather than contribute them directly.[13]

Incumbents consciously use the influence that comes with holding office to raise money from PACs and wealthy individuals who seek political access. Legislators' campaigns first identify potential donors who are most likely to respond favorably to their solicitations. These include PACs that supported the incumbent in a previous race, lobbyists who agree with an incumbent's positions on specific issues, and others who are affected by legislation the incumbent is in a position to influence. Members of Congress who hold party leadership positions, serve on powerful committees, or are recognized entrepreneurs in certain policy areas can easily collect large amounts of money from many wealthy interest group–based financial constituencies. It is no coincidence that the eight House incumbents who raised the most PAC money in 2006, more than $1.7 million each, enjoyed at least one of these assets.[14]

Once an incumbent has identified a financial constituency, the next step is to ask for a contribution. The most effective solicitations describe the member's background, legislative goals, accomplishments, sources of influence (including committee assignments, chairmanships, or party leadership positions), the nature of the competition faced, and the amount of money needed. Incumbents frequently assemble this information in the kits they mail to PACs. Addressed to a member of the PAC's board of directors, usually a lobbyist, these solicitations are customized to tap into the PACs' motives for contributing.

Some PACs require a candidate to meet with one of their representatives, who personally delivers a check. A few require incumbents to complete questionnaires on specific issues, but most PACs rely on members' prior roll-call votes or interest group ratings as measures of their policy proclivities. Some

PACs, particularly ideological committees, want evidence that a representative or senator is facing serious opposition before giving a contribution. Party leaders and Hill committee staff are sometimes called to bear witness to the competitiveness of an incumbent's race.

Parties are another source of money and campaign services. The most important thing incumbents can do to win party support is demonstrate that they are vulnerable. The Hill committees have most of the information they need to make such a determination, but incumbents can give details on the nature of the threat they face that might not be apparent to a party operative who is unfamiliar with the nuances of a member's seat. The National Republican Congressional Committee gives incumbents who request extra party support the opportunity to make their case before a special Incumbent Review Board composed of GOP House members. Once a Hill committee has made an incumbent a priority, it will go to great efforts to supply the candidate with money, campaign services, and assistance in collecting resources from others.

The financing of Rep. Wally Herger's 2006 reelection effort in California is illustrative of most reelection bids involving safe incumbents. Herger raised almost $690,000 and received $287 in contributions from the NRCC and no party coordinated expenditures, a substantially smaller party supplement than the $1,976 received by the typical shoo-in incumbent. He collected more than $65,000 (9 percent of his total resources) in small contributions using campaign newsletters, direct-mail solicitations, and low-dollar fundraising events held in the district. He collected another $182,000 (roughly 26 percent) in individual contributions of $200 or more at high-dollar events. Just over $44,000 (24 percent) was raised from individuals who reside outside California.[15]

Herger raised $410,000 (almost 60 percent) from PACs (excluding leadership PACs). Corporate, trade, and other business-related committees contributed about 92 percent of these funds. Nonconnected committees accounted for 6 percent of Herger's PAC dollars. The candidate collected no contributions from other members' campaign committees or leadership PACs. Indeed, he contributed $47,000 from his campaign committee to other candidates. Most of Herger's PAC money and large individual donations were raised at events held in the district or in Washington and through solicitations coordinated by the candidate's campaign staff. Finally, the campaign raised $32,000 from interest on loans and investments (5 percent of its total campaign receipts). Like most congressional incumbents, Herger contributed no money to his own reelection effort.

Herger was successful at capitalizing on his membership on the House Ways and Means Committee, which writes tax policy. The individuals and groups that are affected by the committee's business make up one of the nation's wealthiest interest group constituencies. Herger's campaign collected more than $122,000 (30 percent of its PAC funds) from PACs associated with the finance, real estate, and insurance industries, and it raised another $25,000 in contributions of $200 or more from individuals who work in this economic sector (14 percent of his total significant individual contributions).[16]

With only two-year terms, House incumbents usually begin raising money almost immediately after they are sworn into office. Sometimes they have debts to retire, but often they use money left over from previous campaigns as seed money for the next election. More than 30 percent of all House incumbents began the 2006 election cycle with more than $400,000 left over from their previous campaigns. In turn, almost 30 percent of all successful 2006 House candidates completed their campaigns with more than $400,000 in the bank, including twenty-eight who had amassed more than $1 million. These funds will provide useful seed money for their reelection campaigns in 2008 or bids for some other office.

Early fundraising is carried out for strategic reasons. Incumbents build substantial war chests early in the election cycle to try to deter potential challengers.[17] An incumbent who had to spend several hundreds of thousands or even millions of dollars to win by a narrow margin in the last election will have a greater compulsion to raise money earlier than someone whose previous election was a landslide victory. Once they have raised enough money to reach an initial comfort level, however, incumbents appear to be driven largely by the threat posed by an actual challenger.[18] Incumbents under duress seek to amass huge sums of money regardless of the source, whereas those who face weak opponents may weigh other considerations, such as developing a "diversified portfolio of contributors."[19]

A typical incumbent's campaign—one waged by a candidate who faces stiff competition in neither the primary nor the general election—will generally engage in heavy fundraising early and then allow this activity to taper off as it becomes clear that the candidate is not in jeopardy. The 2006 Herger campaign exemplifies this pattern. The campaign began the election cycle with more than $578,000 left over from the candidate's last race. Between January 1 and December 31, 2005, it raised $338,000 (about 49 percent of its total receipts). All of this money was raised before A. J. Sekhon, Herger's general election opponent, had collected enough money to need to register his candidacy with the FEC. During the next six months, which included California's June 6 primary, the Herger campaign began to cut back on its fundraising efforts, collecting about $148,000 (21 percent), perhaps in response to the fact that the

Sekhon campaign still had not reported any fundraising receipts. During the next three months the Herger campaign collected an additional $107,000 (16 percent). Between October 1 and November 25 it raised a total of $97,000 (14 percent). The campaign closed out the election year by collecting an additional $3,000 (about 0.4 percent).

Herger's campaign finances help demonstrate that a good deal of incumbent fundraising is challenger driven. Early money is raised to deter a strong opponent from entering the race. If a strong challenger materializes, then an incumbent's fundraising activities will usually increase. If none emerges, they will remain steady or slow down.

The 2006 campaign of Charles Taylor, at the time the Republican representative from North Carolina's 11th district, also supports the generalization that incumbent fundraising is challenger driven: it shows how an incumbent responds to a strong challenger. The campaign collected almost $4.4 million in contributions and almost $20,000 in coordinated expenditures, making it the tenth most expensive House campaign waged by an incumbent that year. It raised almost $497,000 (11 percent of its total resources) from PACs, excluding leadership PACs, and another $664,000 (15 percent) in individual contributions of $200 or more, about three-fourths of which was collected from individuals living in the candidate's home state.[20] The campaign collected almost $217,000 (5 percent) in individual contributions of less than $200. The Republican Party provided $23,000 in contributions and coordinated expenditures (about 0.5 percent). Republican members of Congress and retirees contributed about $36,000, and leadership PACs gave another $132,000 (for a total of 3 percent). What is unusual about the candidate's fundraising, especially for an incumbent in jeopardy, is where the remainder of the campaign's resources came from: the wealthy Taylor contributed $2.8 million (63 percent) to his own campaign.[21]

Taylor began to solicit contributions early and aggressively because he recognized that his less-than-ten-point victory over Buncombe County commissioner Patsy Keever in 2004, some questionable business dealings, and a congressional vote that facilitated the exportation of jobs from the district might make him a target for a strong Democratic challenge. He began the campaign cycle with little more than $46,000 left over from his previous campaign. Between January 1 and December 31, 2005, the Taylor campaign raised $709,000 (roughly 16 percent of its receipts). Between January 1 and June 30, 2006, it collected another $349,000 (8 percent). This money was raised partly in response to Democratic challenger Heath Shuler's ability to attract substantial media coverage and funding. The challenger had raised hundreds of thousands of dollars by this point.

The Democratic candidate's impressive fundraising and outreach and his own campaign's troubles led Taylor to believe he would need to spend more money to hold on to his seat. While most other candidates would have put a great effort into organizing fundraising events and dialing for dollars, Taylor found it easier to lend more of his own money to the campaign. This enabled him to boost the campaign's resources by an additional $2 million between July 1 and September 30 of 2006 (accounting for 45 percent of his receipts) and $1.4 million (31 percent) from October 1 to election day. Between his defeat and the close of the calendar year Taylor was able to raise about $32,000— a drop in the bucket that would be needed for his campaign to repay the funds he had lent it.

The Taylor campaign's fundraising was driven by a situation the candidate had anticipated: unlike the lack of competition that had caused Herger to raise less money than the typical incumbent, stiff competition from Shuler encouraged Taylor, the incumbent, to set a personal record. Unfortunately for him, his personal investment had two negative effects. First, it left his campaign owing him money it is unlikely to repay. And, second, it triggered the BCRA's millionaires' provision, which raised the contribution limits for individuals and allowed the Democratic Party to make unlimited coordinated expenditures in the race. As noted earlier, the Democrats responded by providing Shuler with about $1.6 million in coordinated expenditures, almost doubling the campaign resources under the challenger's control and thereby making the election financially competitive.

HOUSE CHALLENGERS

Challengers have the greatest need for money, but they encounter the most difficulties raising it. The same factors that make it difficult for challengers to win votes also harm their ability to collect campaign contributions. A lack of name recognition, limited campaign experience, a relatively untested organization, and a high probability of defeat discourage most contributors, especially those who give large amounts in pursuit of access, from supporting challengers. The fact that their opponents are established Washington operators who possess political clout does not make challengers' quests for support any easier.

Sources of Funds

Challengers raise less money than incumbents, and their mix of funding sources differs from that of incumbents. House challengers collect a greater portion of their funds from individuals. Challengers competing in the 2006 elections raised an average of about $87,000, or 19 percent of their campaign budgets, in individual contributions of less than $200 (see Figure 6-5). Challengers collected more than twice as much of their funds in the form of individual contributions of $200 or more. Both challengers and incumbents raised substantial funds from individuals, but incumbents raised, on average, more than two times more in individual contributions than did challengers. Moreover, challengers raised a significantly smaller proportion of their funds from out of state.

Challengers garnered a mere 9 percent of their money from PACs, trailing incumbents by a ratio of almost 1 to 12 in terms of the amounts of PAC dollars these candidates typically raised. Challengers also raised substantially less party-connected money, about $30,000, as opposed to the $67,000 raised by the typical incumbent. The distribution of party contributions and coordinated expenditures, by contrast, was more favorable to challengers, who aver-

FIGURE 6-5

Sources of House Challengers' Campaign Receipts in the 2006 Elections

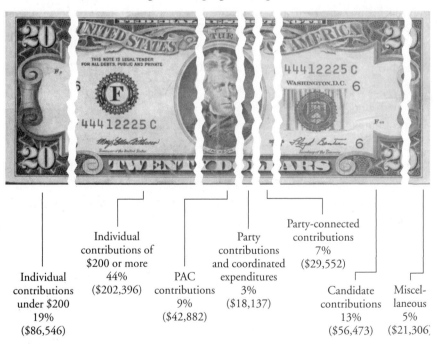

| | Individual contributions of $200 or more | | Party contributions and coordinated expenditures | Party-connected contributions 7% ($29,552) | | |
| Individual contributions under $200 19% ($86,546) | 44% ($202,396) | PAC contributions 9% ($42,882) | 3% ($18,137) | | Candidate contributions 13% ($56,473) | Miscellaneous 5% ($21,306) |

Source: Compiled from Federal Election Commission and Center for Responsive Politics data.

Notes: See notes in Figure 6-4. $N = 345$.

aged better than $5,000 more than incumbents. Finally, challengers dug far deeper into their own pockets than did incumbents. The typical challenger contributed or lent the campaign almost $56,000—more than four times the amount provided by the typical incumbent.

Democratic challengers raised substantially more money from PACs than did their Republican counterparts (see Table 6-2). However, Democratic challengers collected fewer dollars from individuals, with an especially pronounced deficit among those who made large contributions. Republican hopefuls re-

TABLE 6-2

Sources of Support for House Challengers in the 2006 Elections

	Democrats		Republicans	
	Hopefuls	Likely losers	Hopefuls	Likely losers
Individual contributions under $200	$224,120 (20%)	$25,753 (23%)	$101,178 (5%)	$35,933 (29%)
Individual contributions of $200 or more	$538,025 (47%)	$40,085 (36%)	$837,268 (41%)	$45,429 (37%)
PAC contributions	$124,000 (11%)	$14,452 (13%)	$116,375 (6%)	$2,469 (2%)
Party contributions and coordinated expenditures	$54,610 (5%)	$2,084 (2%)	$67,126 (3%)	$1,327 (1%)
Party-connected contributions	$75,612 (7%)	$3,454 (3%)	$194,242 (10%)	$5,241 (4%)
Candidate contributions	$78,789 (7%)	$22,558 (20%)	$583,277 (29%)	$28,125 (23%)
Miscellaneous	$52,975 (4%)	$4,078 (3%)	$134,784 (6%)	$4,015 (3%)

Source: Compiled from Federal Election Commission and Center for Responsive Politics data.

Notes: Figures are averages for general election candidates in major-party contested races. Candidate contributions include loans candidates made to their own campaigns. PAC contributions exclude contributions by leadership PACs. Party-connected contributions are made up of contributions from leadership PACs, candidates, retired members, and members of Congress not up for reelection in 2006. Miscellaneous sources include interest from savings accounts and revenues from investments. Some columns do not add to 100 percent because of rounding. $N = 345$.

ceived more party contributions and coordinated expenditures than did Democrats and enjoyed a 155 percent advantage in party-connected contributions. Republicans also invested substantially more in their own campaigns.

Fundraising Activities

Incumbents may find fundraising a disagreeable chore, but at least their efforts usually meet with success. Challengers put in just as many long, hard hours on the money chase as do incumbents.[22] Yet, as noted above, they clearly have less to show for their efforts. Most challengers start raising early money at home. They begin by donating or lending their campaigns the initial funds needed to solicit contributions from others. They then turn to relatives, friends, professional colleagues, local political activists, and virtually every individual whose name is in their personal organizer or, better, on their holiday card list. Some of these people are asked to chair fundraising committees or host fundraising events. Candidates who have previously run for office are able to turn to past contributors for support. Competitive challengers frequently obtain lists of contributors from members of their party who have previously run for office or from private vendors. In some cases these challengers receive lists from party committees or PACs; however, most of these organizations mail fundraising letters on behalf of selected candidates rather than physically turn over their contributor lists.

Only after enjoying some local fundraising success do most nonincumbents set their sights on Washington. Seed money raised from individuals is especially helpful in attracting funds from PACs, particularly for candidates who have not held elective office.[23] The endorsements of local business, labor, party, or civic leaders have a similar effect, especially if they can be persuaded to serve on a fundraising committee. If the assistance of congressional leaders or members of a candidate's state delegation can be obtained, it can be helpful to challengers who hope to raise money from their party's congressional campaign committee, PACs, or individual large contributors.[24] When powerful incumbents organize luncheons, attend "meet-and-greets," and appear at fundraising events for nonincumbents, contributors usually respond positively. Contributors also look favorably on events attended by high-ranking executive branch officials, particularly the president. The few Republican challengers who benefited from a campaign visit by President Bush in 2006 raised ten times more than other Republican challengers. Although none of them was able to defeat a Democratic incumbent, the President's visit elevated their candidacies among Republican donors and enabled them to wage competitive well-financed campaigns.

Unfortunately for most challengers, their long odds of success make it difficult for them to enlist the help of a president, party leader, or many rank-and-file congressional incumbents. Political leaders focus their efforts on candidates who have strong electoral prospects and may someday be in a position to return the favor by supporting the member's leadership aspirations or legislative goals in Congress.

A knowledge of how party leaders and PAC managers make contribution decisions can improve challengers' fundraising prospects. Political experience and a professional campaign staff often come together, and they are particularly helpful in this regard.[25] Candidates who put together feasible campaign plans, hire reputable consultants, and can present polling figures indicating that they enjoy a reasonable level of name recognition can usually attract the attention of party officials, PAC managers, individuals who make large contributions, and the inside-the-beltway journalists who handicap elections. Political amateurs who wage largely volunteer efforts, in contrast, usually cannot.

During the 2006 congressional elections, House challengers in major-party contested races who had previously held elective office raised, on average, $792,000 in contributions. This includes $27,000 from party committees, and $71,000 in party-connected contributions from other candidates, retired members of Congress, and leadership PACs. Unelected politicians raised an average of $482,000, including $12,000 from party committees and $32,000 in party-connected dollars. Political amateurs raised, on average, only $273,000. Of this, $15,000 came from their party and $12,000 from party-connected sources.

One way in which challengers can increase their chances of success in raising money from PACs is for them to identify the few committees likely to give them support. For Democrats, these committees include labor groups. Challengers can improve their prospects of attracting labor PAC money by showing they have strong ties to the labor community, have previously supported labor issues in the state legislature, or support labor's current goals.[26] Competitive Democratic challengers who were able to make this case in 2006 did quite well with the labor community, raising an average of $89,000 from labor PACs.

Challengers of both parties may be able to attract support from PACs, particularly ideological committees, by convincing PAC managers that they are committed to the group's cause. A history of personal support for that cause is useful. Challengers, and in fact most nonincumbents, typically demonstrate this support by pointing to roll-call votes they cast in the state legislature, to the backing of a PAC's donors or affiliated PACs located in their state or district, or to the support of Washington-based organizations that share some of the PAC's views. Nonincumbents who make a PAC's issues among the central elements of their campaign message and communicate this information in their PAC kits enhance their odds of winning a committee's backing. Properly completing a PAC's questionnaire or having a successful interview with a PAC manager also is extremely important. Taking these steps can help a challenger obtain a contribution and endorsement from a PAC, as well as gain assistance in raising money from individuals and other PACs with shared policy concerns.

Political experience and professional expertise also can help a nonincumbent raise PAC money. In 2006, challengers who had previously held office raised an average of $95,000 from PACs, roughly $22,000 more than the typical unelected politician and $73,000 more than the typical amateur.

Ideological causes have been at the forefront of many candidates' PAC fundraising strategies during the past few decades. Women challengers are able to capitalize on their gender and attract large amounts of money and campaign assistance from EMILY's List, the WISH List (the Republican counterpart of EMILY's List), and other pro-women's groups.[27] Challengers who take a stand on either side of the abortion issue are frequently able to raise money from PACs and individual donors that share their positions. By taking a side on emotionally laden issues, such as handgun control or support for Israel, some challengers are able to attract the contributions of ideological PACs and individuals that identify with those causes.

A perception of competitiveness is critical to challenger fundraising, and a scandal involving an incumbent can help a challenger become competitive. Scandal can be critical in helping primary challengers raise the funds needed to defeat an incumbent. In 2006, it helped Hank Johnson raise the $798,000 he used to knock off Representative Cynthia McKinney in the Democratic primary in Georgia's 4th district and defeat Catherine Davis in the general election.

Sekhon's and Shuler's experiences demonstrate the effect that perceptions of competitiveness have on challenger fundraising. Almost from the beginning, Sekhon's campaign to unseat Herger was in trouble. Despite the fact that Sekhon had run in 2004, he began his 2006 bid for Congress with no money left over from his previous campaign. He also encountered the fundraising doldrums that plague most House challengers, particularly those who would be classified as likely losers. Sekhon's campaign began collecting money more than a year after his opponent's, which is typical in most incumbent-challenger races, and it got off to a very slow start. By September 30, 2006, it had raised only $8,400 (5 percent of its total). It collected another $152,000 (92 percent) between October 1 and November 27, leaving it unable to run a financially viable campaign. Between November 28 and the year's end the campaign raised an additional $6,000 (3 percent) to help it pay off some bills.

Besides getting a late start in raising funds, the Sekhon campaign suffered from having no professional operation to solicit contributions. It had difficulty raising PAC money—collecting only one PAC contribution of $500 from Singh PAC, sponsored by a Michigan real estate firm. The Democratic Party provided no contributions or coordinated expenditures, and the same is true from Democratic politicians and their leadership PACs. The campaign received the rest of its funds from individual donors, raising 87 percent in contributions of $200 or more. The Indian American community was extremely supportive, accounting for a very large proportion of these donations.

The Shuler campaign exemplifies the fundraising dynamics of a challenger who is capable of waging a competitive campaign, and his fundraising experience was typical of most hopeful challengers. As a result of his fame on the gridiron, prominence in the Democrats' Red to Blue Program, and gaining the support of DCCC chair Rahm Emanuel, Shuler was able to capitalize on a variety of techniques and solicit money from a broad array of individuals and groups. Notoriety, party backing, a professional organization, and an effective strategy enabled Shuler to raise more than $1.8 million in contributions. When Taylor triggered the millionaires' amendment, it enabled the DCCC to become heavily involved in the campaign, ultimately spending about $1.6 million in coordinated expenditures—twenty times more than the normal $77,000 limit set for 2006.[28] Shuler raised almost $395,000 from PACs (excluding leadership PACs), $217,000 in party-connected contributions, $203,000 in individual contributions of less than $200, and almost $1.1 million in large individual contributions—48 percent of which were donated by North Carolinians.[29] Shuler neither contributed nor lent any money to his campaign.

The Shuler campaign, unlike the Sekhon organization, began collecting money early in the election season. By December 31, 2005 it had amassed a hefty $441,000 (23 percent of its funding). With the help of Democratic leaders and the party's donor network, the campaign took in an additional $647,000 (34 percent) during the next six months. The campaign raised an additional $756,000 (43 percent) by November 27 and another $6,000 to close out the calendar year.

Taylor's ethical missteps, Shuler's celebrity status and fit for the district, and Shuler's strong party backing helped the challenger attract the support of party committees, PACs, and individual donors who were eager to wrest a seat held by a vulnerable Republican. Taylor and his supporters also responded to the competitiveness of the race, resulting in the incumbent spending more than twice as much as his opponent. The dynamics of the race were somewhat unusual for even close incumbent-challenger contests only in that an incumbent in jeopardy invested an impressive amount of his own money to try to hold on to his seat.

CANDIDATES FOR OPEN HOUSE SEATS

Candidates for open seats possess few of the fundraising advantages of incumbents but also lack the liabilities of challengers. Open-seat candidates rely on many of the same fundraising strategies as challengers but usually have considerably more success. Because most open-seat contests are competitive, they receive a great deal of attention from parties, PACs, and other informed contributors, particularly individuals who make large contributions. This attention places open-seat candidates in a position to convince Washington insiders and other elites that their campaigns are worthy of support.

Sources of Funds

The campaign receipts of open-seat candidates resemble those of both incumbents and challengers. Open-seat candidates typically raise slightly more than do incumbents. Like challengers, however, they usually collect fewer large individual contributions from out of state and more of their funds from parties and party-connected sources (see Figure 6-6). The typical open-seat candidate's PAC receipts lie between those amassed by incumbents and those gathered by challengers. Open-seat candidates contribute more of their own personal funds to their campaigns than do either incumbents or challengers.

Following the GOP takeover of Congress in 1994, more PACs became disposed to support Republican open-seat candidates. In 2006, Republican prospects raised slightly more PAC money than their Democratic opponents. However, Democratic candidates in one-sided open-seat contests collected more PAC money than Republicans, mainly because most of them dominated their races (see Table 6-3). Democratic candidates received significantly more party money than did their Republican counterparts, but Republicans raised more from party-connected sources, as one might expect given the discussion of candidate-to-candidate and leadership PAC contributions in Chapter 4. GOP and Democratic open-seat candidates in close races bankrolled considerable portions of their own campaigns, investing significantly more than did candidates in mismatched contests.

Fundraising Activities

Candidates for open seats put in the longest fundraising hours of all House contestants and, as noted above, with considerable success. Just over 60 percent devote more than one-fourth of their personal campaign schedule to attending fundraising events, meeting in person with potential donors, and di-

FIGURE 6-6

Sources of House Open-Seat Candidates' Campaign Receipts in the 2006 Elections

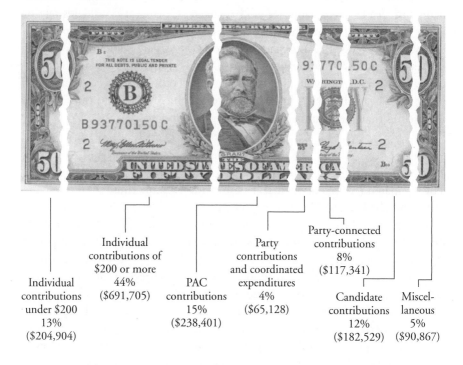

Individual contributions under $200 13% ($204,904)

Individual contributions of $200 or more 44% ($691,705)

PAC contributions 15% ($238,401)

Party contributions and coordinated expenditures 4% ($65,128)

Party-connected contributions 8% ($117,341)

Candidate contributions 12% ($182,529)

Miscel-laneous 5% ($90,867)

Source: Compiled from Federal Election Commission and Center for Responsive Politics data.

Notes: See notes in Figure 6-4. $N = 64$.

aling for dollars.[30] These candidates help their cause by informing potential contributors of their political experience and the assets their campaign organization brings to the race.[31]

Among open-seat candidates, elected politicians raised the most money in 2006, averaging almost $1.3 million, in contrast with the $680,000 raised by unelected politicians and the $338,000 raised by political amateurs. Elected officials did not do particularly well when it came to raising money from party committees, however. They raised, on average, $17,000, which was about the same as amateurs and was $13,000 less than unelected politicians. Nevertheless, they did raise considerable amounts in party-connected contributions—more than $73,000, about $21,000 more than unelected politicians and $57,000 more than amateurs.

TABLE 6-3

Sources of Support for House Open-Seat Candidates in the 2006 Elections

	Democrats		Republicans	
	Prospects	Mismatched	Prospects	Mismatched
Individual contributions				
under $200	$384,468	$144,829	$210,620	$54,997
	(17%)	(14%)	(9%)	(9%)
Individual contributions of				
$200 or more	$982,149	$509,439	$930,552	$274,106
	(43%)	(51%)	(41%)	(46%)
PAC contributions	$304,655	$198,960	$319,577	$110,755
	(13%)	(19%)	(14%)	(18%)
Party contributions and				
coordinated expenditures	$152,555	$7,672	$81,958	$4,424
	(7%)	(1%)	(4%)	(1%)
Party-connected contributions	$155,083	$44,143	$195,676	$58,986
	(7%)	(4%)	(9%)	(10%)
Candidate contributions	$213,131	$58,263	$375,292	$53,648
	(9%)	(6%)	(17%)	(9%)
Miscellaneous	$118,738	$36,828	$151,317	$44,810
	(5%)	(4%)	(6%)	(7%)

Source: Compiled from Federal Election Commission and Center for Responsive Politics data.

Notes: Figures are averages for general election candidates in major-party contested races. Candidate contributions include loans candidates made to their own campaigns. PAC contributions exclude contributions by leadership PACs. Party-connected contributions are made up of contributions from leadership PACs, candidates, retired members, and members of Congress not up for reelection in 2006. Miscellaneous sources include interest from savings accounts and revenues from investments. Some columns do not add to 100 percent because of rounding. $N = 64$.

Winning support from PACs can be a little more challenging. Although open-seat candidates use the same techniques as challengers to identify interest group constituencies and to campaign for PAC support, they usually have greater success. Because their odds of victory are better, open-seat candidates have an easier time gaining an audience with PAC managers and are able to raise more PAC money. Similarly, open-seat candidates point to the same types of information as challengers to make the case that their campaigns will be competitive. Experienced open-seat contestants and those who wage professional campaigns collect more PAC money than do amateurs. In 2006, open-seat candidates who had previously held elective office raised, on average, almost $441,000 from PACs, about $358,000 more than did the typical unelected politician and almost $410,000 more than did the typical amateur.

Like other candidates, open-seat candidates can improve their prospects in the campaign for resources by persuading congressional party leaders and other high-profile politicians to appear at their fundraising events. Of course, nothing helps like a visit by a president. In 2006, Rick O'Donnell in Colorado's 7th district and the few other open-seat prospects who were able to get President Bush to come to their districts raised, on average, 232 percent more dollars than other open-seat candidates.

The fundraising experiences of the candidates in Colorado's 7th district mirror those of most open-seat candidates in competitive races. Both candidates built up considerable war chests. Perlmutter raised about $3 million and received an additional $55,000 in Democratic Party coordinated expenditures. He collected roughly $611,000 (20 percent of his resources) from PACs (excluding leadership PACs) by using contacts he had made while serving as president pro tempore of the Colorado Senate to leverage significant PAC dollars. Labor committees gave Perlmutter about $292,000. PACs sponsored by trade associations, corporations, and cooperatives gave him an additional $173,000, $63,000, and $6,000, respectively.[32] Liberal nonconnected committees gave Perlmutter an additional $76,000.[33]

O'Donnell had not served in the state legislature, but his previous run for Congress in 2002 and experience as Colorado's education commissioner as well as the Republicans' control of Congress made him an appealing candidate to many contributors. He raised more than $2.8 million in cash and an additional $77,000 in party coordinated expenditures. O'Donnell collected $442,000 (15 percent of his total resources) from PACs, receiving $341,000 from business-related committees and $49,000 from conservative nonconnected PACs.[34] Not surprisingly, O'Donnell got no support from PACs affiliated with organized labor.

Both candidates raised significant sums through the mail, the Internet, and at high- and low-dollar receptions. Both Perlmutter and O'Donnell collected about $2 million in individual contributions, accounting for just under 70 percent of their respective campaign funds. Each candidate also raised more than 80 percent of these dollars from their fellow Coloradoans.[35]

O'Donnell raised more party money than did Perlmutter. In addition to the $77,000 he received in coordinated expenditures, he collected $25,000 in Republican Party contributions, $47,000 from Republican members of Congress and retirees, and $220,000 from GOP-sponsored leadership PACs.

Perlmutter's $55,000 in coordinated expenditures was supplemented by another $3,500 in Democratic Party contributions, $96,000 from Democratic legislators and retirees, and $108,000 from leadership PACs. Contributions from formal party organizations and party politicians and their PACs accounted for about 13 percent of O'Donnell's and 9 percent of Perlmutter's total resources.[36] Leaders of both parties clearly viewed this race as important and succeeded in rallying their colleagues to donate funds.

The candidates assumed very different roles in the financing of their campaigns. Perlmutter directly contributed $6,000 to his campaign committee and lent it another $60,000. O'Donnell, on the other hand, chose not to lend or contribute to his campaign.

As is the case with most marginal open-seat contests, Colorado's 7th district race attracted a great deal of attention on the part of party committees, PACs, and other contributors. This attention enabled both candidates to raise large amounts of money once they began fundraising in earnest. Between January 1 and December 31, 2005, O'Donnell and Perlmutter collected $653,000 and $519,000, respectively, accounting for roughly 23 percent and 18 percent of their campaign receipts. O'Donnell amassed an additional $1.7 million (40 percent of his receipts) during the next nine months—a period that included the run-up to the state's August 8 primary. Perlmutter, who was locked in a three-way primary, raised $1.6 million (53 percent) during this same period. The candidates continued their frenetic fundraising between October 1 and November 25, with the advantage going to Perlmutter who collected another $813,000 (27 percent) compared with O'Donnell's $452,000 (16 percent). The victorious Perlmutter collected about $70,000 to close out some of the bills he had accumulated, while the defeated O'Donnell halted his fundraising after the election was over.

SENATE CAMPAIGNS

The differences in the campaigns for resources waged by Senate and House candidates are consistent with other differences that exist between House and Senate elections. Candidates for the Senate need more money, start requesting support earlier, and devote more time to asking for it. About 57 percent of all candidates spend more than one-fourth of their campaign schedule asking potential donors for funds.[37] They often meet with party officials, PAC managers, wealthy individuals, and other sources of money or fundraising assistance three years before they plan to run. Most Senate candidates also attempt to raise money on a more national scale than do House contestants.

The monumental size of the task requires Senate candidates to rely more on others for fundraising assistance. Nonincumbent Senate candidates are more likely than their House counterparts to hire professional consultants to manage their direct-mail and event-based individual and PAC solicitation programs.

Senate candidates raised on average of $4.1 million in large individual contributions in 2006—about 51 percent of their campaign resources (see Figure 6-7). Many of these donations came from out of state. Small individual contributions accounted for 16 percent of their resources, PACs for another 12 percent, and party contributions and coordinated expenditures for 5 percent. Party-connected contributions accounted for a mere 2 percent, reflecting the fact that there are fewer senators than House members to contribute to one another. The candidates themselves provided roughly 9 percent of the money spent directly in Senate campaigns. Compared with can-

FIGURE 6-7

Sources of Senate Candidates' Campaign Receipts in the 2006 Elections

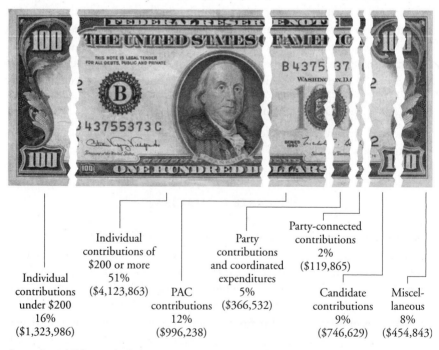

Individual contributions under $200
16%
($1,323,986)

Individual contributions of $200 or more
51%
($4,123,863)

PAC contributions
12%
($996,238)

Party contributions and coordinated expenditures
5%
($366,532)

Party-connected contributions
2%
($119,865)

Candidate contributions
9%
($746,629)

Miscellaneous
8%
($454,843)

Source: Compiled from Federal Election Commission and Center for Responsive Politics data.

Notes: See notes in Figure 6-4. *N* = 60.

didates for the House, candidates for the upper chamber rely more heavily on individuals and formal party organizations and less on PACs and their colleagues for their funding.

Party affiliation affects fundraising for the upper chamber of Congress less than it does for the lower chamber. However, Republican Senate candidates raised more PAC money in the 2006 elections than did the Democrats (see Table 6-4). The GOP's success in this regard was a result of their controlling the majority for the 108th and 109th congresses. Democrats raised more party money than did Republicans, largely as a result of their party's senatorial campaign committee's greater wealth. However, the Republicans were more than compensated by the candidate-to-candidate and leadership PAC contributions they collected from their colleagues.

Important similarities and differences exist among incumbent, challenger, and open-seat candidates. Senate open-seat candidates usually raise more money from every source than do challengers, and, compared to incumbents, they raise more from every source but PACs. The 2006 races exhibited these patterns almost perfectly except that the typical challenger donated more campaign funds than did the typical open-seat candidate. The proportion of funds collected from each source by all three sets of candidates shows many similarities. The major differences are that challengers and open-seat candidates rely substantially less on PAC dollars and depend more on their own resources than do incumbents, reflecting the fact that many access-oriented PACs prefer to support incumbents. Challengers also raise fewer individual contributions in amounts of $200 or more, also probably because their lower odds of winning discourage some access-oriented donors from backing their candidacies.

Incumbency provides members of the Senate with fundraising advantages. Senators, like House members, often begin their quest for reelection with significant sums left over from their previous campaigns and start raising money early. Seven senators each had more than $2 million prior to the start of the 2006 campaign season, and four had in excess of $3 million. Eleven senators scheduled to be up for reelection in 2008 had each raised more than $1 million by March 31, 2007. Sen. John Kerry, D-Mass., led the pack, with a war chest of almost $7.6 million.

Senators, like House members, are able to raise these large sums early because they have a great deal of political clout, which few challengers possess. For example, in 2006 Ohio senator Mike DeWine was able to use his membership on the Senate Appropriations Committee to raise $507,000 from finance, insurance, and real estate PACs and $1.6 million from individuals associated with these financial interests. In addition, PACs and individuals from

TABLE 6-4
Sources of Support for Senate Candidates in the 2006 Elections

	Party		Status			Competitiveness	
	Democrats	Republicans	Incumbents	Challengers	Open-seat candidates	Competitive	Uncompetitive
Individual contributions under $200	$1,648,901 (19%)	$999,072 (13%)	$1,575,243 (16%)	$1,015,740 (18%)	$1,580,437 (13%)	$1,533,313 (13%)	$1,184,435 (20%)
Individual contributions of $200 or more	$4,707,971 (53%)	$3,539,755 (46%)	$5,314,609 (55%)	$2,317,947 (42%)	$6,829,127 (58%)	$6,210,617 (54%)	$2,732,694 (46%)
PAC contributions	$861,444 (10%)	$1,141,400 (16%)	$1,552,802 (15%)	$288,971 (5%)	$967,132 (8%)	$1,263,742 (11%)	$782,234 (13%)
Party contributions and coordinated expenditures	$405,409 (5%)	$327,654 (4%)	$370,974 (4%)	$301,396 (5%)	$639,655 (5%)	$791,884 (7%)	$82,963 (1%)
Party-connected contributions	$142,185 (2%)	$261,982 (3%)	$206,393 (1%)	$146,724 (3%)	$356,484 (3%)	$320,303 (3%)	$103,515 (2%)
Candidate contributions	$616,274 (7%)	$876,983 (12%)	$273,533 (3%)	$1,229,497 (22%)	$702,648 (6%)	$752,133 (7%)	$742,959 (13%)
Miscellaneous	$438,000 (5%)	$472,982 (6%)	$563,695 (6%)	$238,087 (4%)	$723,658 (6%)	$660,039 (5%)	$290,687 (5%)

Source: Compiled from Federal Election Commission and Center for Responsive Politics data.

Notes: Figures are averages for general election candidates in major-party contested races. Candidate contributions include loans candidates made to their own campaigns. PAC contributions exclude contributions by leadership PACs. Party-connected contributions are made up of contributions from leadership PACs, candidates, retired members, and members of Congress not up for reelection in 2006. Miscellaneous sources include interest from savings accounts and revenues from investments. Some columns do not add to 100 percent because of rounding. *N*=60.

a variety of economic sectors that also had the potential to profit from legislation reported out of the Appropriations Committee invested several millions of dollars in DeWine's reelection campaign. PACs and individuals concerned with ensuring that people who receive appointments to the federal courts hold conservative positions on abortion, same-sex marriage, stem cell research, and other issues found DeWine a good target for their contributions. His membership on the Senate Judiciary Committee, which has a critical role in the Senate confirmation process, helped the incumbent raise more than $651,000 from these interests.[38]

SUMMARY

The campaign for resources is an important aspect of contemporary congressional elections. It requires candidates and campaign strategists to identify groups of sympathetic potential donors and fashion a pitch that will appeal to them. The campaign for resources is a campaign among unequals. Incumbent campaigns typically begin the election season with more money in the bank than challengers, who usually start fundraising much later. The levels of skill and resources that incumbents and challengers bring to bear on the fundraising process, including their prospects for success and political clout, also differ markedly. As a result, incumbents raise more money than challengers, and incumbents raise proportionately more funds from PACs and individuals interested in directly influencing the legislative process. Candidates for open seats typically raise about the same, if not slightly more, as incumbents, and open-seat candidates are more likely to wage campaigns that are financially competitive with that of their opponent. Nonincumbents who have significant political experience or who have assembled professional campaign organizations typically raise more money, especially from parties, members of Congress, other party leaders, and PACs than do amateur candidates who assemble unprofessional campaign organizations.

CHAPTER SEVEN

Campaign Strategy

The campaign for votes involves voter targeting, message development, communications, and mobilization. During the heyday of the parties, party organizations formulated and executed campaign strategies. Party leaders, candidates, and activists talked with neighbors to learn about their concerns, disseminated campaign communications to address those concerns, and turned out the vote on election day. The predisposition of voters to support their party's candidates was strong and frequently rewarded with government jobs, contracts, and other forms of patronage.

Contemporary campaigns also involve these aspects of campaigning. Successful candidates craft a message with broad appeal, set the agenda that defines voters' choices, and get their supporters to the polls on election day. In the years in which there is a presidential election, that contest dominates the news and greatly influences most people's thinking about politics. Candidates who stake out positions that correspond to the national political agenda often have an advantage over those who do not.

In this chapter I focus on how voters decide to cast their ballots in congressional elections and on the strategies and tactics that campaigns use to affect those decisions. The primary topics are voting behavior, strategy, public opinion research, voter targeting, and the message.

VOTING BEHAVIOR

Traditional democratic theory holds that citizens should make informed choices when voting in elections. It contends that they should be knowledgeable about the candidates, be aware of the major issues, and take the time to discern which candidate is more likely to represent their views and govern in the nation's best interests. The weight of the evidence, however, suggests that the vast majority of voters in congressional elections fall short of those expectations.[1]

Most voters make their congressional voting decisions on the basis of relatively little information. In a typical House contest between an incumbent and a challenger, for example, only about one in ten voters can recall the names of the two major-party candidates. In open-seat House contests, about 37 percent of all voters can remember both candidates' names.[2] Voters tend to possess more information about contestants in Senate elections: roughly one-third can recall the names of both candidates in contests involving an incumbent and a challenger, and about two-thirds can identify both candidates in open-seat races.[3]

When put to the less-stringent test of merely recognizing House candidates' names, about 60 percent of all voters recognize the names of both major-party contestants in incumbent-challenger races, and 80 percent recognize the names of both candidates in open-seat contests. The levels of name recognition are higher in Senate contests: roughly four out of five recognize the names of the incumbent and the challenger, and more than nine in ten recognize the names of candidates in open-seat races.[4] Thus, the name recognition test, which demands roughly the same minimal amount of knowledge from voters as does actually casting a ballot, shows that a substantial portion of the electorate lacks the information needed to make what might be referred to as "an informed vote choice."[5]

The inability to recall or recognize the candidates' names is indicative of the overall lack of substantive information in congressional elections. Most House election campaigns are low-key affairs that do not convey much information about the candidates' ideological orientations or policy positions.[6] Information on House challengers, most of whom wage underfunded campaigns, is usually scarce. Campaign communications, voters' assessments of the issues, and candidates' qualifications become important only in hard-fought contests.[7]

Incumbency and Voter Information

By and large, the candidates who suffer most from lack of voter interest are House challengers. Whereas nine out of ten voters recognize their House member's name, fewer than 60 percent usually recognize the name of the challenger. Incumbents tend to be viewed favorably. Typically more than half of the voters who recognize their representative's name indicate that they like something about that person; roughly one-third mention something they dislike. The corresponding figures for House challengers are 35 percent and 32 percent.[8] As the high reelection rate for House members indicates, the name recognition and voter approval levels of most incumbents are difficult for opponents to overcome. Only challengers who can overcome their "invisibility problem" and create a favorable image stand a chance of winning.

Senate challengers tend to be less handicapped by voter inattentiveness. They enjoy better name recognition because of their political experience, skill, superior campaign organizations, and greater campaign spending. The newsworthiness of their campaigns also attracts media attention and voter interest. Voters learn more about the ideological orientations and issue positions of Senate challengers than those of their House counterparts.[9] Even though the name recognition of Senate challengers is lower than the near-universal recognition enjoyed by Senate incumbents, it is high enough to make the typical incumbent-challenger race competitive. This helps explain why more electoral turnover occurs in the upper than in the lower chamber of Congress.

The inequalities in candidate information that characterize most incumbent-challenger races generally do not exist in open-seat contests. The major-party candidates in an open-seat race for a marginal seat begin the campaign with similar opportunities to increase their name recognition and convey their messages to voters. Because these contests are more competitive, they receive more press coverage, which helps both candidates become better known to voters. Thus more voters make informed choices in open-seat races than in incumbent-challenger contests.

Voting Decisions

Given their lack of knowledge of the candidates and issues, how do most voters make a decision on election day? Only those voters who know something about the background, political qualifications, party affiliation, and issue stances of both candidates are in a position to sift through the information, weigh the benefits of voting for one candidate over another, and cast their ballots in accordance with classical democratic theory.[10]

Nevertheless, voters who fall short of that ideal level of awareness may respond to the campaign information that candidates and the news media disseminate. Competitive, high-intensity elections that fill the airwaves, newspapers, and voters' mailboxes with campaign information provide some voters, especially those with an interest in politics, with enough information to form summary judgments about the candidates, which they tend to rely on when deciding which candidate to support.[11]

In the absence of spirited, high-intensity elections, most voters use "voting cues"—shortcuts that enable them to cast a ballot without engaging in a lengthy decision-making process. The most frequently used voting cue is incumbency. Knowing only an incumbent's name is sufficient for an individual to cast an adequately informed vote, some scholars argue.[12] Reasoning that the incumbent should be held accountable for the government's performance, the state of the economy, the nation's foreign involvements, or other issues, these voters quickly determine whether to support the status quo and vote for the incumbent or to advocate change and cast their ballot for the challenger.

Other voters pin the responsibility for the state of the nation on the president. When these voters are satisfied with how things are being run in Washington, they support the congressional candidate who belongs to the president's party. When they are dissatisfied with the state of the nation's affairs, as in 1994 and 2006, they vote for the candidate whose party does not occupy the White House. The connection between presidential and congressional voting can help a congressional candidate when a popular president is running for reelection, but belonging to the president's party usually has more harmful than beneficial effects in midterm elections.[13] Belonging to the party that has the majority in the House or Senate also can help or harm a congressional candidate.[14] The party cue, like the incumbency cue, enables voters to make retrospective voting choices without having much knowledge about the candidates or their issue positions. Under conditions of unified government, party cues are stronger because voters can more readily assign credit or blame for the state of the nation to the party that controls both the executive and legislative branches.[15] The power-sharing arrangements of divided government, in contrast, obscure political responsibility because they enable politicians to blame others in power.

The party cue also enables voters to speculate about a candidate's ideological orientation and issue positions. Republicans are generally identified as more conservative than Democrats and are associated with free-market economics, deregulation, lower taxes, traditional family values, hawkish foreign policy, and the wealthier elements of society. Most Republicans profess to be for limited government, and some campaign as though they are antigovernment. Democrats are often viewed as the party of government. They are associated with greater economic intervention; the social safety net; environmental protection; public education; acceptance of alternative lifestyles; a more dovish foreign policy; and protecting the interests of senior citizens, minorities, the poor, and working people. Some voters project the parties' images onto candidates and use those projections to guide their congressional voting decisions.[16] Others habitually support a party's nominees regardless of their credentials, issue positions, or opponents.

Partisanship and incumbency can affect the voting decisions of people who possess even less political information than the individuals described above.

The voting behavior of people who go to the polls out of a sense of civic responsibility or habit, and who lack much interest in or knowledge about politics, can in many ways be equated with the behavior of shoppers at a supermarket. Individuals in both situations select a product—either a consumer good or a congressional candidate—with relatively little information. Except for first-time shoppers and newly enfranchised voters, the individuals have made similar selections before. Previous decisions and established preferences often strongly influence their current decisions. Shoppers, lacking a good reason to try a new product, such as a sale or a two-for-one giveaway, are likely to purchase the same brand-name product that they previously purchased. Voters are likely to cast a ballot for the candidates or party that they supported in previous elections.[17] If a voter recognizes one candidate's name, which is almost always the incumbent's, that candidate usually gets the individual's vote. If the voter recognizes neither candidate but tends to be favorably predisposed toward one party, then most often the person votes for that party's candidate. Situations in which voters have little information, then, usually work to the advantage of incumbents and of candidates who belong to the district's or state's dominant party.

However, if the recognized candidate or favored party is associated with scandal or a domestic or foreign policy failure, many relatively uninformed voters, as well as some who are informed, break old habits and cast their ballots against that candidate or party, or they may not vote at all. During the elections of the 1990s, for example, many challengers, with the support of Washington-based party committees and interest groups, sought to make control of Congress itself a major campaign issue. That strategy is credited with enabling the Republicans to take over Congress in 1994 and end forty uninterrupted years of Democratic control of the House. Attacking the performance of Congress and the Bush administration also was a major tactic for many in 2006. It is credited with enabling Democratic candidates to wrest control over Congress back from the GOP. Regardless of which party has been in control, attacking Congress has contributed to the electoral success of many challengers, and some incumbents, for much of recent history.

VOTERS AND CAMPAIGN STRATEGY

Candidates and political consultants generally do not plan election campaigns on the basis of abstract political theories, but they do draw on a body of knowledge about how people make their voting decisions. Politicians' notions about voting behavior have some ideas in common with the findings of scholarly research. Among them are the following: (1) most voters have only limited information about the candidates, their ideologies, and the issues; (2) voters are generally more familiar with and favorably predisposed toward incumbents than they are toward challengers; and (3) voters tend to cast their ballots in ways that reflect their party identification or previous voting behavior. Candidates and consultants also believe that a campaign sharply focused on issues can be used to motivate supporters to show up at the polls and to win the support of undecided voters. They try to set the campaign agenda so that the issues that politically informed voters use as a basis for casting their ballots are the most attractive issues for their candidate.

Politicians' and consultants' beliefs account for some of the differences among the campaigns waged by incumbents, challengers, and open-seat candidates, as well as many of the differences between House and Senate campaigns. Generally, members of Congress use strategies that capitalize on the advantages of incumbency. They discuss the services and the federal projects they have delivered to their constituencies.[18] They focus on elements of their public persona that have helped make them popular with constituents and draw on strategies that they have used successfully in previous campaigns.[19]

Some incumbents capitalize on their advantages in name recognition and voter approval by virtually ignoring their opponents. They deluge the district with direct mail, e-mail, radio advertisements, television commercials, yard signs, or other communications that make no mention of their opponent, so as to minimize the attention the challenger gets from the local media and voters. An alternative strategy is to take advantage of a challenger's relative invisibility by attacking his or her qualifications, performance while holding a prior office, or issue positions early in the campaign. Incumbents who succeed in defining their opponents leave them in the unenviable position of being invisible to most voters and negatively perceived by others. Republican incumbent Wally Herger's campaign pursued the former strategy, treating Democratic challenger A. J. Sekhon as if his candidacy would have no impact on the outcome of their 2006 California House race. The campaign waged by GOP senator Mike DeWine in Ohio used the latter strategy, airing TV ads criticizing some of Sherrod Brown's votes in the House of Representatives on issues related to homeland security and taxes.

House challengers are in the least enviable position of any candidates. Not only are they less well known and less experienced, but they are also without the campaign resources of their opponents. To win, challengers must force their way into voters' consciousness and project a message that will give voters a reason to cast a ballot for a little-known commodity.

Many challengers try to make the election a referendum on some negative aspect of the incumbent's performance. They portray the incumbent as incompetent, corrupt, an extreme ideologue, or out of touch with the district. They magnify the impact of any unpopular policy or scandal with which the incumbent can be associated. Challengers often try to link the current officeholder to unpopular policies or trends and present themselves as agents of change, often using negative or comparative ads to do so. The goals of this approach are twofold: first, to win the backing of undecided voters and individuals who previously had voted for the incumbent, and second, to discourage the incumbent's supporters from going to the polls.

Without the advantages of an incumbent or the disadvantages of a challenger, both candidates in an open-seat race face the challenge of making themselves familiar to voters and becoming associated with themes and issues that will attract electoral support. Both also have the opportunity to define their opponent. Some open-seat candidates seek to define themselves and their opponent on the basis of issues or their previous performance in some other office. Others, particularly those running in districts that favor their party, emphasize partisan or ideological cues. Both candidates for the House in Colorado's 7th district used a variety of means to set the agenda and define their opponent. The Democrat, Ed Perlmutter, proclaimed himself the candidate for change. He tried to define opponent Rick O'Donnell as an extremist because O'Donnell had advocated eliminating Social Security, in a paper he wrote for a Washington think tank, and also advocated that seventeen-year-old boys skip their last semester of high school to guard the U.S.-Mexico border. Perlmutter also frequently linked O'Donnell to President Bush. O'Donnell tried to present himself as a man of the people, deriding Perlmutter as a politician, dishonest, and a hypocrite on the issue of renewable energy. Perlmutter was the more successful of the two candidates in framing the debate and creating more positive associations for himself among voters.[20]

GAUGING PUBLIC OPINION

Campaigns use many different instruments to take the public's pulse. Election returns from previous contests are analyzed to locate pockets of potential strength or weakness. Geodemographic analysis enables campaigns to identify individuals who voted in previous elections and classify them according to their gender, age, ethnicity, race, religion, occupation, and economic background. By combining geodemographic information with polling data and election returns, campaigns are able to identify potential supporters and formulate messages that will appeal to them. Increasingly, candidates' campaign organizations have gone door to door to discern whether those voters are indeed supporters and to learn how they can be motivated to vote for their candidate. With the assistance of party committees and some interest groups, some have employed lists developed through microtargeting. These approaches, discussed in Chapter 4, enable campaigns to concentrate their efforts on supporters or persuadable voters.

Polls are among the most common means of gauging public opinion. Virtually every Senate campaign and roughly seven out of ten House campaigns take at least one poll to learn about voters. Benchmark polls, which are taken early in the election season, inform candidates about the issue positions, partisanship, and initial voting preferences of people living in their state or district. House campaigns commonly commission benchmarks a year prior to the election, and Senate candidates have been known to commission them as early as three years before election day. Benchmark polls also measure the levels of name recognition and support that the candidates and their opponents or prospective opponents enjoy. They help campaigns learn about the types of candidates voters prefer, the types of messages likely to attract support, and to whom they should direct specific campaign communications.

Campaigns also use benchmark polls to generate support. Challenger and open-seat candidates disseminate favorable benchmarks to attract media coverage and the support of campaign volunteers and contributors. Incumbents typically publicize benchmarks to discourage potential challengers. When poll results show a member of Congress to be in trouble, however, the incumbent quietly uses them to convince parties, PACs, and other potential contributors that he or she needs extra help to win.

Trend polls are taken intermittently throughout the campaign season to discover changes in voters' attitudes. Some senators use them to chart their public approval throughout their six-year term. These polls are more narrowly focused than are benchmarks. They feature detailed questions designed to reveal whether a campaign has been successful in getting voters to associate its candidate with a specific issue or theme. Trend polls help campaigns determine whether they have been gaining or losing ground with particular segments of the electorate. They can reassure a campaign that its strategy is working or indicate that a change in message is needed.

Whereas trend and benchmark polls present "snapshots" of public opinion, tracking polls provide campaigns with a "motion picture" overview. Tracking polls typically ask samples of 150 to 200 voters per night to discuss their reactions to a few key advertisements, issue statements, or campaign events. The interviews are pooled and used to calculate rolling averages based on the responses from the three most recent nights. Changes in rolling averages can be used to reformulate a campaign's final appeals. Because tracking polls are expensive, most House campaigns wait until the last three weeks of the campaign to use them.

Candidates may supplement their polling with focus groups. Focus groups usually consist of one to two dozen participants and a professional facilitator, who meet for two to three hours. The participants are selected not to be a scientifically representative sample but to represent segments of the population whose support the campaign needs to reinforce or attract. Campaigns use focus groups to learn how voters can be expected to respond to different messages or to pretest actual campaign advertisements. Some high-priced consultants, such as Wirthlin Worldwide, a prominent Republican firm, employ computerized audience response techniques to obtain a precise record of how focus group participants react to specific portions of campaign advertisements.[21] These techniques enable an analyst to plot onto the ad itself a line that represents the participants' reactions, pinpointing exactly which portions the participants liked or disliked. Focus group research is useful in fine-tuning the visuals and narratives in television communications.

Finally, candidates learn about public opinion through a variety of approaches that do not require the services of public opinion experts. Newspaper, magazine, radio, and television news stories provide information about voters' positions on major issues. Exchanges with local party leaders, journalists, political activists, and voters can also help candidates get a sense of the public mood. Blogs have been used increasingly to learn about, and influence the views of, politically engaged, computer-savvy voters.

When asked about the significance of different forms of information, House candidates and campaign aides typically rank direct contact with voters first, indicating that they consider it very important to extremely important (see Table 7-1). Voter contact is followed by public opinion polls, which are generally considered moderately helpful to very helpful in learning about voters' opinions. News stories come next, followed by discussions with local party activists and mail from voters. Although their role is bigger than those of PACs and other interest groups, national party officials and the materials they publish are less important than local information sources.

Incumbents and candidates for open seats make greater use of surveys than do challengers. Candidates in competitive contests of all types make greater use of them than do those in lopsided races. Challengers, and open-seat candidates in one-sided contests, often cannot afford to buy polls and must rely heavily on news reports, party publications, and the advice of national party leaders. Incumbents, who are often sensitized to issues by the constituent mail that floods their offices, value letters as a significant indicator of public sentiment more than other candidates do. Incumbents in safe seats show a greater

TABLE 7-1

Campaigners' Perceptions of the Importance of Different Sources
of Information for Gauging Public Opinion in House Campaigns

		Incumbents		Challengers		Open-seat candidates	
	All	In jeopardy	Shoo-ins	Hope-fuls	Likely losers	Pros-pects	Mis-matched
Candidate contact with voters	4.37	4.23	4.41	4.44	4.44	4.16	4.59
Public opinion surveys	3.53	4.23	3.54	3.68	2.88	3.96	3.09
Newspaper, radio, TV	3.05	2.69	3.13	3.08	3.27	2.86	3.17
Local party activists	2.63	2.78	2.74	2.69	2.41	2.45	2.80
Mail from voters	2.45	2.65	3.43	2.19	1.99	2.00	2.29
National party publications	2.28	1.83	1.96	2.39	2.75	2.12	2.65
National party leaders	2.14	1.80	1.94	2.31	2.32	2.20	2.30

Source: The 1992 Congressional Campaign Study, Center for American Politics and Citizenship, University of Maryland.

Notes: Candidates and campaign aides were asked to assess the importance of each source on the following scale: 1 = not important or not used; 2 = slightly important; 3 = moderately important; 4 = very important; 5 = extremely important. The values listed are the arithmetic means of the scores. Figures are for major-party candidates in contested general elections, excluding a small number of atypical races. $N = 325$.

preference than others for learning about public opinion through the mail and other forms of unmediated voter contact.

VOTER TARGETING

Campaigns are not designed to reach everyone. Targeting involves categorizing different groups of voters, identifying their political preferences, and designing appeals to which they are likely to respond. Targeting is the foundation of virtually every aspect of campaign strategy. Candidates and campaign managers consider many factors when devising targeting strategies, including the underlying partisan and candidate loyalties of the groups that reside in the district, the size and turnout levels of those groups, and the types of issues and appeals that will attract their support.[22] Using this information, they formulate a strategy designed to build a winning coalition.

Partisanship is the number-one consideration in the voter targeting of most campaigns. It subsumes all other factors. Almost one-half of all campaigns focus on individuals who identify with their party, independent voters, or both (see Table 7-2). About 2 percent of campaigns primarily target voters who identify with the opposing party. The campaigns of former Republican representative Constance Morella, who represented Maryland's strongly Democratic-leaning 8th district, are an example of those. Morella was able to hold her seat for eight terms by building bipartisan support. Like many incumbents, she routinely sent letters of congratulation to constituents who had recently registered to vote in her district. Unlike most other incumbents, however, she often sent letters to voters who had registered in the opposing party, in this case as Democrats.[23]

TABLE 7-2

Partisan Component of Targeting Strategies in House Campaigns

		Incumbents		Challengers		Open-seat candidates	
	All	In jeopardy	Shoo-ins	Hope-fuls	Likely losers	Pros-pects	Mis-matched
Own party	9%	17%	9%	9%	7%	9%	17%
Opposing party	2	—	1	6	2	—	—
Independents	3	3	1	3	5	—	6
Both parties	2	—	—	—	2	3	6
Own party and independents	36	35	43	38	30	40	39
Opposing party and independents	2	7	—	3	2	3	5
All voters	45	38	46	41	50	43	28
Did not target	1	—	—	—	2	3	—

Source: The 2002 Congressional Campaign Study, Center for American Politics and Citizenship, University of Maryland.

Notes: Figures are for general election candidates in major-party contested races, excluding those in incumbent-versus-incumbent races. — = less than 0.5 percent. Some columns do not add to 100 percent because of rounding. $N = 320$.

Campaigns by challengers are the most likely to target voters who identify with the opposing party. Many of these candidates recognize that the one-sidedness of their district makes it impossible for them to compete without winning some of the opposing party's supporters. For example, as a Democratic challenger, Heath Shuler made many appeals to war veterans, most of whom are Republicans, in his successful race against incumbent Charles Taylor in North Carolina's 11th district. Some challengers do not have the resources to carry out even a basic, party-oriented targeting strategy. Lacking a poll or a precinct-by-precinct breakdown of where Republican, Democratic, and independent voters live, some amateurs resort to unorthodox strategies, such as focusing on the precincts that had the highest turnout in the previous election.

Other factors that campaigns consider when designing targeting strategies include demography and issues. Sixty-two percent of all House campaigns target demographic, geographic, or occupational groups: 53 percent concentrate on specific ethnic, racial, religious, gender, or age groups; 4 percent focus on counties, suburbs, cities, or other geographic locations; and 5 percent target union members, blue-collar workers, small-business owners, or voters involved in particular industries.[24] Issues and political attitudes, including intention to vote and partisanship, are central to the targeting strategies of roughly 36 percent of all campaigns.

Group-oriented and issue- or attitude-oriented targeting strategies offer campaigns distinct advantages. The group-oriented, or geodemographic, approach is based on the idea that there are identifiable segments of the population whose support the campaign needs to attract and that specific communications can be tailored to win that support. Just as soliciting money from a readily identifiable fundraising constituency is important in the campaign for resources, communicating a message to identifiable groups of supporters and undecided voters is important in the campaign for votes. Group-based targeting strategies emphasize different aspects of the campaign's message depending on the intended audience for a particular campaign advertisement. By tailoring their messages to attract the votes of specific population groups, the campaigns hope to build a winning coalition. In recent years, many campaigns have stressed the effect of the economy on children and families in literature mailed to women, whereas they emphasized tax cuts and economic growth issues in literature sent to business executives and upper-class and upper-middle-class voters. Tailoring messages to particular groups can help persuade some group members to support a candidate and boost the group's turnout.[25]

Candidates focus on many groups, reflecting the diverse segments of the population that the two major parties represent, especially the Democrats.[26] More Democrats than Republicans target women, racial and ethnic minorities, and senior citizens; Democratic candidates target senior citizens more than any other segment of the population. More Republicans focus on frequent churchgoers.[27] The 2006 contest between Perlmutter and O'Donnell gives some insight into the dynamics of targeting. Perlmutter and his allies anticipated winning support from the Democratic base and independents, and they focused much of their efforts on Democratic women who had voted in only one of the three previous elections, Republican women domiciled with Democratic men, Hispanics, and African Americans. O'Donnell also aggressively courted Republican women (and GOP voters generally), swing voters, and Hispanics.[28] An overlap of targets is typical of a close election because both campaigns go after the same swing voters.

The issue- or attitude-oriented strategy is based on the premise that issues and ideas should drive the campaign. Campaigns that target on the basis of specific policies or a broad ideology, such as conservatism or progressivism, hope to win the support of single-issue or ideological voters who favor those positions. In many cases, one or two specific issues are emphasized to attract the support of swing voters whose ballots a candidate believes will be a deciding factor in the election outcome. Some candidates target pro-life or pro-choice voters, believing their ballots will be decisive. Others target pro-environment or anti–gun control voters. Republicans who employ such strategies focus mainly on voters who are concerned about moral values, taxes, the size of government, government regulation, and crime. Democrats who use them focus on voters who care about public education, jobs, the environment, health care, and the protections and services that government provides for the elderly, children, and underprivileged groups. In 2006, Republicans also targeted voters especially concerned about national security, and the Democrats focused on constituencies who were upset about the Iraq War, corruption in government, and the failures of the Republican-controlled Congress and the Bush administration. In 2006, in California's 2nd congressional district, Sekhon focused on veterans' issues, inequities in the tax code, and the failure of Republican leadership at home and abroad. Herger concentrated on the war on terror, illegal immigration, and reforming Social Security, Medicare, and other government entitlement programs.[29]

Targeting strategies based on issues or voter attitudes lend themselves better to the communication of a coherent campaign message than group-oriented strategies. They are especially effective at mobilizing single-issue voters and political activists who have strong ideological predispositions. But they run the risk of alienating moderate voters who agree with the candidate on most policy matters but disagree on the issues the campaign has chosen to emphasize. Campaigns waged by policy amateurs and ideologues are the most likely to suffer from this problem. Often these candidates become boxed in by their own message, are labeled "ultra-liberals" or "right wingers" by their opponents, and ultimately lose.

Incumbents target demographic, geographic, and occupational groups more than challengers and open-seat candidates do. Most incumbents have a detailed knowledge of the voting blocs that supported them in the past and target constituents who belong to those groups. Many challengers, especially those unable to mount competitive campaigns, do not have this information. Lacking good voter files, and recognizing that they need to peel away some of their opponent's supporters, they target on the basis of issues.[30]

THE MESSAGE

A candidate's message gives substance to a campaign. It helps to shape the political agenda, mobilize backers, and win votes. In a well-run campaign, the same coherent message pervades every aspect of the candidate's communications—from paid television advertisements to impromptu remarks. Campaign messages can be an essential ingredient for victory in close elections because they activate supporters and strongly influence the decisions of persuadable voters.

Campaign messages rely heavily on imagery. The most successful campaigns weave the candidate's persona and policy stances into thematic messages.[31] These form the core of the image the candidate seeks to project. According to Joel Bradshaw, president of the Democratic consulting firm Campaign Design Group, good campaign messages are clear and easy to communicate, are short, convey a sense of emotional urgency, reflect voters' perceptions of political reality, establish clear differences between the candidate and the opponent, and are credible.[32]

The precise mix of personal characteristics, issues, and broad themes that candidates project depends on their political views, the groups they target, and the messages that they anticipate their opponents will communicate. Good strategic positioning results in the transmission of a message that most voters will find appealing; when both candidates achieve this result, an election becomes what strategists refer to as a "battle for the middle ground."[33] In designing a message, campaign decision makers consider a variety of factors, which J. Toscano, of the Democratic media firm Greer, Margolis, Mitchell, and Burns, refers to as "the five Cs of strategy": commitments on issues that drive votes; competence, as exhibited by the candidate's professional accomplishments; cultural connections that "shortcut" voters' need for information; a core message that describes what drives the candidate, often exemplified by the candidate's personal experiences; and contrast with opponents to foster a clear choice.[34] Ladonna Lee, a leading Republican political strategist, emphasizes the importance of consistency.[35] The different components of the message must add up to a coherent public image. Otherwise, a campaign's communications will get lost in an environment that is saturated by commercial advertisers that spend billions every year finding new, interesting, and entertaining ways to engage audiences.

Campaigns endeavor to create a favorable image for their candidates by identifying them with decency, loyalty, honesty, hard work, and other cherished values.[36] Campaign communications interweave anecdotes about a candidate's personal accomplishments, professional success, family, or ability to overcome humble origins to portray him or her as the living embodiment of the American dream—someone whom voters should be proud to have represent them in Washington. Campaigns frequently emphasize elements of their candidate's persona that point to an opponent's weakness. In 2006, many veterans used their military experience to increase the credibility of their positions on the Iraq War and raise questions about the qualifications of their opponents on this key voting issue.

Incumbents frequently convey image-oriented messages. They seek to reinforce or expand their base of support by concentrating on those aspects of their persona that make them popular with constituents.[37] Their messages convey images of competent, caring individuals who work tirelessly in Washington to improve the lives of the folks back home they represent. Incumbents' campaign communications often describe how they have helped constituents resolve problems, brought federal programs and projects to the district, and introduced or cosponsored popular legislation. Some discuss their efforts to prevent a military base or factory from closing. Those whose districts have experienced the ravages of floods, earthquakes, riots, or other disasters almost always highlight their roles in bringing federal relief to victims.

Many challengers and open-seat contestants also seek to portray themselves as caring, hard working, and experienced. Nonincumbents who have held elective office frequently contrast their accomplishments with those of their opponent. During the elections held at the turn of the century, many challengers who were state legislators blamed their opponents for contributing to the federal deficit, while pointing to their own budget-cutting efforts.

Political amateurs usually discuss their successes in the private sector, seeking to make a virtue of their lack of political experience. Many blame the "mess in Washington" on the "career politicians" and discuss how someone who has succeeded in the private sector is needed to make government work for the people again. Still, a challenger who focuses on experience rarely wins. As one consultant explained, "By virtue of their being the current officeholder, an incumbent can 'out-experience' a challenger to death."

Issues

Most House candidates and campaign aides maintain that the bulk of their messages focus on policy concerns rather than the candidate's personality, a claim borne out by examinations of their campaign materials.[38] More than half of all House campaigns make issues—either their own issue positions or their opponents'—the primary focus of their message; 44 percent, mostly incumbent campaigns, emphasize candidate imagery (see Table 7-3). Challengers and open-seat candidates run the most issue-oriented campaigns, reflecting the belief that taking policy stances is a useful way to draw support away from their opponents. Challengers run the most opposition-oriented campaigns. They point to incumbents' ethical lapses, congressional roll-call votes that are not in accord with constituents' views, or federal policies that have harmed local voters or the national interest. About 24 percent of all challengers try to make their opponent or their opponent's actions in office a defining campaign issue. A few incumbents holding marginal seats respond in kind by pointing to unpopular aspects of their challenger's background or policy stances. Twelve

TABLE 7-3

Major Focus of Advertising in House Campaigns

		Incumbents		Challengers		Open-seat candidates	
	All	In jeopardy	Shoo-ins	Hope-fuls	Likely losers	Pros-pects	Mis-matched
Candidate's image	39%	54%	58%	31%	22%	44%	50%
Candidate's issue positions	47	42	39	31	59	44	44
Opponent's image	5	—	1	6	9	6	6
Opponent's issue positions	9	4	1	31	11	6	—

Source: The 2002 Congressional Campaign Study, Center for American Politics and Citizenship, University of Maryland.

Notes: Figures are for general election candidates in major-party contested races, excluding those in incumbent-versus-incumbent races. — = less than 0.5 percent. Some columns do not add to 100 percent because of rounding. *N* = 308.

percent of open-seat candidates in close contests also make their opponent the central focus of their message.

Almost all candidates take policy stands that identify them with "valence" issues, which are policies that are universally viewed in a favorable light. They include a strong economy, job creation, domestic tranquility, and national security. Some make these the centerpiece of their campaign. They either ignore or soft-pedal "positional" issues (sometimes referred to as "wedge" issues), which have two or more sides.[39] When both candidates campaign mainly on valence issues, the dialogue can be like a debate between the nearly identical Tweedledee and Tweedledum. That would be unusual, as most candidates select policy positions associated with their party and so are on opposing sides on most issues.[40]

When candidates communicate dissimilar stands on positional issues, political debate becomes more meaningful. Issues such as illegal immigration, the economy, taxes, gun control, crime, abortion, and civil rights have for several years had the potential to draw the attention of voters and affect elections. Health care, environmental issues, and social entitlement programs also have the ability to influence elections. During the 2006 elections, the war in Iraq, political scandals, and the failures of the federal government were important.

Challengers are especially likely to benefit from emphasizing positional issues. By stressing points of disagreement between themselves and the incumbent, challengers can help their image crystallize, attract media attention, and strip away some of their opponent's support.[41] Incumbents may not derive the same electoral benefits from running on positional issues because they are usually evaluated in personal terms.[42] Candidates who campaign on positional issues hope to attract the support of ideological voters or to overcome some weakness in their image. Some liberal Democrats emphasize crime fighting or their war records to project "tougher" images. Some conservative Republicans discuss health care to show their compassionate side. Both groups of candidates seek to convince the voters that they share their concerns.

Candidates try to anticipate the issues their opponents will emphasize before taking a strong policy stance. Candidates who run against police officers rarely mount "law-and-order" campaigns because of the obvious disparities in credibility between themselves and their opponents on crime-related issues.[43] Sherrod Brown is an example of a candidate who would have been at a disadvantage had he sought to focus on street crime, as Mike DeWine had worked as a county prosecutor before running for Congress. Instead, Brown made scant mention of the subject.

Perlmutter focused on a variety of issues that traditionally favor Democratic candidates. On health care, he championed stem cell research; on the environment, he called for more advances in renewable energy; he also made clear his support for abortion rights. O'Donnell focused on issues that typically work to the advantage of his party, including border security, taxes, and supporting the military. Both candidates discussed government fiscal responsibility.[44] Although that is an issue traditionally associated with the GOP, it has become increasingly available to Democrats as a result of the rising federal deficits under the Reagan and Bush administrations.[45]

Brown made improving the situation of middle-class Americans the central theme of his campaign. He ran television ads that indicated his support for increasing the minimum wage, stem cell research, tightening U.S. borders, and a balanced budget amendment and on other issues. Regardless of the combination of issues discussed in the ad, or whether it was positive or negative, his ads always ended with the candidate stating, "It's time to put the middle class first." DeWine's campaign communications were not as tightly structured around one message. His ads emphasized his support for programs for children, seniors, the military, firefighters, and others, but they did not present a consistent theme or identifying phrase. As a result, at least one political observer commented that "DeWine looks like an incumbent in search of a message."[46]

Candidates who learn that their opponent is vulnerable on a salient issue generally make it a major focus of the campaign to try to win the support of independents or pry voters from their opponent's camp. Democrats and some moderate Republicans lure women's votes by making abortion rights a major part of their campaign platforms. Democrats who adopt this position during presidential election years typically receive the added benefit of being able to coordinate their message with their party's presidential campaign. Divisions within the Republican Party have made abortion an issue to avoid for GOP candidates from the Northeast and other less-conservative areas. Women who run against men are the most likely to campaign as pro-choice and discuss women's concerns, and those who campaign on these issues and target women voters enjoy greater electoral success.[47] Nevertheless, some male candidates, like Perlmutter and Brown, also stake out pro–abortion rights positions to attract the support of women and liberal voters.

Economic issues—inflation, unemployment, taxes, jobs, the federal budget, or the national deficit—have been the number-one concern of voters in most elections since the Great Depression. Virtually all candidates make some aspect of the economy part of their campaign message. Democratic candidates often discuss the economy as a fairness issue. In 2006, many linked federal trade policies to the loss of manufacturing jobs and the federal deficit. Some also discussed the increased tax burdens that Bush administration policies placed on the middle class and the tax breaks Republicans gave to wealthy Americans. Many also chastised Republicans for proposing to cut popular social safety net programs to give a tax break to the rich.

Republican candidates usually focus on economic growth and the deficit. Throughout the 1980s and early 1990s they sought to blame the economic woes of the country on wasteful government subsidies, excessive regulation, and profligate pork-barrel spending approved by the Democratic-controlled Congress. Their message gained supporters in 1994, as Republican candidates proclaimed tax cuts the crown jewel of their vaunted Contract with America.[48] More recently, Republican arguments for tax cuts have lost much of their persuasiveness as a result of public perceptions that GOP tax cuts do little to improve the situations of the middle class and less-well-off Americans.[49]

Political reform also has been an important issue for both Democrats and Republicans, reflecting the anti-Washington mood of the country. Many House challengers raise corruption in government or campaign finance reform as campaign issues, frequently contrasting their reform positions with their opponent's vote for a congressional pay raise, taking junkets at the expense of wealthy lobbyists, or dependence on PAC contributions. Incumbents address political reform differently. Some seek to defend Congress, whereas others try to impress upon voters that they are part of the solution and not the problem. One House member said he "neutralized" the reform issue by arguing that he "was constructively working to improve government from the inside, while [his opponent] was content to merely lob stones from a distance." Another popular incumbent strategy is to campaign for reelection to Congress by attacking the institution itself.[50]

Most candidates prefer themselves, not their opponents, to be the ones whom voters associate with valence issues, but candidates can also find it profitable to take strong stands on positional issues. That is especially true when their stances are welcomed by voters in their district or occupy a prominent place on the national agenda. The national campaign agenda in 2006 featured several domestic policy debates that enabled the candidates to take opposing sides.[51] Perhaps the most powerful debate was about government corruption and mismanagement as they related to congressional scandals and the federal response to Hurricane Katrina. Other prominent domestic policy debates involved immigration reform; the environment; stem cell research, abortion, and other so-called moral issues; the loss of manufacturing jobs and the increasing gap between the rich and the middle class; and social safety net issues, such as health care and prescription drug affordability, Medicare, and Social Security. There was some debate over homeland security, but the Republicans did not enjoy the same advantages they did in the 2002 and 2004 elections for a

number of reasons, including growing concern about the war in Iraq and un-
ease over warrantless government eavesdropping on telephone conversations
and e-mails.

Partisanship, incumbency, and geography are critical in determining
whether a candidate makes an issue a priority in the campaign, as well as the
position he or she takes on it.[52] Most candidates' issue priorities and substantive issue positions dovetail with those of their party's core voters. Thus in
2006 more Democratic candidates focused on corruption and government
mismanagement, the Iraq War, and issues related to the middle-class squeeze
and the social safety net. More Republican candidates, on the other hand,
sought to make the war on terrorism, traditional values, and taxes the central
issues. More incumbents of both parties, but especially Republicans, focused
on terrorism. Elected officials are notorious for capitalizing on the stature that
comes with holding office and "wrapping themselves in the flag" during times
of crisis. Geography and local political culture also are important. Candidates
from the Midwest, home of the nation's declining automobile industry, were
somewhat more likely to focus on job loss and the economy, as were candidates running in the South and Northeast, which have lost jobs in textiles and
other manufacturing industries. By focusing on these issues, the candidates
tried to tap into the job insecurities and frustrations of voters. Regional differences on these issues show that geography still matters in congressional campaign politics. Locally reinforced policy divisions pose considerable obstacles
to the nationalization of congressional elections.

Partisanship, Populism, and Progressivism

Candidates who run in districts made up overwhelmingly of people who identify with their party normally emphasize partisan themes and messages. They
frequently mention their party in speeches and campaign literature. They all are
required by the Bipartisan Campaign Reform Act of 2002 to include "authori-
zation lines," stating who approved the message, somewhere in their television
or radio advertisements. Campaigns that are run in "hostile" or divided districts
typically use nonpartisan strategies, avoiding mention of party affiliation.

Progressive strategies have become increasingly popular with Democrats
who run as agents of change. These candidates avoid the term *liberal* because
voters associate it with government regulations and high taxes, which are unpopular.[53] They instead choose to call themselves "progressives" or "new"
Democrats.

Many candidates of both parties use populist strategies. Republican populists, like Herger of California, rail against the government, taxes, and special

interests in Washington, even when they are in control of the government. Democratic populists also champion the cause of ordinary Americans. Rather than oppose big government, however, these candidates run against big business. For example, Democrat Byron Dorgan, who was elected North Dakota's at-large representative in 1980 and its junior senator in 1992, earned his populist credentials when, as state tax commissioner, he sued out-of-state corporations doing business in North Dakota to force them to pay taxes there.[54] Running campaigns based on populism has served Dorgan well, as he has served in Congress for roughly three decades.

Negative Campaigning

Negative campaigning has always been, and will probably always be, a part of U.S. elections. Just as positive campaigning attempts to build up a candidate, negative campaigning endeavors to tear down an opponent. Negative campaigning can be a legitimate form of campaign communication that has the potential to increase voter knowledge and otherwise enhance the electoral process. Campaign ads that question a candidate's qualifications or point to unpopular, wasteful, or unethical practices bring a measure of accountability to the political system.[55] Still, much negative campaigning amounts to little more than character assassination and mudslinging. Whether negative campaigning turns off voters and discourages them from participating in elections, thereby demobilizing a portion of the electorate, or captures voters' attention and stimulates voter turnout, thus serving to mobilize the electorate, is of secondary concern to candidates.[56] What matters is that more of their supporters than their opponent's show up at the polls.

One or both candidates use negative campaigning in almost three-quarters of all House contests and virtually every Senate election. As election day approaches, the probability that someone will feature negative ads goes up.[57] The sense of urgency that pervades a close contest encourages the contestants to figuratively tar and feather each other because it is easier to discredit an opponent than to build loyalty.[58]

Attack ads can be an important component of challenger campaigns because they can help break voters of the habit of casting their ballots for the incumbent.[59] However, some incumbents have made negative advertising a central element of their strategies in recent years, using early attacks to define their challengers for voters before the challengers can define themselves.[60] Because of their competitiveness, open-seat campaigns tend to be the most negative of all.

The most effective negative ads are grounded in fact, document their sources, focus on some aspect of the opponent's policy views rather than personality, use ridicule, are delivered by a surrogate, and avoid discussing the plight of unfortunate citizens.[61] Many negative ads feature actors depicting incumbents voting themselves pay raises or attending lavish parties with lobbyists. Some use fancy graphics to show opponents literally "flip-flopping" when the ads discuss the issues. Ridicule is a powerful weapon in politics because it is difficult for people to vote for a candidate they have just laughed at. Campaign attacks that do not adhere to these guidelines tend to be less effective and can backfire, making the candidate who makes the charges look dishonest or mean-spirited.

The hazards of "crossing the line" with negative campaigning are something that the O'Donnell campaign learned the hard way. In early September, O'Donnell's campaign attacked Perlmutter for representing a life insurance company whose bankruptcy was financially damaging to elderly and disabled policyholders. A local media investigation of the charge, however, reported that Perlmutter had actually helped the people recover some of their funds. The O'Donnell campaign's failure to research their claim carefully resulted in an attack that was meant to undermine Perlmutter's credibility actually harming the credibility of their own candidate. That attack was one of several that raised questions about O'Donnell's trustworthiness during an election season when dishonesty and corruption in government were major issues.[62]

Opposition research provides the foundation for negative campaigning. Campaigns begin with a thorough examination of the opponent's personal and professional background. Current members of Congress are qualified to serve in the House or Senate by virtue of their incumbency, although the 2006 elections, which saw twenty-three House members and six Senators defeated, poignantly demonstrated that incumbency can also be used as a weapon against them. The backgrounds of challengers and open-seat candidates are often more open to question, especially if the candidate has no political experience or has pursued a career that most constituents would view with skepticism. Junk bond traders and dogcatchers, for example, are at risk of being labeled unqualified because of their professions.

The candidate's public record is the next thing that is usually explored. Challengers often study their opponent's attendance records, roll-call votes, and floor speeches. Incumbents and open-seat candidates usually study their opponent's political record. If an opponent has never held office, then a campaign will usually turn to newspaper or trade magazine accounts of speeches made to civic organizations, trade associations, or other groups.

Virtually all campaigns search for activities that can be construed as illegal or unethical. The 2006 elections provided some challengers with a mountain of dirt they could throw at their opponents. Some incumbents were vulnerable because of their own actions. They included Rep. Don Sherwood, R-Pa., who was accused of assaulting his mistress; Rep. Cynthia McKinney, D-Ga., who allegedly assaulted a Capitol Hill police officer (among other things); Sen. George Allen, R-Va., who was accused of using racial epithets; and Rep. William Jefferson, D-La., who was under investigation by the FBI for allegations of bribery and fraud in connection with $90,000 in cash found in his freezer. Of the four, only Jefferson was reelected. Many others, all Republicans, lost their seats because of their ties to the convicted lobbyist Jack Abramoff. Another group of members of Congress became vulnerable because of their connections to other disgraced politicians. For example, National Republican Campaign Committee chair Tom Reynolds and some other Republican leaders were implicated in the Rep. Mark Foley page scandal because of their failure to take proper action in response to Foley's inappropriate behavior before it made headlines. A few candidates who were even farther removed from scandal were harmed by the wrongdoing of others. Rep. Mike Sodrel, R-Ind., was criticized in a TV ad not for his connections to Mark Foley, but for accepting contributions from Republican House leaders who allegedly knew of Foley's inappropriate behavior and did nothing about it. Senator DeWine was hurt by a series of scandals from which he was far removed but that involved Ohio's Republican governor and other high-ranking GOP politicians in Columbus, the state capital. Even some open-seat Republican candidates, competing in what are usually very reliably Republican districts, lost because their district's seat had previously been occupied by a GOP member who had resigned under a cloud. As the 2006 elections demonstrate, opposition research can uncover wrongdoing and relationships with those accused of wrongdoing—including distant ones—that can be used to attack a candidate.

Most congressional candidates, regardless of incumbency, routinely search for unethical business transactions, evidence of tax dodging, and other questionable activities that could be used to discredit their opponent. Sometimes ex-spouses, estranged children, former friends, colleagues, and neighbors are interviewed to find examples of improper behavior or character flaws. Sometimes, investigations of military records, driving records, and campaign finance reports reveal that an opponent has lied about his or her service in the armed forces, is vulnerable to charges of having lived in the state or district for only a few years, or can be charged with being a tool of some wealthy special interest.

Most opposition research is tedious. Researchers scour the *Congressional Record,* search records of the floor proceedings of state legislatures, look through newspapers, surf the web, and turn to other public sources to show that a candidate is out of touch with the district, has flip-flopped on an issue, has taken an inordinate number of government-financed trips, or has committed some other questionable act. Opposition researchers often pore over campaign finance reports so that a candidate can claim that an opponent is too beholden to PACs, wealthy individuals from out of state, or donors with questionable reputations to represent the views of constituents.

The widespread use of negative advertising also has encouraged most campaigns to search for their own candidate's weaknesses. As one campaign manager involved in a close race explained, "We need to be prepared for the worst. We have to spend a lot of time looking at the things our opponent may try to pin on us."[63] Campaigns investigate their own candidates in anticipation of attacks they expect to be made against them.

Some campaigns discuss a potential liability with members of the press before an opponent has had a chance to raise it. Preemption is an effective tactic for "inoculating" a candidate against an attack. Another approach is to hire one of the consulting firms that stake their reputation on the ability to prepare a televised response to an attack in less than half a day. Many well-financed Senate and House contenders in tight races go so far as to record television commercials that present responses to particular charges before their opponent actually makes them.

A large number of incumbents were defeated in the 2006 congressional elections, and negative advertising played a role in the defeat of most of them. One of the lessons to be drawn from the congressional elections of the past three decades is that, if used skillfully, negative campaigning can be a potent weapon.

SUMMARY

The campaign for votes, like the campaign for resources, requires candidates and strategists to identify groups of supporters and potential supporters and communicate to them a message they will find appealing. Campaign strategists recognize that most voters have little interest in politics, possess little information about congressional candidates, are more familiar with incumbents than with challengers, and know more about candidates for the Senate than about those for the House. They also understand that voters tend to cast their ballots for candidates whom they have previously supported or who share their party identification.

Candidates and their advisers consider these factors when plotting strategies. Most campaigns use voting histories, census data, and polls to target voters. Demography and geography are often major considerations; sometimes microtargeting techniques are used. Campaigns consider the partisan advantages associated with specific policy stances, the positions likely to be staked out by the opponent, the opinions of the blocs of supporters they need to mobilize, and the views of undecided voters they need to win. Most candidates make issues a major component of their message, but incumbents have a greater tendency to focus on imagery and their performance in office. Most candidates also seek to hold their opponent accountable for perceived weaknesses in the person's record. However, competitive elections usually produce the most negative campaigns.

CHAPTER EIGHT

Campaign Communications

Campaign communications range from sophisticated television advertisements and Internet web sites to old-fashioned knocking on doors. The resources at a candidate's disposal, the types of media available, and the competitiveness of the election are the factors that most strongly influence how campaigns reach voters. In this chapter I examine the techniques that campaigns use to disseminate their messages and get their supporters to the polls.

Campaign communications are meant to accomplish six objectives: to improve a candidate's name recognition, project a favorable image, set the campaign agenda, exploit the issues, undermine an opponent's credibility or support, and defend the candidate against attacks. These objectives, of course, are designed to advance the campaign's broader goals of shoring up and expanding its bases of support and getting its supporters sufficiently interested in the election to vote.

Campaign communications usually proceed through four short phases that begin in the summer and continue until election day. In the first, often called the biography phase, candidates introduce themselves to voters by highlighting their experience and personal background. Next, in the issue phase, candidates use issues to attract the support of uncommitted voters, energize their supporters, and further define themselves to the public.

The attack phase often begins after one candidate learns that he or she is slipping in the polls or failing to advance on an opponent. During this phase, candidates contrast themselves with their opponent, point to inconsistencies between an opponent's rhetoric and actions, try to exploit unpopular positions the opponent has taken, or just plain sling mud at one another. In the final weeks of the campaign, most successful candidates pull their message together by reminding voters who they are, why they are running, and why they are more worthy of being elected than their opponent. At this final, or summation, phase they commonly emphasize phrases and symbols presented earlier in the campaign.

TELEVISION ADVERTISING

Virtually every household in the United States possesses at least one television set, and the average adult watches three and one-half to four hours of television per day.[1] About three-fourths of all voters maintain that television is their most important source of information about elections.[2] These factors make television an important vehicle for campaign communications and have encouraged congressional campaigners in cheap, moderate-priced, and sometimes extremely expensive media markets to utilize it.

There was so much use of television during the 2006 congressional elections that TV stations reportedly earned $2.25 billion from political advertising.[3] Voters in states and districts with competitive elections were undoubtedly exposed to hundreds of TV ads during the final weeks of the campaign. Television is the best medium for conveying image-related information to a mass audience. It is also extremely useful in setting the campaign agenda and associating a candidate with popular issues.[4] Television ads enable candidates to transmit action-oriented visuals that demonstrate desirable qualities such as leadership. Images of candidates meeting with voters or attending groundbreaking ceremonies convey more powerfully than do written or verbal statements the message that these individuals are actively involved in community affairs and have close ties to voters. Images also have a stronger emotional impact than words. Republican strategist Robert Teeter explains that "80 or 90 percent of what people retain from a TV ad is visual.... If you have the visual right, you have the commercial right. If you don't, it almost doesn't matter what you're saying."[5] Television advertisements have the extra advantage of enabling the campaign to control its message. Unlike interactive modes of communication, such as debates and speeches, paid advertisements do not allow an opponent or disgruntled voter to interrupt. Message control makes TV a potent means for increasing name recognition.[6]

Roughly nine out of ten Senate campaigns and 65 percent of House campaigns use either broadcast or cable television, and the percentage would be larger if the costs were not so high.[7] Although candidates pay lower rates than commercial advertisers, these ads still can be prohibitively expensive. In November 2006, Democratic representative José Serrano or his Republican opponent, Ali Mohamed, would have had to spend $70,000 to broadcast a single thirty-second advertisement at 9:00 p.m., during the airing of the popular TV show *Grey's Anatomy,* to reach voters in New York's 16th congressional district. The cost of broadcasting an ad to this South Bronx district is exorbitant because the seat is in a media market that spans the entire New York metropolitan area. By contrast, Wally Herger or A. J. Sekhon would only have paid $840 to air an ad that would blanket California's 2nd district during that same time slot. Ed Perlmutter or Rick O'Donnell would have paid $9,000 to cover Colorado's 7th district. Of course some campaigns, including many in major metropolitan areas, save money and improve targeting by substituting cable TV for broadcast stations.

High costs and the misalignment of media markets and the boundaries of congressional districts discourage House candidates in the highly urbanized areas of the Mid-Atlantic, the West Coast, and southern New England from using television advertising. The distribution of media markets and relatively low advertising rates in most southwestern states and many rural areas, by contrast, enable many House candidates there to use television extensively.[8] Senate candidates tend to make greater use of television than candidates for the House because the configurations of state borders and media markets make television relatively cost-efficient in statewide contests. That Senate campaigns have more money and the expectation that Senate candidates will rely on television also contribute to its greater use in contests for the upper chamber.

Televised campaign advertisements have come a long way since the days when candidates appeared as talking heads that spouted their political experience and issue positions. Six trends define the evolution of the modern television campaign commercial: a movement toward greater emphasis on imagery, the use of action-oriented themes and pictures, the employment of emotionally laden messages, a decrease in the length of ads, an increase in negative advertising, and a reduction in the amount of time required to create an ad.[9] Gimmicky, ten- and fifteen-second spots punctuated by twenty-or-so words have recently become popular with congressional candidates and other political groups. The ability to counterattack rapidly has become a selling point for the nation's top media firms. Campaign advertisements broadcast in the guise of independent expenditures and issue advocacy ads by parties and interest groups are relatively recent phenomena.[10]

During the biography phase of the campaign, incumbents' ads typically depict them as experienced leaders who know and care about their constituents. Challengers and candidates for open seats also try to present themselves as capable and honorable by pointing to their accomplishments in politics, family life, or the private sector. Regardless of incumbency, candidates broadcast advertisements that repeatedly mention and display their names, and they frequently end their commercials with the line, "Vote for [candidate's name] for Congress" to boost their name recognition and support. Federal law requires that they state who paid for the ad, and that statement frequently comes last.

Candidates who have led remarkable lives, have come from humble origins, or have compiled impressive records of public service often broadcast what are called "mini-docudramas" to showcase their war record, community activism, or road to professional success. The ad that a campaign selects to introduce its candidate depends both on the candidate's experiences and on the competition in the race.

O'Donnell had the stage entirely to himself when he began his bid for Congress in 2006. As the sole contender in the Republican primary in Colorado's 7th district, who had won 31 percent of the vote in the 2002 GOP primary, he started the race recognizable to at least some Republican voters. O'Donnell is extremely telegenic, and his campaign decided to introduce him with a lighthearted and slightly humorous, if not formulaic, thirty-second television commercial. His biography ad opens with a head shot of the candidate looking directly into the camera and stating, "I'm Rick O'Donnell, and I grew up here in a big, Irish family." At this point, a "Rick O'Donnell for Congress" emblem reappears in the upper left corner of the screen, and the candidate remarks, "Boy that was hard work." While he is speaking two video clips of him and his siblings appear. The first features a caption that states, "Lifelong resident of Jefferson County." The caption on the other reads, "Youngest of 5 kids." The candidate goes on to explain, "I worked hard to overcome dyslexia; then I became a bit of a nerd." At this moment, he is standing in front of lockers in a school hallway. Next, a picture taken when the candidate was an awkward-looking teenager with huge round glasses appears, along with the chuckle-inspiring caption, "Clearly." The candidate goes on to say, "I bagged groceries [to] put myself through school…keeps you looking young." The backdrop is a small grocery store, which is followed by a picture of fourteen-year-old Rick with the caption, "Started working at 14." This is replaced by a current picture of the candidate with the caption, "Still looks 14 (actually he's 36)." The candidate then continues, "In Congress, I'm going to do what I did at the end of the day at the grocery store—clean up!" Then an announcer says, "Rick O'Donnell for Congress," and a picture of O'Donnell talking to a group of people at a conference table appears, along with the caption, "A New Generation of Leadership." Next, the visual changes to a shot of the candidate and a woman holding hands while walking in a grassy park. This is followed by the candidate's reappearance in front of the school lockers, where he puts a personal spin on the ad's required disclaimer when he states, "I'm Rick O'Donnell and I approve this message because we're desperate for new blood in Washington!" At this point, the "Rick O'Donnell for Congress" emblem reappears in the upper left corner, and a required caption appears on the bottom of the screen that reads, "Paid for by Coloradans for Rick O'Donnell and approved by Rick O'Donnell."[11]

The ad helped establish O'Donnell as a likable young man who had managed to overcome some early obstacles through hard work. The references to cleaning up Congress and providing new blood in Washington were intended to portray him as a political outsider. This was an important message in 2006 because most voters were unhappy with the performance of the national government and looking for candidates who would bring about political change.

O'Donnell's general election opponent, Ed Perlmutter, a former state senator, faced a different type of challenge in introducing his candidacy because he had first to defeat two Democratic opponents in the primary. His strongest opponent was former state representative Peggy Lamm, who shares the same last name as her brother-in-law, popular former Colorado governor Richard Lamm. A lesser opponent was Herbert Rubenstein, a political amateur who owns a leadership development consulting firm. Perlmutter presented himself to voters in a thirty-second ad titled "Dad," which portrayed him as a moderate, pragmatic politician whose views were strongly in tune with the district. The ad introduced the candidate by way of a conversation between him and his three daughters. It opens with the Perlmutter daughters stating, "He's always been there for us. Now Dad's running for Congress to change things. Like fighting the dumping of nuclear waste in Adams County, pushing to develop renewable energy, and investing in stem cell research. He'd be a great congressman, and he's a great dad!" The ad closes with Perlmutter giving his required approval of the ad and his daughters cheerfully concurring, "And so do we!"

Like O'Donnell's ad, Perlmutter's bio spot is full of attractive footage of the candidate and his family, filmed with appropriate backdrops. It also has the required caption acknowledging that the candidate approved the ad and his campaign committee paid for it. The ad is different in that it weaves together narratives from the candidate's political and personal life. His daughters' discussion of the issues makes subtle references to both. The candidate had built a reputation as an environmentalist and a champion of renewable energy while in the Colorado legislature. His interest in stem cell research is inspired by his eldest daughter's having epilepsy. As is the case with many candidates who have political experience, the Perlmutter campaign chose to draw on that experience when introducing its candidate.

Some incumbents, and a few nonincumbents with political experience, use "community action" spots to show the impact of their efforts on behalf of constituents. As noted in Chapter 7, Ohio senator Mike DeWine used that approach extensively, employing testimonials by emergency first responders, nurses, senior citizens, and military families to develop the theme early in the race. Some of these messages were repeated in the closing days of the campaign, along with the senator's relevant congressional votes, in an effort to show the breadth of his concern for voters and the scope of his influence.[12]

"Feel-good" ads are virtually devoid of issues and are designed to appeal to the electorate's sense of community pride or nationalism. They feature visuals of a candidate marching in parades, on horseback in the countryside, or involved in some other popular local activity. "Passing the torch" ads manipulate symbols to depict the concept of succession, to make the case that a candidate is the right person for the job. The most effective spot of this kind in recent years was broadcast in 1992 by a presidential rather than a congressional candidate. It featured then-teenager Bill Clinton shaking hands with President John F. Kennedy on the grounds of the White House.

During the issue phase, campaign ads communicate candidates' policy stances on valence or positional issues.[13] The O'Donnell campaign ran an ad highlighting his support for Social Security, mainly to try to inoculate the candidate against attacks it foresaw that the Perlmutter campaign would mount based on O'Donnell's think tank paper attacking the program. The Perlmutter campaign stressed their candidate's desire to shield children from online predators and protect families. Fortunately for Perlmutter, the Foley page scandal broke a few days after they had begun broadcasting the ad, prompting his campaign to keep the ad running for several additional days to take advantage of the latest congressional scandal to dominate the news. Both DeWine and challenger Sherrod Brown focused on a number of issues during this phase of the campaign season. Most of Brown's issue ads focused on Democratic positional issues, including affordable health care, fighting the exportation of American factories and jobs, and funding stem cell research. DeWine's ads primarily focused on Republican positional issues, such as tax cuts, national defense, and support for the military. Both candidates mentioned some issues customarily associated with the opposing party. For Brown, they included a balanced budget amendment, tightening U.S. borders, and national security. For DeWine, they were Social Security and regulating prescription drug companies. Although most voters have only limited interest in any single issue, ads that focus on positional issues, such as taxes and health care reform, can help candidates pick up the support of uncommitted voters, mobilize single-issue activists, or emphasize certain aspects of their image.[14]

In the attack phase of the campaign, candidates use TV ads to point to their opponent's shortcomings. Television is ideally suited to comparative ads because it enables candidates to present pictures of themselves and their opponent side by side and roll lists of issues down the screen to show themselves on the popular side of salient policies and their opponent on the unpopular side. That less-than-flattering pictures of the opponent are usually used is an understatement. Sometimes the opponent's head is reduced in size, "phased out," or distorted, to keep voters' attention and subtly imply that faulty issue positions are only the beginning of the opponent's weaknesses. Advertisements that feature images of the opponent somersaulting back and forth across the screen or debating himself or herself are useful for highlighting inconsistencies among an opponent's speeches, campaign positions, or congressional roll-call votes. Ominous or flighty music can reinforce the visuals and language.

Of course, candidates are not responsible for all comparative and negative advertising. Much of it comes from the independent expenditures and issue advocacy ads of party committees and interest groups. All three—candidates, parties, and interest groups—broadcast attack ads in the Perlmutter–O'Donnell contest. The Democratic Congressional Campaign Committee ran four TV ads linking O'Donnell to President Bush and another three criticizing him for "radical ideas," including his early stand on Social Security. A local 527 committee called Too Extreme for Colorado also attacked O'Donnell on Social Security. The National Republican Congressional Committee ran an ad characterizing Perlmutter as a hypocrite on renewable energy and protecting children from sex offenders. The 527 committee, Americans for Honesty on the Issues, ran two ads attacking Perlmutter. Ironically, the first had to be pulled from the airwaves because it inaccurately claimed that while a state senator Perlmutter had sponsored legislation to provide benefits to *illegal* immigrants. The second ad was merely a corrected version of the first and claimed that Perlmutter sought to provide benefits to *legal* immigrants.

In the summation phase of the campaign, eleventh-hour television blitzes are used to solidify a candidate's message in the minds of voters. Key phrases and visuals from earlier commercials are repeated, as candidates who are ahead shore up support and those running behind appeal to undecided voters. Sometimes the ads are supplemented by endorsements from local news outlets.

RADIO ADVERTISING

Radio is an extremely popular medium for congressional campaign communications. Almost two-thirds of all House candidates and virtually all Senate contestants purchase radio ads.[15] During the last week of the congressional campaign season, voters typically hear four to five radio ads per day.[16] Inexpensive to record and broadcast, radio commercials are ideal for building a candidate's name identification. Another advantage is that some candidates—whether they are intimidated by the television camera, not telegenic, novices to the spotlight, or products of the pretelevision era—perform better on radio. For many incumbents, taping radio commercials is an easy extension of the radio shows they regularly send back to stations in their district. Like television, radio is an excellent vehicle for emotion-laden messages.[17]

Radio allows candidates to target voters with great precision. Radio stations broadcast to smaller, more homogeneous audiences than television stations, enabling campaigns to tailor their messages to different segments of the population. Campaigns can reach Hispanic voters in the Southwest, Florida, or the inner cities of the Northeast by advertising on Spanish-language stations. "Golden oldies" stations, which feature music from the 1960s and 1970s, are ideal for reaching middle-aged voters. Radio talk programs, such as the *Rush Limbaugh Show,* are excellent vehicles for reaching voters who are committed to particular ideologies. The commuting hours furnish near-captive audiences of suburbanites who travel to work.

NEWSPAPER ADVERTISING

Newspaper advertisements dominated campaign communication for much of American history but became less important with the decline of the partisan press in the late 1800s.[18] Congressional campaigns still purchase newspaper ads, but they are not as widely used as radio and many other media. Sixty-three percent of all House and 80 percent of all Senate campaigns purchase ads in local or statewide newspapers.[19]

Newspapers as a campaign medium have some advantages but many shortcomings. Their major advantages are that they provide plenty of opportunity to deliver a detailed message, and their readers are educated and likely to vote. On the other hand, newspapers do not communicate images or convey emotion as well as television. They also cannot be used to deliver a personalized message. Moreover, only a few congressional districts and states have minority communities large enough to sustain independent newspapers that can be used to target communications to those groups. The effectiveness of campaign advertisements that appear in newspapers is also somewhat limited.[20]

If such shortcomings exist, why do most campaigns place ads in newspapers? One reason is that they are inexpensive. Newspaper advertisements cost less than ads transmitted via television, radio, mail, or virtually any other medium. Newspaper ads can also be useful in announcing the times and locations of campaign events, which can help attract coverage by other media. Finally, some candidates and campaign aides believe that purchasing advertising space from a local newspaper can help them secure the paper's endorsement.

DIRECT MAIL AND NEWSLETTERS

Newsletters and direct mail can be used to raise money, convey a message, or encourage people to vote, but the key to success in all three areas is a good mailing list. A good fundraising list is made up of previous donors or persons who have a history of contributing to like-minded candidates; a good advertising list includes supporters and persuadable voters; and a good voter mobilization list includes only those who intend to vote for the candidate.

Direct-mail pieces and newsletters (sometimes referred to as "persuasion" or "mobilization" mail, depending on its main purpose) are among the most widely used methods of campaign advertising in congressional elections. Roughly 80 percent of all House candidates and virtually all Senate candidates use them.[21] During the 2006 congressional elections, 71 percent of all registered voters received at least one piece of direct mail.[22] Individuals living in areas with competitive contests typically receive dozens. Mail is a one-way communications tool that offers significant advantages in message control and delivery. Precise targeting is its main advantage. Campaigns can purchase lists that include information such as a voter's name, address, gender, age, race or ethnicity, employment status, party registration, voting history, and estimated income.[23] This information enables campaigns to tailor the candidate profiles, issue positions, and photographs that they include in their mailings to appeal to specific segments of the population. Lists developed through microtargeting, which include a variety of consumer preference data, allow a campaign to fine-tune its message to individual voters. The ability to narrowcast a message makes mail excellent for staking out positional issues and for campaigning in heterogeneous states or districts. Campaigns in highly diverse areas, such as New York's 12th district, which is 49 percent Hispanic and includes most of Chinatown, often use the mail to campaign in more than one language.

Another advantage of mail is that it is relatively inexpensive. Letters produced using personal computers and laser printers can be mailed to voters for little more than the price of a stamp. Campaigns can also take advantage of postal service discounts for presorted mailings. Finally, mail campaigns often fly under the radar for a while. As long as an adversary does not detect them, his or her campaign will not respond.

Nevertheless, direct mail has some disadvantages, including the fact that it is often tossed out as junk mail. Another disadvantage is that it rests principally on the power of the printed word. Whereas television and radio enable campaigns to embellish their messages with visual images or sound effects, mail depends primarily on written copy to hold voters' attention and get a message across. This makes it a less-effective medium for communicating image-related information.

Direct-mail experts rely on many techniques to combat the weaknesses of their medium. Personalized salutations, graphs, and pictures are often used to capture and hold voters' attention. Other gimmicks include the use of post-scripts designed to look as though they were handwritten.

Direct mail is an especially powerful medium for challengers and candidates who have strong ideological positions because it is ideal for negative advertising or for making appeals that stir voters' emotions. Yet mail also offers some advantages to incumbents. Many members of Congress send out letters early in the election cycle to reinforce voter support without mounting a highly visible campaign.[24] These mailings often include messages reinforcing the ones that incumbents communicate in congressionally franked mass mailings (500 or more of the same letter) to constituents, which are prohibited during the ninety days before a primary or general election for House members and for sixty days before an election for senators.

Direct mail plays a prominent role in many congressional elections. In Colorado's 7th district race in 2006, the Perlmutter campaign sent two unique pieces of direct mail, the Colorado Democratic Party and the DCCC mailed nine pieces, and various advocacy groups sent out an additional nine pieces. Meanwhile, the O'Donnell campaign mailed two letters, the Colorado Republican Party sent at least sixteen, and various advocacy groups sent out four. Not surprisingly, the direct mail distributed in conjunction with the Ohio Senate race far outpaced that in most House elections. The Brown campaign was responsible for eight direct-mail pieces; various Democratic Party committees sent out another thirty; and several unions, environmental groups, and other progressive organizations distributed an additional fifty-eight pieces. The DeWine campaign distributed only three pieces of direct mail, but the Ohio Republican Party sent out another thirteen. Various interest groups, including the U.S. Chamber of Commerce and the National Right to Life Committee, sent out a dozen more pieces. Clearly, candidates, parties, and interest groups make significant efforts to provide their supporters and persuadable voters with opportunities to read about the candidates and the major issues in the race.

MASS TELEPHONE CALLS

Just over 70 percent of all House campaigns and most Senate campaigns use mass telephone calls to communicate with voters.[25] Campaigns make personal calls, referred to as "telemarketing" in the business world, for a variety of reasons, including identifying voters' political predispositions and candidate preferences. This information is often added to a database so that core supporters and swing voters can be contacted later. Other uses of mass telephone calls are to try to win the support of undecided voters and to contact supporters to ask them to volunteer, make a contribution, or attend an event. Of course, a major purpose of mass telephone calls is voter mobilization. Campaigns that can afford it, or that receive the assistance of a party committee or interest group equipped with the appropriate resources, use microtargeting to make this outreach more effective. Automated mass telephone calls, sometimes referred to as "robo-calls," can provide a less labor-intensive alternative to person-to-person calls for voter mobilization. During the 2006 campaign season, almost two-thirds of all registered voters received at least one robo-call, and another 24 percent received phone calls from a live person.[26]

The Perlmutter campaign benefited from some twenty waves of targeted phone calls, most of them during the final week. O'Donnell benefited from considerably fewer. His campaign organization made one round of calls, but few other groups joined in. The lack of telephone calls by Republican Party organizations and conservative interest groups was probably due to the Republican candidate's inability to close Perlmutter's considerable lead and tactical decisions to deploy the resources elsewhere, particularly in contests where GOP incumbents were in serious danger of losing. Not surprisingly, more mass telephone calls were made in conjunction with the Ohio Senate race: The Brown and DeWine campaigns made five rounds of calls each, Democratic Party committees made one, and their Republican counterparts made seventeen. Liberal advocacy groups made another six calls, and conservative organizations made two. This race demonstrates the greater centralization of GOP voter mobilization efforts compared with the Democrats'.

Although personal calls are much more effective than recorded ones, and can be made by volunteers, recorded messages also can be effective in mobilizing voters. Some candidates, particularly challengers, ask prominent politicians for assistance with these. During the elections held during George W. Bush's presidency, many Republican candidates in close races benefited from prerecorded voter mobilization messages featuring President Bush, First Lady Laura Bush, and various other GOP leaders. Of course, most of these candidates' opponents benefited from similar messages by senators Hillary Rodham

Clinton and Barack Obama, former president Bill Clinton, and other Democratic leaders. In many cases, party committees financed these efforts.

Live and prerecorded telephone calls also have been used for less-noble purposes. Campaigns have been known to leave prerecorded messages attempting to implicate an opponent in scandal. They also have been known to hire telephone firms to conduct "push polls," which seem to be normal telephone surveys used for collecting information but soon degenerate into allegations and attacks phrased as questions. Another "dirty trick" involves making automated phone calls in the middle of the night in the name of an opposing candidate. These types of activities are intended to keep voters away from the polls rather than learn about or mobilize them.

THE INTERNET

Although it was unheard of for much of the 1990s, many contemporary political campaigns, party committees, other political organizations, and activists have a presence on the Internet. The best web sites are integrated into the candidate's campaign. They provide a place for voters to collect information that is often available elsewhere, but to do so in a more convenient and reliable way than telephoning campaign headquarters, scouring newspapers, or contacting local political activists. They help meet the needs of the roughly 40 percent of Americans who say that they get political and other news online.[27] Campaigns save money and effort, and avoid mistakes, when they direct voter, donor, and press inquiries to their web site. They also increase the audiences for their television and radio advertisements, speeches, and other events when they post them as streaming video or audio. Although only 14 percent of registered voters report having contact with streaming video and/or campaign e-mails, the number is likely to increase in future elections.[28]

Good campaign web sites are easy to navigate, feature attractive home pages that immediately tell voters about the candidate and his or her reasons for running, feature discussions of the candidate's issue positions, present attractive photographs, display the candidate's schedule, and are updated regularly. They include online areas that permit individuals to volunteer for campaign activities; make a contribution; register to vote; look up directions to their polling place; or sign up for the campaign's e-mail list, which itself is a valuable communications tool. These data are usually integrated into the campaign's computerized volunteer and finance databases.[29]

Some web sites encourage "viral" campaigning, which often takes place without the involvement of the candidate's campaign organization. They feature information that voters can send to their friends or use to write op-ed articles, send letters to the editor, or call radio talk shows. The inclusion of the names, addresses, and telephone numbers of local media outlets further encourages political activists to express their support for a candidate to the news media. Other aspects of campaign web sites that encourage viral campaigning are pages for voters to write endorsements and chat rooms that can help stimulate "meet-ups," house parties, and other grassroots activities. Opportunities for interactivity are particularly useful in helping a candidate attract a coterie of web-savvy supporters, many of whom are young people.

Internet web logs, commonly referred to as "blogs," also can motivate politically engaged supporters. Those sponsored by a candidate's campaign organization often afford the campaign almost as much control over the flow of information as television and other one-way communication from the campaign to voters. Blogs allow the candidate to regale supporters with his or her experiences on the campaign trail or answer voters' questions online. Should an entry cause a problem at a later date, the campaign can always delete it. Blogs sponsored by a candidate's supporters also are usually very helpful, but because they are not the property of the campaign, it has less control over the online conversation. Independent blogs, ranging from the widely read and influential Daily Kos to a teenager's postings on MySpace or BlogSpot, afford the campaign no control over their content. As is the case with other forms of free media (discussed below), the best a campaign typically can do in response to a negative posting is to request that its rebuttal be posted.

How widespread is Internet use in congressional elections? During the 2006 election cycle, almost every major-party general election candidate for Congress had their own campaign web site. Candidate web sites are far from identical; incumbency and the competitiveness of the race have a noteworthy impact on web site quality and features, including those having to do with fundraising, communications, and voter mobilization.

Virtually every House candidate's web site has some provision or instructions for making a contribution. In 2006 about 85 percent made it possible for supporters to give a contribution online using a credit card (see Table 8-1). web sites created for incumbents in jeopardy are more likely to possess this feature than those representing shoo-in incumbents. The web sites of virtually all hopeful challengers provide this option, in contrast to 83 percent of the challengers who stand little chance of victory. In open-seat contests, where every candidate web site appears to have a link for online contributions, differences based on electoral competitiveness disappear.

Nearly two-thirds of all Democratic and Republican House candidates enhance their campaign communications by giving voters the opportunity to

TABLE 8-1

Internet Use in House Campaigns in 2006

	All	Incumbents		Challengers		Open-seat candidates	
		In jeopardy	Shoo-ins	Hope-fuls	Likely losers	Pros-pects	Mis-matched
Online fundraising	85	87	76	100	83	100	100
Request e-mail newsletter	64	74	60	74	51	86	69
Streaming video	24	22	19	39	14	54	38
Poll data	8	5	1	18	6	26	5
Comparative or negative information about opponent	44	39	9	83	58	56	38
Volunteer recruitment	88	96	85	97	79	93	100
Voter registration	35	36	39	46	22	41	33
E-mail information from web site	17	13	15	31	11	21	23
Chat room	5	1	5	7	4	10	0

Source: Project E-Voter, University of Maryland.

Notes: Figures are for general election candidates in major-party contested races, excluding those in incumbent-versus-incumbent races. Percentages reflect the campaigns that participated in these activities. The numbers do not add to 100 percent because campaigns could pick as many of these activities as applied. *N* ranges from 436 to 507.

sign up online to receive newsletters via e-mail. About one-fourth of the web sites feature streaming video of TV ads or campaign events. Competition is a key determinant of the presence of both features, but the candidate's office-holding status is the most important factor in explaining the availability of streaming video. More web sites designed for open-seat prospects and hopeful challengers have streaming video than sites belonging to incumbents in jeopardy. This pattern is not surprising, as nonincumbent candidates for other offices have shown the greatest penchant for embracing web innovations.[30]

The content and tone of the information posted on House candidates' web sites also vary according to incumbency and competitiveness. Although few incumbents post information about their standings in the polls, substantial numbers of open-seat candidates and challengers in close contests do, presumably because the nonincumbents recognize that this information can help generate more voter and donor support and can attract additional media coverage. Similarly, nonincumbents, particularly challengers in neck-to-neck races, are the most likely to post comparative and negative information about their opponents. Recall from Chapter 7 that this information can be useful in peeling away support from sitting members of Congress. Of course, incumbents who are in danger of losing the election also are liable to perceive advantages in going on the offensive; about 40 percent of them posted unflattering information about their opponents in 2006.

Internet web sites may be the most cutting-edge technological innovation in campaign politics, but a large number of contemporary campaigns use them to enhance traditional grassroots campaign efforts. Almost nine out of ten House campaigns use the web to recruit campaign volunteers, and more than one-third use it to provide supporters with information about how to register to vote. Candidates in competitive contests typically make the greatest use of the Internet for these purposes.

Finally, a small number of House candidates' web sites have features designed to encourage viral campaigning. Roughly one-third of all hopeful challengers and one-fifth of all open-seat candidates enable voters to e-mail web site information to others, as opposed to only 14 percent of all incumbents. About one out of twenty House candidates' web sites hosts a chat room that voters can use to express their opinions and communicate directly with one another. Most of these are sponsored by challengers and open-seat candidates in close races, demonstrating once again that nonincumbents tend to be more innovative than those already in office.

FREE MEDIA

One of the major goals of any campaign is to generate free, or "earned," media—radio, television, newspaper, or magazine coverage that candidates receive when news editors consider their activities newsworthy. "Earned media" has other advantages besides free advertising. Because it is delivered by a neutral observer, it has greater credibility than campaign-generated communications.[31] Its major disadvantage is that campaigns cannot control what news correspondents report. Misstatements and blunders are more likely to appear in the news than in the candidate's major policy speeches.

News coverage of congressional elections consists of stories based on press releases that campaigns issue; stories about events, issues, campaign ads, or time that a reporter has spent with a candidate; and analytical or editorial stories about a candidate or campaign.[32] Most analysis focuses on the "horse-race" aspect of the election. The stories that get beyond handicapping the race usually discuss candidates' political qualifications, personal characteristics, or campaign organizations. Fewer stories focus on the issues.[33] Coverage by television and radio tends to be shorter, more action oriented, and less detailed than print journalism.

Most journalists strive to cover politics objectively, but that does not mean that all candidates are treated the same. Reporters follow certain norms when pursuing leads and researching and writing their stories—norms that usually work to the advantage of incumbents.[34] Moreover, editorials are largely exempt from the norms of objectivity that apply to news stories. Newspaper owners and their editorial boards do not hesitate to voice their opinions on the editorial page. Radio and television stations also air programs that feature pundits discussing the virtues and foibles of specific candidates. Most consumers of news have come to expect newspaper editors and political talk show hosts to endorse specific candidates shortly before the election. Media endorsements and campaign coverage can have a significant impact on the outcome.[35]

Attracting Coverage

Attracting media coverage requires planning and aggressiveness. Besides issuing streams of press releases, campaign offices distribute copies of the candidate's schedule to correspondents, invite them to campaign events, and make special efforts to grant interviews. Candidates also submit themselves to interrogations by panels of newspaper editors, with the goal of generating good press coverage or winning an endorsement.

Successful campaigns carefully play to the needs of different news media. Press releases that feature strong leads, have news value, provide relevant facts, and contain enough background information for an entire story are faxed to print reporters. Advance notice of major campaign events, including information about predicted crowd size, acoustics, and visual backdrops, goes to television and radio correspondents in the hope that the event will be one of the few they cover.[36] Interpretive information is provided to journalists in all the news media to try to generate campaign stories with a favorable news spin. News organizations routinely report stories based on materials distributed by campaigns, and because few of them have the resources to research or even verify the information, most free press is uncritical.

Newspapers and radio stations are more likely than television stations to give candidates free coverage. Television stations devote little time to covering congressional elections, particularly House races. Television news shows occasionally discuss the horse-race aspect of campaigns, cover small portions of campaign debates, or analyze controversial campaign ads, but few are willing to give candidates air time to discuss issues. Radio stations are more generous with air time. Many invite candidates to participate in call-in shows and public forums. Newspapers usually give the most detailed campaign coverage. Small, understaffed newspapers frequently print portions of candidates' press releases and debate transcripts verbatim.

Senate candidates attract more free media coverage than House candidates. Incumbents and open-seat contestants usually get more—and more favorable—press coverage than challengers, regardless of whether they are running for the House or the Senate. Inequities in campaign coverage are due to the professional norms that guide news journalists and to inequalities among candidates and campaign organizations. The preoccupation of journalists with candidates' personalities, qualifications, campaign organizations, and probable success is to the advantage of incumbents because they are almost always better known, more qualified, in possession of more professional organizations, and more likely to win than their opponents.[37]

Newspaper coverage in House contests between an incumbent and a challenger is so unequal that veteran Democratic political adviser Anita Dunn believes "the local press is the unindicted coconspirator in the alleged 'permanent incumbency.'" As Dunn explains, "A vicious circle develops for challengers— if early on, they don't have money, standing in the polls, endorsements, and the backing of political insiders, they—and the race—are written off, not covered, which means the likelihood of a competitive race developing is almost nonexistent."[38]

The reporting policies of many national and local newspapers can contribute to this conundrum. One such policy is to provide no news coverage to challengers in uncontested primaries until the actual primary date has passed and they are officially nominated. Ignoring these challenger campaigns is particularly harmful to candidates in states that hold late primaries, some of which hold midterm congressional primaries as late as eight weeks before election day. The delay in press coverage makes it impossible for many challengers to receive the free media coverage they need to become viable candidates. Local news reporting policies and late primary dates combine to contribute to high incumbent retention rates.

Although many challengers can usually count on getting only four stories— the announcement of their candidacy, coverage of their primary victory, a candidate profile, and the announcement of their defeat—it is still worth pursuing free media coverage. Those few challengers who are able to make the case to journalists that they have the capacity to mount a strong campaign are able to attract significant coverage, often enough to become known among the local voters. Challengers who have held elective office or had other significant political experience, and who have assembled professional campaign organizations and raised substantial funds, are in a better position to make this case than those who have not. They typically receive extra press coverage, which helps them raise more money, hire additional help, become more competitive, and attract even greater attention from the media.[39] A similar set of relationships exists for open-seat candidates, except that it is usually easier for them to make the case that they are involved in a close contest.

Scandal can help candidates attract more media coverage. Underdogs are taken more seriously when their opponent has been accused of breaking the law or of ethical misconduct. During the 2006 elections, dozens of congressional candidates were either directly implicated in a scandal or touched by one because of their association with tainted incumbents. As noted in Chapter 7, such associations can be the result of knowing about a scandal, accepting campaign contributions from someone who knew, or even running for a seat formerly held by a person accused of wrongdoing. The negative news stories generated by scandal or an association with scandal can put a campaign on the defensive and prevent it from communicating the candidate's message for the remainder of the race. They also can result in a little-known contender's receiving enough favorable media coverage to become competitive and eventually win. Scandal was critical in helping Virginia Democrat Jim Webb receive the news coverage that helped to vault him from a likely congressional "also-ran" to U.S. senator. It had a similar impact on the candidacies of Chris Carney, who defeated Rep. Don Sherwood in Pennsylvania, Hank Johnson, who defeated Rep. Cynthia McKinney in a Democratic primary in Georgia, and numerous other incumbents who were swept from the hallways in the 2006 and previous elections.

Campaign Debates

Debates are among the few campaign activities that receive extensive press coverage and can place a challenger on equal footing with an incumbent. The decision to participate in a debate is a strategic one. Front-runners, who are usually incumbents, generally prefer to avoid debating because they understand that debates have the potential to do them more harm than good. Nevertheless, incumbents recognize that the public expects them to debate; most do so to avoid being blasted for shirking their civic responsibility. Candidates who are running behind, usually challengers, have the most to gain from debating. They prefer to engage in as many debates as possible and to hold them when they will attract the most media coverage.

Before debates are scheduled, the candidates or their representatives negotiate certain matters in regard to them. In addition to the number and timing of debates, candidates must agree on whether independent or minor-party candidates will participate, on the format, and on where the debate or debates will be held. All these factors can influence who, if anyone, is considered the winner.[40] Negotiations about debates can become heated but are almost always successfully resolved. Roughly nine out of ten House and Senate contestants debate their opponents.[41] The few who refuse usually enjoy insurmountable leads, lack verbal agility, or both.

Media Bias

House challengers and incumbents disagree over the nature of the coverage the news media give to House campaigns (see Table 8-2).[42] Challengers, particularly those in uncompetitive contests, are the most likely to perceive a bias for the incumbent, reflecting the one-sided nature of press coverage in elections for safe seats. To some extent these perceptions are a product of the norms that guide the distribution of media endorsements, which favor incumbents by almost nine to one.[43]

Partisan differences also exist in perceptions about media coverage. More Republican campaigners than Democrats maintain that the press gives more coverage and endorsements to their opponent, reflecting an opinion widely shared among Republican politicians and voters that the media corps is made up of members of a liberal establishment. Nevertheless, equal numbers of campaigners from each party believe the media covered their campaign fairly. That

TABLE 8-2

Campaigners' Perceptions of Media Coverage in House Campaigns

	Incumbents		Challengers		Open-seat candidates	
	All	In jeopardy	Shoo-ins	Hope-fuls	Likely losers	Pros-pects	Mis-matched
Favored your campaign	9%	—	11%	10%	9%	12%	12%
Favored your opponent's campaign	37	18%	5	48	62	24	47
Equally fair	54	82	84	42	29	65	41

Source: The 2002 Congressional Campaign Study, Center for American Politics and Citizenship, University of Maryland.

Notes: Figures are for general election candidates in major-party contested races, excluding those in incumbent-versus-incumbent races. — = less than 0.5 percent. Some columns do not add to 100 percent because of rounding. $N = 312$.

almost four out of ten campaigners from both parties believe that the news media are biased against them, however, highlights the adversarial relationship that exists between politicians and the press.[44]

FIELD WORK

Field work involves voter registration and get-out-the-vote drives, literature drops, the distribution of yard signs and bumper stickers, and other grassroots activities. It also includes candidate appearances at town meetings and in parades, speeches to Rotary Clubs and other civic groups, door-to-door campaigning, and other forms of direct voter contact. Grassroots politics was the major means of campaigning during the golden age of parties, and it remains important in modern congressional elections. Sophisticated targeting plans—similar to those used in direct mail, mass e-mails, and mass telephone calling—guide many grassroots activities. They also inform tactics concerning early and absentee voting, which occurs over an extended period before election day. The number of people using these forms of voting has increased substantially in recent years, from 14 percent of the electorate in 2000 to more than 20 percent in 2006.[45] The distribution of early voting varies greatly. In 2006, an estimated 40 percent of Florida's voters cast their ballots early, and all of Oregon's voters cast their ballots by mail. For many campaigns in these and other states, an effective early voting program is crucial for success.

Field work is the most labor-intensive and volunteer-dependent aspect of congressional elections. Candidates, their supporters, and local party workers knock on doors and make telephone calls to learn whether citizens intend to vote, whom they support, and whether they have any specific concerns they would like the candidate to address. These individuals receive follow-up contacts late in the campaign season to encourage them to vote. Such direct voter contact boosts voter turnout.[46] Supporters and potential supporters who express an interest in a policy area, need to register to vote, desire help in getting to the polls, state a preference for casting an absentee or early ballot, or are willing to work in the campaign typically receive earlier follow-up calls to address those issues.

Person-to-person communication is probably the most effective means of political persuasion and boosting turnout, especially communication directly between the candidate and a voter. It also provides a campaign with useful feedback. Candidates routinely draw on conversations with people they meet along the campaign trail to develop anecdotes that humanize issues.

Field work is relatively inexpensive because volunteers can carry out much of the actual labor. Local party activists, union members, and other volunteers are often called on to deliver campaign literature, register voters, or drive voters to the polls. In 2006, more than four out of ten registered voters received a phone call or visit at home from a volunteer or someone hired by a campaign during the election season.[47] Many of them were contacted several times during the final week before the election. The development of coordinated campaigns, including the Republican National Committee's 72-Hour Program, the Colorado Republicans' 96-Hour Program, and the Colorado Democrats' Colorado Victory 2006, has allowed many congressional candidates to rely in part on party organizations to carry out their field work, when those organizations believe the candidate has at least a fighting chance.[48] The Sekhon campaign in California's 2nd district could not rally the support or money to conduct a get-out-the-vote drive, and the campaign of the opponent, Rep. Wally Herger, did not feel the need to mount a massive voter mobilization effort. But the O'Donnell and Perlmutter campaigns received extensive assistance from parties and interest groups in Colorado's 7th district contest, and Taylor and Shuler benefited from substantial party help in North Carolina's 11th district race. These and other campaigns for hotly contested congressional seats were able to conduct extensive voter mobilization activities, and they benefited from the efforts of party committees and interest groups. Sixty percent of all House campaigns report that local party committees played a moderately important to extremely important role in their registration and GOTV drives, and almost three-quarters of the campaigns say that local parties were a moderately important to extremely important source of campaign volunteers.[49]

THE IMPORTANCE OF DIFFERENT COMMUNICATION TECHNIQUES

Congressional campaigns disseminate their messages through a variety of media, each having its advantages and disadvantages. Door-to-door campaigning is inexpensive but time consuming. Television advertising requires little commitment of the candidate's time, but it is rarely cheap. Radio advertising, direct mail, and mass telephone calls require accurate targeting to be effective.

Most campaigners believe that direct contact with voters is the best way to win votes (see Table 8-3). A firm handshake and a warm smile, accompanied by an explanation of why one wants to serve in Congress, perhaps followed by a direct response to a voter's question, are the best way to convey politically relevant information and build trust—two key ingredients to winning votes.[50] Indeed, other campaign communications intended to win undecided voters or mobilize supporters—whether television, radio, or direct mail, or biography or

TABLE 8-3

Campaigners' Perceptions of the Importance of Different Communications Techniques in House Campaigns

		Incumbents		Challengers		Open-seat candidates	
	All	In jeopardy	Shoo-ins	Hope-fuls	Likely losers	Pros-pects	Mis-matched
Direct contact with voters	91%	86%	92%	91%	91%	94%	94%
Broadcast TV ads	50	72	47	84	23	91	72
Cable TV ads	36	55	32	52	23	58	47
Newsletters or direct mail	70	83	83	84	51	77	83
Radio ads	50	69	51	66	38	57	65
Newspaper ads	33	17	30	38	35	34	53
Free media	77	83	83	81	71	76	76
Door-to-door campaigning	68	72	54	81	69	77	78
Mass telephone calls	54	79	54	62	39	77	56
Billboards or yard signs	65	59	67	72	62	60	88
Debates and forums	52	48	36	72	54	63	56
Internet web sites or e-mail	62	38	48	62	77	54	67

Source: The 2002 Congressional Campaign Study, Center for American Politics and Citizenship, University of Maryland.

Notes: Figures are for general election candidates in major-party contested races, excluding those in incumbent-versus-incumbent races, responding that a technique was moderately, very, or extremely important. The number of cases varies slightly because some respondents did not answer every question. $N = 318$.

issue-focused ads—aim to fulfill those same objectives. However, with the typical congressional district containing approximately 693,000 residents, candidates who wish to run competitive races cannot rely solely on direct voter contact, to say nothing of the challenges faced by Senate candidates, who must win the support of half their state's voters.

The next most popular communications techniques among candidates in close races are broadcast television, newsletters, direct mail, and free media. Incumbents find television (broadcast or cable) more important than challengers do, reflecting the fact that more incumbents can afford to broadcast TV commercials. But open-seat candidates most consistently evaluate television as very important, if not essential, to their campaigns. As shown in Chapter 6, the overwhelming majority of open-seat candidates can afford the high cost of broadcast time, and their races are usually competitive enough to warrant purchasing it.

Incumbents (regardless of the closeness of their elections), competitive challengers, and open-seat candidates also rely heavily on direct mail, newsletters, mass telephone calls, and free media to get out their message. Door-to-door campaigning, newspaper ads, candidate debates and forums, and web sites and e-mail are favored more by challengers and open-seat campaigns than by incumbents. Presumably nonincumbents depend more on door-to-door campaigning and newspaper ads because they are inexpensive. Similarly, they look to debates and forums because they are free and allow voters to make side-by-side comparisons between them and their opponent.

District characteristics and campaign strategy also affect how candidates use media. Television is a more important communication medium for House campaigns in rural districts than it is for those in urban and suburban settings because of cost and the mismatch between media markets and House districts in metropolitan areas. Greater population density allows campaigns waged in urban and suburban districts to make greater use of field activities, including distributing campaign literature and canvassing door to door, than can campaigns in rural areas. Campaigns that target individuals who live in particular neighborhoods, work in certain occupations, or belong to specific segments of the population (such as women, the elderly, or members of an ethnic group) make greater use of direct mail than do campaigns that focus their efforts on less easily identifiable groups, such as single-issue voters.[51]

INDEPENDENT, PARALLEL, AND COORDINATED CAMPAIGN COMMUNICATIONS

Not all of the communications that influence congressional elections are under a candidate's control. The independent, parallel, and coordinated campaigns waged by party committees and interest groups also can influence the messages voters receive. Indeed, party and interest group parallel campaigns are believed to have a greater impact on setting the campaign agenda in some elections than the candidates, largely because those organizations spend more money than the candidates' campaign committees. As one would expect, parties and groups are active only in some races. Incumbent shoo-ins, likely-loser challengers, and open-seat candidates competing in similarly lopsided elections typically maintain that outside groups had no impact on their campaign agenda.[52] Candidates in close races, by contrast, hold a different point of view. About two-thirds of them typically state that parties and interest groups sought to set the campaign agenda, and about one-half report that such organizations' efforts either helped or harmed their candidacy.[53] Open-seat contestants were significantly more likely than incumbents and challengers to describe party and interest group communications as having had an impact on the campaign agenda in their races. Parties and interest groups are more uniformly active in open-seat contests, in which outcomes are typically less predictable. They limit their agenda-setting activities in incumbent-challenger contests largely to competitive contests, viewing the results of the other races as virtually predetermined. Similarly, and as noted in Chapters 4 and 5, most of the independent expenditure and issue advocacy ads that party committees and interest groups broadcast on television, as well as the voter mobilization efforts that are at the heart of the coordinated campaigns, are in competitive elections.

SUMMARY

Campaign communications are the centerpiece of any bid for elective office. Congressional candidates disseminate their messages using a variety of media. Television and radio allow candidates to powerfully convey emotional messages. Direct mail and the Internet are less expensive and enable campaigns to disseminate targeted, customized messages. Free media coverage is highly sought after, but it can be difficult for some candidates to attract, and it affords campaigns less control over their message than other forms of communication. web sites are relatively inexpensive and can convey a great deal of information, but voters must actively search them out. Old-fashioned person-to-person contacts between candidates, campaign and local party activists, other volunteers, and voters, augmented by sophisticated targeting methods, are among the most effective means of communication.

Of course, the specific media mix that a campaign uses depends on the size of its war chest, the match between the district's boundaries and local media markets, and the talents and preferences of the individual candidate and the campaign's consultants. Another factor that influences candidates' campaign communications is the role that political parties and interest groups choose to play in their elections. Candidates whose elections are characterized by significant party or interest group agenda-setting activity have to compete for control over the election agenda not only with their opponent but also with these organizations. Party and group agenda-setting efforts in close races often require candidates to respond by adjusting their messages and the media they use to convey them. Nevertheless, as is the case in most aspects of congressional elections, incumbents enjoy tremendous advantages when it comes to communicating with voters.

CHAPTER NINE

Candidates, Campaigns, and Electoral Success

During the golden age of parties, party loyalties dominated the voting decisions of the vast majority of citizens and were the chief determinants of the outcome of most congressional elections. The decline of voter partisanship in the 1960s and 1970s paved the way for incumbency to have a greater effect on election outcomes.[1] Reelection rates routinely exceeded 90 percent for members of the House, as legislators began to make better use of the resources that the institution put at their disposal. Senators, capitalizing on the perks of their office, also enjoyed impressive reelection rates.[2] Although challenger victories were rare, the types of campaigns that individual candidates mounted, especially in open-seat contests, could make the difference between victory and defeat.

Incumbency, money, district partisanship, and other factors pertaining to individual candidates and their campaigns are usually the major determinants of modern congressional election outcomes. National forces have occasionally been important. They were important in 1994 and 2002, when congressional elections were nationalized in favor of the Republicans, and in 2006, when they favored the Democrats.

What separates winners from losers in contemporary congressional elections? How great an impact do candidate characteristics, political conditions, campaign strategy, campaign effort, media coverage, and party and interest group activities have on the percentage of the votes that candidates receive? Do these factors affect incumbents, challengers, and open-seat contestants equally? Or do different candidates need to do different things to win elections? This chapter addresses those questions. It also contains a discussion of the differences between what winners and losers think determines the outcomes of elections.

HOUSE INCUMBENT CAMPAIGNS

Incumbency is highly important in regard to the types of campaigns that candidates mount, and it is the most important determinant of congressional election outcomes.[3] Virtually all House incumbents begin the general election campaign with higher name recognition and voter approval levels, greater political experience, more money, and a better campaign organization than their opponent. Nearly all incumbents also benefit from the fact that most constituents and political elites in Washington expect them to win and act accordingly. For the most part, voters cast ballots, volunteers donate time, contributors give money, and news correspondents provide coverage in ways that favor incumbents. Most strategic politicians also behave in ways that contribute to high incumbent success rates. They usually wait until a seat becomes open, rather than take on a sitting incumbent and risk a loss that could harm their political career.

The big leads most incumbents enjoy at the beginning of the election season make defending those leads the major objective of their campaigns. Incumbent campaigns usually focus more on reinforcing and mobilizing existing bases of support than on winning new ones. The overwhelming advantages that most members of Congress possess make incumbency an accurate predictor of election outcomes in more than nine out of ten House races and three-quarters of all Senate races in which incumbents seek reelection.

Incumbency advantages are sometimes reduced in post-redistricting House elections. This is especially the case when incumbents are forced to compete against one another, run in a newly created district, or compete in a district that has been heavily redrawn, sometimes to their disadvantage. These members must introduce themselves to large numbers of voters who are unfamiliar with their records.

Even in elections that do not follow a redistricting, some incumbents find themselves in jeopardy, and a few challengers have realistic chances of winning. Incumbents who are implicated in a scandal, have cast roll-call votes that are not in accord with constituent opinions, or possess other liabilities need to mount more aggressive campaigns. They must begin campaigning early to reinforce their popularity among supporters, to remind voters of their accomplishments in office, and to set the campaign agenda. They also must be prepared to counter the campaigns of the strong challengers who are nominated to run against them and the independent, parallel, and coordinated campaigns that party committees and interest groups wage in support of those challengers. Many incumbents in jeopardy face experienced challengers, some of whom amass sufficient financial and organizational resources to mount a serious campaign. A few of the challengers capitalize on their opponent's weaknesses and win.

Because most incumbents have established a firm hold on their district, there is little they can do to increase their victory margins. Incumbents as a group, whether Democrat or Republican; Caucasian, Hispanic, or African American; old or young; male or female, have tremendously favorable odds of being reelected. Few variables (those identified as such in Table 9-1) have a significant, direct effect on the percentage of the vote that incumbents win. Such characteristics as gender, age, race, and occupation, which Chapter 2 showed to be so influential in separating House candidates from the general population, typically have no impact on the votes incumbents receive.[4] Primary challenges from within their own party rarely harm the reelection prospects of House incumbents who defeat primary opponents. Moreover, incumbents' targeting strategies, issue stances, and spending on campaign communications do not significantly increase their share of the vote in the general election.[5] Party and interest group outside communications efforts also rarely spell the difference between success and defeat in incumbent-challenger races.

The first figure in Table 9-1, labeled the base vote, represents the percentage of the vote that a House incumbent in a typical, two-party, contested race would have received if all the other factors were set to zero.[6] That is, a hypothetical incumbent who runs for reelection in a district that was not recently

TABLE 9-1

Significant Predictors of House Incumbents' Vote Shares

	Percentage of vote
Base vote	57.28
District is very different or completely new	−1.96
Partisan bias (per one-point advantage in party registration)	+0.15
Incumbent's ideological strength	+0.92
Incumbent implicated in scandal	−3.71
Challenger spending on campaign communications (per $100,000)	−0.84
Incumbent received most endorsements from local media	+5.22
National partisan tide	+2.02

Sources: The 2002 Congressional Campaign Study, Center for American Politics and Citizenship, University of Maryland; Federal Election Commission; and Political Money Line.

Notes: The figures were generated using ordinary least squares regression to analyze data for general election candidates in major-party contested races. Complete regression statistics are presented in note 6. $N = 97$.

altered by redistricting and comprises roughly equal numbers of registered Democratic and Republican voters; who has developed a reputation as a moderate member of Congress; and who spends no money, faces a challenger who spends no money, is not endorsed by most local editorial boards, and is in a race not affected by a national partisan tide would win about 57 percent of the vote.

Certain districts and states lend themselves to the election of particular types of candidates. Districts that are heavily affected by redistricting are usually less favorable to incumbents than are others. Incumbents who run in newly drawn districts or ones that are very different from those in which they previously competed typically suffer a net loss of about 2 percent of the vote that is not experienced by incumbents who run in seats that are largely unchanged by redistricting.

Partisanship also is important. Districts populated mainly by Democratic voters (often urban districts that are home to many lower-middle-class, poor, or minority voters) typically elect Democrats; those populated by Republican voters (frequently, rural, suburban, and more affluent districts) usually elect Republicans. The partisan bias of the district (the difference between the percentage of registered voters who belong to a candidate's party and the percentage who belong to the opponent's party) has a positive impact on incumbents' electoral prospects.[7] As the third figure in the table indicates, for every 1 percent increase in the partisan advantage that incumbents enjoy among registered voters, they receive a 0.15 percent boost at the polls (controlling for the other factors in the table). A Democratic incumbent who represents a one-sided district, with seventy-five registered Democratic voters for every twenty-five registered Republicans, typically starts out the election with a 7.5 percentage point (a fifty-point advantage in party registration multiplied by 0.15) vote advantage over a Democratic incumbent in a district that is evenly split between Democratic and Republican voters. Partisan bias is an important source of incumbency advantage because most House members represent districts that are populated primarily by members of their party.

Most incumbents begin the general election campaign relatively well known and liked by their constituents. Many voters have a general sense of where their House member falls on the ideological spectrum. Like Wally Herger, the shoo-in incumbent in California's 2nd district, most House members come from districts made up primarily of individuals who generally share their party and ideological preferences. As a result, these House members rarely face a strong general election challenge from the opposing party, though some Republican members must be concerned with facing a stiff primary test from the right, and their Democratic counterparts must be wary of a challenge from the left.[8] It is moderate members of Congress, who usually represent less ideologically consistent, more middle-of-the-road voters, who are at greater political risk in the general election. They need to build broader electoral coalitions, and they often face centrist challengers who are able to position themselves to compete aggressively for the same swing voters. These representational dynamics work to the advantage of staunch conservatives, such as Herger and most Republican House leaders, and unabashedly liberal Democrats, including most Democratic congressional leaders. They collect about three points more than do moderate House incumbents of either party.[9]

Of course, not all incumbents begin their reelection campaigns with clean slates. Members of Congress who are caught up in a scandal run the risk of angering or disappointing constituents, attracting strong opposition, or both. Some scandals involve many members of Congress. In a 1992 House banking scandal, for example, revelations that more than 325 House members had made 8,331 overdrafts at the House bank undermined the reelection campaigns of many of them. Other scandals involve only one or a few legislators. The 2006 elections featured many of those. Among them were the extramarital affair that appears to have cost Rep. Don Sherwood reelection in Pennsylvania and the cover-up of the Foley page scandal, which created difficulties for several Republican House leaders. The scandals concerning the receipt of vacations, meals, and other gifts from Jack Abramoff and other lobbyists also were important. They implicated several, mostly Republican members of the House and Senate. Incumbents typically pay a price of about 4 percent of the vote for being implicated in or closely associated with a scandal. Republican National Committee chairman Ken Mehlman maintains that in 2006, twelve GOP House incumbents lost their seats because of scandal.[10]

Scandal, ideology, and district conditions (usually in place before the start of the campaign season) can be important in determining an incumbent's vote share. But most of the aspects of incumbent campaigning that voters normally associate with elections do not have much influence in incumbent-challenger races. The targeting approaches that incumbents use and the themes and issues they stress do not significantly affect their vote margins. Nor do the dollars incumbents spend on direct mail; television, radio, and newspaper advertising; field work; or other communications make a significant contribution to the percentage of the vote that they win.[11]

Following the usual pattern, incumbent spending in 2006 increased in direct response to the closeness of the race.[12] Shoo-ins, such as Herger, who ran against underfunded challengers undertook fairly modest reelection efforts by incumbents' standards, assembling relatively small organizations and spending moderate sums of money. Those who were pitted against well-funded challengers, however, followed the example of Charles Taylor in North Carolina's 11th district and mounted expensive campaigns.

Although the communications expenditures and other campaign activities of incumbents are not significantly related to higher vote margins, they are not inconsequential. A more accurate interpretation is that incumbent campaigning generally works to reinforce rather than to expand a candidate's existing base of support. Incumbents who are in the most trouble—because they represent marginal districts, have been redistricted in ways that do not favor them, have been implicated in a scandal, have failed to keep in touch with voters, or are ideologically out of step with their constituents—usually spend the most. Most either succeed in reinforcing their electoral bases or watch their share of the vote dip slightly from those of previous years. Others watch their victory margins become perilously low. The high-powered campaigns these incumbents wage might make the difference between winning and losing. In a few cases, probably no amount of spending would make a difference. Scandal, poor performance, and other factors simply put reelection beyond the reach of a few House members. Whether an incumbent in a close race wins or loses, however, that individual would undoubtedly have done worse without an extensive campaign effort.

House challengers' expenditures do reduce incumbents' vote shares somewhat. The typical challenger spent roughly $280,000 on campaign communications in 2006, shaving about 2 percent more off the typical incumbent's vote share than a challenger who spent no money or just a few thousand dollars.[13] Strong challengers who ran against weak incumbents were able to raise and spend substantially more. Hopeful challengers committed an average of $1.1 million to campaign communications, which drove down the portion of the vote won by the typical incumbent in jeopardy by about seven percentage points. Individual challengers who spent even more generally drew greater numbers of votes away from incumbents, although the impact of campaign spending may diminish in the most expensive races.[14]

Attracting favorable media coverage can help an incumbent's reelection efforts. Editorial endorsements in local newspapers can be extremely influential because many voters read them and some take them into the voting booth. Incumbents who receive the lion's share of the endorsements from local media outlets are likely to benefit at the polls.[15] Roughly 85 percent of incumbents in races contested by both major parties benefit from this advantage. It improved their electoral performance by roughly five points over incumbents who did not enjoy such positive relations with the fourth estate. The efforts that House candidates and their press secretaries make to cultivate relationships with news correspondents are clearly worthwhile.

National partisan tides, which are beyond any one candidate's control, can affect how an incumbent fares in an election. The terrorist attacks of September 11, 2001, and the war in Afghanistan encouraged voters to focus on national security, which worked to the advantage of President Bush and his party in 2002 and 2004. However, in 2006 the unpopularity of the war in Iraq, growing numbers of American fatalities in the Middle East, and perceptions of widespread corruption and mismanagement in the Republican-controlled Congress and executive branch hung like an albatross around the necks of GOP candidates. National partisan tides gave Republican incumbents a two-point boost in 2002 and presumably a similar lift in the next election, but they worked against GOP House members in 2006. Indeed, candidates, party officials, and opinion leaders associated with both parties, as well as more neutral observers of politics, widely believe that the national mood was critical in bringing about the tidal wave that washed away many Republican members of the House and Senate.

These generalizations hold for the vast majority of incumbent campaigns waged throughout the 1990s and 2000s. However, a relatively small but important group of incumbent-challenger races illustrate the power of outside campaigning. As described in Chapters 4 and 5, the independent, parallel, and coordinated campaigns that political parties and interest groups mount are by and large outside a candidate's control. These campaigns often involve significant sums. Outside campaigning has the potential to change the dynamics of individual campaigns because it forces candidates to compete with other organizations, as well as with each other, when trying to set the election agenda and influence the political debate. Party and interest group communications often result in contests becoming more competitive and contentious.

Approximately 38 percent of all candidates competing in two-party, contested incumbent-challenger races in 2006 were the subject of independent expenditures by a party, PAC, or some other group. The vast majority of them were in competitive contests. The independent and parallel campaigns of political parties and interest groups had a variety of effects on these contests.[16] Most of the expenditures tried to link an incumbent to a scandal or some negative aspect of the national political agenda. Not surprisingly, this spending depressed those candidates' vote shares. Moreover, challenger spending on campaign communications took on heightened importance in races where outside groups were active, even though the effects of incumbent spending were the same as in other incumbent contests. Newspaper endorsements also brought incumbents somewhat fewer benefits, presumably because the plethora of political advertising to which voters were exposed weakened the endorsements' effects, as well as the influence of the candidates' own communications. Even independent expenditures and issue advocacy ads intended to help a candidate can cloud voters' perceptions of the race if the ads are "off message," presenting information that is inconsistent with the imagery and issue stances the campaign is seeking to project. Outside communications are more likely to harm than help incumbents, who generally win when their elections are low-key affairs that are ignored by national party committees and interest groups.

HOUSE CHALLENGER CAMPAIGNS

Most challengers begin the general election at a disadvantage. Lacking a broad base of support, these candidates must build one. Challengers need to mount aggressive campaigns to become visible, build name recognition, give voters reasons to support them, and overcome the initial advantages of their opponent. Most challenger campaigns also must communicate messages that not only will attract uncommitted voters but also will persuade some voters to abandon their pro-incumbent loyalties in favor of the challenger. The typical House challenger is in a position similar to that of a novice athlete pitted against a world-class sprinter. The incumbent has experience, talent, professional handlers, funding, equipment, and crowd support. The challenger has few, if any, of these assets and has a monumental task to accomplish in a limited amount of time. Predictably, most challengers end up eating their opponent's dust. Still, not every novice athlete or every congressional challenger is destined to suffer the agony of defeat. A strong challenger who is able to assemble the money and organization to devise and carry out a good game plan may be able to win if the incumbent stumbles.

Even though the vast majority of challengers ultimately lose, the experience and resources that they bring to their races have an impact on their ability to win votes. In short, challenger campaigning matters. The figures in Table 9-2 reveal that challengers' nomination contests, election expenditures, targeting, strategies, campaign messages, and media relations affect their vote shares in meaningful ways.[17] The same is true of national forces that may be working to favor the candidates of one party over the candidates of the other.

The table shows that a hypothetical House challenger will finish with about 25 percent of the vote—far from victory—under the following circumstances: The candidate runs in a district that is evenly split between registered Republicans and Democrats and is handed a major-party nomination without a primary fight; the candidate uses an unorthodox targeting strategy, fails to offer voters a clear choice on the issues, runs a race bereft of all candidate campaign spending, and receives few endorsements from the local news media; and the contest is unaffected by national partisan forces.

TABLE 9-2

Significant Predictors of House Challengers' Vote Shares

	Percentage of vote
Base vote	25.29
Partisan bias (per one-point advantage in party registration)	+0.13
Contested primary	+2.46
Targeted own party members, independents, or both	+2.50
Advertising focused on challenger or incumbent's issue positions	+1.84
Challenger spending on campaign communications (per $100,000)	+0.31
Incumbent spending on campaign communications (per $100,000)	+0.56
Challenger received most endorsements from local media	+5.50
National partisan tide	+2.50

Sources: The 2002 Congressional Campaign Study, Center for American Politics and Citizenship, University of Maryland; Federal Election Commission; and Political Money Line.

Notes: The figures were generated using ordinary least squares regression to analyze data for general election candidates in major-party contested races. Complete regression statistics are presented in note 17. $N = 138$.

Challengers who run under more favorable circumstances fare better. In most cases the partisan composition of the district works to the advantage of the incumbent, but a few challengers are fortunate enough to run in districts that include more members of their party. Challengers in districts in which the balance of registered voters favors their party by 10 percent begin the general election with a 1.3 percent advantage over those who run in neutral districts. Those few challengers who run in districts that favor their party by 20 percent possess an advantage of between 2 percent and 3 percent of the vote.

Political experience and campaign professionalism have indirect effects on a challenger's ability to win votes. As explained in Chapters 2 and 3, challengers with office-holding or significant nonelective political experience are more likely than political amateurs to run when their odds of winning are best, to capture their party's nomination, and to assemble organizations that draw on the expertise of salaried professionals and political consultants. Moreover, political experience and campaign professionalism help challengers raise money, as Chapter 6 demonstrated. They also help challengers attract free media coverage and endorsements, as well as favorable outside communications by party committees and interest groups, as shown in Chapters 4 and 5. Challenger campaigns that are staffed with experienced political operatives also are presumably better at targeting, message development, communications, and grassroots activities than those run by amateurs.[18]

Contested primaries, which only rarely have negative general election consequences for the incumbents who survive them, have a positive impact on the prospects of House challengers who emerge from them victorious. It should be recalled from Chapter 2 that primaries in which an incumbent is challenged are often hotly contested when the incumbent is perceived to be vulnerable; they are usually won by strategic candidates who know how to wage strong campaigns. The organizational effort, campaign activities, and media coverage associated with contested primaries provide the winners with larger bases of support and more name recognition than they would have attained had the primary not been contested. The momentum that House challengers get from contested primaries and the incumbent weaknesses that give rise to these primaries in the first place lead to stronger performances in general elections. Challengers who have had to defeat one or more opponents in a primary typically wind up winning between two and three percentage points more than challengers who were merely handed their party's nomination.

General election campaign strategy is critical. Challengers who target members of their own party, independents, or both win more votes than those who use less-conventional strategies, such as targeting all registered voters, or no strategy at all. Challengers who run issue-oriented campaigns that focus on their or their opponent's policy stances win more votes than those who focus on character and experience or who fail to deliver a clear campaign message. Heath Shuler, in his successful challenge to the incumbent, Taylor, in North Carolina's 11th district, for example, aggressively courted Democrats and swing voters. He campaigned on a variety of issues, including education, health care reform, the environment, the war in Iraq, and job creation. However, he drew the sharpest line between himself and Taylor when he focused on corruption in Washington and explained that the most important thing voters could do was to send a new leader who had integrity to Washington.[19] Challengers who use partisan targeting strategies receive, on average, a 2 percent to 3 percent boost in their vote share. Those who draw issue-oriented distinctions between themselves and their opponents receive a 2 percent boost.

Not surprisingly, campaign spending is another factor that has a significant impact on the vote shares challengers receive. For every $100,000 that House challengers spent on television, radio, campaign literature, direct mail, mass telephone calls, the Internet, campaign field work, or some other form of campaign communication, they won an additional 0.31 percent of the vote. Challengers in 2006 spent an average of $278,000 on campaign communications, garnering the typical challenger an additional 0.84 percent of the ballot. Incumbent spending on campaign communications, largely a reaction to the closeness of the race and the efforts of strong challengers and their supporters, is not significantly related to challengers' vote shares.

Large communications expenditures by both candidates are strongly associated with closely decided incumbent-challenger races. Taylor spent $3.4 million, and Shuler spent approximately $1.1 million on campaign communications in their 2006 contest. Because Taylor's contributions to his own campaign triggered the millionaires' provision of the Bipartisan Campaign Reform Act of 2002, the Democratic Party was free to make unlimited coordinated expenditures in the race. Party coordinated spending increased by almost $1.6 million the amount the Shuler campaign could use to disseminate its message to voters, and it brought the two campaigns' communications spending near parity. Shuler's and the Democrats' communications expenditures undoubtedly played an important role in the challenger's eight-point victory.[20]

Low-spending incumbent-challenger campaigns tend to produce very lopsided results. A. J. Sekhon spent only about $130,000 to communicate with voters in his twenty-eight-point loss to Herger, who spent about $187,000 in their California House race. That the typical 2006 House challenger spent roughly $280,000 on campaign communications helps to explain why so few of them won and why challengers generally fare poorly.[21]

Media relations, which involve a courtship of sorts between candidates and local media outlets, also can have significant consequences for an election. The 5 percent or so of all House challengers who are endorsed by the local press typically watch their vote shares increase between 5 percent and 6 percent. National partisan tides, over which challengers have no control, can be important. The pro-Republican trend of 2002 provided the typical GOP challenger with an extra two to three percentage points; the pro-Democratic tide of 2006 gave Democratic challengers a similar boost.

How best to allocate scarce financial resources is a constant concern for strategists in challenger campaigns. Are radio or television commercials more effective than campaign literature? How effective is direct mail at influencing voters compared with less precisely tailored and less well-targeted forms of advertising? Is it worthwhile to invest money in newspaper ads or the grassroots activities commonly referred to as "campaign field work"?

Direct mail and campaign literature, which can be directed to specific voting blocs, are among the most cost-effective campaign activities.[22] For every $10,000 a challenger campaign spends on direct mail, it gains an average of about 0.24 percent of the vote. The typical challenger campaign spent about $15,000 on direct mail, helping to increase its share of the vote by 0.36 percent.

Campaign literature provides a somewhat lower return, yielding 0.14 points per $10,000. Challengers spend an average of $21,000 on literature, which is associated with a net pickup of 0.28 points at the polls. Hopeful challengers spend considerably more on some of these activities. Shuler spent roughly $225,000 on direct mail, which is associated with a 1.1 percentage point increase in the vote.

Television commercials are less targeted, are considerably more expensive, and bring somewhat lower returns per dollar than do the activities already mentioned. The typical House challenger campaign spends about $60,000 on television ads, which is associated with an increase of about 0.42 percent of the vote. Hopeful challengers spend an average of about $280,000 on TV ads, bringing them roughly two points more at the polls. Shuler and the few other challengers who had the wherewithal to spend about $850,000 on television advertising saw their vote shares increase by 5.5 points. Of course, Democratic Party coordinated spending on TV ads increased this return. Because the candidate's campaign and the party jointly designed the ads, they blended seamlessly with the campaign's other communications. Radio ads, which fall between direct mail and newspaper ads in terms of targeting, can have a positive impact on some challenger races, but they do not significantly increase challengers' vote shares overall.

Newspaper advertisements, purchased by little more than half of all challenger campaigns, are typically a low-priority, low-budget item. The typical challenger spent about $740 on newspaper ads, for no net increase in vote returns.

Field work is the most labor-intensive form of electioneering. It differs from direct mail and television advertising in that, if done properly, it requires both skillful targeting and a corps of committed campaign workers. It also is performed in cooperation with parties and interest groups. Thus the money that the typical challenger spends on field work does not perfectly describe the candidate's field operations. Contacts between candidates and voters and other field activities, which are often coordinated by specialized consultants and carried out by volunteer workers, do not have a statistically measurable impact on challengers' vote shares, although they are believed to be effective forms of campaigning.

Finally, the independent, parallel, and coordinated campaign efforts of party committees and interest groups work to the advantage of the challengers they are intended to help. Challengers in elections where parties or advocacy groups try to set the campaign agenda do five points better at the polls than challengers in general, even absent any candidate spending or other activities.[23] Despite the benefit challengers gain from these party and group efforts, many are ambivalent about them, and with good reason. Outside spending can neutralize the effects of some important elements of challenger strategy, including those associated with voter targeting and campaign advertising. It takes control away from the campaign and puts it in the hands of others, blurring the message the campaign intends to convey.

In sum, most House challengers lose because the odds are so heavily stacked against them. Those few who run in favorable or competitive districts, compete against a vulnerable incumbent, assemble the resources needed to communicate with voters, develop and implement a sound campaign strategy that blends partisan targeting with an issue-oriented message, and spend their money wisely win more votes than those who do not. The same is true of those who curry favor with the media and benefit from party and interest group outside spending. Despite doing all of these things correctly, these challengers rarely win enough votes to defeat an incumbent. The partisan composition of most House districts, the preelection activities that incumbents undertake to cultivate the support of constituents, and their success in warding off talented and well-funded challengers are critical in determining the outcome of most incumbent-challenger races.

Nevertheless, politics is a game that is often played at the margins. Not all House incumbents begin the general election as shoo-ins and go on to win. The few who hold competitive seats, are implicated in scandal, are out of step with their constituents, draw a strong major-party opponent, or are targeted for defeat by the opposing party and independent-spending interest groups often find themselves in a precarious position. Many of these incumbents spend huge sums of money, sometimes to no avail. If the challengers who run against them are able to apply the lessons learned while working in politics (or imparted by a political consultant) and assemble the money and organizational resources to wage a strong campaign, they can put their opponents on the defensive. Challengers have some chance of winning if they set the campaign agenda, carefully target their base and groups of potential supporters, tailor their messages to appeal to those voters, and communicate their messages through paid ads, free media, and strong field operations. Challengers who can attract newspaper endorsements and considerable outside spending by parties and interest groups have even better odds. A win by a challenger is typically the result of both incumbent failure and a strong challenger campaign. Numerous House members were anxious about their reelection prospects before the 2006 campaign. Some incumbents retired. Others sought reelection, and few of those were defeated. The challengers who beat an incumbent were successful primarily as a result of their own efforts, including their successful campaigns for resources and their successful campaigns for votes. Party and interest group independent, parallel, and coordinated campaigns and a strong national partisan tide also helped Democratic challengers defeat Republican incumbents in the 2006 general election.

HOUSE OPEN-SEAT CAMPAIGNS

Elections for open House seats are usually won by much smaller margins than incumbent-challenger races. Once a seat becomes open, several factors come into play. The partisanship of the district and the skills and resources of the candidates and their organizations have a greater influence on elections when there is no incumbent who can draw on established voter loyalties. Because voters usually lack strong personal loyalties to either candidate, campaigning becomes more important. The same is true of local media endorsements and national partisan trends. The factors that significantly affect the outcome of open-seat House races are listed in Table 9-3.[24]

The partisan bias of open seats is important. Candidates who run for open seats in districts where the balance of voter registration favors their party do much better than others. Those who run for open seats in districts where the registration balance favors their party by 10 percent have, on average, a 1.7 percent vote advantage over those who compete in districts with the same number of Democrats and Republicans.

Campaign strategy is critical to the outcome of an open-seat contest. Campaigns that target party members, independents, or both typically increase their votes by five percentage points over those that do not consider partisanship when formulating their targeting plans. Candidates' issue positions also have a large impact. Unlike incumbents, open-seat candidates do not have to defend a congressional voting record, nor are they in a position to emphasize their performance in office. Unlike challengers, they are not in a situation where they can attack a sitting House member for failing to tend adequately to constituents' needs, nor can they use a member's congressional roll-call votes to contrast the incumbent's issue positions with their own. Open-seat candidates are usually best served when they put together an issue-based message that is powerful enough to inspire a strong turnout by voters who identify with their party and to attract the support of swing voters. In 2002, the Republicans who campaigned on homeland security, defense-related issues, or taxes—issues that are favorably associated with the GOP—performed better than Republicans who focused on other issues. In 2006 the Democrats who focused on government corruption and mismanagement, the Iraq War, jobs and the economy, health care, and other Democratic positional issues also

TABLE 9-3
Significant Predictors of House Open-Seat Candidates' Vote Shares

	Percentage of vote
Base vote	24.15
Partisan bias (per one-point advantage in party registration)	+0.17
Targeted own party members, independents, or both	+4.68
Republican ran on Republican issues	+7.42
Open-seat candidate spending on campaign communications:	
$400,000	+25.44
$600,000	+26.98
$800,000	+28.08
$1,000,000	+28.93
$2,000,000	+31.57
$3,000,000	+33.11
Opponent spending on campaign communications:	
$400,000	−20.46
$600,000	−21.70
$800,000	−22.58
$1,000,000	−23.27
$2,000,000	−25.39
$3,000,000	−26.63
Candidate received most endorsements from local media	+6.70
National partisan tide	+8.52

Sources: The 2002 Congressional Campaign Study, Center for American Politics and Citizenship, University of Maryland; Federal Election Commission; and Political Money Line.

Notes: The figures were generated using ordinary least squares regression to analyze data for general election candidates in major-party contested races. Complete regression statistics are presented in note 24. $N = 50$.

were very successful in attracting votes. This is to be expected given the salience of those issues and the impact they had on individuals' congressional voting decisions (discussed in Chapter 4).

Candidates in open-seat elections stand to make large gains in name recognition and voter support through their campaign communications. In contrast to candidates in incumbent-challenger races, both candidates in open-seat elections clearly benefit from spending on campaign advertising and voter contact. A campaign's initial expenditures are particularly influential because they help voters become aware of a candidate and his or her message. Further expenditures, although still important, have a lower rate of return; as more voters learn about the candidates and their issue positions, the effects of campaign spending diminish. An open-seat candidate facing an opponent who spends virtually no money gains, on average, an additional 25 percent above the base vote of 24 percent for the first $400,000 spent to communicate with voters. That same candidate gains an additional 1.5 percent of the vote (a total increase of almost 27 percent) when he or she increases spending by $200,000. An expenditure of $3 million would increase a candidate's vote share by about 1.5 percent over the amount gained for the first $2 million in communications expenditures—the same increase a candidate wins when moving from $400,000 to $600,000.

Lopsided spending is unusual in open-seat contests; rarely does a candidate spend $3 million, $2 million, $600,000, or even $100,000 against an opponent who spends virtually nothing. More often, these elections feature two well-funded opponents. When the campaigns spend nearly the same amount on communications, their expenditures come close to offsetting each other. Once the campaigns have completely saturated the airwaves, overstuffed the mailboxes, and left about half a dozen or so voice mail and e-mail messages, the quality and timing of their communications may have a bigger influence on the election outcome than the dollars each ultimately spends to reach out to voters. In the 2006 race in Colorado's 7th district, for example, Rick O'Donnell spent about $2.8 million on campaign communications to Ed Perlmutter's approximately $1.6 million, in a race where Perlmutter defeated O'Donnell by a 12 percent vote margin.[25]

The amounts that open-seat campaigns spend on most forms of campaign communication are positively related to the number of votes they receive, but the precise effects of the communications are difficult to evaluate because relatively few open-seat contests take place in any given election year. It is possible, however, to make some generalizations about the relative importance of the techniques open-seat candidates use to get out their message. Open-seat candidates spend substantial portions of their campaign budgets on campaign literature, direct mail, TV, and radio. Of these, literature, direct mail, and radio—which can be directed to specific individuals or voting blocs—have the greatest electoral impact.[26]

The mass media also play an important role in open-seat House races. Experienced politicians who have strong campaign organizations and run for open seats in districts that are made up mostly of voters who belong to their party usually receive better treatment from the media than their opponents. Open-seat candidates, such as Perlmutter, who win the endorsements of the local press typically pick up an additional 7 percent of the vote.

The partisan tides that lifted some House candidates in incumbent-challenger races in 2002 and 2006 had even greater influence on campaigns for open seats. Republican open-seat candidates in 2002 benefited from an eight-to-nine-point boost in their vote shares, giving them a considerable edge over their Democratic opponents. Four years later, the tsunami that took with it many House GOP incumbents gave many Democratic candidates for open seats a boost, resulting in Democrats capturing nine formerly Republican open seats.

Competitive open-seat contests usually attract substantial independent, parallel, and coordinated campaign activity by parties and interest groups. Voters in Colorado's 7th congressional district, for example, were exposed to appreciably more campaign activities than voters nationally in 2006. The Perlmutter campaign, the Colorado Democratic Party, and Too Extreme for Colorado (the Democratic-leaning interest group) aired ten unique television spots, and these organizations and a variety of progressive interest groups were responsible for no less than twenty pieces of direct mail, nineteen e-mails, twenty mass phone calls, two radio ads, and five personal voter contacts from volunteers and paid campaign aides. The O'Donnell campaign and its allies were no less aggressive in seeking to get out their message. The campaign, various Republican Party committees, and some conservative interest groups broadcast at least a dozen unique TV ads. These same organizations also disseminated roughly nineteen direct-mail pieces, twenty-eight e-mails, one wave of mass phone calls, one radio ad, one newspaper advertisement, and two personal contacts. Much of this activity took place during the last week or so before the election.[27] One of the effects of this saturation advertising is that even many of the least politically engaged voters learn something about the election; another effect is that most voters become weary of being bombarded with messages and look forward to the election being over.

Just as party and interest group independent and parallel campaigns can change the dynamics of incumbent-challenger races, they can influence the conduct of open-seat elections.[28] Such outside spending on campaign communications rewards candidates whose campaigns use party affiliation to guide their tactics. Both Democratic and Republican campaigns in districts that were inundated by significant outside advertising received a greater boost from their use of voter partisanship to guide their targeting than did campaigns where parties and groups did not seek to influence the campaign agenda. Republicans campaigning in contests featuring a high volume of party and interest group activity in 2002 and 2004 reaped greater electoral benefits from emphasizing pro-Republican issues, including the war on terrorism, national defense, and tax cuts, than GOP candidates who did so in elections free of outside spending. The same lesson appears to have applied in 2006: Democrats who campaigned on Democratic positional issues, such as an unpopular war in

Iraq, protecting American jobs, and health care, and on holding the Republicans accountable for government corruption and mismanagement enjoyed greater success than those who focused on other issues.

Party and advocacy group independent, parallel, and coordinated campaign efforts in open-seat contests tend to reduce the impact of communications that concentrate voters' attention on the candidates and issues involved in a particular race. Local newspaper endorsements also have little effect under such circumstances, presumably because they lose their potency when voters are saturated with political information.

SENATE CAMPAIGNS

The small number of Senate elections that occur in a given election year and the differences in the size and politics of the states in which they take place make it difficult to generalize about Senate campaigns. Nevertheless, a few broad statements are possible. Chief among them is that incumbents possess substantial advantages over challengers. The advantages of incumbency in Senate elections are similar to those it bestows in House elections. Most Senate incumbents enjoy fundraising advantages, greater name recognition, and more political experience—particularly in running a statewide campaign—than their opponents.

Yet the advantages that senators enjoy are not as great as those that House members have over their opponents. Most Senate challengers and open-seat candidates have previously served in the House, as governor, or in some other public capacity and are more formidable opponents than their House counterparts. Their previous political experience helps Senate challengers assemble the financial and organizational resources and attract the media coverage needed to run a competitive campaign.[29]

One of the most important differences between Senate and House contests is the effect of incumbent expenditures on election outcomes. Although increased challenger spending has a negative effect on incumbents' margins in both Senate and House elections, it is only in Senate races that spending by incumbents is positively related to the number of votes they receive. Incumbent expenditures on campaign communications are not as important as challenger expenditures, but the amounts that both sides spend are influential in determining the victor in Senate elections.[30] This difference is due to three major factors. First, because Senate challengers are usually better qualified, Senate elections tend to be closer than House contests. Second, senators' six-year terms and greater responsibilities in Washington result in their meeting less frequently with voters than House members do, so the bonds that they establish with their constituents are not as strong. Senators' larger constituencies also prevent them from establishing the kinds of personal ties with voters that House members have.[31] Third, the greater diversity of their constituencies means that senators are more likely to offend some voters in the course of their legislative activities. Because of these differences, campaign spending and campaigning in general are more likely to affect the electoral prospects of Senate than House incumbents.

Senate elections bear further comparison with House contests. Scandal and the partisan bias of the constituency influence the results of elections for both the upper and lower chambers. Senate campaigns' targeting strategies and issue selection also are believed to be important.[32] Primary challenges, which have no detrimental effects on the election prospects of House incumbents, harm those of incumbents in Senate campaigns.[33]

The 2006 Senate election in Ohio illustrates many of the preceding generalizations. In particular, it highlights the importance of incumbency, an experienced challenger, issues, voter targeting, message, and field work.[34] In that campaign a Democratic House member, Sherrod Brown, sought to defeat the sitting Republican senator, Mike DeWine. Even though DeWine had won his previous election by a twenty-point margin, several factors combined to make him appear vulnerable in 2006. One source of vulnerability is the diversity of the state. Ohio has five distinct regions, each with a unique political culture. This makes building a political coalition challenging and maintaining one over a long time difficult. A moderate on some issues and conservative on others, DeWine had cast some votes during his twelve years in the Senate that probably strained his relations with some voters, making him vulnerable to defections under certain circumstances. For example, DeWine's pro-life position (to allow abortion when the life of the mother is in danger or in cases involving incest or rape) would probably not fully satisfy voters on either side of the abortion debate; his support for gun control laws did little to endear him to the highly organized membership of the National Rifle Association; and his support for the Iraq War and the Bush administration did not help him as the war's and the president's popularity declined. Moreover, Ohio was a poor venue in which to be a Republican running for reelection in a year when corruption and scandal were major political issues. As noted in Chapter 7, political scandals involving Ohio's Republican governor and other prominent GOP politicians in the Buckeye State added to Ohioans' desire for a change in political leadership. Although DeWine was not directly implicated in any national or state scandal, merely that he was running for reelection as a Republican increased his vulnerability.

DeWine had an easy route to his party's nomination. He faced token opposition by two Republicans, who combined raised less than $23,000. Things were not so straightforward in the Democrat's nominating contest. After initially resisting the recruitment efforts of the Democratic Senatorial Campaign Committee, Brown jumped into the contest in October 2005. By that time Paul Hackett, an Iraq War veteran who had come within four percentage points of winning a special election to a Republican-held House seat in August 2005, had entered the contest. After months of behind-the-scenes maneuvering, Hackett withdrew from the primary, enabling Brown to handily defeat Merrill Keiser, a socially conservative Democrat with no political experience. Once the primary season was over, both Brown and DeWine entered the general election campaign in earnest. Although the incumbent had a financial advantage, outspending the challenger by $14.2 million to $10.8 million, both had substantial resources at their disposal. The DeWine campaign spent about $7.6 million on television ads to Brown's approximately $5 million. Both also spent large sums on direct mail, mass telephone calls, and other campaign communications.

The DeWine campaign's strategy consisted primarily of mobilizing the Republican base. Given the competitiveness of the state, which is fairly evenly divided between Democrats and Republicans, DeWine's moderate positions on some issues, and the scandals plaguing GOP politicians in Ohio and nationwide, the campaign made it a priority to shore up its support among Republican voters. The Brown campaign also sought to mobilize its base, but the issue environment provided it with advantages in reaching out to swing voters. As indicated in Chapters 7 and 8, Brown emphasized issues of importance to the middle class and his opposition to congressional Republicans and President Bush. DeWine's campaign communications were not as thematically focused and including appeals to a variety of constituencies.

Political parties and interest groups were very active in the Ohio race. As discussed in Chapter 4, the parties invested millions in contributions and coordinated expenditures, and national party organizations transferred millions of dollars to the state to help finance independent, parallel, and coordinated campaigns. Much of the money was spent on television, radio, direct mail, and voter identification, registration, and get-out-the-vote efforts. Interest groups also contributed more millions of dollars and committed huge sums to finance similar campaign activities. Indeed, parties and interest groups spent more on television advertising than the candidates did.

One result of all of this outside spending was that Ohio voters were deluged with campaign communications. Television expenditures in the Senate contest alone reached more than $26 million, and candidate, parties, and groups spent tens of millions of dollars more in the state's gubernatorial, U.S. House, and state legislative contests. Candidates, parties, and interest groups also mailed 134 unique pieces of direct mail focused on the Senate contest, with some voters receiving similar numbers of letters in connection with other elections. Party and interest group electronic media ads and direct mail added considerably to the negativity of the race.

National party leaders assumed prominent roles in the race. Visits by President George W. Bush, former president Bill Clinton, and Senators McCain, Biden, Clinton, and Obama served to remind voters of the national implications of the contest. DeWine's ties to Bush and McCain may not have been as helpful as Brown's links to Clinton and the Democratic aspirants to the White House. Ohioans who questioned the war in Iraq, the movement of manufacturing jobs abroad, and the overall performance of the Republican-led U.S. and Ohio governments were apparently more motivated to come to the polls on behalf of Brown than voters who favored Republican positional issues and supported DeWine.

It is impossible to tell exactly what contribution specific factors made to the outcome of a race decided by twelve percentage points. The candidates' experience and political records and their campaign communications, as well as those of the political parties and interest groups, all were probably important. The same can be said of the stumping by the parties' national leaders and Brown's more tightly focused message.

CLAIMING CREDIT AND PLACING BLAME

Once the election is over, candidates and their campaign staffs have a chance to reflect. Their main interest, naturally, is what caused the election to turn out as it did. Winners and losers have very different ideas about what factors influence congressional election outcomes. Some differences are obvious. Losing candidates almost always obsess about money, particularly the funds that they and their opponents spent on campaigning. Unsuccessful candidates for the House generally considered the funds that they and their opponents spent to have been very important in determining the outcome of their elections, whereas the winners believed money was only moderately important (see Table 9-4).[35] Defeated candidates also placed greater emphasis on the impact of party and interest group spending on their elections than did winners. Some had strong beliefs about the influence of the parties' and groups' independent, parallel, and coordinated campaigns.

Unsuccessful candidates frequently assert that if they had had more money—or if their party or interest group allies had spent more money on

TABLE 9-4

Winners' and Losers' Opinions of the Determinants of House Elections

	Winners	Losers
Money spent by campaigns	2.95	3.90
Money spent by political parties	2.11	2.97
Money spent by advocacy groups	1.79	2.60
Candidate's image and personality	4.53	3.53
Incumbent's record	4.10	2.79
Incumbency advantages	3.51	4.51
Local issues	3.53	2.74
National domestic issues	3.69	3.05
Foreign affairs and defense	3.36	2.96
Party loyalty	3.11	3.65
Newspaper endorsements	2.23	2.25
U.S. Senate election	1.96	2.58
State or local elections	1.96	2.55
Negative campaigning	1.86	2.04
Debates	1.72	1.85
Political scandal in own race	1.36	1.47

Source: The 2002 and 1998 Congressional Campaign Studies, Center for American Politics and Citizenship, University of Maryland.

Notes: Candidates and campaign aides were asked to assess the importance of each factor on the following scale: 1 = not important; 2 = slightly important; 3 = moderately important; 4 = very important; 5 = extremely important. The values listed are arithmetic means. Figures for the impact of incumbent's record and incumbency advantages exclude responses from candidates and campaign aides from open seats. Figures are for general election candidates in major-party contested races, excluding those in incumbent-versus-incumbent races. See note 35 for more details.

their behalf—they would have reached more voters and won more votes. The better than three-to-one advantage in campaign resources that victorious House incumbents had over losing challengers in 2006 supports their point (see Figure 9-1). The 63 percent spending advantage that successful open-seat candidates had over their opponents is not as large, but it also lends credence to the view that money matters. The fact that successful House challengers in two-party contested races spent almost $2 million, on average, in the 2006 elections demonstrates that the cost of admission is fairly high.

The patterns of spending in competitive House elections further reinforce the importance of money (see Figure 9-2). Moreover, they show that these contests attract substantial attention from outside groups. Incumbents in jeopardy who managed to hold onto their seats attracted, on average, $50,000 in outside spending advocating their reelection, mainly indepen-

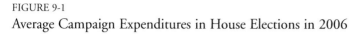

FIGURE 9-1

Average Campaign Expenditures in House Elections in 2006

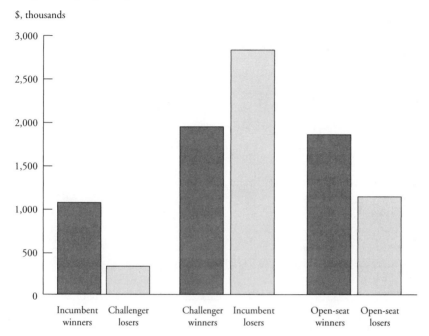

$, thousands

Source: Compiled from Federal Election Commission data.

Notes: Figures are for major-party candidates in contested general elections. They include candidate expenditures and party coordinated expenditures; they exclude funds candidates donated to other candidates and party committees. $N = 754$.

dent expenditures by parties or PACs or internal communications by corporations, trade associations, labor unions, or other groups.[36] These candidates also benefited from another $321,000 that these organizations spent to attack their opponents. The hopeful challengers who lost to these candidates benefited from similar amounts of outside spending, which helped them compensate for the better than two-to-one campaign spending advantage enjoyed by the incumbents. Candidate and outside spending was considerably higher in the races where a challenger defeated a House incumbent, such as the Shuler-Taylor contest, but even in those cases incumbents and their allies typically held a financial advantage. Not surprisingly, elections between open-seat prospects, who are usually equally matched in many respects, are financially competitive and attract considerable outside spending. The 2006 Perlmutter-O'Donnell race was typical in that the winner and his

FIGURE 9-2

Average Campaign Spending in Competitive House Elections in 2006

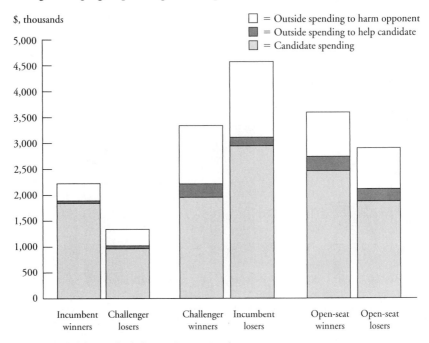

Source: Compiled from Federal Election Commission data.

Notes: Figures are for major-party candidates in contested general elections. Candidate spending includes candidate expenditures and party coordinated expenditures (over which candidates exercise some influence); they exclude funds candidates donated to other candidates and party committees. Outside spending includes independent expenditures and interest group internal communications to members, either to help a candidate or harm an opponent. $N = 244$.

allies enjoyed a financial advantage over the loser. The patterns for Senate elections further corroborate the importance of money in elections and substantiate the claim that outside spending can help level the playing field between challengers and incumbents, especially in contests where the challenger emerges victorious (see Figure 9-3).

There are differences of opinion about the extent to which factors other than money influence election outcomes. Successful House candidates have a strong tendency to credit their victories to their own attributes and to factors that were largely under their campaign's control. They believe that the candidate's image was the most important determinant of their election. Successful incumbents credit their record in office next. They also acknowledge the advantages they derived from incumbency.

FIGURE 9-3

Average Campaign Spending in Senate Elections in 2006

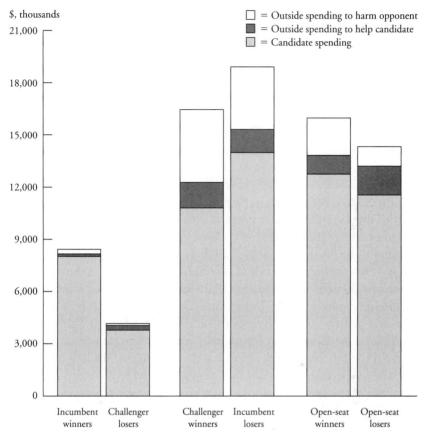

Source: Compiled from Federal Election Commission data.

Notes: Figures are for major-party candidates in contested general elections. Candidate spending includes candidate expenditures and party coordinated expenditures (over which candidates exercise some influence); they exclude funds candidates donated to other candidates and party committees. Outside spending includes independent expenditures and interest group internal communications to members, either to help a candidate or harm an opponent. $N = 60$.

The winners of House races rank issues as having been moderately to very influential in producing the outcomes of their elections. Democratic winners in recent elections believed that they benefited from focusing on jobs and the economy, Social Security, Medicare and health care generally, education, the environment, or some other traditional Democratic issue. Many successful Republican candidates believed they helped themselves by concentrating on tax cuts, moral values, national defense, and other issues that have traditionally formed the core of the GOP's communication efforts. Candidates of both parties considered local concerns to have been roughly as important as national domestic issues, followed by foreign affairs or defense. Winning candidates rate the partisan loyalties of voters in their districts as moderately important.

Finally, winners generally believe that newspaper endorsements; the influence of U.S. Senate, state, or local elections; negative campaigning; debates; and political scandal were much less important to the outcome of their contests. The winners' opinions reflect a tendency to attribute their victories to their own efforts and the wisdom of voters.[37] These beliefs stand in stark contrast to political science theories that suggest that congressional election outcomes are primarily a function of national conditions and events.[38]

Defeated House candidates have very different views about what caused their candidacies to conclude as they did. First and foremost, losing challengers point to the incumbent's perquisites of office, which they believe to have been very to extremely important. Next, unsuccessful candidates point to money—specifically, the financial advantages of their opponent. They rank the partisanship of voters in their district third. Candidate images came in fourth, followed by national domestic issues, foreign affairs and defense-related issues, and party and interest group spending. Unsuccessful candidates typically believe that local issues and debates are less important than these other factors. They place more emphasis on the influence of Senate, state, and local elections than do winners. Defeated candidates prefer to rationalize their defeats by blaming them on factors over which neither they nor their campaigns had any control.[39] The losers' views bear similarities to political science theories that downplay the importance of individual candidates and campaigns.[40]

Senate candidates have a somewhat different view of the causes of their election outcomes than do House contestants. Both the winners and losers in Senate contests emphasize factors that are largely under their control. Contestants generally believe that the images they projected to the voters were the number-one determinant of the election outcome. Winners typically maintain that candidate imagery was extremely important, whereas losers believe it was moderately important. Winners are more likely to emphasize the importance of issues, ranking them second only to imagery. Losing challengers, in contrast, believe that the advantages of office holding are substantially more important. Winning and losing incumbents are equally likely to view incumbency as a two-edged sword, agreeing that the anger that many voters direct at Washington reduces their vote margins.

Senate incumbents place greater emphasis on the importance of their voting records than do Senate challengers, but both acknowledge that job performance was at least a moderately important determinant of the outcome of Senate elections. Both winners and losers also place moderate importance on the partisan loyalties of state voters. Senate candidates attribute less influence to such factors as debates, negative campaigning, local issues, and state and local elections than do House contestants.

SUMMARY

The efforts that candidates make to communicate with voters can have an impact on congressional elections, but they are especially important for House challengers and open-seat contestants. Challengers who carefully target their campaign resources, run on issues that draw distinctions between themselves and the House members they seek to unseat, spend significant sums on campaign advertising and voter mobilization, and attract local media endorsements can significantly increase the number of votes they receive. House challengers who must defeat an opponent to secure their party's nomination, who run in districts that have many members of their party, who oppose vulnerable incumbents, and who attract significant outside campaigning by their party and supportive interest groups also increase their share of the vote. House incumbents can do little to substantially increase their standing in the polls. The efforts they make to serve their constituents and deter a strong challenger result in most incumbents' beginning and ending their campaigns with a commanding lead. Most House incumbent campaign communications, like most incumbent fundraising, are driven by the threat that an opponent poses and are directed at shoring up the candidate's support. Campaigns for open House seats are usually very competitive. Voter targeting, issue selection, and candidate communications can be decisive in these races, even in districts that are inundated by outside campaign advertisements aired by parties and interest groups. Senate elections bear many similarities to House contests, but they are usually both more expensive and more competitive. Moreover, although contested primaries hurt Senate incumbents and incumbents' spending has a positive impact on their vote shares, these factors do not have the same effects on House incumbents' shares of the vote.

Congressional campaigners have divergent views about the causes of their election outcomes. Successful campaigners credit their candidates' abilities and their organizations' strategic and tactical efforts for their wins. House losers focus on money, incumbents' perks of office, voter partisanship, and other factors outside of their control. Senate losers are somewhat more likely to acknowledge that candidate characteristics and some aspects of their campaigns contributed to their loss.

CHAPTER TEN

Elections and Governance

"The election is over, and now the fun begins." Those were the words of one new House member shortly after being elected to Congress. Others have more sober, if not more realistic, visions of what lies ahead. Although getting elected to Congress is difficult, especially for those who have to topple an incumbent, staying there also requires great effort. The high reelection rates that members of Congress enjoy are not guarantees; they are the result of hard work, the strategic deployment of the resources that Congress makes available to its members, and the campaign dynamics discussed in previous chapters.

This chapter addresses the question: What impact does the electoral process have on the activities of members of Congress and the operation of Congress as a policy-making institution? It examines the efforts that members of Congress make to stay in office and the resources and strategies they use to shore up their electoral coalitions and participate in the legislative process. First, I discuss the goals and activities of members of Congress and their congressional staffs. I then discuss the committees, issue caucuses, party organizations, and other groups that influence congressional activity. Finally, I comment on the policy-making process.

THE PERMANENT CAMPAIGN

As locally elected officials who make national policy, members of Congress almost lead double lives. The main focus of their existence in Washington, D.C., is framing and enacting legislation, overseeing the executive branch, and carrying out other activities of national importance. Attending local functions, ascertaining the needs and preferences of constituents, and explaining their

Washington activities are what legislators do at home. Home is where members of Congress acquire their legitimacy to participate in the legislative process. The central elements of legislators' lives both at home and in Washington are representing the voters who elected them, winning federally funded projects for their state or district, and resolving difficulties that constituents encounter when dealing with the federal government. The two aspects of members' professional lives are unified by the fact that much of what representatives do in Washington is concerned with getting reelected, and a good deal of what they do at home directly affects the kinds of policies and interests they seek to advance in Washington.[1] In a great many respects, the job of legislator resembles a permanent reelection campaign.

Members of Congress develop home styles that help them to maintain or expand their bases of electoral support. One common element of these home styles concerns how legislators present themselves to voters. Members build bonds of trust between themselves and voters by demonstrating that they are capable of handling the job, that they care about their constituents, and that they are living up to their campaign promises.[2]

A second component of home style is concerned with discussing the Washington side of the job. Members describe, interpret, and justify what they do in the nation's capital to convey the message that they are working relentlessly on their constituents' behalf.[3] Many respond to the low opinion that people have of Congress by trying to separate themselves from the institution in the minds of voters. Members frequently portray themselves as protectors of the national interest locked in combat with powerful lobbyists and feckless colleagues.

Members of Congress and their staffs spend immense amounts of time, energy, and resources advertising the legislator's name among constituents, claiming credit for favorable governmental actions, and taking strong but often symbolic issue positions to please constituents.[4] Their offices provide them with abundant resources for these purposes. House members are annually entitled to roughly $1.3 million for office expenses, including funds for staff, travel, and one or more district offices. They also get a suite of offices in the Capitol complex and virtually unlimited long-distance telephone privileges. Members who are assigned to certain committees, occupy committee chairs, or hold party leadership positions receive extra staff, office space, and operating funds. Senators are allowed even greater budgets, reflecting their larger constituencies and the greater responsibilities associated with representing an entire state. Senators' staffs, office space, and budget allocations are determined by their state's population and by their committee assignments. The annual administrative and clerical allowance for a senator ranges from $2.7 million to $4.3 million.[5]

Although few legislators consume all the resources they are allocated, many come close. The average House member hires approximately fifteen full-time aides; the average senator hires about thirty-four.[6] Among these aides are administrative assistants, legislative assistants, legislative correspondents, schedulers, office managers, caseworkers, press secretaries, receptionists, staff assistants, and interns. Each performs a different set of functions, but nearly all are somehow related to building political support among constituents. Legislative correspondents and legislative assistants are highly conscious of the electoral connection when they send franked mail to constituents or prepare materials for their boss's web site.[7]

Caseworkers are often called upon to help constituents resolve problems with the federal bureaucracy, knowing that their performance can directly affect the reelection prospects of the legislator for whom they work. Receptionists, staff assistants, and schedulers are well aware that the tours they arrange for visitors to Washington contribute to the support their member maintains in the district. Those who forget that constituents come first are quickly reminded of this by the member's administrative assistant, who is responsible for making sure that the office runs smoothly and frequently serves as the member's chief political adviser.

The most reelection-oriented staffers tend to be congressional press secretaries (sometimes called communications directors). Most members of Congress have at least one press secretary, and some have two or three deputy press assistants.[8] The press secretary is the chief public relations officer in a congressional office. Press secretaries write newsletters and press releases and are heavily involved in crafting the targeted mass mailings that most legislators send to constituents. They also produce copy for radio and television spots, which they arrange to have aired on local stations. Press secretaries help to organize town meetings, arrange interviews with correspondents, and disseminate to the media transcripts and videotapes of their boss's floor and committee speeches. A good press secretary is often able to arrange for local media outlets to print or air a legislator's remarks verbatim or with minimal editing.

Many factors led to the emergence of the press secretary as a key congressional aide, including the election since the mid-1970s of highly media-conscious members, increased television coverage of politics, the opening of Congress to greater media scrutiny, the growth in the size of the congressional press corps, and the availability of new communications technologies. These changes created both pressures and opportunities to increase the public relations side of congressional offices. Members of Congress, who work in a resource-rich institution, responded by allowing themselves to hire specialized staff who could help them advance their political careers.

Congress also has allowed its members to exploit new computer technologies to firm up their relations with voters. Legislative aides use computerized databases to target large volumes of mail to specific audiences. Information about constituents who write, telephone, or e-mail their legislator about an issue is routinely entered into a computerized database that includes the constituent's name, contact information, and the subject of their communication. These individuals are then sent periodic communications that update them on what their legislator is doing in the area of concern. Constituents who contact members' offices via e-mail often receive e-mails in return.[9]

Subsidized House and Senate recording studios and party-owned recording facilities also help legislators reach out to voters. Many members use the studios to record radio shows and television briefings or to edit floor speeches for local media outlets. Some make use of satellite technology to hold live "town meetings" with constituents located on the other side of the country.

A DECENTRALIZED CONGRESS

The candidate-centered nature of congressional elections provides the foundation for a highly individualized, fragmented style of legislative politics. Members are largely self-recruited, are nominated and elected principally as a result of their own efforts, and know that they bear the principal responsibility for ensuring that they are reelected. Local party organizations, Washington-based party committees, political action committees, and other groups and individuals may have helped convince them to run for office and assisted with fundraising and campaign communications, but politicians arrive in Congress believing that their election is a direct result of the efforts they made to win the support of their constituents.

Reelection Constituencies

Legislators' first loyalties are to their constituents, and most members staff their offices, decide which committee assignments to pursue, and choose areas of policy expertise with an eye toward maintaining voter support. Campaign contributors, including those who live outside a legislator's district or state, form another important constituency. Local elites and interest groups that provide campaign support or political advice routinely receive access to members of Congress, further encouraging legislators to respond to forces outside of the institution rather than within.[10] Other personal goals, including advancing specific policies, accruing more power in the legislature, or positioning themselves to run for higher office, also have a decentralizing effect on the legislative process.[11] Much of the work done to advance these goals—conducting policy research; disseminating press releases; drafting bills; attending committee meetings; overseeing the bureaucracy; and meeting with constituents, campaign contributors, and lobbyists—is done by staffers who owe their jobs and their loyalties to individual legislators more than to the institution.[12] This, in turn, makes their bosses less dependent on congressional leaders and encourages members to march to their own beat.

Congressional Committees

The dispersal of legislative authority among twenty standing committees and their 102 subcommittees in the House, and sixteen standing committees and their seventy-two subcommittees in the Senate, four joint committees, and a small number of select committees in each chamber adds to the centrifugal tendencies that originate from candidate-centered elections. Each committee and subcommittee is authorized to act within a defined jurisdiction. A chair and a ranking member, who are among the majority and minority parties' senior policy experts, head each committee and subcommittee. Each also has its own professional staff, office, and budget to help it carry out its business.

The committee system was designed to enable Congress to function more efficiently. It allows Congress to investigate simultaneously a multitude of issues and to oversee a range of executive branch agencies. Although committees and subcommittees are Congress's main bodies for making national policy, much of what they do revolves around local issues, the distribution of federal grants and programs, and activities that could boost the reelection of individual legislators. Most members of Congress serve on at least one committee or subcommittee with jurisdiction over policies of importance to their constituents. Members use their committee assignments to develop expertise in policy areas, to actively promote their constituents' interests, to build reputations as champions of popular issues, and to attract political support.

Congressional committees can be categorized according to the objectives they enable members to pursue: reelection, prestige, and policy.[13] "Reelection committees," such as the House Transportation and Infrastructure Committee and the Senate Environment and Public Works Committee, enable their members to work directly on the policy areas that are most important to constituents. Reelection committees usually rank high among the assignments that new members of Congress seek. More than half of all first-term House members seek appointment to one or more of them.[14]

"Prestige committees" give their members influence over legislative activities that are of extraordinary importance to their congressional colleagues. The House and Senate Appropriations Committees are the ultimate prestige, or power, committees. They are responsible for funding federal agencies and programs and have the ability to initiate, expand, contract, or discontinue the flow of federal money to projects located across the country. This gives their members the power to affect the lives of the beneficiaries of those programs and the ability to influence the reelection prospects of legislators who represent them. The House Ways and Means and Senate Finance Committees' jurisdiction over tax-related matters, particularly their ability to give tax breaks to various interests, gives members of these panels sway with their colleagues. Members of prestige committees can help their constituents by acting directly or, by wielding their clout with other legislators, indirectly. Membership on one of the appropriating or tax-writing committees is particularly helpful when it comes to raising campaign funds from individuals and PACs associated with a wide array of economic interests.

In contrast to reelection and prestige committees, "policy committees," such as those that deal with criminal justice, education, or labor issues, are sought by legislators who have a strong interest in a particular policy area. These committees are among the most divisive because they are responsible for some highly charged issues, such as education, health insurance, and welfare reform, and many members use them to stake out conservative or liberal stands. Ambitious legislators who seek a career beyond Congress often use policy committees as platforms for developing a national reputation on salient issues. Thus the committee system gives expression to the differing goals and viewpoints of representatives and senators and their constituents. By so doing, it decentralizes Congress.

Congressional Caucuses

Congressional caucuses—informal groups of members who share legislative interests—have a similar but less powerful effect on Congress. Even though caucuses have been prohibited from having their own congressional staffs and office space since the 104th Congress, they continue to function as competing policy centers, alternative suppliers of information, and additional sources of legislative decision-making cues.[15] Groups such as the Congressional Black Caucus and the Congressional Women's Caucus are recognized as advocates for specific segments of the population. The Northeast-Midwest Senate Coalition, Western States Senate Coalition, and other geographically based groups seek to increase the clout of legislators from particular regions. Steel, auto, and textile caucuses have ties to outside industries and work to promote their interests in Congress. Although they do not hold any formal legislative powers, caucuses further add to the fragmentation of Congress by advancing disparate goals.

Interest Groups

Privately funded interest groups, which form an important part of the political environment with which Congress interacts, also have decentralizing effects on the legislative process. Like caucuses, interest groups are sources of influence that compete with congressional leaders for the loyalty of legislators on certain issues. Roughly 35,000 registered lobbyists work in the Washington area.[16] They are assisted by tens of thousands of others in trade associations, public relations firms, and other agencies, who work to advance the political interests of particular groups, and Congress is their number one target.

Interest groups work to influence the legislative process in many ways. Participation in elections is usually considered an important first step. It should be recalled from Chapter 5 that access-oriented groups make campaign contributions, provide campaign services, or carry out other campaign activities to create or maintain strong relationships with legislators. Ideological groups primarily become involved in campaigns to elect members of Congress who share their issue concerns rather than to gain political access. Groups motivated by both ideological and access concerns participate in elections both to influence the membership of Congress and to enjoy good relations with the legislators they consider key to the achievement of their organization's goals.

Once the election is over, groups use many methods to influence the legislative process. Some groups advertise on television, on radio, in newspapers, on the Internet, or through the mail to influence the political agenda or stimulate grassroots support for or opposition to specific pieces of legislation. Their efforts often resemble election campaigns in that they involve both targeted and mass communications to influence the policy-making process.

The pharmaceutical industry, with its associated companies and trade associations, ranks among the wealthiest and best represented industries in the United States. Its targeted communications, often spearheaded by the trade association Pharmaceutical Research and Manufacturers of America, include millions of dollars in spending intended to influence the decision making of members of Congress and executive branch officials. Some of the money is spent to lobby policy makers directly; some is used to advertise in specialized periodicals, including *Roll Call* and *The Hill,* which are widely read by members of Congress and others working on Capitol Hill. Those expenditures are in addition to the more than $70 million that PACs and individuals associated with this economic sector contributed to federal candidates and parties during the five elections held between 1998 and 2006.[17] The pharmaceutical industry's mass communications include televised issue advocacy ads and print ads appearing in major newspapers and magazines. The industry is among the nation's leaders in generating grassroots support for its interests. One of its most effective tactics is to establish shell groups with innocuous names, such as Citizens for Better Medicare, the Seniors Coalition, and the United Seniors Association, to blanket the airwaves with television ads intended to gin up backing for public policies or candidates who support the interests of drug companies. The pharmaceutical industry has been largely successful in its endeavors, helping to defeat President Clinton's health care reform plan in 1994 and undermine a variety of prescription drug reforms that would have been unfavorable to its interests. One of its most recent triumphs was the enactment of the Medicare Prescription Drug, Improvement, and Modernization Act, which has been criticized by some as providing more benefits to the pharmaceutical industry than to the senior citizens it is supposed to serve.[18]

Most interest groups also advocate their positions in less-visible ways, designed to play to the legislative and electoral needs of individual members of Congress. Representatives of interest groups testify at committee hearings and meet with legislators at their offices and informally at social events. Lobbyists use a variety of forums to provide members and their staffs with technical information, impact statements of how congressional activity (or inactivity) can affect their constituents, and insights into where other legislators stand on the issues. Sometimes they go so far as to draft a bill or help design a strategy to promote its enactment.[19]

Many groups supplement these "insider" techniques with approaches that focus more directly on the electoral connection. Trade and business associations ask their members to contact their legislators. Labor unions, churches, and other groups with large memberships frequently organize telephone and letter-writing campaigns. These communications show members of Congress that important blocs of voters and their advocates are watching how they vote on specific pieces of legislation.[20] Interest group–sponsored issue advocacy advertising intended to influence the legislative process or elections has resulted in some groups contributing to the permanent campaigns that consume a significant portion of the professional lives of many members of Congress.

Interest groups, congressional subcommittee members, and executive branch officials form collegial decision-making groups, which are frequently referred to as "iron triangles," "issue networks," or "policy subgovernments."[21] These issue experts often focus on the minutiae of arcane, highly specialized areas of public policy. Because they form small regimes within a government, they further contribute to the decentralization of Congress.

POLITICAL PARTIES AS CENTRALIZING AGENTS

Unlike the structural, organizational, and political factors that work to decentralize Congress, political parties act as a glue—albeit sometimes a weak one—to bond members together. A party's ability to unite its members in support of a legislative program, or even a single bill, depends on the situation, especially the partisan balance of power. A party's prospects for success are better when it controls both chambers of Congress and the White House, when the party's members in the two chambers share a common agenda and ideological perspective, and when Congress overall is made up mostly of moderates.[22] The presence of many moderates means the majority party can look beyond its own ranks when building coalitions.

Congressional parties lay the foundation for cooperation among their members through a number of activities. They socialize new members to Congress's norms and folkways, distribute committee assignments, set the legislative agenda, disseminate information, and carry out other tasks that are essential to Congress's lawmaking, oversight, and representative functions. Although they are not the central actors in elections, party committees help individual candidates develop their campaign messages. Party campaign efforts on behalf of individual candidates and election agenda-setting efforts encourage legislators to vote for bills that are at the core of their party's agenda when Congress is in session.[23] Party issue advocacy that takes place outside of the campaign season is meant to increase or reduce support for specific bills or damage the reputations of members who voted against them.

The congressional parties' leadership organizations are structured similarly to those of legislative parties in other countries. The Democrats and Republicans are each headed by a leader in each chamber—the Speaker and minority leader in the House and the majority and minority leaders in the Senate. Each party has several other officers and an extensive whip system to facilitate communications between congressional party leaders and rank-and-file legislators. Legislative parties convene caucuses and task forces to help formulate policy positions and legislative strategy. Providing campaign assistance, giving out committee assignments and other perks, setting the congressional agenda, structuring debate, and persuading legislators that specific bills are in the best interests of their constituents and the nation are tools that congressional leaders use to build coalitions.[24]

Nevertheless, party leaders have less control over the policy-making process than do their counterparts in other democracies.[25] The persuasive powers of party leaders are usually insufficient to sway members' votes when party policy positions clash with those of legislators' constituents and campaign supporters. Recognizing the primacy of the electoral connection, party leaders generally tell legislators to respond to constituents rather than "toe the party line" when the latter could endanger their chances of reelection. Even with the centralization of power under congressional party leaders that began following the Republicans' takeover of Congress, party leaders still are probably less important in how party members cast their roll-call votes than are commonalities in the political outlooks of a party's legislators or similarities among legislators' constituents.[26] The nomination of candidates by partisans whose views are more ideologically extreme than those of the public has contributed to this phenomenon. It has resulted in the election of more conservative Republicans, more liberal Democrats, and fewer moderates of either party. Members of the majority party who are strongly motivated by ideology, particularly in the House, have enhanced the power of congressional party leaders to help the party achieve its electoral and policy goals. When strong House Speakers, such as Newt Gingrich, Dennis Hastert, and most recently Nancy Pelosi, have exploited these powers they have been able to structure the congressional debate and control political outcomes. The result is that parties in Congress have acted more programmatically in recent years.[27]

Traditionally, party leaders are most able to overcome the forces that fragment Congress when they seek to enact policies that have widespread bipartisan support or when the majority party possesses many more seats than the opposition and proposes popular legislation that advances its core principles. As the historic 104th Congress showed, a change in party control can also act as a catalyst for party unity. Members of the new House and Senate majorities in 1995 were aware that their accomplishments as a party would directly influence their individual reelection campaigns and their party's ability to maintain control of Congress. They empowered their leaders to use extraordinary measures to encourage party discipline. The leadership, in turn, restructured some aspects of how the House did business. The Republicans cut the number of House committees and subcommittees and committee staffs, enacted term limits for committee chairs and the Speaker, and made other formal changes aimed at strengthening the majority-party leadership. Legislative study organizations, which had formerly enhanced the representation of specific—mostly Democratic—constituencies, were eliminated. GOP House leaders relied on partisan task forces instead of the normal committee process to write several major pieces of legislation, used highly restrictive rules to prevent Democrats (and others) from amending it, and held some close roll-call votes open for hours beyond their allotted time until they had enough votes to pass the legislation. When reconciling bills with the Senate, Republican leaders excluded Democrats from some conference committees. Although some of these tactics had been used before, including by Democratic-controlled congresses, politicians and observers from both sides of the aisle agree that the Republicans took them to new lengths. They also agree that the tactics facilitated coalition building within the majority party and greatly reduced minority party input. The GOP's tactics made possible some legislative victories using a "right in" rather than a "center out" approach to coalition building.[28]

Republican members of ensuing congresses also demonstrated an understanding of the importance of party unity and a record of performance in keeping control of a closely divided legislature. Their unity increased even more once George W. Bush was elected president. From that point on, GOP House and Senate leaders largely followed the White House's lead on legislative matters and virtually abdicated responsibility for oversight of the executive branch. The Democrats' initial response to Republican rule was to unify in opposition to the Republicans and to seek to portray the GOP as presiding over "do-nothing" congresses. Leading up to the 2006 election, the Democrats broadened their criticism to include the Iraq War and allegations of corruption and incompetence in Congress and the executive branch.

Following their takeover of Congress, the Democrats pledged to return to a more open and inclusive style of legislating that respected the rights of the minority party. Yet before the Democrats in the House took steps toward keeping that promise they used a series of restrictive rules to pass their so-called "6 for '06" policy agenda. This led a number of Republicans to complain about hypocrisy on the part of the new majority party, but it enabled the Democrats to pass their core policy program during the first one hundred hours of the 110th Congress. Other changes that the Democratic leadership instituted included a return to some of the norms that the party had been accustomed to during its previous, forty-year reign over the House, including an emphasis on seniority when making committee assignments and abandonment of the Republicans' system of term limits for committee and subcommittee chairs. Given the Democrats' greater diversity, they are unlikely to display levels of cohesion equal to those of the Republicans when they were Congress's majority party. The Republicans, on the other hand, probably will remain united in opposition to most Democratic policy initiatives.

RESPONSIVENESS, RESPONSIBILITY, AND PUBLIC POLICY

In representative democracies, elections are the principal means of ensuring that governments respond to the will of the people and promote their interests. Voters, through elections, hold public officials accountable for their actions and for the state of the nation as a whole. Elections are a blunt but powerful instrument of control that enables people to inform their individual representatives, or the government collectively, of how political action or inaction has affected the quality of their lives. Elections are the primary means that democracies use to empower or remove political leaders at all levels of government. Campaigns help to establish standards by which officeholders are judged. Other paths of influence, such as contacting members of Congress and giving campaign contributions, are usually used to advance narrower goals, are more demanding, and are in practice less democratic.

Despite the extensive resources for building and maintaining relationships with constituents that Congress and the rest of the Washington establishment put at the disposal of representatives and senators, members cannot fully insulate themselves or Congress as an institution from the impact of electoral forces. Voters can, and occasionally do, expel large numbers of incumbents, leading to changes in the membership, leadership, operations, and output of Congress. The 1994 elections resulted in a new Republican majority taking control of Congress for the first time in forty years and led to the selection of Gingrich—a relative newcomer to his party's leadership—as House Speaker. The elections also empowered the Republicans to claim a mandate to change some of the ways in which Congress operated and to overturn Democratic programs that had originated more than sixty years earlier during the New Deal. The Democrats made similar claims after winning control of the House and Senate in the 2006 elections, promising to move the nation in a different direction from the one Republicans began to chart in 1994.

Individuals whose public service is contingent on being reelected often straddle the fuzzy line that demarcates responsiveness and responsibility in government. On some occasions, legislators are highly responsive, functioning as delegates who advance their constituents' views. On others, they take the role of trustee, relying on their own judgment, sometimes informed by cues from their party, to protect the welfare of their constituents or the nation.[29] Responsible legislators must occasionally vote against their constituents' wishes to best serve the interests of the nation.

Election Systems and Public Policy

The type of political system in which elected officials function influences whom they answer to. The U.S. candidate-centered system is unique, and it results in a style of governance that contrasts sharply with the parliamentary systems that govern most democracies. Parliamentary systems feature party-focused elections that tend to hold elected officials accountable to national political majorities.[30] Members of the British Parliament, for example, perform casework and are attentive to their constituents, but they are inclined to vote for legislation fashioned to please national rather than local constituencies. They support party initiatives because they know that their prospects for re-election are tied closely to their party's ability to enact its legislative program. The candidate-centered nature of the U.S. system, in contrast, encourages elected officials to be responsive to the desires of constituents and organized groups that support their campaigns, sometimes in opposition to their party's leadership. Indeed, members who represent the most diverse constituencies often respond to the mixed signals they receive by adopting no public position on controversial issues and avoid casting roll-call votes on them altogether.[31] The separation of powers reinforces legislators' predisposition to support district voters first and their campaign's financial supporters second when making public policy. Even when one party controls the White House and both chambers of Congress, it may find it difficult to unify legislators because they can disagree with one another without fear of losing control of the government.

Members of the majority party in Congress cast roll-call votes secure in the knowledge that they will remain in office for their full two- or six-year terms even if their party suffers a major legislative defeat. In parliamentary systems, majority-party members understand that a major policy defeat may be interpreted as a vote of no confidence in their party and may force an election that could turn them out of office in less than a month. The separation of powers also affects the behavior of legislators who are in the minority party. They have little incentive to vote against legislation that could benefit their constituents just because it was sponsored by the other party, since even a smashing legislative defeat would not force a snap election.

The defeat of President George W. Bush's immigration policy in the closing days of the 109th Congress demonstrates the difficulties that parties encounter when they try to overcome the centrifugal forces influencing members of Congress. Bush, who had made immigration reform one of his major priorities, was unable to get his program enacted, despite Republican majorities in the House and Senate, his having campaigned aggressively for congressional Republicans in previous elections, and his emerging as one of the most partisan presidents in recent U.S. history. Bush pushed hard for an immigration package that included a guest worker program. However, GOP members of Congress had other ideas. House Republicans were primarily interested in cutting off the flow of immigrants. Led by House Judiciary Committee chairman James Sensenbrenner Jr., R-Wis., they passed a bill that focused on border security and tough enforcement of immigration laws and pointedly left out the president's guest worker program. The bill passed by a largely party-line vote in December 2005, with GOP legislators emphasizing the importance of giving voice to their constituents' views. As Rep. Tom Tancredo, R-Colo., pronounced, "For the first time, I can go out on the stump and say our party has done right on the issue of immigration. And I feel good about it."[32] Addressing the immigration issue five months later, the Senate passed a bill that was consistent with the broader approach proposed by Bush. The bill enjoyed bipartisan backing from conservatives and liberals, including that of Senate Judiciary Committee chairman Arlen Specter, R-Pa., Sen. Edward Kennedy, D-Mass., Republican majority leader Bill Frist, R-Tenn., and Democratic minority leader Harry Reid, D-Nev. However, it lacked the backing of most Senate Republicans. Passed by a vote of sixty-two to thirty-six, it had the support of only twenty-three Republican senators and was opposed by another thirty-two. The disparities between the House and Senate bills were so great that House Republicans refused to participate in a conference with the Senate to negotiate a final bill. Instead, House members sought to play to their political base: they held two dozen hearings on the issue in sympathetic parts of the country during the August 2006 recess and passed a series of mostly symbolic bills late in the session. As a result of the opposition of members of his own party, the president failed to accomplish one of his major policy initiatives.[33]

Most acts of Congress are not as monumental as the defeat of a major presidential initiative involving one of the most salient issues on the political agenda during the period leading up to an election. The separation of powers, bicameralism, federalism, and a fixed-date system of elections make it difficult for legislators to enact longer-term, more nationally focused policies. Members of Congress who believe that their individual images, policy positions, and public records were decisive in their election are less likely than legislators in party-centered democracies to sacrifice the interests of constituents or to compromise on salient issues to enact policies advocated by party leaders. House members, who must run for reelection every two years, respond strongly to parochial concerns.

The effects of parochialism are most apparent in distributive politics, which provide tangible benefits to private individuals or groups. Building coalitions in support of spending on roads, bridges, universities, museums, and other projects is relatively simple in a decentralized legislature such as the U.S. Congress. Bill sponsors can add new programs and projects, referred to as "earmarks," as a way to win enough legislative supporters to pass their plan.[34] A farm advocate who is hoping to subsidize northern sugar beets, for example, might build support for this cause by expanding the number of subsidized crops in a bill to include sugar cane, rice, corn, wheat, and even tobacco, thereby expanding support that began with representatives from Minnesota to include colleagues from Hawaii, Massachusetts, virtually every southern state, and the states of the Midwest.[35] Subsidies for ostrich farmers can be left out because they will not draw many legislative votes, but food stamps can be added to attract the support of legislators from poor urban districts.[36] Trading subsidies for votes is a simple example of logrolling. Other deals are cut over tax breaks, budget votes, and even appointments to the federal judiciary.

Logrolling and other forms of compromise usually do not allow individual legislators to get all the federal "pork" they would like for their constituents. Nevertheless, these compromises enable most legislators to insert enough pork into a bill to claim credit for doing something to help their constituents. A broadly supported distributive bill is an easy candidate for congressional enactment because, like a Christmas tree decorated by a group of friends, everyone can see his or her handiwork in it and find something to admire in the finished product.

Distributive politics is problematic because it is practiced with both eyes focused on short-term gain and little attention to long-range consequences. Broadening programs that were originally intended to provide benefits to one group to include others usually causes the programs to become ineffectively targeted, watered down, and too expensive. When large sums are spent to benefit many groups, overall spending rises, and fewer funds remain available to help the group originally targeted for assistance. This does little to promote the original goals of a bill and leads to deficit spending.[37] Pork-barrel spending and logrolling, which are at the heart of distributive politics, contribute heavily to the U.S. national debt. Distributive politics is a prime example of what happens when independently elected officials seek to promote the interests of their constituents and campaign supporters, without giving much thought to the effect of their collective actions on the nation. Recent congresses have enthusiastically taken on the task of distributing pork, and the number of earmarks grew from about 3,000 to more than 13,000 between 1996 and 2006.[38] Working with President Clinton, the congresses elected between 1994 and 2000 took steps to reduce government spending, lowering the national debt and generating budget surpluses in 1998 and 1999. However, constant wrangling over tax cuts, military spending, and other federal programs has hindered further attempts at debt reduction. The war on terrorism and the wars in Afghanistan and Iraq also have contributed to the national debt, which had ballooned to almost $9 trillion as of August 2006.

Policy Gridlock and Political Cycles

Parochialism also leads to a reactive style of government and incremental policy making. Congress is better at making short-term fixes than at developing long-term initiatives. Congressional leaders often find it difficult to develop a vision for the future. During the 1980s House Democrats took steps to outline, publicize, and act on a partisan agenda. Parts of this effort were successful, but much of it was not. Differences in legislators' political philosophies, the diversity of their constituencies, and the limited resources available to party leaders made it difficult to develop and implement a Democratic plan for the nation's future.[39] House Republicans also tried on several occasions in the 1980s to develop a partisan agenda, but prior to the Contract with America they, too, enjoyed only limited success.[40]

Under most circumstances, election outcomes, constituent demands, interest group pressures, and White House initiatives support the continuation of the status quo or suggest only small changes in public policies. When pressure for change exists, Congress generally initiates limited reform, but only after a period of some delay. On some occasions, however, the federal government enacts comprehensive programs that significantly affect people's lives.

Major policy change is most likely to occur during periods of crisis and is frequently associated with partisan realignments. Realignments traditionally occur when a critical event polarizes voters on a major issue, the two major parties take clear and opposing stands on that issue, and one party succeeds in capturing the White House and large majorities in both the House and Senate. The ascendant party then has an electoral mandate to enact major policy change.[41]

The events leading up to, and continuing through, Franklin Roosevelt's presidency exemplify federal policy making during a period of crisis. The seeds of Roosevelt's New Deal programs were sown in the Great Depression of the 1930s. Republicans controlled the White House, the House of Representatives, and the Senate when the stock market crashed in 1929. The Democrats made a major campaign issue out of the Republicans' failure to initiate economic reforms to reverse the depression. After winning the White House and both chambers of Congress, the Democrats used their mandate to replace laissez-faire economics with Keynesian policies, which relied on government intervention to revive the economy. Other partisan and policy realignments took place during the late 1820s, the Civil War era, and the 1890s.

Some major policy changes have been instituted in the absence of partisan realignments, but most of those were less sweeping than the ones that followed critical elections. The civil rights and Great Society programs of the 1960s and the U.S. withdrawal from Vietnam are examples of major policy changes that occurred in the absence of a partisan realignment. Historical perspective is needed before scholars can conclude whether the 1994 congressional elections constituted a first step toward a full-scale political realignment, but the Democrats' long-term hegemony over Congress clearly ended.[42] Regardless of whether a realignment was constituted in 1994, the GOP was able to use its stunning electoral success to institute major changes in public policy and shift the national policy debate.

Under Gingrich's leadership, the GOP-controlled Congress passed legislation aimed at rewarding its constituents. It cut federal programs and regulations, reduced federal mandates on the states, and changed the welfare system from a federally mandated program to one run by each state independently with a block grant from the federal government. The Republicans also shifted the policy debate from how to improve the efficiency and performance of the federal government to how to decrease its scope. For the first time since the New Deal, the subject of reducing entitlement benefits dominated public debate. This debate continued when President George W. Bush proposed to privatize Social Security and succeeded in revamping Medicaid.

After they claimed control of the Senate in 2003, the Republicans were poised to advance even more policy change. With control of the White House and both chambers of Congress, the GOP had the ability to dominate the political agenda. Partly as repayment for the extraordinary campaign efforts the president made on behalf of GOP congressional candidates in 2002 and 2004, Republican members of Congress were strongly inclined to back the administration's policy initiatives. That enabled the GOP to pass more tax cuts, including those targeted predominantly to the wealthy; ease pollution restrictions for factories and power plants; and outlaw certain abortion procedures. As noted above, the Republicans also enacted prescription drug reforms that are highly favorable to the pharmaceutical industry. Republican control of the Senate brought with it the additional ability to introduce lasting change in the federal judiciary. Bush's judicial appointments enjoyed relatively smooth sailing in the confirmation process, and once confirmed they shifted the balance of the federal courts—including the U.S. Supreme Court—in a conservative direction.

After winning majorities in the House and Senate, the Democrats sought to chart a new direction for the federal government—one that rewarded Democratic constituencies. The first set of bills passed by the House, the "6 for '06" agenda, consisted of an increase in the minimum wage, a cut in student loan interest rates, improvements in security screening at seaports, support for stem cell research, a reduction in drug prices under the Medicare program, and increased research on renewable energy funded through repeal of some tax breaks for oil companies. The Democrats also reinvigorated congressional oversight to look into allegations of impropriety, neglect, and partisan abuse by numerous members of the administration. That included investigations into the firing of nine U.S. attorneys, unauthorized domestic wiretapping by the FBI, and the taxpayer-funded travel by drug czar John Walters to help Republican candidates in the 2006 elections. Future congressional oversight and legislative cohesion will be strongly influenced by the outcome of the 2008 congressional and presidential elections.

Elections that result in a shift in partisan control and the swearing in of many new members can be catalysts for Congress to overcome its normal state of decentralization, especially when a widespread consensus for change exists among the American people. When such partisan turnover occurs, congressional parties in the United States resemble both parliamentary parties in other countries and an idealized system of responsible party government.[43] However, once public support for sweeping change erodes, the centrifugal forces that customarily dominate Congress reassert themselves, and the legislature returns to its normal, incremental mode of policy making. The natural parochialism of members of Congress, bicameralism, the internal decentralization of the House and Senate, and other centrifugal forces promote political cycles marked by long periods of incremental policy making followed by short periods of centralized power and major policy change.

SUMMARY

The candidate-centered congressional election system has a major impact on how Congress functions. The electoral connection encourages members of Congress to develop home styles that result in their building bonds of trust with local voters. Congress, as an institution, provides its members with resources to help them accomplish this objective. The candidate-centered system also finds expression in the highly individualistic legislative behavior exhibited by most representatives and senators and in Congress's decentralized style of operation. Although political parties occasionally overcome the legislature's naturally fragmented state, the centrifugal forces exerted on Congress by constituents, campaign contributors, interest groups, committees, and other organizations within Congress itself cause the institution to return to its normal decentralized operations after short periods of centralization. The result is that national policy making in the United States is characterized by prolonged periods of gradual policy modification followed by brief episodes of sweeping political change.

CHAPTER ELEVEN

Campaign Reform

Congress has come under assault in recent years for its inability to solve some of the nation's most pressing problems, its perceived shortcomings in representing the general public, and its failure to keep its own house in order. Gridlock, deficit spending, indictments and convictions of some of its members, scandal, the personal foibles of individual legislators, and the operations of Congress itself have led many to champion congressional reform.[1] Reformers have called for a variety of changes, ranging from internal reforms to consolidate the authorizing committees that create federal programs with the appropriations committees that fund them, to term limits, which would restructure the political careers of members and would-be members. Campaign reform falls somewhere between these measures: it requires the passage of new legislation but does not require a constitutional amendment. Given that it only requires a bill to survive the legislative process, one might ask, why aren't campaign reforms enacted more often? And, why isn't the process Americans use to elect their national legislators better? I address these questions by first reviewing the politics surrounding the enactment and implementation of the Bipartisan Campaign Reform Act of 2002, and its impact on congressional elections to date. I also speculate on how the Supreme Court's decision in 2007 to overturn part of the law will affect future elections. This is followed by a discussion of some additional reform proposals and their prospects for passage.

THE CASE FOR REFORM

Numerous arguments are routinely made for reforming congressional elections. Some proposals are quite sweeping, revolving around the question: Is this any way to elect a member of Congress? When this question was put to major-party candidates and campaign aides competing in congressional elections, 35 percent responded that the campaign process prepares candidates "poorly" or "not at all" for holding office. The defeated candidates were more critical than the winners, but 24 percent of the winners also shared that view. Similarly, 58 percent of the campaigners agreed with the statement, "There are only a few important connections between being a good candidate and being a good public official," and 21 percent maintained that "there is little or no connection" between the two roles. Only one out of five candidates felt that "the best candidates are usually the best public officials." Only 28 percent of the winners took the position that the best congressional candidates make the best members of Congress, and losers perceived even fewer links between campaigning and governing.[2]

These respondents also voiced skepticism about the substantive policy links between campaigning and governing. Ten percent agreed that "issues raised in political campaigns are almost never the most important for future governing," and another 60 percent held that campaign issues are "occasionally" the most important. Only 30 percent felt they were "usually" the most important. Moreover, the winners were no more likely than the losers to maintain that issues raised in campaigns were usually the most important for governing.[3]

Congressional contestants' dissatisfaction with the limited connections between campaigning and governing are important, but they are too amorphous to provide a basis for reform. How does one begin to write a law to ensure that the issues candidates discuss on the campaign trail are the same issues they act on when in office? Elections are the means voters use to hold government officeholders accountable. The disenchantment that politicians feel about the campaign process may be important, but most political reformers are consumed with more concrete shortcomings. Many reformers point out that the campaign system stacks the cards so much against challengers that incumbents almost always win, sometimes calling attention to congressional perks and the politics of redistricting. Even more reformers zero in on money and politics, taking issue with the large sums routinely spent in congressional elections and bemoaning the fact that most of the money comes from wealthy individuals and interest groups. That most incumbents raise and spend so much money, making it impossible for their opponents to compete, is another frequent complaint.

Enterprising politicians, party leaders, interest group executives, and political consultants have found many ways to work around federal campaign finance laws, including the BCRA's predecessor, the Federal Election Campaign Act. As the FECA was progressively weakened by court decisions and administrative rulings, reform groups and the public became more vociferous in their objections to the campaign finance system. More than eight out of ten

TABLE 11–1

Assessments of the Campaign Finance System by Congressional Candidates, Significant Donors, and the General Public

	Congressional candidates	Significant donors	General public
It is broken and needs to be replaced.	40%	32%	12%
It has problems and needs to be changed.	39	46	70
It has some problems but is basically sound.	21	21	14
It is all right just the way it is and should not be changed.	1	2	4
N	*326*	*1,027*	*807*

Sources: Paul S. Herrnson, The Congressional Donors Survey, 1996; the Campaign Assessment and Candidate Outreach Project, Center for American Politics and Citizenship, University of Maryland, 2000 survey; *Washington Post* poll, January 14–19, 1997.

Notes: Congressional candidates include 2000 major-party primary and general election candidates. Significant donors are individuals who contributed $200 or more to a congressional candidate. Some columns do not add up to 100 percent because of rounding. *N* = 326 for the candidates; *N* = 1,027 for the donors; *N* = 807 for the public.

members of the public agreed with the statement that the campaign finance system "is broken and needs to be replaced" or that "it has problems and needs to be changed"; less than two out of ten said that "it has some problems but is basically sound" or that "it is all right just the way it is and should not be changed" (see Table 11–1). Individuals who were active in the campaign finance system—those who contributed $200 or more to at least one congressional candidate—were as critical of the system as the rest of the public, if not more so. Among the criticisms that contributors to congressional campaigns routinely levied were that "donors regularly pressure officeholders for favors," "officeholders regularly pressure donors for money," and "money has too big an impact on the outcomes of elections." Finally, congressional candidates were the most disparaging of the financing of elections prior to the enactment of the BCRA. Of course voters, donors, and candidates of different political parties were critical of different aspects of the system. The same was true of incumbents, challengers, and candidates for open seats.[4]

OBSTACLES TO REFORM

Enacting legislation is never easy, but it is particularly challenging when a bill promises to affect the political careers and livelihoods of those whose support is required to pass it. Mustering sufficient support to pass the BCRA was difficult, and any future reform will be similarly challenging. It requires winning the support of individuals who have succeeded under the current campaign finance system, who view politics in light of their personal experiences, and who consider themselves experts on campaigns and elections. Members of Congress, and the party and interest group officials who contribute to their campaigns, possess a keen understanding of the provisions of the election system that work to their advantage and disadvantage. They can readily speculate on how different reform packages may affect their ability to participate in elections and influence the policy-making process. Although these individuals often portray themselves as reformers, they frequently advocate changes that reflect their own self-interest. Not surprisingly, incumbents and challengers are likely to support different reform packages, at least until the challengers become incumbents. Republicans and Democrats also take different positions. Members of the GOP favor high contribution limits or no limits at all, which would enable them to take advantage of their superior fundraising prowess and larger donor base. Democrats are more favorably disposed toward public funding for campaigns and free media time and postage, which would reduce the impact of the Republicans' traditional financial advantages.[5] Some of the differences are based on philosophical orientation: Republicans tend to favor marketplace approaches with few limits on campaign contributions; Democrats generally prefer regulatory measures and government programs, such as limits on contributions, accompanied by public subsidies.

Additional differences of opinion derive from the demands that campaigning makes on different types of candidates. Because of the dissimilarities in their term lengths and the sizes of their constituencies, as well as other structural factors, members of the House and Senate disagree on some issues. Many women, African Americans, ethnic minorities, and members of other traditionally underrepresented groups, who depend on national donor networks, hold preferences different from those of most white male candidates. Candidates from wealthy urban districts tend to have fundraising opportunities, spending needs, and views on reform that differ from those of candidates from poor rural states or districts.

The diversity of views and the complexity of the issue make it difficult for legislators to find the common ground needed to pass meaningful campaign reform. The sometimes questionable recommendations and inflammatory public relations campaigns of reform groups often widen, rather than close, gaps between members of Congress. Not surprisingly, legislators often find it challenging to move beyond public posturing and engage in serious reform efforts. From the late 1970s through the turn of the century House members and senators of both parties introduced comprehensive packages that they knew would never be adopted by their respective chambers, survive a conference committee, and be signed into law by the president. Their efforts were largely geared toward providing political cover for themselves rather than enacting campaign finance reform.

THE BIPARTISAN CAMPAIGN REFORM ACT OF 2002

The BCRA is typical of a successfully enacted campaign finance reform in many ways. It was limited in scope, passed under somewhat unique circumstances and using unusual procedures, and was immediately challenged in the courts by its opponents. Its effects were more modest than many had anticipated, and it may have had some unanticipated consequences. As is often the case with political reforms, parts of it were weakened not long after its enactment.

Enactment

The BCRA's enactment was made possible by a confluence of factors. They included public pressure arising from political scandal and the growing amounts of unregulated soft money spent in politics, skillful bipartisan coalition building and the use of unorthodox approaches to lawmaking, resourceful insider lobbying and outside grassroots mobilization by reform groups, and sympathetic portrayal of the struggle for reform by the mass media.[6] The efforts, over several congresses, of the BCRA's sponsors, senators John McCain, R-Ariz., and Russell Feingold, D-Wis., and representatives Christopher Shays, R-Conn., and Martin Meehan, D-Mass., were essential to its passage.

The political setting was critical. The Democrats' reclaiming control of the Senate in the 107th Congress, and a small but important increase in the number of legislators in support of reform, improved its prospects. McCain's discussion of campaign finance reform during the 2000 Republican presidential nominating contest and a major corporate scandal involving the now-defunct energy giant Enron raised the issue's profile. These factors increased the number of legislators who believed a vote for the BCRA was a good vehicle for showing their willingness to act against corporate abuse and corruption in general.[7]

The sequencing of events also was extremely important. In both the 105th and 106th Congresses the House had passed a campaign reform package first, with a significant number of signatories to the bill anticipating that the Senate would scuttle it. In the 107th Congress, the Senate passed the BCRA first. Because President Bush had previously announced that if given the opportunity he would sign a campaign finance reform bill into law, it became up to the House to determine the bill's future. The House Republican leadership fiercely opposed the reform, but when the BCRA's supporters gathered backing sufficient for a discharge petition to force a floor vote the leadership relented. This left representatives who had previously voted for reform, but did not actually want the BCRA to become law, in an awkward position. They could cast their votes consistently and in support of the bill and live with the consequences of the new law, or they could reverse their positions on previous votes, deny the bill passage, and look like hypocrites. Most chose to support reform. After the House voted to pass a slightly different version of the bill than had been passed by the Senate, McCain and Feingold successfully pressed their colleagues to accept the House version as a substitute for the Senate version, and on March 27, 2002, President Bush signed the BCRA into law.

Major Provisions

The BCRA was intended to close some of the loopholes in the FECA, not restructure the campaign finance system. It sought to prevent political parties and interest groups from circumventing federal contribution and expenditure limits and avoiding federal disclosure requirements. It also aimed to reduce corruption and the appearance of corruption associated with federal candidates' raising huge unregulated donations from wealthy interests for the political parties.[8]

The act's major provisions banned party soft money, increased contribution limits, and restricted issue advocacy advertising. The soft money provisions prohibit national party organizations, including the Democratic National Committee, the Republican National Committee, the four Hill committees, or any entity they establish or control from raising, spending, or transferring funds that are not subject to federal regulation. They also prohibit federal officeholders or candidates, or their agents, from raising, spending, or transferring nonfederal funds in connection with a federal election. National party committees, state and local party committees, federal officeholders, and candidates for federal office also are prohibited from raising nonfederal funds for political organizations. State and local parties can use only federal funds for all communications that feature a federal candidate. The same is true of voter registration drives that are conducted during the last 120 days before a federal election and mention a federal candidate. State and local party voter registration drives that do not mention a federal candidate can be financed using a mix of federally regulated hard money and unregulated soft money.

The law increased hard money contribution limits to partially compensate political parties for the loss of soft money as a potential source of revenue and expenditures. The BCRA's ceiling of $95,000 per election cycle for individual contributions to federal candidates, party committees, and PACS replaced the $25,000 annual contribution limit that existed under the FECA. The $37,500 limit for contributions to all party committees, combined with the overarching limit of $57,500 on contributions to party committees and PACs, ensures that an individual will contribute more to the former than the latter. Most of the law's other contribution limits, detailed in Chapter 1, represent increases from the ceilings imposed by the FECA. Most also were indexed to inflation, so that they would rise along with the costs of campaigning. The limits for PAC contributions to candidates and individual contributions to PACs, however, were neither increased nor indexed to inflation.

The BCRA's provisions on issue advocacy advertising were designed to bring under federal regulation broadcast communications intended to affect the outcomes of federal elections. The law required interest group–sponsored broadcast, cable, or satellite television or radio ads that feature a federal candidate and are aired thirty days before a primary or sixty days before the general election be financed with federally regulated funds. In practice this meant that only PACs could sponsor ads during these periods, and organizations such as 527 committees were limited to airing them earlier in the election cycle. Party issue advocacy ads were deemed legal only if they were financed with hard money and aired up to ninety days before a primary or the general election.

Post–BCRA Challenges

Challenges to the BCRA were mounted before the ink from the president's signature on the law had even dried. In fact, the BCRA's opponents were lining up to contest its constitutionality even before it was officially enacted. Leading the charge was Sen. Mitch McConnell, R-Ky., who while still filibustering against reform, stated, "Should the bill become law, I will be the lead plaintiff."[9] Among the dozens of others who joined the effort to overturn the law were the RNC, then-House Speaker Dennis Hastert, the California Democratic and Republican Parties, the Cato Institute, the American Civil Liberties Union (ACLU), the AFL-CIO, the National Rifle Association, and eight state attorneys general. These plaintiffs maintained that the law's ban on issue advocacy advertising and restrictions on party financial activity were unconstitutional violations of free speech rights. The National Voting Rights Institute, the U.S. Public Interest Research Group (associated with consumer advocate Ralph Nader), and some other voter groups joined the suit for a different reason, claiming that its increased contribution limits were unconstitutional because they favored the wealthy. Writing in defense of the law were the Committee on

Economic Development (comprising many of the nation's business leaders), almost every living former member of the ACLU leadership, and twenty-one state attorneys general.[10]

In addition to legal wrangling that was destined to find its way to the U.S. Supreme Court on two separate occasions, the BCRA encountered another set of challenges when the Federal Election Commission began drafting the regulations for administering the law. The BCRA was not warmly received by some members of the FEC, including Commissioner Bradley Smith and Chairman David Mason, who had made speeches and released statements challenging the bill during the congressional debate.[11] Numerous party committees, interest groups, and others—including supporters and opponents of the law—worked to influence the rule-making process. Some of the FEC regulations weakened provisions of the law designed to prevent soft money from influencing federal campaigns. Among them were rules exempting Internet communications from the law's soft money prohibitions and allowing federal candidates to be involved in state party soft money fundraising events.

On May 2, 2003, a special three-judge panel of the U.S. District Court for the District of Columbia handed down a 1,638-page verdict in *McConnell v. FEC*. The verdict upheld most of the BCRA's main provisions. Almost as soon as the panel handed down its decision, numerous parties filed appeals to the Supreme Court. In a five-to-four decision the Court upheld most of the provisions of the BCRA. However, it overturned the law's prohibition against a political party making both coordinated and independent expenditures in conjunction with one election, freeing the parties to do both. It also overturned the BCRA's prohibition against contributions by minors, allowing infants, toddlers, and other children (perhaps with the influence of their parents) to once again contribute to the candidates of their choice.

Just four years after the BCRA survived its first constitutional challenge and five years after its passage, the act was significantly weakened by a ruling of a differently constituted Supreme Court headed by Chief Justice John Roberts Jr., one of President George W. Bush's appointees. In a combined decision, addressing *FEC v. Wisconsin Right to Life* and *McCain et al. v. Wisconsin Right to Life* (jointly referred to as *WRTL*), the Court overturned part of the law that regulated soft-money spending by interest groups. Specifically, the Court ruled unconstitutional the law's prohibitions against the use of soft (or unregulated) money to finance issue advocacy advertisements featuring the name or likeness of a federal candidate during the last thirty days leading up to a primary or the sixty days preceding the general election. The Court's ruling appears to put interest groups in the same situation with regard to issue ads that they were in prior to the BCRA's enactment. That is, they can finance such ads with soft money throughout the election season, and they no longer need to switch to federally regulated independent expenditures during the closing weeks of a nomination or general election contest.

In justifying the ruling, Chief Justice Roberts argued that issue advocacy ads might be about issues, as opposed to the sham candidate-focused ads that were one of the reasons for the BCRA's enactment, and "where the First Amendment is implicated, the tie goes to the speaker, not the censor." The likely effect of the ruling is to increase the amount, volume, and impact of electioneering financed by corporations, trade associations, unions, and other groups and reduce the impact of the campaign communications financed by candidates, parties, and individuals. The former organizations are in the privileged position of using money collected from sources, and in amounts, that are prohibited to candidates and parties. As a result, interest groups will be able to collect money from virtually any source in the United States, whereas these others can only raise and spend money that originates from limited contributions made by U.S. citizens. Moreover, interest group soft money is not subject to the same strict and timely disclosure as the hard money regulated under the BCRA. Ironically, on the same day that the ruling was handed down, championing the speech rights of wealthy corporations, unions, and other groups, the Supreme Court limited the free speech of ordinary citizens when, in *Morse v. Frederick,* it held that a high school student had no right to display a cheap handmade banner proclaiming "Bong Hits 4 Jesus."

THE BCRA'S IMPACT

Prior to the Supreme Court's ruling in the *WRTL* case, the BCRA had had some predictable and some not-so-predictable effects on the financing of congressional elections. The immediate impact on political parties, interest groups, individual contributors, candidates, and the public can be analyzed, but the long-term effects are more difficult to discern, given that the 2006 election was the first midterm contest to take place after the BCRA. That part of the law was voided as a result of the Wisconsin case adds to the uncertainty, but some speculation about its impact is possible.

Political Parties

Perhaps the BCRA's major goal was to eliminate party soft money. Following its enactment, numerous party leaders complained that party organizations would become so impoverished that they would become irrelevant in congressional elections. The act's ban on soft money certainly reduced the parties' roles in some aspects of elections, particularly in airing issue ads, but claims about their demise turned out to be hyperbole. Congressional elections have remained candidate centered, with parties continuing to have influential supplemental roles, as has been demonstrated in earlier chapters in this book.

Formal party organizations began preparing to adapt to the BCRA as soon as it was enacted. They entered a new phase of party building that involves expanding their donor networks and solicitation techniques to raise more money from individuals who give small and medium-sized contributions; advising candidates about how to participate in the altered campaign finance system; and instructing state and local party leaders how to further develop their organizations' institutional capacities, fundraising, and campaign service programs without violating the law. These developments, bearing names like the Democratic National Committee's Fifty State Program and the RNC's microtargeting project, parallel those that took place shortly after passage of the FECA.[12]

As a result of their adaptation, Democratic and Republican Party organizations, especially the congressional and senatorial campaign committees, have continued to raise large sums of money and carry out tasks that are important to congressional campaigns. They remain important sources of campaign contributions, coordinated expenditures, and independent expenditures. They also recruit candidates and provide them with assistance in campaign management, fundraising, and the other aspects of campaigning that require technical expertise, in-depth research, and connections with the political consultants who possess the knowledge and skills needed to run a contemporary congressional campaign. The congressional and senatorial campaign committees also continue to have a hand in coordinating the contributions and campaign efforts of politicians, wealthy interest groups, and individuals.

During the 2006 midterm elections, the first held after the BCRA, the parties raised more hard money than in any previous midterm election. The Democrats raised $392.1 million and the Republicans $511.4 million. The sums fall slightly short of the combined hard and soft money totals raised in 2002, but they hardly represent the catastrophic impact forecast. Moreover, as noted in Chapter 4, the parties continued to make substantial contributions and coordinated expenditures in the 2006 House and Senate elections. Members of Congress and other politicians also continued to redistribute the wealth to other needy candidates, as party-connected contributions increased by almost one-third over 2002. This increase was probably offset by the prohibition against federal candidates raising soft money for 527 and 501(c) committees.

One particularly noteworthy change was that the parties increased their independent expenditures dramatically, from $1.7 million in 2002 to $108.1

million in 2006 for the Democrats and from $1.9 million to $115.6 million for the Republicans. The massive increase in the parties' independent campaigns was accompanied by decreases in their coordinated campaigns and especially their parallel campaigns, both of which had been funded largely by soft money. Another important change was that the Democrats reduced the GOP's fundraising advantage by almost two-thirds. This is a significant development because the Democrats had been substantially more dependent on soft money than the Republicans. Overall, these developments suggest that the parties will continue to fare well under the BCRA.

Interest Groups

A second major goal of the BCRA was to direct more interest group activity through federally regulated PACs. One short-lived success involved independent expenditures. The prohibition against the airing of soft-money-funded issue advocacy ads during the month before a primary and the two months before the general election forced groups that wished to continue broadcasting ads during these periods to switch from issue advocacy to independent expenditures. As noted in Chapter 5, this encouraged PAC independent expenditures to increase from $13.5 million in 2002 to $35.7 million in 2006. The trend is likely to be short-lived because of the *WRTL* case's reversal of the BCRA's issue advocacy prohibitions.

Another unsuccessful aspect of the BCRA concerns the expansion of existing interest group organizations and the formation of new ones to raise and spend unregulated soft money. This may have been an unanticipated consequence of the BCRA. Among the groups that expanded their soft money activities are EMILY's List and the Club for Growth. Several new soft-money-financed groups also emerged in response to the ban on party soft money. They include the pro-Democratic America Coming Together and the pro-Republican Progress for America. Many of the new groups were started by individuals with strong ties to the parties, including former White House officials, former members of Congress, and former party officials, for the purpose of collecting soft money and spending it on issue ads, voter mobilization activities, and other campaign efforts formerly conducted with party soft money.

Individual Donors

Few members of the public contribute to political campaigns. Roughly 7 percent of all voters claim to have made a contribution to any candidate for public office, and only 0.2 percent donated $200 or more to a congressional candidate. The average individual contribution is less than $75, and the top 1 percent of all individual donors account for roughly 10 percent of all individual donations. The BCRA's ban on party soft money, its limits on interest group issue advocacy advertising, and its increased ceilings for individual contributions led some party organizations, PACs, and candidates to broaden their donor bases and increase the number of small, medium, and large individual contributions they raise. This may have led to a small increase in the numbers of individuals who make contributions. However, it is likely that heightened political competition and innovations in fundraising, including fundraising via the Internet, are equally responsible for any increase in individual donations in congressional elections.

Congressional Candidates

One of the immediate effects of the BCRA was to inspire a major jump in the fundraising activity of congressional candidates. It is doubtful that this was one of the reformers' goals, but it is not surprising given that most politicians tend to be cautious and like to protect themselves from the impact of change. House candidates raised almost 37 percent more money in the 2006 elections than in the 2002 cycle. Senate candidates increased their take by a whopping 71 percent.

Increasing congressional candidates' dependence on large individual contributions was not one of the reformers' goals, but it is one of the BCRA's results. Many wealthy donors and candidates appear to have capitalized on the law's higher ceilings for individual contributions. They have influenced incumbents', challengers', and open-seat candidates' receipts, but incumbents continue to raise the most in individual contributions of $200 or more. The trend is evident in both House and Senate campaign financing.

The Public

An underlying objective of all campaign finance reforms is the restoration of public trust in the campaign finance system and in politics more generally. Most voters do not understand the differences between hard and soft money or independent expenditures, coordinated expenditures, and issue advocacy ads. They are unlikely to notice the law's impact on campaign finance or the broader conduct of congressional elections. Rather, most voters will continue to adhere to their preconceived notions about the role of money in politics. News stories about campaign spending, lavish fundraising events, and the power of high-priced lobbyists will continue to feed those negative preconceptions. Public opinion is difficult to change, and Americans traditionally have had a healthy skepticism about politics.

The growing disconnection between the campaign for votes and the campaign for resources contributes to voters' skepticism. During the golden age of parties, when local party activists were among the most important campaign resources, an intimate connection existed between the two campaigns. Elections were neighborhood affairs, and campaigns involved personal contact between candidates, party activists, other volunteers, and voters. Personal contact between voters and campaigners existed before, during, and after the election season. Parties provided ordinary voters and campaigners with ongoing relationships with politicians and others involved in the political system. The relationships often revolved around jobs, contracts, social clubs, and opportunities to improve oneself or one's neighborhood. Such relationships humanized government for voters and built bonds of trust between people and political institutions.[13]

Contemporary campaigns encourage fewer meaningful ties between voters and candidates. Despite the efforts of political parties, interest groups, and candidate organizations, the campaign for votes is still relatively impersonal, consisting largely of television, radio, direct mail, mass telephone calls, and the free media they generate. Fleeting contacts occasionally take place among citizens, candidates, and party and campaign activists, but they rarely lead to enduring personal relationships. Moreover, campaigns for resources rarely focus on ordinary voters, turning instead toward national party organizations, PACs, and wealthy individuals in a position to provide the wherewithal needed to mount a contemporary campaign. Corporations, unions, and other organizations that finance independent, parallel, and coordinated campaigns also have become important targets in the campaign for resources.

Many voters believe that the elite special interests that spend large sums in elections, rather than the individuals who vote in them, possess the strongest and most beneficial relationships with members of Congress and others in government.[14] Because members of Congress and the organizations that elect them have relatively little patronage, few government contracts, and hardly any opportunities for social advancement to distribute to their constituents, many voters have come to believe that these "goodies" are being distributed instead to wealthy campaign contributors in Washington and the nation's other financial centers. Transformations in the way that campaigns are conducted at home and in Washington have contributed to the public's belief that the operation of the federal government has changed in ways that favor special interests in Washington over the folks back home.

BEYOND THE BCRA

Although the reform community hailed the enactment of the BCRA as a major victory, most members of that community consider it a short step on a long road to a model election system. Indeed, the BCRA as enacted is a mere shadow of the first campaign reform bill introduced by McCain and Feingold. That bill proposed to ban PACs, prohibit bundling, require candidates to raise 60 percent of their funds from within their state, and offer candidates free television time and reduced postage in exchange for voluntary spending limits.

Other measures entertained by a variety of reform groups include term limits, the creation of multimember House districts, and public funding for candidates and parties. Among the reforms that have received more serious consideration are improved disclosure of campaign expenditures intended to influence federal elections; free or subsidized campaign communications for candidates and political parties; tax credits for individual contributors; restructuring of the FEC; revamping of state redistricting processes; initiatives to increase voter turnout; and most recently, measures to improve voting machines, ballots, and election administration.

Regardless of their goals, reformers should base their proposals on an understanding that elections are fought primarily between candidates and that party committees, PACs, other organizations, and individuals have important supplemental roles in them. Reformers need to appreciate the different goals and resources that individuals and groups bring to elections and to consider how their proposals will affect those groups.

Campaign reform should be predicated on the assumption that highly participatory, competitive elections are desirable because they are the best way to hold elected officials accountable to voters, enhance representation, and build trust in government. Reform should make congressional elections more competitive by encouraging talented candidates to run and by improving the ability of candidates, particularly nonincumbents, to communicate with voters. Campaign reform should also seek to increase the number of people who vote and contribute to campaigns. It should attempt to minimize the amount of unregulated money spent to influence federal elections. The recommendations that follow are not a comprehensive reform package but a series of proposals that would make congressional elections more participatory and more competitive and perhaps eventually instill greater public confidence in the political system.

Disclosure

One of the most important and broadly supported provisions of the original FECA and its amendments concerns the full disclosure of receipts and expenditures made in federal elections. Disclosure enables the public to track the money flow in election campaigns. Timely publication of a campaign's financial transactions allows voters to hold candidates accountable for where they raise their funds and how they spend them, making it possible for campaign financing to become an issue in an election. Moreover, combined with information about legislators' roll-call votes, candidates' campaign finances provide citizens with information they can use to gauge whether an incumbent appears to be held captive by one or more specific interests. Similarly, publication of a party committee's or PAC's receipts, contributions, and other expenditures enables interested voters to develop a sense of whom these organizations depend on for their resources and how they seek to influence elections, legislators, and policy making in general.

For much of its history, the FECA was largely successful in enabling voters to follow the money trail in federal elections. Watchdog groups, particularly the Center for Responsive Politics and Political Money Line, improved on the FEC's disclosure efforts by making it possible for individuals and reporters to easily visit a web site containing detailed information about candidates' reliance on various interests and organizations for their campaign finances. As a result, news reports on campaign finance have become at least as prevalent as stories about substantive campaign issues.

However, the emergence of soft money and outside spending by interest groups on issue advocacy ads weakened disclosure. Although the FECA required national party committees to disclose their soft money receipts, and the BCRA prohibits national parties from collecting such funds, disclosure requirements for state and local parties vary by state and usually are not as rigorous. Moreover and as noted earlier, some interest group entities that participate in congressional and presidential elections are not subject to the same rigorous disclosure requirements as are federal candidates, party committees, and PACs. As a result, the exact expenditures that some interest groups undertake to influence congressional elections, their sources and amounts, are largely hidden from public view. This becomes especially problematic when interests hide their identity by forming shadow groups with innocuous-sounding names, such as America Coming Together, Progress for America, and

Americans for Honesty on Issues, for the purpose of spending large sums on issue advertisements. That most members of the public are unable to distinguish these ads from candidate ads further blurs accountability. The BCRA originally addressed some undisclosed or partially disclosed expenditures by shadow groups by outlawing issue advocacy ads during the federal spending periods. As noted above, this aspect of the law was overturned in the *WRTL* case. The law could be improved by subjecting to strict disclosure laws any organization that spends money at any time to influence federal elections, regardless of that group's designation under the federal election law or the federal tax code.

Free or Subsidized Communications

Free or subsidized campaign communications—whether in the form of postage, television or radio time, or communications vouchers—would give candidates, particularly challengers, the opportunity to present their messages to the public. The promise of free or heavily discounted communications resources would probably encourage better candidates to run for Congress because it would guarantee access to some of the resources needed to campaign.[15] By encouraging the entry of better candidates and providing them with communications resources, this reform should lead to more competitive congressional elections.

The availability of communications resources also might indirectly encourage greater electoral competition. Congressional challengers and open-seat candidates who use these resources effectively would be in a position to attract the attention of local journalists, and that would help the candidates communicate more effectively with voters and help voters cast their ballots on the basis of more information. Because campaign communications help stimulate public interest in elections, reforms that ensure that both candidates have adequate communications resources also probably would increase voter turnout.[16] A perception of greater competitiveness also might encourage some PACs and wealthy individuals to contribute to challengers, although most would likely continue to employ access or mixed strategies, which dictate contributing primarily to incumbents.

Free or subsidized mailings would give candidates opportunities to present targeted, detailed information about their qualifications, issue positions, and political objectives. Giving congressional candidates free postage for three or four first-class mailings—including postage for one or two newsletters of six to ten pages—is a simple reform that would improve the quality of the information that voters receive and could increase voter turnout and electoral competitiveness.

Parties also could be offered free postage to mobilize current supporters and attract new ones. Minor parties and their candidates, as well as candidates who run as independents, could be given free postage if they persuaded a threshold number of voters to register under their label prior to the current election, if the candidates had received a minimum number of votes in the previous contest, or if they met some other threshold requirement. Minor parties and their candidates and independent candidates also could be reimbursed retroactively for postage if they reached some threshold level of votes in the current election. Extending free postage to candidates and parties is justified by the fact that it would contribute to the education of citizens—the same argument used to justify congressional franked mail and reduced postage for party committees and nonprofit educational groups.

Giving candidates access to radio and television broadcast time would be more complicated because of disparities in the cost and because congressional districts and media markets often do not match one another.[17] One solution is to require local broadcasters to provide Senate candidates with free television time and to require local radio stations to give free radio time to both House and Senate candidates. Broadcasters could be required to provide back-to-back, prime-time segments to opposing candidates. Candidates could be issued five-minute blocks of time early in the campaign season, which they could use to air "infomercials." These time slots would be lengthy enough for candidates to communicate some information about their personal background, political qualifications, issue positions, and major campaign themes. Later in the campaign season, two- or one-minute time slots could be distributed so that candidates could reinforce the images and campaign themes they introduced earlier. Thirty- or fifteen-second time slots could be made available during the summation phase of the election for candidates to pull together their campaign messages and rally their supporters.

This system of structured, free media time would give candidates the opportunity to communicate positive, substantive messages. It also would encourage voters to compare the messages. The differences in requirements for each chamber reflect the fact that television is an efficient and heavily used medium in virtually all Senate elections but is less practical and less frequently used in House contests, especially ones in major metropolitan areas.

The Democratic and Republican national, congressional, and senatorial campaign committees also should be given free blocks of television and radio time, so that each could have the opportunity to remind voters of their party's accomplishments, philosophy, and objectives. Giving parties resources that they can use to influence the political agenda during and after an election could introduce more collective responsibility into the political system.[18] Minor parties and candidates should receive free broadcast time on terms similar to those for free postage.

Requiring local broadcasters to provide free political advertisements is justifiable because the airwaves are public property, and one of the conditions of using them is that broadcasters "serve the public interest, convenience, and necessity."[19] The United States is the only major industrialized democracy that does not require broadcasters to contribute air time to candidates for public office—a distinction that should be eliminated.[20] Cable and satellite television operators also should be required to distribute advertising time to House and Senate candidates and parties, with the justification that much of what is viewed on cable television passes through the public airwaves or over publicly maintained utility lines.

An alternative to providing candidates and parties with communications resources is government distribution of communications vouchers. Such a program would allow campaigners more freedom in designing their communications strategies. Campaigns desiring to allocate more resources to setting the agenda could use their vouchers to purchase mass media ads. Campaigns that wished to focus on mobilizing specific population groups could devote a greater portion of their vouchers to targeted direct mail or telephone calls.

The Political Campaign Broadcast Activity Improvements Act that senators McCain, Feingold, and Richard Durbin, D-Ill., introduced during the 107th Congress includes some of these ideas.[21] It provides House candidates who raise at least $25,000 in individual contributions of $250 or less, and who do not spend more than $125,000 in personal funds (including funds from immediate family members), with $3 in broadcast vouchers for every $1 the candidate raises in individual contributions in amounts not exceeding $250. It provides Senate candidates who raise at least $25,000 in individual contributions of $250 or less, and who do not spend more than $500,000 in personal funds, with $3 in broadcast vouchers for every $1 they raise in individual contributions not exceeding $250. The ceiling for vouchers for House candidates is $375,000, and the ceiling for vouchers for Senate candidates is $375,000 multiplied by the number of House districts in the state. Candidates who receive vouchers but do not wish to use them can exchange them with their party for an equivalent amount of cash, which they could then spend on other campaign activities.

The proposal sets aside an aggregate total of up to $100 million in broadcast vouchers to be divided among the political parties. Major political parties (defined as those that received 25 percent or more of the popular vote in the preceding presidential election) automatically qualify for vouchers. Minor parties qualify once they have fielded candidates who qualify for vouchers in twenty-two House races or five Senate races. A minor party would receive vouchers proportionate to the number of qualified candidates it fields. A minor party that fields candidates who qualify for vouchers in at least 218 House elections or seventeen Senate elections is eligible for the same number of vouchers as a major party.

The bill also has some public affairs programming requirements. It requires all radio and television broadcast stations to devote a minimum of two hours per week to candidate-centered or issue-focused programming for a total of six weeks before a primary or general election. This programming must be aired during popular time slots: one-half must be between 5 p.m. and 11:35 p.m.; none may be broadcast between midnight and 6 a.m. The bill requires that during the forty-five days before a primary and the sixty days before the general election, candidates and parties be charged the lowest rate that the station has charged any other advertiser during the 120 days preceding a candidate's or party's request. Finally, the bill prohibits stations from preempting air time purchased by candidates or parties on behalf of a candidate in favor of other customers.

Tax Incentives

Tax incentives should be used to broaden the base of campaign contributors and to offset the impact of funds collected from wealthy and well-organized segments of society. Prior to the tax reforms introduced in 1986, individuals were able to claim a tax credit of $50 if they contributed $100 or more to federal candidates. (Couples who contributed $200 could claim a tax credit of $100.) Although some taxpayers took advantage of these credits, the credits themselves were not sufficient to encourage many citizens to contribute to campaigns.[22]

A system of graduated tax credits similar to those used in some other western democracies might accomplish that goal.[23] If they could claim a 100 percent tax credit for up to $100 in campaign contributions, individuals would be more likely to contribute. Credits of 75 percent for the next $100 and 50 percent for the following $100 would encourage further contributions. Tax credits would encourage candidates and parties to pursue small and moderate contributions more aggressively. Because being asked is one of the most important determinants of who actually makes a contribution, tax credits for individual donations are likely to have a positive impact on the number of taxpayers who make them.[24] Using taxpayer dollars to increase the number of individuals who give money to federal candidates is an expensive proposition, but it would probably be the most effective way to increase the number of people who participate in the financing of congressional elections. Increasing the base of small contributors is the best way to offset the influence of individuals and groups that make large contributions while maintaining a tie between a candidate's levels of popular and financial support.

The Federal Election Commission

The FEC should be strengthened. The commission is currently unable to investigate many of the complaints brought before it, has a backlog of cases that is several years old, and has been criticized for its failure to dispense quickly with frivolous cases and pursue more important ones. Some of these shortcomings are the result of the commission's being micromanaged by its oversight committees in Congress and of underfunding. Other shortcomings are due to the FEC's structure—it has three Democratic and three Republican commissioners, all political appointees. In recent years, the commissioners have ignored the opinions of the FEC's professional legal staff. All of this has led to indecision and stalemate.[25]

It is essential that the FEC be restructured so that it operates in a more decisive fashion. Only strong enforcement by the FEC, with backup from the Justice Department and a specially appointed independent counsel on appropriate cases, can discourage unscrupulous politicians from violating the law. Recent failures by the FEC to enforce the law adequately have encouraged members of Congress to spend tens of millions of dollars on partisan investigations. Such investigations, which may be useful for embarrassing political opponents, are an inadequate substitute for impartial administration of the law.

Redistricting

As a result of redistricting, 2002 set a contemporary record for the number of uncompetitive House elections. Deals cut between Democratic and Republican House members have resulted in an absence of competition in most incumbent-challenger races. Only a few states, most notably Iowa, feature a significant number of competitive House races in most election years. The contrast between Iowa and most other states suggests that competition would increase if more states passed reforms emulating Iowa's redistricting commission, which does not take into account partisanship or incumbency when drawing congressional districts.

Another reform related to redistricting is to prohibit state legislatures from redrawing House seats following the initial redistricting that takes place after reapportionment. Republicans in Texas and Colorado sought to do precisely that after they won control of both the legislature and the governorship in those states in the 2002 elections. The GOP succeeded in Texas, but not until after

Democratic legislators left the state to avoid a vote on the plan, and Republicans called on a variety of law enforcement agencies and the Federal Aviation Administration to track them down. Colorado Republicans also succeeded in a midcycle redistricting of their state's House seats, but that plan was ruled unconstitutional because the state's constitution explicitly mandates that congressional seats only be drawn once per decade. Midcycle redistricting is a bad idea. Allowing politicians to create new district boundaries anytime, including whenever party control of a state's government changes hands, rather than wait until the normal census, reapportionment, and redistricting cycle runs its course, can only inject more discord into an already conflict-ridden process and increase the number of lawsuits that accompany the drawing of congressional districts.

Voter Turnout Initiatives

Campaign reform should address low voter turnout in elections. In the 2006 congressional elections about 40 percent of all eligible voters turned up at the polls—a figure in line with those for other recent midterm elections.[26] Citizen apathy and disenchantment with the political system are probably responsible for some voter abstention, but voter registration laws are believed to depress turnout by about 9 percent.[27] The "motor-voter" law, enacted in 1993, has eased some barriers to voter registration. Requiring all states to include a check-off box on their income tax forms to enable citizens to register to vote when they file their tax returns could further reduce the barriers to voting.

Other measures that make it easier for voters to exercise the franchise also should be considered. Making election day a national holiday is one possibility. Making wider use of mail-in ballots, such as those used exclusively in Oregon, is another. "Early," "countywide," and "mobile" voting procedures also should be considered. Such procedures currently allow voters in Texas to cast their ballots over a seventeen-day period commencing twenty days before an election, at any of numerous locations in the county in which they are registered. The locations include mobile units that are dispatched to parks and other popular locations on weekends. Measures that make it easier to register to vote or cast a ballot will not cause a groundswell in voter turnout, but they should increase it, especially when combined with increased competition and greater efforts by candidates and parties to mobilize voters.[28]

Improving the Way Americans Vote

The 2000 presidential election was a wake-up call for voters, election administrators, and candidates for public office. It showed that something was amiss with the way Americans vote. Between 4 million and 6 million presidential votes and as many as 3.5 million senatorial and gubernatorial votes were lost in the balloting process. Approximately 7.4 percent of the forty million registered voters who did not vote stated that they did not cast a ballot because of problems with their registration. An additional 2.8 percent of all registered voters who did not vote attributed their failure to turn up at the polls to long lines, inopportune hours, or inconveniently located polling places.[29]

Discussions of "butterfly ballots," "chads," "undervotes," "overvotes," and partisan decision making by election officials and the courts also left many people unsettled. Reports that substantial numbers of the poor and members of minority groups were supplied with faulty information about their proper polling place, subjected to intimidation, or turned away at the polls raised alarm among civil rights groups. Evidence that the votes cast by members of these groups were less likely to be counted than votes cast by wealthy or middle-class white voters raised concerns about adherence to the principle of one person, one vote. Learning about the absence of clearly delineated procedures for vote recounts in many states and localities also was cause for some anxiety. The fact that 1960s technology was still being widely used in twenty-first-century elections was another cause of voter dissatisfaction.[30]

Congress responded to public pressure for reform by passing the Help America Vote Act (HAVA), which the president signed into law on October 29, 2002. The HAVA requires the states to replace outdated voting machines, employ computerized voting registration systems, and improve poll worker training, among other things, and it authorizes federal subsidies for these purposes. Each polling place is required to have at least one voting machine that is accessible to individuals with disabilities. All polling places are to provide provisional ballots to individuals whose names do not appear on the voter rolls and to count those ballots once the voter's registration is verified. The law also requires first-time voters who registered by mail to provide identification the first time they show up to cast their ballots.

The HAVA depends on state governments, and ultimately the county governments that administer elections in most states, for implementation. Thus, its success depends largely on the capabilities and resources of those governments. Complicating the picture is the fact that these governments depend on private manufacturers and vendors for voting equipment, poll worker training, and much of the software to run the new voting machines and manage voter rolls. Most of the voting systems currently available for purchase perform well. Nevertheless, there is room for improvement, including improvement of paper ballot/optical scan systems and "direct recording electronic" systems that employ touch screens, buttons, or other interface features. One step that could improve voter satisfaction, reduce voters' need for help, and increase voters' ability to cast their ballots as intended would be for those states that use ballots that have a straight-party-voting option to do away with them.[31] Another possibility for improving the election process would be to recruit younger, more technologically proficient poll workers—perhaps by providing higher pay or allowing citizens to substitute duty as poll workers for jury duty. The HAVA is an important step in improving how Americans vote, but actions must be taken by many governmental and private institutions for it to be effective. As the 2000 elections demonstrated, voting technology, ballot design, and election administration are important, especially when elections are competitive.

CONCLUSION

The rules and norms that govern congressional elections resemble those that structure any activity: they favor some individuals and groups at the expense of others. In recent years the number of Americans who believe that the electoral process is out of balance and provides too many advantages to incumbents, interest groups, wealthy individuals, and other "insiders" has grown tremendously. Their views are reflected in growing citizen distrust of government, the sense of powerlessness expressed by many voters, and the public's willingness to follow the lead of insurgent candidates and reformers without scrutinizing their qualifications or objectives. These are signs that the prestige and power of Congress are in danger. They also are signs that meaningful campaign reform is in order.

Campaign reform should make congressional elections more competitive and increase the number of citizens who participate in them, both as voters and as financial contributors. Campaign reform should enable candidates to spend less time campaigning for resources and more time campaigning for votes. Reform also should seek to enhance representation, accountability, and trust in government.

Without major campaign reform, incumbency will remain the defining element of most congressional elections. Challengers, particularly those who run for the House, will continue to struggle to raise money and attract the attention of the news media and voters. The dialogues in House incumbent-challenger contests will remain largely one-sided, whereas those in open-seat contests and Senate races will be more even. Interest groups will continue to spend outside money on issue ads designed to influence elections. Party and interest group issue advocacy and independent expenditure ads may continue to overshadow the election activities of candidates in very close races. Congress, elections, and other institutions of government will remain targets for attack both by those who have a sincere wish to improve the political process and by those seeking short-term partisan gain.

Elections are the most important avenue of political influence afforded to the citizens of a representative democracy. They give voters the opportunity to hold public officials accountable and to reject politicians with whom they disagree. Respect for human rights and political processes that allow for citizen input are what make democratic systems of government superior to others. Yet all systems of government have their imperfections, and some of these are embodied in their electoral processes. Sometimes the imperfections are significant enough to warrant major change. Such change should bring the electoral process closer in line with broadly supported notions of liberty, equality, and democracy, as well as with the other values that bind the nation. Despite the enactment of the BCRA and the HAVA, the current state of congressional elections demonstrates that change is warranted in the way Americans elect those who serve in Congress.

Notes

INTRODUCTION

1. Abraham Lincoln, Gettysburg Address.

1. THE STRATEGIC CONTEXT

1. Thomas A. Kazee, "The Emergence of Congressional Candidates," in *Who Runs for Congress?* ed. Thomas A. Kazee (Washington, D.C.: Congressional Quarterly, 1994), 1–14; L. Sandy Maisel, Linda L. Fowler, Ruth S. Jones, and Walter J. Stone, "Nomination Politics," in *The Parties Respond: Changes in the American Party System,* 2d ed., ed. L. Sandy Maisel (Boulder, Colo.: Westview Press, 1994), 145–168.

2. Leon D. Epstein, *Political Parties in Western Democracies* (New York: Praeger, 1967), chap. 8.

3. Kenneth Martis, *The Historical Atlas of U.S. Congressional Districts, 1789–1983* (New York: Free Press, 1982), 5–6.

4. See, for example, Frank J. Sorauf, "Political Parties and Political Action Committees," *Arizona Law Review* 22 (1980): 445–464.

5. Jerrold B. Rusk, "The Effect of the Australian Ballot Reform on Split Ticket Voting," *American Political Science Review* 64 (1970): 1220–1283.

6. See, for example, V. O. Key, *Politics, Parties, and Pressure Groups* (New York: Thomas Y. Crowell, 1964), 371.

7. Ibid., 389–391.

8. Committee on Political Parties, American Political Science Association, "Toward a More Responsible Two-Party System," *American Political Science Association Review* 44, no. 3, part 2 (1950): 21.

9. For more on the BCRA, see Anthony Corrado, Thomas E. Mann, Daniel Ortiz, and Trevor Potter, *The New Campaign Finance Sourcebook* (Washington, D.C.: Brookings Institution, 2005). See also Paul S. Herrnson, "The Bipartisan Campaign Reform Act and Congressional Elections," in *Congress Reconsidered,* 8th ed., ed. Lawrence C. Dodd and Bruce I. Oppenheimer (Washington, D.C.: CQ Press, 2005), 107–135.

10. The exception to this is so-called Levin funds, contributions to state and local parties of up to $10,000 per donor per year from sources and in amounts that are permissible under a state's laws. These funds can be used for voter registration, identification, and mobilization activities. The ratio of

federally regulated funds and Levin funds that can be spent in a given election is based on an allocation formula determined by the Federal Election Commission.

11. Karl-Heinz Nassmacher, "Comparing Party and Campaign Finance in Western Democracies," in *Campaign and Party Finance in North America and Western Europe,* ed. Arthur B. Gunlicks (Boulder, Colo.: Westview Press, 1993), 233–263.

12. Arthur B. Gunlicks, "Introduction," in *Campaign and Party Finance,* 6.

13. Sorauf, "Political Parties and Political Action Committees," 445–464.

14. Paul S. Herrnson, *Party Campaigning in the 1980s* (Cambridge: Harvard University Press, 1988), 82.

15. Anthony Corrado, *Campaign Finance Reform: Beyond the Basics* (New York: The Century Foundation Press, 2000), 93.

16. Louis Hartz, *The Liberal Tradition in America* (New York: Harcourt, Brace, 1955).

17. See, for example, Robert A. Dahl, *Democracy in the United States* (Chicago: Rand McNally, 1967), 252; Herbert McClosky and John Zaller, *The American Ethos* (Cambridge: Harvard University Press, 1984), 62–100.

18. See Rusk, "The Effect of the Australian Ballot."

19. Key, *Politics, Parties, and Pressure Groups,* 342, 386; Nelson W. Polsby, *The Consequences of Party Reform* (Oxford: Oxford University Press, 1983), 72–74; William J. Crotty, *American Parties in Decline* (Boston: Little, Brown, 1984), 277–278.

20. Lee Ann Elliot, "Political Action Committees—Precincts of the '80s," *Arizona Law Review* 22 (1980): 539–554; Kay Lehman Schlozman and John T. Tierney, *Organized Interests and American Democracy* (New York: Harper and Row, 1986), 75–78.

21. John R. Petrocik, *Party Coalitions* (Chicago: University of Chicago Press, 1981), chaps. 8 and 9; Paul Allen Beck, "A Socialization Theory of Partisan Realignment," in *Controversies in American Voting Behavior,* ed. Richard G. Niemi and Herbert F. Weisberg (Washington, D.C.: CQ Press, 1984), 396–411; Martin P. Wattenberg, *The Decline of American Political Parties, 1952–1988* (Cambridge: Harvard University Press, 1990), chap. 4.

22. Austin Ranney, *Channels of Power* (New York: Basic Books, 1983), 110; Doris Graber, *Mass Media and American Politics,* 4th ed. (Washington, D.C.: CQ Press, 1993), 250–252.

23. Jack Dennis, "Support for the Party System by the Mass Public," *American Political Science Review* 60 (1966): 605.

24. CBS News/*New York Times* poll, October 1986, cited in Bruce E. Keith, David B. Magleby, Candice J. Nelson, Elizabeth Orr, Mark C. Westlye, and Raymond E. Wolfinger, *The Myth of the Independent Voter* (Berkeley: University of California Press, 1992), 8.

25. "Cooperative Congressional Election Study," University of Maryland and Brigham Young University modules (Palo Alto, Calif.: Polimetrix, 2006).

26. This group includes independents who "lean" toward one of the parties. Figures for party identification and voting behavior are compiled from Nancy Burns, Donald R. Kinder, and National Election Studies, *American National Election Study, 2002: Post-Election Survey* (Ann Arbor: University of Michigan, Center for Political Studies, 2003).

27. Sorauf, "Political Parties and Political Action Committees," 447.

28. Robert Agranoff, "Introduction," in *The New Style in Election Campaigns,* ed. Robert Agranoff (Boston: Holbrook Press, 1972), 3–50; Larry J. Sabato, *The Rise of the Political Consultants* (New York: Basic Books, 1981).

29. See Ranney, *Channels of Power,* 110; and Graber, *Mass Media,* 250.

30. Agranoff, "Introduction."

31. Sorauf, "Political Parties and Political Action Committees."

32. Cornelius P. Cotter and John F. Bibby, "Institutional Development and the Thesis of Party Decline," *Political Science Quarterly* 95 (1980): 1–27; Herrnson, *Party Campaigning,* chaps. 3 and 4;

Stephen E. Frantzich, *Political Parties in the Technological Age* (New York: Longman, 1989), 81–90, 182–186.

33. See, for example, Key, *Politics, Parties, and Pressure Groups,* 421.

34. David R. Butler and Bruce Cain, *Congressional Redistricting* (New York: Macmillan, 1992), 10, 87; Michael Lyons and Peter F. Galderisi, "Incumbency, Reapportionment, and U.S. House Redistricting," *Political Review Quarterly* 49 (1995): 857–873. For another view, see Richard Niemi and Alan I. Abramowitz, "Partisan Redistricting and the 1992 Elections," *Journal of Politics* 56 (1994): 811–817.

35. Donald Ostdiek, "Congressional Redistricting and District Typologies," *Journal of Politics* 57 (1995): 533–543.

36. Bruce I. Oppenheimer, James A. Stimson, and Richard W. Waterman, "Interpreting U.S. Congressional Elections, *Legislative Studies Quarterly* 11 (1986): 227–247; J. W. Koch, "Candidate Status, Presidential Approval, and Voting for U.S. Senator," *Electoral Studies* 19 (2000): 479–492; James E. Campbell, *The Presidential Pulse of Congressional Elections* (Lexington: University of Kentucky Press, 1993), 7–11.

37. Michael S. Lewis-Beck and Tom W. Rice, *Forecasting Elections* (Washington, D.C.: CQ Press, 1992), chaps. 4–6.

38. Jerome M. Clubb, William H. Flanigan, and Nancy H. Zingale, *Partisan Realignment* (Beverly Hills, Calif.: Sage Publications, 1980), 258–260.

39. On coattail effects, see Barry C. Burden and David C. Kimball, *Why Americans Split Their Tickets* (Ann Arbor: University of Michigan Press, 2002), esp. 78–96, 134–138; Randall L. Calvert and John A. Ferejohn, "Coattail Voting in Recent Presidential Elections," *American Political Science Review* 77 (1983): 407–419; Richard Born, "Reassessing the Decline of Presidential Coattails," *Journal of Politics* 46 (1980): 60–79; James E. Campbell, "Predicting Seat Gains from Presidential Coattails," *American Journal of Political Science* 30 (1986): 397–418; Gary C. Jacobson, *Electoral Origins of Divided Government, 1946–1988* (Boulder, Colo.: Westview Press, 1990), 80–81.

40. Edward R. Tufte, "Determinants of the Outcomes of Midterm Congressional Elections," *American Political Science Review* 69 (1975): 812–826; Lewis-Beck and Rice, *Forecasting Elections,* 60–75.

41. Morris P. Fiorina, *Retrospective Voting in American National Elections* (New Haven: Yale University Press, 1981), 165; Eric M. Uslaner and M. Margaret Conway, "The Responsible Electorate," *American Political Science Review* 79 (1985): 788–803.

42. Gerald Kramer, "Short-Term Fluctuations in U.S. Voting Behavior," *American Political Science Review* 65 (1971): 131–143; Gary C. Jacobson and Samuel Kernell, *Strategy and Choice in Congressional Elections* (New Haven: Yale University Press, 1983), chap. 6; Gary C. Jacobson, "Does the Economy Matter in Midterm Elections?" *American Journal of Political Science* 34 (1990): 400–404. For alternative interpretations, see Robert S. Erikson, "Economic Conditions and the Vote," *American Journal of Political Science* 34 (1990): 373–399; Patrick G. Lynch, "Midterm Elections and Economic Fluctuations," *Legislative Studies Quarterly* 227 (2002): 265–294.

43. Norman Nie and Kristi Andersen, "Mass Belief Systems Revisited," *Journal of Politics* 36 (1974): 540–591; Crotty, *American Parties in Decline,* 49–50.

44. Richard A. Brody and Benjamin I. Page, "The Assessment of Policy Voting," *American Political Science Review* 66 (1972): 450–458; Norman H. Nie, Sidney Verba, John R. Petrocik, *The Changing American Voter* (New York: Twentieth Century Fund, 1979), esp. chap. 18.

45. David R. Mayhew, *Congress: The Electoral Connection* (New Haven: Yale University Press, 1974); Morris P. Fiorina, *Congress: Keystone of the Washington Establishment* (New Haven: Yale University Press, 1978), 19–21, 41–49, 56–62; Bruce Cain, John Ferejohn, and Morris Fiorina, *The Personal Vote* (Cambridge: Harvard University Press, 1987), 103–106; Gary C. Jacobson, *The Politics of Congressional Elections,* 4th ed. (New York: Longman, 1997), 28–33; George Serra and Albert

Cover, "The Electoral Consequences of Perquisite Use," *Legislative Studies Quarterly* 17 (1992): 233–246.

46. Harrison W. Fox and Susan Webb Hammond, *Congressional Staffs* (New York: Free Press, 1977), 88–99, 154–155.

47. Herrnson, *Party Campaigning,* chap. 4; Frank J. Sorauf, *Inside Campaign Finance* (New Haven: Yale University Press, 1992), 80–84.

48. *Thornburg v. Gingles,* 478 U.S. 30 (1986).

49. Redistricting Task Force for the National Conference of State Legislatures, "Action on Redistricting Plans: 2001–02," February 12, 2003, www.senate.leg.state.mn.us/departments/scr/redist/redsum2000/action01-02.htm, May 14, 2003.

50. Richard F. Fenno Jr., *Home Style* (Boston: Little, Brown, 1978), 164–168.

51. Gary C. Jacobson, "The 1994 House Elections in Perspective," in *Midterm,* ed. Philip A. Klinkner (Boulder, Colo.: Westview Press, 1996), 1–20; John R. Hibbing and Elizabeth Theiss-Morse, *Congress as Public Enemy: Public Attitudes toward American Political Institutions* (Cambridge: Cambridge University Press, 1995), 31–33, 69–71, 96–100; Adam Nagourney and Janet Elder, "Only 25% in Poll Approve of the Congress," *New York Times,* September 21, 2006.

52. Klinkner, *Midterm;* James G. Gimpel, *Fulfilling the Contract* (Boston: Allyn and Bacon, 1996).

53. Richard F. Fenno Jr., "If, as Ralph Nader Says, Congress Is 'the Broken Branch,' How Come We Love Our Congressmen So Much?" in *Congress in Change,* ed. Norman J. Ornstein (New York: Praeger, 1975).

54. Paul S. Herrnson and Irwin L. Morris, "Presidential Campaigning in the 2002 Congressional Elections," *Legislative Studies Quarterly* 32 (2007); Luke J. Keele, Brian J. Fogarty, and James A. Stimson, "Presidential Campaigning in the 2002 Congressional Elections," *PS: Political Science and Politics* 37 (2004): 827–832.

55. "President Bush—Overall Job Rating," PollingReport.com, www.pollingreport.com/BushJob.htm.

56. "Congress—Job Rating," PollingReport.com, www.pollingreport.com/CongJob.htm.

57. "Generic Ballot—U.S. House of Representatives," PollingReport.com, http://pollingreport.com/2006.htm.

58. Twenty percent is an appropriate victory margin given the heightened level of uncertainty in contemporary congressional elections. A narrower margin, such as 15 percent, would have eliminated campaigns that were competitive for part of the election season but were ultimately decided by more than 15 percent of the vote. Slightly changing the boundaries for the competitiveness measure does not significantly change the results. Moreover, the twenty-point classification produces results similar to the forecasts of political journalists who handicap Democratic elections. When the seats the *Cook Political Report* classifies as "lean," "likely," or "toss-up" races (based on ten reports from September 1, 2006, through November 2, 2006) are combined into one category, 90 percent of those races fall into the twenty-point classification for competitiveness used here. For more discussion of the classification scheme, see the appendix to the first edition of this book.

2. CANDIDATES AND NOMINATIONS

1. E. E. Schattschneider, *Party Government* (New York: Holt, Rinehart, and Winston, 1942), 99–106.

2. Thomas A. Kazee, "The Emergence of Congressional Candidates," in *Who Runs for Congress?* ed. Thomas A. Kazee (Washington, D.C.: Congressional Quarterly, 1994), 1–14; L. Sandy Maisel, Walter J. Stone, and Cherie Maestas, "Quality Challengers to Congressional Incumbents," in *Playing Hardball,* ed. Paul S. Herrnson (Upper Saddle River, N.J.: Prentice Hall, 2001), 12–40.

3. Joseph A. Schlesinger, *Ambition and Politics* (Chicago: Rand McNally, 1966), 11–12, 16–19, 198–199; Gary C. Jacobson and Samuel Kernell, *Strategy and Choice in Congressional Elections* (New Haven: Yale University Press, 1983), chap. 3; Kazee, "The Emergence of Congressional Candidates"; David T. Canon, *Actors, Athletes, and Astronauts* (Chicago: University of Chicago Press, 1990), 76–79.

4. Jamie L. Carson, "Strategy, Selection, and Candidate Competition in U.S. House and Senate Elections," *Journal of Politics* 67 (2005): 1–28; and Cherie D. Maestas, Sarah Fulton, L. Sandy Maisel, and Walter J. Stone, "When to Risk It? Institutions, Ambitions, and the Decision to Run for the U.S. House," *American Political Science Review* 100 (2006): 195–208.

5. Gary C. Jacobson and Samuel Kernell, "National Forces in the 1986 U.S. House Elections," *Legislative Studies Quarterly* 15 (1990): 65–87; Canon, *Actors, Athletes, and Astronauts,* 106–108.

6. Richard F. Fenno Jr., *Home Style* (Boston: Little, Brown, 1978), 164–168.

7. Walter J. Stone, L. Sandy Maisel, and Cherie D. Maestas, "Quality Counts," *American Journal of Political Science* 48 (2004): 479–495.

8. Peverill Squire, "Preemptive Fundraising and Challenger Profile in Senate Elections," *Journal of Politics* 53 (1991): 1150–1164; Janet M. Box-Steffensmeier, "A Dynamic Analysis of the Role of War Chests in Campaign Strategy," *American Journal of Political Science* 40 (1996): 352–371. For another viewpoint, see Jay Goodliffe, "The Effect of War Chests on Challenger Entry in U.S. House Elections," *American Journal of Political Science* 45 (2001): 830–844.

9. Sara Fritz and Dwight Morris, *Gold-Plated Politics* (Washington, D.C.: Congressional Quarterly, 1992), esp. chap. 2.

10. On redistricting, see Richard G. Niemi and Laura R. Winsky, "The Persistence of Partisan Redistricting Effects in Congressional Elections," *Journal of Politics* 54 (1992): 565–571.

11. Stephen E. Frantzich, "De-Recruitment," *Western Political Quarterly* 31 (1978): 105–126; Michael K. Moore and John R. Hibbing, "Is Serving in Congress Fun Again?" *American Journal of Political Science* 36 (1992): 824–828; Eric M. Uslaner, *The Decline of Comity in Congress* (Ann Arbor: University of Michigan Press, 1993), esp. chap. 2.

12. Ed Patru, deputy director of communications, NRCC, interview, November 30, 2006.

13. Frantzich, "De-Recruitment," 105–126; John R. Hibbing, "Voluntary Retirement from the U.S. House," *Legislative Studies Quarterly* 8 (1982): 57–74.

14. John B. Gilmour and Paul Rothstein, "Early Republican Retirements," *Legislative Studies Quarterly* 18 (1993): 345–365; D. Roderick Kiewiet and Langche Zeng, "An Analysis of Congressional Career Decisions, 1947–1986," *American Political Science Review* (1993): 928–941; Richard L. Hall and Robert P. Van Houweling, "Avarice and Ambition in Congress," *American Political Science Review* 89 (1995): 121–136.

15. Darrell M. West and John Orman, *Celebrity Politics* (Upper Saddle River, N.J.: Prentice Hall, 2003), 2–4.

16. For a comprehensive assessment of these conditions, see Canon, *Actors, Athletes, and Astronauts,* 103–110.

17. On the effects of redistricting, see Marc J. Hetherington, Bruce Larson, and Suzzanne Globetti, "The Redistricting Cycle and Strategic Candidate Decisions in U.S. House Races," *Journal of Politics* 65 (2003): 1221–1234.

18. On the impact of term limits, see Richard J. Powell, "The Impact of Term Limits on the Candidacy Decisions of State Legislators in U.S. House Elections," *Legislative Studies Quarterly* 25 (2000): 645–661; on the number of states with term limits, see "The Term Limited States," National Conference of State Legislatures, February 2006, www.ncsl.org.

19. On ambitious, policy, and experience-seeking or hopeless amateurs, see Canon, *Actors, Athletes, and Astronauts,* xv, 26–32.

20. Throughout this chapter, seats are categorized according to their status (open or incumbent occupied) at the beginning of the election cycle. Seats that began the election cycle as incumbent occupied but featured two nonincumbents in the general election are classified as open from chap. 3 forward.

21. See, for example, E. J. Dionne Jr., *Why Americans Hate Politics* (New York: Simon and Schuster, 1991).

22. On the decision making of quality challengers, see Gary W. Cox and Jonathan N. Katz, "Why Did the Incumbency Advantage in U.S. House Elections Grow?" *American Journal of Political Science* 40 (1996): 478–497.

23. The term incumbent-opposing primary is from Canon, *Actors, Athletes, and Astronauts.*

24. An exception to this rule occurs in Texas, where an individual can appear on the ballot for two offices simultaneously.

25. Harold D. Lasswell, *Power and Personality* (Boston: Norton, 1948), 39–41.

26. The generalizations that follow are drawn from responses to question 18 of the 1992 Congressional Campaign Study; see the appendix to the first edition of this book and the book's web site, http://herrnson.cqpress.com. See also L. Sandy Maisel, *From Obscurity to Oblivion: Running in the Congressional Primary* (Knoxville: University of Tennessee Press, 1982), 31–32; Paul S. Herrnson, *Party Campaigning in the 1980s* (Cambridge: Harvard University Press, 1988), 86; and Kazee, "The Emergence of Congressional Candidates."

27. Thomas A. Kazee and Mary C. Thornberry, "Where's the Party? Congressional Candidate Recruitment and American Party Organizations," *Western Political Quarterly* 43 (1990): 61–80; Steven H. Haeberle, "Closed Primaries and Party Support in Congress," *American Politics Quarterly* 13 (1985): 341–352.

28. Herrnson, *Party Campaigning,* 51–56.

29. Taylor claimed his no vote went unrecorded as the result of a technical error. Ken Coriale, "The Fighting Eleventh" (unpublished paper, University of Maryland, College Park, December 6, 2006); Karin Johanson, executive director, Democratic Congressional Campaign Committee, interview, November 29, 2006.

30. Janet Hook, "Meet the Powers behind the Democrats' Strategy," *Los Angeles Times,* July 5, 2006, Sec. A.

31. Coriale, "The Fighting Eleventh"; Johanson, interview, November 29, 2006.

32. Mark Stephens, executive director, National Republican Senatorial Committee, interview, December 13, 2006.

33. Ibid.

34. See, for example, Linda L. Fowler and Robert D. McClure, *Political Ambition* (New Haven: Yale University Press, 1989), 205–207.

35. On WISH List, see Mark J. Rozell, "WISH List," in *After the Revolution: PACs and Lobbies in the New Republican Congress,* ed. Robert Biersack, Paul S. Herrnson, and Clyde Wilcox (Boston: Allyn and Bacon, 1991), 184–191. See also Christine L. Day and Charles D. Hadley, *Women's PACs* (Upper Saddle River, N.J.: Prentice Hall, 2005).

36. Walter J. Stone and L. Sandy Maisel, "The Not So Simple Calculus of Winning," *Journal of Politics* 65 (2003): 951–977.

37. Jackie Koszcsuk and H. Amy Stern, eds., *CQ's Politics in America 2006* (Washington, D.C.: CQ Press, 2005), 76–77.

38. Brian Nutting and H. Amy Stern, eds., *CQ's Politics in America 2002: The 107th Congress* (Washington, D.C.: Congressional Quarterly, 2001), 992–993.

39. Ibid.

40. "The Post Endorses Herger for Congress," *Paradise Post,* October, 29, 2006, www .paradisepost.com.

41. Fenno, *Home Style,* 176–189.

42. See Paul S. Herrnson, "National Party Organizations and the Postreform Congress," in *The Postreform Congress,* ed. Roger H. Davidson (New York: St. Martin's Press, 1992), 48–70.

43. See, for example, Schlesinger, *Ambition and Politics,* 99; Canon, *Actors, Athletes, and Astronauts,* 50–53, 56–58; Maisel et al., "Quality Challengers to Congressional Incumbents."

44. Koszcsuk and Stern, *CQ's Politics in America 2006,* 288.

45. "Hank Johnson Announces Congressional Campaign against Cynthia McKinney," American Chronicle, December 21, 2005, www.americanchronicle.com.

46. Dave Williams, "Low-Key Primary Turns into High-Profile Runoff," *Gwinnett (Georgia) Daily Post,* August 4, 2006.

47. Jeffrey L. Austin, "Johnson Draws in Dollars as Runoff with McKinney Nears," August 4, 2006, CQPolitics.com.

48. Ibid.

49. Success rates for previous elections can be found in earlier editions of this book.

50. Stephanie Wood, "The 50 Richest Members of Congress," *Roll Call,* September 11, 2006.

51. R. Darcy, Susan Welch, and Janet Clark, *Women, Elections, and Representation* (New York: Longman, 1987), 93–108.

52. Linda L. Fowler, *Candidates, Congress, and the American Democracy* (Ann Arbor: University of Michigan Press, 1993), 127–136.

53. Barbara Burrell, "Women Candidates in Open-Seat Primaries for the U.S. House: 1968–1990," *Legislative Studies Quarterly* 17 (1992): 493–508.

54. Richard L. Fox and Jennifer L. Lawless, "To Run or Not to Run for Office," *American Journal of Political Science* 49 (2005): 642–659.

55. On the impact of religious participation on the development of political and civic skills, see Sidney Verba, Kay Lehman Schlozman, and Henry E. Brady, *Voice and Equality* (Cambridge: Harvard University Press, 1995), 333.

56. On the effect of race on candidate selection, see Fox and Lawless, "To Run or Not to Run for Office"; and Fowler, *Candidates, Congress, and the American Democracy,* 136–142.

57. Kevin A. Hill, "Does the Creation of Majority Black Districts Aid Republicans?" *Journal of Politics* 57 (1995): 384–401; Charles Cameron, David Epstein, and Sharyn O'Halloran, "Do Majority-Minority Districts Maximize Substantive Black Representation in Congress?" *American Political Science Review* 90 (1996): 794–812.

58. David T. Cannon, *Race, Redistricting, and Representation* (Chicago: University of Chicago Press, 1999).

59. Wood, "The 50 Richest Members of Congress."

60. See, for example, Richard L. Fox, Jennifer L. Lawless, and Courtney Feeley, "Gender and the Decision to Run for Office," *Legislative Studies Quarterly* 26 (2001): 411–435.

61. Alan Ehrenhalt, *The United States of Ambition* (New York: Random House, 1991), 225–226.

62. Mildred Ames, "Membership of the 110th Congress: A Profile," Congressional Research Service, December 15, 2006, http://opencrs.cdt.org/document/RS22555.

63. Beginning with the U.S. House, and proceeding in the order listed, only the highest office is included.

64. Charlie Cook, "On Your Mark. . . ," Cook Political Report, March 15, 2005, www.cookpolitical.com.

65. Guy Cecil, political director, DSCC, interview, December 4, 2006.

66. Ibid.

67. Stephens, interview, December 13, 2006.

68. This generalization is drawn from responses to question 18 of the 1992 Congressional Campaign Study; see the appendix to the first edition of this book and the book's web site, http://herrnson.cqpress.com.

3. THE ANATOMY OF A CAMPAIGN

1. See, for example, Edie N. Goldenberg and Michael W. Traugott, *Campaigning for Congress* (Washington, D.C.: CQ Press, 1984), 19–24.

2. Committee on Political Parties, American Political Science Association, "Toward a More Responsible Two-Party System," *American Political Science Association Review* 44, no. 3, part 2 (1950): 21; Robert Agranoff, "Introduction," in *The New Style in Election Campaigns,* ed. Robert Agranoff (Boston: Holbrook Press, 1972), 3–50; Larry J. Sabato, *The Rise of the Political Consultants* (New York: Basic Books, 1981).

3. R. Sam Garrett, Paul S. Herrnson, and James A. Thurber, "Perspectives on Campaign Ethics," in *The Electoral Challenge: Theory Meets Practice,* ed. Stephen C. Craig (Washington, D.C.: CQ Press, 2006), 203–226; Bill Hamilton and Dave Beattie, "The Big Metamorphosis: How Campaigns Change Candidates," *Campaigns & Elections,* August 1999, 34–36.

4. Compiled from data provided by Political Money Line, www.tray.com/. Note: In August 2007, the Political Money Line web site was changed to CQ MoneyLine, http://moneyline.cq.com/pml/home.do.

5. There have been important exceptions to this generalization in recent years. See David T. Canon, *Actors, Athletes, and Astronauts* (Chicago: University of Chicago Press, 1990), 3, 36.

6. Paul S. Herrnson, *Party Campaigning in the 1980s* (Cambridge: Harvard University Press, 1988), 61–63, 92–94.

7. "Charities on the Hill," *Washington Post,* March 7, 2006, Sec. A.

8. Peter L. Francia, John C. Green, Paul S. Herrnson, Lynda W. Powell, and Clyde Wilcox, *The Financiers of Congressional Elections* (New York: Columbia University Press, 2003), 69–98.

9. Political consultant (anonymous), interview, April 5, 2002.

10. Michael Margolis, David Resnick, and Chin-chang Tu, "Campaigning on the Internet," *Harvard International Journal of Press/Politics* 2 (1997): 59–78; David A. Dulio, Donald L. Groff, and James A. Thurber, "Untangled Web: Internet Use during the 1998 Election," *PS: Political Science and Politics* 32 (1999): 53–58.

11. As noted in Chapter 8, research conducted in 2006 demonstrates that virtually every major-party general election candidate possesses a web site and uses it for many purposes.

12. Paul S. Herrnson, "The Professionalization of Election Campaigns" (presentation at "Conference on the 2006 U.S. Elections and the Road Ahead for American Politics and Canada-U.S. Relations," sponsored by the Center for United States Studies, University of Quebec at Montreal, October 5, 2006).

13. This finding supports Fenno's observation that the explanatory power of challenger quality and political experience is largely the result of the quality of the candidates' campaign organizations. See Richard F. Fenno Jr., *Senators on the Campaign Trail: The Politics of Representation* (Norman: University of Oklahoma Press, 1996), 100.

14. "The List," *Campaigns & Elections,* December 2006.

15. Arjinderpal Sekhon, candidate for the U.S. House of Representatives, interview, February 12, 2007.

16. "The List," *Campaigns & Elections,* December 2006; Ken Coriale, "The Fighting Eleventh" (unpublished paper, University of Maryland, College Park, December 6, 2006); Karin Johanson, executive director, Democratic Congressional Campaign Committee, interview, November 29, 2006.

17. Coriale, "The Fighting Eleventh"; Johanson, interview, November 29, 2006.

18. Senior staff member (anonymous), NRCC, interview, November 30, 2006.

19. Danielle Kogut, "Democrats on the Rampage: Perlmutter Takes Colorado 7" (unpublished paper, University of Maryland, College Park, December 6, 2006).

20. Kyle L. Saunders and Robert J. Duffy, "Volatility and Volition: The Pendulum Swings High and Hard in Colorado's Seventh District," in *War Games,* ed. David B. Magleby and Kelly D.

Patterson (Provo, Utah: Brigham Young University, Center for the Study of Elections and Democracy, 2007), 74–75; and Kogut, "Democrats on the Rampage."

21. Figures are from Political Money Line, www.tray.com/.

22. In states with only one representative, House campaigns must reach out to as many voters as Senate campaigns.

4. THE PARTIES CAMPAIGN

1. Frank J. Sorauf, "Political Parties and Political Action Committees," *Arizona Law Review* 22 (1980): 447.

2. See, for example, Robert Agranoff, "Introduction," in *The New Style in Election Campaigns,* ed. Robert Agranoff (Boston: Holbrook Press, 1972), 3–50.

3. Joseph A. Schlesinger, "The New American Political Party," *American Political Science Review* 79 (1985): 1151–1169; Paul S. Herrnson, *Party Campaigning in the 1980s* (Cambridge: Harvard University Press, 1988), chaps. 2–3.

4. Herrnson, *Party Campaigning,* chap. 2.

5. For more on the concept of party issue ownership, see John R. Petrocik, "Issue Ownership in Presidential Elections, with a 1980 Case Study," *American Journal of Political Science* 40 (1996): 825–850; and George Rabinowitz and Stuart McDonald, "A Directional Theory of Voting," *American Political Science Review* 65 (1989): 93–122.

6. Paul S. Herrnson, Kelly D. Patterson, and John J. Pitney Jr., "From Ward Heelers to Public Relations Experts" in *Broken Contract? Changing Relationships between Citizens and Government in the United States,* ed. Stephen C. Craig (Boulder, Colo.: Westview Press, 1996), 251–267.

7. Richard K. Armey, Jennifer Dunn, and Christopher Shays, *It's Long Enough: The Decline of Popular Government under Forty Years of Single Party Control of the U.S. House of Representatives* (Washington, D.C.: Republican Conference, U.S. House of Representatives, 1994); Richard K. Armey, *Under the Clinton Big Top: Policy, Politics, and Public Relations in the President's First Year* (Washington, D.C.: Republican Conference, U.S. House of Representatives, 1993); James G. Gimpel, *Fulfilling the Contract* (Boston: Allyn and Bacon, 1996); Robin Kolodny, "The Contract with America in the 104th Congress," in *The State of the Parties,* ed. John C. Green and Daniel M. Shea (Lanham, Md.: Rowman and Littlefield, 1996), 314–327.

8. Paul S. Herrnson and Irwin L. Morris, "Presidential Campaigning in the 2002 Congressional Elections," *Legislative Studies Quarterly* 32 (2007); Luke J. Keele, Brian J. Fogarty, and James A. Stimson, "Presidential Campaigning in the 2002 Congressional Elections," *PS: Political Science and Politics* 37 (2004): 827–832.

9. Some polls had jobs and the economy rated higher; see Greenberg Quinlan Rosner Research, "Election 2006," www.americanprogress.org.

10. Even though the reports that candidates filed with the Federal Election Commission indicate that some received large national committee contributions and coordinated expenditures, this spending is almost always directed by a congressional or senatorial campaign committee's election strategy.

11. The term *Hill committees* probably originates from the fact that the congressional and senatorial campaign committees were originally located in congressional office space on Capitol Hill.

12. These figures include only hard dollars, which can be spent directly on individual federal campaigns. See "Party Financial Activity Summarized for the 2006 Election Cycle," Federal Election Commission, press release, March 7, 2006.

13. Zachary A. Goldfarb, "Bush Raises $27 Million for GOP," *Washington Post,* June 20, 2006.

14. Leadership PACs are political action committees associated with members of Congress and other politicians. Figures are compiled from data provided by the Center for Responsive Politics, www.opensecrets.org.

15. Figures are compiled from data provided by the Center for Responsive Politics.

16. Rep. Chris Van Hollen, D-Md., interview, March 26, 2007.

17. On party donor networks, see Peter L. Francia, John C. Green, Paul S. Herrnson, Lynda W. Powell, and Clyde Wilcox, *The Financiers of Congressional Elections* (New York: Columbia University Press, 2003).

18. Herrnson, *Party Campaigning*, 46; Robin Kolodny, "Electoral Partnerships," in *Campaign Warriors*, ed. James A. Thurber and Candice J. Nelson (Washington, D.C.: Brookings Institution Press, 2000), 121; David B. Magleby, Kelly D. Patterson, and James A. Thurber, "Campaign Consultants and Responsible Party Government," in *Responsible Partisanship?* ed. John C. Green and Paul S. Herrnson (Lawrence: University Press of Kansas, 2003), 101–119.

19. Karin Johanson, executive director, DCCC, interview, November 29, 2006; Guy Cecil, political director, DSCC, interview, December 4, 2006; Ed Patru, deputy communications director, NRCC, interview, November 30, 2006; Mark Stephens, executive director, NRSC, interview, December 13, 2006; Michael DuHaime, political director, RNC, interview, December 4, 2006.

20. Gary C. Jacobson, "Party Organization and Campaign Resources in 1982," *Political Science Quarterly* 100 (1985–1986): 604–625.

21. On the use of congressional and senatorial campaign committee chairmanships as vehicles for advancing in the congressional leadership, see Paul S. Herrnson, "Political Leadership and Organizational Change at the National Committees," in *Politics, Professionalism, and Power*, ed. John Green (Lanham, Md.: University Press of America, 1993), 186–202; Brooks Jackson, *Honest Graft: Big Money and the American Political Process* (New York: Alfred A. Knopf, 1988), 286–290; Robin Kolodny, *Pursuing Majorities* (Norman: University of Oklahoma Press, 1998), 175–195.

22. Gary C. Jacobson and Samuel Kernell, *Strategy and Choice in Congressional Elections* (New Haven: Yale University Press, 1983), 39–43, 76–84.

23. The information on committee strategy, decision making, and targeting is from numerous interviews conducted with high-ranking officials of the congressional and senatorial campaign committees before, during, and after various election cycles dating back to 1984.

24. On the 1990 election, see Les Frances, "Commentary," in *Machine Politics, Sound Bites, and Nostalgia*, ed. Michael Margolis and John Green (Lanham, Md.: University Press of America, 1993), 58; on the 1994 election, see Paul S. Herrnson, "Money and Motives," in *Congress Reconsidered*, 6th ed., ed. Lawrence C. Dodd and Bruce I. Oppenheimer (Washington, D.C.: CQ Press, 1996), 106–107; on the 1992 and 1996 elections, see previous editions of this book.

25. The forecasts of specialized journalists who handicap congressional elections parallel those of party leaders. See Chapter 1, note 58, for information on those forecasts.

26. Robert Biersack and Paul S. Herrnson, "Political Parties and the Year of the Woman," in *The Year of the Woman?* ed. Elizabeth Adell Cook, Sue Thomas, and Clyde Wilcox (Boulder, Colo.: Westview Press, 1994), 173–174.

27. Van Hollen, interview, March 26, 2007.

28. Dan Balz and Jim VandeHei, "GOP Redirects Funds from Faltering Races," *Washington Post*, October 13, 2006; Michael Powell, "Upstart Leaves the Campaigning to Congressman," *Washington Post*, October 19, 2006.

29. These are considered separate elections under the BCRA. Party committees usually give contributions only to general election candidates.

30. The coordinated expenditure limit for states with only one House member was originally set at $20,000 and reached $79,200 in 2006. Also, as is noted in Chapter 1, in the event that a candidate breaks the threshold amount associated with the millionaires' provision of the BCRA, the coordinated expenditure limits for parties increase.

31. Jennifer A. Steen, "Self-Financed Candidates and the 'Millionaires' Amendment,'" in *The Election after Reform*, ed. Michael J. Malbin (Lanham, Md.: Rowman & Littlefield, 2006);

"Millionaires' Amendment," Federal Election Commission, March 2004, updated January 2007, www.fec.gov.

32. Herrnson, *Party Campaigning,* 43–44.

33. For data on prior elections see the previous editions of this book, and Paul S. Herrnson and Kelly D. Patterson, "Financing the 2000 Congressional Elections," in *Financing the 2000 Election,* ed. David B. Magleby (Washington, D.C.: Brookings Institution, 2002), 106–132. See also Herrnson, "Money and Motives"; Paul S. Herrnson, "National Party Decision Making, Strategies, and Resource Distribution in Congressional Elections," *Western Political Quarterly* 42 (1998): 301–323; Jacobson, "Party Organization and Campaign Resources in 1982," 604–625.

34. The major recipient of these funds was Democrat Amy Klobuchar, who defeated Rep. Mark Kennedy in the 2006 Minnesota Senate election.

35. Ross K. Baker, *The New Fat Cats: Members of Congress as Political Benefactors* (New York: Priority Press Publications, 1989), 31.

36. After testing the waters, Warner opted not to run for president in 2008. Figures are from the Center for Responsive Politics.

37. The coverage of these topics draws heavily from Herrnson, *Party Campaigning,* chaps. 4 and 5.

38. Andrew Grossman, political director, DSCC, interview, February 27, 2003.

39. Cecil, interview, December 4, 2006.

40. Information provided by Anne Marie Habershaw, chief operating officer, DCCC, February 16, 2007.

41. Johanson, interview, November 29, 2006.

42. Patru, interview, November 30, 2006.

43. Cecil, interview, December 4, 2006.

44. Stephens, interview, December 13, 2006.

45. Habershaw; Stephens, interview, December 13, 2006.

46. DuHaime, interview, December 4, 2006; see also Matt Bai, "The Multilevel Marketing of the President," *New York Times Magazine,* April 25, 2004.

47. Habershaw; Johanson, interview, November 29, 2006.

48 Patru, interview, November 30, 2006.

49. DSCC staff; Grossman, interview, February 27, 2003.

50. Stephens, interview, December 13, 2006.

51. Typical PAC kits include information about the candidate's personal background, political experience, campaign staff, support in the district, endorsements, issue positions, and campaign strategy.

52. David Maraniss and Michael Weisskopf, "Speaker and His Directors Make the Cash Flow Right," *Washington Post,* November 27, 1995.

53. Herrnson, *Party Campaigning,* 75.

54. These generalizations are drawn from responses to questions VI.1 through VI.7 of the 2002 Congressional Campaign Study.

55. Cornelius P. Cotter, James L. Gibson, John F. Bibby, and Robert J. Huckshorn, *Party Organizations in American Politics* (Pittsburgh: University of Pittsburgh Press, 1989), 20–25.

56. Ibid.; Herrnson, *Party Campaigning,* 102–106; Robert Huckfeldt and John Sprague, "Political Parties and Electoral Mobilization," *American Political Science Review* 86 (1992): 70–86; Gregory A. Caldeira, Samuel C. Patterson, and Gregory A. Markko, "The Mobilization of Voters in Congressional Elections," *Journal of Politics* 47 (1985): 490–509; Michael A. Krassa, "Context and the Canvass," *Political Behavior* 10 (1988): 233–246; Peter W. Wielhower and Brad Lockerbie, "Party Contacting and Political Participation, 1952–90," *American Journal of Political Science* 38 (1994): 211–229.

57. John Lapp, head of independent expenditure group, DCCC, interview, November 29, 2006; Habershaw.

58. Patru, interview, November 30, 2006.

59. Cecil, interview, December 4, 2006; Stevens, interview, December 13, 2006.

60. Paul Freedman and Ken Goldstein, "Measuring Media Exposure and the Effects of Negative Campaign Ads," *American Journal of Political Science* 43 (1999): 1189–1208; Ken Goldstein and Paul Freedman, "Campaign Advertising and Voter Turnout," *Journal of Politics* 64 (2002): 721–740.

61. Kim Fridkin Kahn and Patrick J. Kenney, *No Holds Barred* (Upper Saddle River, N.J.: Prentice Hall, 2004), 74–84, 91–107.

62. Ken Goldstein and Joel Rivlin, "Political Advertising in the 2002 and 2004 Elections," University of Wisconsin at Madison, Wisconsin Advertising Project, 2002, updated February 2005, chap. 5, www.polisci.wisc.edu/tvadvertising.

63. Cecil, interview, November 30, 2006.

64. Quote from Curt Anderson, RNC, in Dan Balz and David S. Broder, "Close Election Turns on Voter Turnout," *Washington Post,* November 1, 2002.

65. Herrnson and Morris, "Presidential Campaigning in the 2002 Congressional Elections."

66. Karen Finney, communications director, DNC, interview, January 19, 2007; Johanson, interview, November 29, 2006; Cecil, interview, November 30, 2006.

67. Michael DuHaime, quoted in David B. Magleby and Kelly D. Patterson, "War Games," in *War Games,* ed. David B. Magleby and Kelly D. Patterson (Provo, Utah: Brigham Young University, Center for the Study of Elections and Democracy, 2007), 34.

68. Figures include expenditures from 527 organizations that raised or spent $200,000 or more during the 2006 congressional election cycle; compiled from Stephen R. Weissman and Kara D. Ryan, "Soft Money in the 2006 Election and the Outlook for 2008," Campaign Finance Institute, Washington, D.C., 2007, www.cfinst.org.

69. These generalizations are drawn from responses to questions VI.1 through VI.7 of the "2002 Congressional Campaign Study," Center for American Politics and Citizenship, University of Maryland. To some degree the assessments also reflect the propensity of campaign managers and candidates in the candidate-centered system to view themselves as the nucleus of all campaign activity and to understate the contributions others make to the campaign.

70. The discussion of the congressional election in Colorado's 7th district draws heavily from Kyle L. Saunders and Robert J. Duffy, "Volatility and Volition: The Pendulum Swings High and Hard in Colorado 7th Congressional District Race," in Magleby and. Patterson, *War Games,* 69–85; see also Danielle Kogut, "Democrats on the Rampage: Perlmutter Takes Colorado 7" (unpublished paper, University of Maryland, College Park, December 6, 2006).

71. Patru, interview, November 30, 2006.

72. See note 70 for this chapter.

73. The discussion of the Senate race in Ohio draws heavily from Stephen Brooks, Michael John Burton, David B. Cohen, Daniel Coffey, Anne C. Hanson, Stephen T. Mockabee, and John C. Green, "The Battle for Ohio," in *War Games,* ed. Magleby and Patterson, 162–178.

74. Cecil, interview, December 4, 2006.

75. Ibid.

5. THE INTERESTS CAMPAIGN

1. See, for example, Herbert E. Alexander, *Financing Politics* (Washington, D.C.: CQ Press, 1992), 10–17.

2. Although it was referred to as a political action committee from its inception, COPE operated somewhat differently from modern (post-1974) PACs until the enactment of the FECA. See Clyde Wilcox, "Coping with Increasing Business Influence: The AFL-CIO's Committee on Political

Education," in *Risky Business? PAC Decisionmaking in Congressional Elections,* ed. Robert Biersack, Paul S. Herrnson, and Clyde Wilcox (Armonk, N.Y.: M. E. Sharpe, 1994), 214–223.

3. PACs that do not meet these requirements are subject to the same $1,000 contribution limit as are individuals.

4. The number of nonconnected PACs excludes leadership PACs.

5. On EMILY's List, see Christine L. Day and Charles D. Hadley, *Women's PACs* (Upper Saddle River, N.J.: Prentice Hall, 2005).

6. Stephen R. Weissman and Kara D. Ryan, "Soft Money in the 2006 Election and the Outlook for 2008," Campaign Finance Institute, Washington, D.C., 2007.

7. Center for Responsive Politics, Washington, D.C., www.opensecrets.org.

8. Weissman and Ryan, "Soft Money in the 2006 Election and the Outlook for 2008."

9. Ibid.

10. Ibid.

11. Ibid.; Catalist, www.catalist.us/index.html.

12. See, for example, Theodore J. Eismeier and Philip H. Pollock III, *Business, Money, and the Rise of Corporate PACs in American Elections* (New York: Quorum Books, 1988), 27–30; J. David Gopoian, "What Makes PACs Tick," *American Journal of Political Science* 28 (May 1984): 259–281; Craig Humphries, "Corporations, PACs, and the Strategic Link between Contributions and Lobbying Activities," *Western Political Quarterly* 44 (1991): 353–372; Frank J. Sorauf, *Inside Campaign Finance* (New Haven: Yale University Press, 1992), 64–65, 74–75; and the case studies in Biersack, Herrnson, and Wilcox, eds., *Risky Business?*

13. Laura Langbein, "Money and Access," *Journal of Politics* 48 (1986): 1052–1062; Richard Hall and Frank Wayman, "Buying Time," *American Political Science Review* 84 (1990): 797–820.

14. John Frendreis and Richard Waterman, "PAC Contributions and Legislative Behavior," *Social Science Quarterly* 66 (1985): 401–412; Janet M. Grenzke, "PACs and the Congressional Supermarket," *American Journal of Political Science* 33 (1989): 1–24; John Wright, "Contributions, Lobbying, and Committee Voting in the U.S. House of Representatives," *American Political Science Review* 84 (1990): 417–438; Kevin B. Grier and Michael C. Munger, "Comparing Interest Group PAC Contributions to House and Senate Incumbents, 1980–1986," *Journal of Politics* 55 (1993): 615–643; Thomas Romer and James M. Snyder Jr., "An Empirical Investigation of the Dynamics of PAC Contributions," *American Journal of Political Science* 38 (1994): 745–769; Andrew J. Taylor, "Conditional Party Government and Campaign Contributions," *American Journal of Political Science* 57 (2003): 293–304; Kevin M. Esterling, "Buying Expertise," *American Political Science Review* 101 (2007): 93–109.

15. Gary C. Jacobson and Samuel Kernell, *Strategy and Choice in Congressional Elections* (New Haven: Yale University Press, 1983), esp. chap. 4.

16. Theodore J. Eismeier and Philip H. Pollock III, "The Tale of Two Elections: PAC Money in 1980 and 1984," *Corruption and Reform* 1 (1986): 189–207; Sorauf, *Inside Campaign Finance,* 67–77; Brooks Jackson, *Honest Graft* (New York: Alfred A. Knopf, 1988), 69–70, 77–81, 90–93.

17. Paul S. Herrnson, "Money and Motives," in *Congress Reconsidered,* 6th ed., ed. Lawrence C. Dodd and Bruce I. Oppenheimer (Washington, D.C.: CQ Press, 1996), 122–124; Thomas J. Rudolph, "Corporate and Labor PAC Contributions in House Elections," *Journal of Politics* 61 (1999): 195–206; Gary W. Cox and Eric Mager, "How Much Is Majority Status in the U.S. Congress Worth?" *American Journal of Political Science* 93 (1999): 299–309.

18. Sorauf, *Inside Campaign Finance,* 61–71.

19. See the case studies in Biersack, Herrnson, and Wilcox, eds., *Risky Business?;* Robert Biersack, Paul S. Herrnson, and Clyde Wilcox, eds., *After the Revolution: PACs and Lobbies in the New Republican Congress* (Boston: Allyn and Bacon, 1991).

20. Clyde Wilcox, "Organizational Variables and the Contribution Behavior of Large PACs: A Longitudinal Analysis," *Political Behavior* 11 (1989): 157–173.

21. John Wright, "PACs, Contributions, and Roll Calls," *American Political Science Review* 79 (1985): 400–414.

22. Larry J. Sabato, *PAC Power: Inside the World of Political Action Committees* (New York: W. W. Norton, 1984), 44–49; Robert Biersack, "Introduction," in *Risky Business?*

23. The information on the Realtors PAC is from Anne H. Bedlington, "The Realtors Political Action Committee," in *After the Revolution,* 170–183.

24. On AT&T's PAC, see Robert E. Mutch, "AT&T PAC: A Pragmatic Giant," in *Risky Business?*; and Robert Mutch, "AT&T PAC," in *After the Revolution.* On AMPAC, see Michael K. Gusmano, "The AMA in the 1990s," in *After the Revolution.*

25. The information on WASHPAC is from Barbara Levick-Segnatelli, "WASHPAC," in *Risky Business?*

26. Brett Kappel, legal counsel, Powell, Goldstein, Frazer, and Murphy PAC, interview, August 17, 1999.

27. Ibid.

28. On lead PACs, see the introduction to part I in *Risky Business?,* 17–18. On the NCEC, see Paul S. Herrnson, "The National Committee for an Effective Congress," in *Risky Business?* On COPE, see Clyde Wilcox, "Coping with Increasing Business Influence," in *Risky Business?*; and Robin Gerber, "Building to Win," in *After the Revolution,* 77–93. On BIPAC, see Candice J. Nelson, "The Business-Industry PAC," in *Risky Business?*; and Candice J. Nelson and Robert Biersack, "BIPAC," in *After the Revolution,* 36–46.

29. See previous editions of this book.

30. Theodore J. Eismeier and Philip H. Pollock III, "Political Action Committees," in *Money and Politics in the United States,* ed. Michael J. Malbin (Washington, D.C.: American Enterprise Institute, 1984), 122–141; Margaret Ann Latus, "Assessing Ideological PACs," in *Money and Politics in the United States,* 150–160; Sabato, *PAC Power,* 93–95.

31. On abortion rights PACs, see, for example, Sue Thomas, "NARAL PAC," in *Risky Business?*; and Day and Hadley, *Women's PACs.*

32. Linda L. Fowler and Robert D. McClure, *Political Ambition* (New Haven: Yale University Press, 1989), 205–207.

33. Ronald G. Shaiko and Marc A. Wallace, "From Wall Street to Main Street," in *After the Revolution*; James G. Gimpel, "Peddling Influence in the Field," in *Risky Business?*

34. Herrnson, "The National Committee for an Effective Congress," in *Risky Business?*

35. See, for example, Sabato, *PAC Power,* 44–49.

36. Peter L. Francia, "Early Fundraising by Noincumbent Female Congressional Candidates," *Women & Politics* 23 (2001): 7–20; Day and Hadley, *Women's PACs.*

37. Peter L. Francia, John C. Green, Paul S. Herrnson, Lynda W. Powell, and Clyde Wilcox, *The Financiers of Congressional Elections: Investors, Ideologues, and Intimates* (New York: Columbia University Press, 2003).

38. EMILY's List, www.emilyslist.org.

39. Club for Growth, www.clubforgrowth.org/index1.php.

40. Francia et al., *The Financiers of Congressional Elections.*

41. Center for Responsive Politics, www.opensecrets.org.

42. Ibid.

43. In addition, because groups have to report the costs of only the small portion of the communication that discusses an election, FEC reporting requirements understate the true value of these communications.

44. See, for example, Political Money Line, www.tray.com.

45. Compiled from data on web site of Center for Responsive Politics, www.opensecrets.org.

46. David B. Magleby and Kelly D. Patterson, "War Games," in *War Games,* ed. David B. Magleby and Kelly D. Patterson (Provo, Utah: Brigham Young University, Center for the Study of Elections and Democracy, 2007), 54–55.

47. Ibid., 22–38.

48. Ibid.

49. Mass media advertising is the one campaign activity where Democratic and Republican House campaigns report receiving equal amounts of help from interest groups. These generalizations are drawn from questions VI.1 through VI.7 of the "2002 Congressional Campaign Study," Center for American Politics and Citizenship, University of Maryland.

50. All individual contributions referred to in this section were made in amounts of $200 or more. Figures are from the Center for Responsive Politics, www.opensecrets.org.

51. The discussion of the congressional election in Colorado's 7th district draws heavily from Kyle L. Saunders and Robert J. Duffy, "Volatility and Volition: The Pendulum Swings High and Hard in Colorado 7th Congressional District Race," in *War Games,* ed. Magleby and Patterson.

52. Figure includes contributions from corporations without stock.

53. Center for Responsive Politics, www.opensecrets.org.

54. Magleby and Patterson, "War Games," in *War Games.*

55. The discussion of the Ohio Senate race draws heavily from Stephen Brooks, Michael John Burton, David B. Cohen, Daniel Coffey, Anne C. Hanson, Stephen T. Mockabee, and John C. Green, "The Battle for Ohio," in *War Games.*

6. THE CAMPAIGN FOR RESOURCES

1. Quoted in David Adamany and George E. Agree, *Political Money* (Baltimore, Md.: Johns Hopkins University Press, 1975), 8.

2. George Thayer, *Who Shakes the Money Tree?* (New York: Simon and Schuster, 1973), 25.

3. The figures for House and Senate campaign contributions and coordinated expenditures include funds raised by all candidates involved in major-party contested general elections.

4. The denominator used to calculate the percentages is the candidates' total receipts plus any coordinated spending the parties made on the candidates' behalf. Coordinated expenditures are included because candidates have some control over the activities on which they are spent.

5. Frank J. Sorauf, *Inside Campaign Finance* (New Haven: Yale University Press, 1992), 47.

6. Figures are compiled from Paul S. Herrnson, *The Campaign Assessment and Candidate Outreach Project, 2000 Survey* (College Park, Md.: Center for American Politics and Citizenship, University of Maryland, 2000).

7. On direct-mail fundraising, see Kenneth R. Godwin, *One Billion Dollars of Influence* (Chatham, N.J.: Chatham House, 1988).

8. Center for Responsive Politics, www.opensecrets.org.

9. Figures are from question IV.2 of the "2002 Congressional Campaign Study," Center for American Politics and Citizenship, University of Maryland.

10. As noted in Chapter 1, individual contribution limits are $2,000 plus an adjustment for inflation.

11. Peter L. Francia, John C. Green, Paul S. Herrnson, Lynda W. Powell, and Clyde Wilcox, *The Financiers of Congressional Elections* (New York: Columbia University Press, 2003), esp. chap. 3.

12. Ibid., chaps. 3 and 5.

13. See, for example, Sorauf, *Inside Campaign Finance,* 124–127.

14. The figure for PACs excludes contributions by leadership PACs. The House members were Dennis Hastert, R-Ill. (Speaker), Deborah Pryce, R-Ohio (chair, Domestic and International Monetary Policy, Trade and Technology Subcommittee of the Financial Services Committee), John Boehner, R-Ohio (chair, Education and Workforce Committee), Henry Bonilla, R-Texas (chair, Agriculture, Rural Development and FDA Subcommittee of the Appropriations Committee), Roy Blunt, R-Mo. (House Republican whip and member of the Energy and Commerce Committee), Nancy Johnson, R-Conn. (chair, Health Subcommittee of the Ways and Means Committee), Joe L. Barton, R-Texas (chair, Energy and Commerce Committee), and Eric Cantor, R-Va. (assistant Republican whip and member, Ways and Means Committee).

15. Center for Responsive Politics, www.opensecrets.org.

16. Ibid.

17. Some argue that preemptive fundraising by incumbents may not discourage quality challengers from running. See Jonathan S. Krasno and Donald Philip Green, "Preempting Quality Challengers in House Elections," *Journal of Politics* 50 (1988): 920–936; Peverill Squire, "Preemptive Fundraising and Challenger Profile in Senate Elections," *Journal of Politics* 53 (1991): 1150–1164.

18. Gary C. Jacobson, *Money in Congressional Elections* (New Haven: Yale University Press, 1980), 113–123; Jonathan S. Krasno, Donald Philip Green, and Jonathan A. Cowden, "The Dynamics of Fundraising in House Elections," *Journal of Politics* 56 (1994): 459–474.

19. Sorauf, *Inside Campaign Finance,* 75.

20. Center for Responsive Politics, www.opensecrets.org.

21. The remainder came from interest on investments and miscellaneous funds.

22. Forty-eight percent of all challengers spent one-fourth of their personal campaign schedule fundraising. See note 6 for this chapter.

23. Robert Biersack, Paul S. Herrnson, and Clyde Wilcox, "Seeds for Success," *Legislative Studies Quarterly* 18 (1993): 535–553; Krasno, Green, and Cowden, "The Dynamics of Fundraising in House Elections."

24. Paul S. Herrnson, *Party Campaigning in the 1980s* (Cambridge: Harvard University Press, 1988), 75.

25. Paul S. Herrnson, "Campaign Professionalism and Fundraising in Congressional Elections," *Journal of Politics* 54 (1992): 859–870.

26. Clyde Wilcox, "Coping with Increasing Business Influence," in *Risky Business? PAC Decision-making in Congressional Elections,* ed. Robert Biersack, Paul S. Herrnson, and Clyde Wilcox (Armonk, N.Y.: M. E. Sharpe, 1994), 214–223; Robin Gerber, "Building to Win," in *After the Revolution,* ed. Robert Biersack, Paul S. Herrnson, and Clyde Wilcox (Boston: Allyn and Bacon, 1991), 77–93; Denise L. Baer and Martha Bailey, "The Nationalization of Education Politics," in *Risky Business?,* 65–78.

27. See Craig A. Rimmerman, "New Kids on the Block," in *Risky Business?;* Rimmerman, "The Gay and Lesbian Victory Fund Comes of Age," in *After the Revolution;* and Mark J. Rozell, "WISH List" in *After the Revolution.*

28. As noted in Chapter 1, the normal coordinated expenditure limit is $2,000 for all party committees, plus an adjustment for inflation.

29. Center for Responsive Politics, www.opensecrets.org.

30. See note 6 for this chapter.

31. Herrnson, "Campaign Professionalism and Fundraising in Congressional Elections."

32. Corporate contributions include $2,200 from corporations without stock.

33. The figure for nonconnected PAC contributions excludes contributions from leadership PACs.

34. The figures exclude contributions by leadership PACs.

35. Figures for out-of-state money are from the Center for Responsive Politics, www.opensecrets .org.

36. Total resources include party-coordinated expenditures and receipts. See note 4 for this chapter.

37. The corresponding figure for all House candidates is 49 percent (see note 6 for this chapter). The figure for Senate candidates also draws from Paul S. Herrnson, *The Campaign Assessment and Candidate Outreach Project, 1998 Survey* (College Park, Md.: Center for American Politics and Citizenship, University of Maryland, 1998).

38. Center for Responsive Politics, www.opensecrets.org.

7. CAMPAIGN STRATEGY

1. Angus Campbell, Philip E. Converse, Warren E. Miller, and Donald E. Stokes, *The American Voter* (New York: John Wiley, 1960), 541–548; and Donald R. Kinder and David O. Sears, "Public Opinion and Political Action," in *Handbook of Social Psychology,* 3rd ed., ed. Gardner Lindzey and Elliot Aronson (New York: Random House, 1985), 659–741.

2. Figures compiled from Virginia Sapiro, Stephen J. Rosenstone, and National Election Studies, *American National Election Study, 1998: Post-Election Survey* (Ann Arbor: University of Michigan, 1999).

3. On Senate elections, see Alan I. Abramowitz and Jeffrey A. Segal, *Senate Elections* (Ann Arbor: University of Michigan Press, 1992), 39; Peverill Squire, "Challenger Quality and Voting Behavior," *Legislative Studies Quarterly* 17 (1992): 247–263.

4. Figures compiled from Nancy Burns, Donald R. Kinder, and National Election Studies, *American National Election Study, 2002: Post-Election Survey* (Ann Arbor: University of Michigan, Center for Political Studies, 2003).

5. For the importance of information in democratic politics in general and American politics in particular, see, for example, Michael X. Delli Carpini and Scott Keeter, *What Americans Know about Politics and Why It Matters* (New Haven: Yale University Press, 1996), 1–16, 22–61.

6. Alan I. Abramowitz, "A Comparison of Voting for U.S. Senator and Representative in 1978," *American Political Science Review* 74 (1980): 633–640; Gerald C. Wright and Michael B. Berkman, "Candidates and Policy in United States Senate Elections," *American Political Science Review* 80 (1986): 567–588; Mark C. Westlye, *Senate Elections and Campaign Intensity* (Baltimore: Johns Hopkins University Press, 1992), 122–151.

7. Robert D. Brown and James A. Woods, "Toward a Model of Congressional Elections," *Journal of Politics* 53 (1991): 454–473; John R. Zaller, *The Nature and Origins of Mass Opinion* (Cambridge: Cambridge University Press, 1992), chap. 10.

8. See note 4 for this chapter.

9. Wright and Berkman, "Candidates and Policy in United States Senate Elections"; Westlye, *Senate Elections and Campaign Intensity,* chap. 6.

10. See, for example, Raymond E. Wolfinger and Steven J. Rosenstone, *Who Votes?* (New Haven: Yale University Press, 1980), 34–36, 58–60, 102–114.

11. Zaller, *The Nature and Origins of Mass Opinion,* chap. 10; Westlye, *Senate Elections and Campaign Intensity,* esp. chap. 5; Milton Lodge, Marco R. Steenbergen, and Shawn Brau, "The Responsive Voter," *American Political Science Review* 89 (1995): 309–326; Jon K. Dalager, "Voters, Issues, and Elections," *Journal of Politics* 58 (1996): 496–515.

12. See Morris P. Fiorina, *Retrospective Voting in American National Elections* (New Haven: Yale University Press, 1981); Edward R. Tufte, "Determinants of the Outcomes of Midterm Congressional Elections," *American Political Science Review* 69 (1975): 812–826; James E. Campbell, "Explaining Presidential Losses in Midterm Congressional Elections," *Journal of Politics* 47 (1985): 1140–1157; Samuel C. Popkin, *The Reasoning Voter* (Chicago: University of Chicago Press, 1991), esp. chaps. 3 and 4.

13. Alan I. Abramowitz, Albert D. Cover, and Helmut Norpoth, "The President's Party in Midterm Elections," *American Journal of Political Science* 30 (1986): 562–576; Henry W. Chappell Jr. and Motoshi Susuki, "Aggregate Vote Functions for the U.S. Presidency, Senate, and House," *Journal of Politics* 55 (1993): 207–217. See also the studies cited in n. 12.

14. David R. Jones and Monika L. McDermott, "The Responsible Party Government Model in House and Senate Elections," *American Journal of Political Science* 48 (2004): 1–12.

15. Morris P. Fiorina, *Divided Government* (Boston: Allyn and Bacon, 1996), 109–110; Stephen P. Nicholson and Gary M. Segura, "Midterm Elections and Divided Government," *Political Research Quarterly* 52 (1999): 609–629.

16. Alan I. Abramowitz and Kyle L. Saunders, "Ideological Realignment in the U.S. Electorate," *Journal of Politics* 61 (1998): 634–652.

17. Raymond E. Wolfinger, "Candidates and Parties in Congressional Elections," *American Political Science Review* 74 (1980): 622–629; Gary C. Jacobson, *The Politics of Congressional Elections,* 4th ed. (New York: Longman, 1997), 106–108.

18. David R. Mayhew, *Congress: The Electoral Connection* (New Haven: Yale University Press, 1974); Stephen Ansolabehere, James M. Snyder Jr., and Charles Stewart III, "Old Voters, New Voters, and the Personal Vote," *American Journal of Political Science* 44 (2000): 17–34.

19. Richard F. Fenno Jr., *Home Style* (Boston: Little, Brown, 1978), esp. chaps. 3 and 4.

20. The discussion of the congressional election in Colorado's 7th district draws from Kyle L. Saunders and Robert J. Duffy, "Volatility and Volition," in *War Games,* ed. David B. Magleby and Kelly D. Patterson (Provo, Utah: Brigham Young University, Center for the Study of Elections and Democracy, 2007), 74–75; Danielle Kogut, "Democrats on the Rampage" (unpublished paper, University of Maryland, College Park, December 6, 2006); and the candidates' web pages and television advertisements.

21. Bryce Bassett, director of marketing support, Wirthlin Worldwide presentation to the Taft Institute Honors Seminar in American Government, June 15, 1993.

22. See, for example, Robert Axelrod, "Where the Votes Come From," *American Political Science Review* 66 (1972): 11–20.

23. Manuel Perez-Rivas, "Opponent Tries to Make Party Label Stick to Morella," *Washington Post,* March 7, 1996.

24. These generalizations are drawn from responses to question III.3 of the 2002 Congressional Campaign Study, Center for American Politics and Citizenship, University of Maryland.

25. See, for example, Brian F. Schaffner, "Priming Gender," *American Journal of Political Science* 49 (2005): 803–817.

26. Axelrod, "Where the Votes Come From," 11–20; Henry C. Kenski and Lee Sigelman, "Where the Vote Comes From," *Legislative Studies Quarterly* 18 (1993): 367–390.

27. This generalization is from question III.3 of the 2002 Congressional Campaign Study.

28. Saunders and Duffy, "Volatility and Volition"; and Kogut, "Democrats on the Rampage."

29. Ryan Sabalow, "Incumbents Dominate in Congress, State Races," Redding.com, www.redding.com.

30. See note 7 for this chapter.

31. See, for example, Patrick J. Sellers, "Strategy and Background in Congressional Campaigns," *American Journal of Political Science* 92 (1998): 159–171.

32. Joel C. Bradshaw, "Who Will Vote for You and Why," in *Campaigns and Elections American Style,* ed. James A. Thurber and Candice J. Nelson (Boulder, Colo.: Westview Press, 1995), 30–46.

33. The logic behind the battle for the middle ground is presented in Anthony Downs, *An Economic Theory of Democracy* (New York: Harper and Row, 1957), chap. 8.

34. J. Toscano, Greer, Margolis, Mitchell, and Burns, interview July 1, 2007.

35. Ladonna Y. Lee, "Strategy," in *Ousting the Ins,* ed. Stuart Rothenberg (Washington, D.C.: Free Congress Research and Education Foundation, 1985), 18–19.

36. Kathleen Hall Jamieson, *Dirty Politics* (New York: Oxford University Press, 1992), esp. chap. 2.

37. Interview with an anonymous political consultant, December 1992.

38. See Peter Clarke and Susan H. Evans, *Covering Campaigns* (Stanford: Stanford University Press, 1983), 38–45.

39. On the differences between valence issues and position issues, see Donald E. Stokes, "Spatial Models of Party Competition," in *Elections and the Political Order,* ed. Angus Campbell, Philip E. Converse, Warren E. Miller, and Donald E. Stokes (New York: John Wiley, 1966), 161–169.

40. See John R. Petrocik, "Issue Ownership in Presidential Elections, with a 1980 Case Study," *American Journal of Political Science* 40 (1996): 825–850; Owen G. Abbe, Jay Goodliffe, Paul S. Herrnson, and Kelly D. Patterson, "Agenda-Setting in Congressional Elections," *Political Research Quarterly* 56 (2003): 419–430; Constantine Spiliotes and Lynn Vavreck, "Campaign Advertising," *Journal of Politics* 64 (2007): 249–261. For a different perspective, see Noah Kaplan, David K. Park, Travis N. Ridout, "Dialogue in American Campaigns?"*American Journal of Political Science* 50 (2006): 724–736.

41. See, for example, Gary C. Jacobson and Samuel Kernell, "National Forces in the 1986 U.S. House Elections," *Legislative Studies Quarterly* 15 (1990): 65–87.

42. Jacobson, *The Politics of Congressional Elections,* 112–116.

43. On the role of candidates' backgrounds in campaign strategy, see Sellers, "Strategy and Background in Congressional Campaigns."

44. Saunders and Duffy, "Volatility and Volition"; Kogut, "Democrats on the Rampage"; and candidates' web sites, www.perlmutter2006.com and www.odonnellforcongress.com.

45. Wes Anderson, Curt Anderson, and Brian Todd, *A Study of Swing Districts* (Crofton, Md.: On Message Inc., 2006).

46. Jennifer Duffy, "And Now There Are Seven," *National Journal,* http://election.nationaljournal .com/features/110106njpolitics.htm.

47. See, for example, Paul S. Herrnson, J. Celeste Lay, and Atiya Kai Stokes, "Women Running 'as Women,' " *Journal of Politics* 64 (2003): 244–255.

48. James G. Gimpel, *Fulfilling the Contract: The First 100 Days* (Boston: Allyn and Bacon, 1996); Robin Kolodny, "The Contract with America in the 104th Congress," in *The State of the Parties,* ed. John C. Green and Daniel M. Shea (Lanham, Md.: Rowman and Littlefield, 1996), 314–327.

49. Anderson, Anderson, and Todd, *A Study of Swing Districts.*

50. Richard F. Fenno, "If, as Ralph Nader Says, Congress Is 'The Broken Branch,' How Come We Love Our Congressmen So Much?" in *Congress in Change,* ed. Norman J. Ornstein (New York: Praeger, 1975).

51. For a discussion of partisan divergence on the issues, see Spiliotes and Vavreck, "Campaign Advertising," 249–261.

52. See note 40 for this chapter.

53. Fred Hartwig, vice president, Peter Hart and Associates, presentation to the Taft Institute Honors Seminar in American Government, June 15, 1993.

54. Phil Duncan, ed., *Politics in America, 1992* (Washington, D.C.: Congressional Quarterly, 1991), 1133.

55. See, for example, James Innocenzi, "Political Advertising," in *Ousting the Ins,* 53–61; Barbara G. Salmore and Stephen A. Salmore, *Candidates, Parties, and Campaigns* (Washington, D.C.: CQ Press, 1989), 159.

56. On the demobilization thesis see, for example, Stephen Ansolabehere and Shanto Iyengar, *Going Negative* (New York: Free Press, 1995), esp. chap. 5. On the mobilization thesis, see Steven Finkel and John G. Geer, "Spot Check," *American Journal of Political Science* 42 (1998): 573–595; Richard R. Lau and Gerald M. Pomper, "Effects of Negative Campaigning on Turnout in U.S. Senate Elections, 1988–1998," *Journal of Politics* 63 (2001): 804–819; Ken Goldstein and Paul Freedman, "Campaign Advertising and Voter Turnout," *Journal of Politics* 64 (2002): 721–740; Paul Freedman,

Michael Franz, and Kenneth Goldstein, "Campaign Advertising and Democratic Citizenship," *American Journal of Political Science* 48 (2004): 723–741; Martin P. Wattenberg and Craig Leonard Brians, "Negative Campaign Advertising," *American Political Science Review* 93 (1999): 891–900. Also see Richard P. Lau, Lee Sigelman, Caroline Heldman, and Paul Babbitt, "The Effects of Negative Political Advertisements," *American Political Science Review* 93 (1999): 851–875; Kim Fridkin Kahn and Patrick J. Kenney, "Do Negative Campaigns Mobilize or Suppress Turnout?" *American Political Science Review* 93 (1999): 877–889; Paul Freedman and Ken Goldstein, "Measuring Media Exposure and the Effects of Negative Campaign Ads," *American Journal of Political Science* 43 (1999): 1189–1208; Kim Fridkin Kahn and Patrick J. Kenney, *No Holds Barred* (Upper Saddle River, N.J.: Prentice Hall, 2004), 74–84, 91–107.

57. These generalizations are drawn from responses to question 11 of the 1998 Congressional Campaign Study and question 28 of the 1992 Congressional Campaign Study. See also Ken Goldstein and Paul Freedman, "Lessons Learned: Campaign Advertising in the 2000 Elections," *Political Communication* 19 (2002): 5–28.

58. Richard R. Lau, "Negativity in Political Perception," *Political Behavior* 4 (1982): 353–377; Richard R. Lau, "Two Explanations for Negativity Effects in Political Behavior," *American Journal of Political Science* 29 (1985): 110–138; Jamieson, *Dirty Politics,* 41.

59. On differences in the effects of negative campaigning on incumbents and challengers, see Richard R. Lau and Gerald M. Pomper, "Effectiveness of Negative Campaigning in U.S. Senate Elections," *American Journal of Political Science* 46 (2002): 47–66.

60. Lee, "Strategy," 22.

61. Jamieson, *Dirty Politics,* 103.

62. Kogut, "Democrats on the Rampage."

63. Interview with an anonymous campaign manager for a 1992 House candidate, December 1992.

8. CAMPAIGN COMMUNICATIONS

1. Matthew Katz, "Living without TV," *Washington Times,* September 17, 1998.

2. Pew Research Center, "Election Pleases Voters despite Mudslinging," November 1998, www.people-press.org/nov98que.htm.

3. Meredith McGehee, "Election Costs Add Up," *Political Standard,* March 2007.

4. Darrell M. West, *Air Wars* (Washington, D.C.: Congressional Quarterly, 1993), esp. chap. 6.

5. Quoted in Frank I. Luntz, *Candidates, Consultants, and Campaigns* (Oxford: Basil Blackwell, 1988), 77.

6. Darrell M. West, "Political Advertising and News Coverage in the 1992 California U.S. Senate Campaigns," *Journal of Politics* 56 (1994): 1053–1075.

7. This generalization is drawn from responses to question IV.1 of the 2002 Congressional Campaign Study. For Senate campaigns, which are few in number in a given election year, additional information is drawn from the 1992 Congressional Campaign Study, Center for American Politics and Citizenship, University of Maryland; and Paul S. Herrnson, The Campaign Assessment and Candidate Outreach Project, 1999 and 2001, Center for American Politics and Citizenship, University of Maryland.

8. John R. Alford and Keith Henry, "TV Markets and Congressional Elections," *Legislative Studies Quarterly* 9 (1984): 665–675.

9. Luntz, *Candidates, Consultants, and Campaigns,* 76.

10. As noted in Chapters 4 and 5, the BCRA prevents political parties from broadcasting issue advocacy ads using soft money, and it prohibits them from airing such ads ninety days before a primary

and ninety days before the general election. The restrictions on interest groups in place in 2004 and 2006 (later overturned by the Supreme Court) prevented them from broadcasting issue ads thirty days before a primary and sixty days before the general election.

11. The discussion of the congressional election in Colorado's 7th district draws from Kyle L. Saunders and Robert J. Duffy, "Volatility and Volition," in *War Games,* ed. David B. Magleby and Kelly D. Patterson (Provo, Utah: Brigham Young University, Center for the Study of Elections and Democracy, 2007), 74–75; Danielle Kogut, "Democrats on the Rampage" (unpublished paper, University of Maryland, College Park, December 6, 2006); and the candidates' web pages and television advertisements.

12. Stephen Brooks, Michael John Burton, David B. Cohen, Daniel Coffey, Anne C. Hanson, Stephen T. Mockabee, and John C. Green, "The Battle for Ohio," in *War Games,* ed. Magleby and Patterson, 162–178.

13. As discussed in Chapter 7, whereas valence issues, such as a strong economy, have only one side and are universally viewed by voters in a favorable light, position issues, which would include either position in the abortion rights debate, divide voters because they have two or more sides.

14. Jay Bryant, "Paid Media Advertising," in *Campaigns and Elections American Style,* ed. James A. Thurber and Candice J. Nelson (Boulder, Colo.: Westview Press, 2004), 100–102.

15. West, "Political Advertising."

16. Figure provided by J. Quin Monson, Department of Political Science, Brigham Young University, April 16, 2003.

17. Luntz, *Candidates, Consultants, and Campaigns,* 108.

18 Frank Luther Mott, *American Journalism* (New York: Macmillan, 1947), 411–430.

19. West, "Political Advertising."

20. Luntz, *Candidates, Consultants, and Campaigns,* 109–110.

21. West, "Political Advertising."

22. Lee Rainie, "There's a Robot on the Line for You," Pew Research Center, December 20, 2006 (http://pewresearch.org/).

23. Kenneth R. Godwin, *One Billion Dollars of Influence* (Chatham, N.J.: Chatham House, 1988), chaps. 1–3; Jonathan Robbin, "Geodemographics," in *Campaigns and Elections,* ed. Larry J. Sabato (Glenview, Ill.: Scott Foresman, 1989), 105–124.

24. Barbara G. Salmore and Stephen A. Salmore, *Candidates, Parties, and Campaigns* (Washington, D.C.: CQ Press, 1989), 86–87.

25. West, "Political Advertising."

26. Rainie, "There's a Robot on the Line."

27. Lee Rainie, Michael Cornfield, and John Horrigan, *The Internet and Campaign 2004,* Pew Internet and American Life Project, March 6, 2005 (www.pewinternet.org).

28. Rainie, "There's a Robot on the Line."

29. See, for example, Emiliene Ireland and Phil Tjitsu Nash, *Winning Campaigns On Line* (Bethesda, Md.: Science Writers Press, 2001), 3–48.

30. Paul S. Herrnson, Atiya Kai Stokes-Brown, and Matthew Hindman, "Campaign Politics and the Digital Divide," *American Politics Research* 60 (2007): 31–42.

31. Peter Clarke and Susan Evans, *Covering Campaigns* (Stanford: Stanford University Press, 1983), chap. 6.

32. Xandra Kayden, *Campaign Organization* (Lexington, Mass.: D. C. Heath, 1978), 125.

33. Clarke and Evans, *Covering Campaigns,* 60–62; Doris A. Graber, *Mass Media and American Politics,* 4th ed. (Washington, D.C.: CQ Press, 1993), 262, 268–270.

34. Richard Born, "Assessing the Impact of Institutional and Election Forces on Evaluations of Congressional Incumbents," *Journal of Politics* 53 (1991): 764–799.

35. Kim Fridkin Kahn and Patrick J. Kenney, "The Slant of the News," *American Political Science Review* 96 (2002): 381–394.

36. Kayden, *Campaign Organization,* 126; Brian F. Shaffner, "Local News Coverage and the Incumbency Advantage in the U.S. House," *Legislative Studies Quarterly* 31 (2006): 491–511.

37. Clarke and Evans, *Covering Campaigns,* 60–62; Edie N. Goldenberg and Michael W. Traugott, *Campaigning for Congress* (Washington, D.C.: CQ Press, 1984), 127.

38. Anita Dunn, "The Best Campaign Wins," in *Campaigns and Elections American Style,* ed. James A. Thurber and Candice J. Nelson (Boulder, Colo.: Westview Press, 1995), 115.

39. These generalizations are drawn from the following four sources, which together demonstrate that political experience, campaign professionalism, and campaign receipts are positively related to the free media coverage that campaigns receive: (1) candidates' campaign receipts, (2) the political experience measure developed in Chapter 2, (3) the measure of campaign professionalism developed in Chapter 3 (total number of campaign activities performed by paid staff or consultants), and (4) responses to question I.6 of the 2002 Congressional Campaign Study and to question 25 of the 1992 Congressional Campaign Study.

40. See Ronald A. Faucheux, ed. *The Debate Book* (Washington, D.C.: Campaigns & Elections, 2003).

41. West, "Political Advertising."

42. See also Clarke and Evans, *Covering Campaigns,* chap. 4.

43. This generalization is drawn from responses to question I.8 of the 2002 Congressional Campaign Study. See also Kahn and Kenney, "The Slant of the News."

44. On media bias see Herbert J. Gans, "Are U.S. Journalists Dangerously Liberal?" *Columbia Journalism Review* 24 (1985): 29–33. On politicians and the press, see also Lance W. Bennett, *News: The Politics of Illusion* (New York: Longman, 1983), 76–78.

45. John M. Broder, "Growing Absentee Voting Is Reshaping Campaigns," *Washington Post,* October 27, 2006.

46. Alan S. Gerber and Donald P. Green, "The Effects of Canvassing, Telephone Calls, and Direct Mail on Voter Turnout," *American Political Science Review* 94 (2000): 653–664; and Kosuke Imai, "Do Get-Out-the-Vote Calls Reduce Turnout," *American Political Science Review* 99 (2005): 283–300.

47. Rainie, "There's a Robot on the Line."

48. Paul S. Herrnson, "National Party Organizations and the Postreform Congress," in *The Postreform Congress,* ed. Roger H. Davidson (New York: St. Martin's, 1992), 65–66.

49. These generalizations are drawn from responses to questions V.15 and V.16 of the 2002 Congressional Campaign Study.

50. On the effectiveness of personal campaigning see Gerber and Green, "The Effects of Personal Canvassing."

51. See Table 8-3 in the third edition of this book.

52. See Table 8-4 in the fourth edition of this book.

53. Using a narrower victory margin to measure competitiveness did not substantively alter the findings.

9. CANDIDATES, CAMPAIGNS, AND ELECTORAL SUCCESS

1. Larry M. Bartels, "Partisanship and Voting Behavior, 1952–1996," *American Journal of Political Science* 44 (2000): 42–43.

2. Morris P. Fiorina, *Congress* (New Haven: Yale University Press, 1978); John A. Ferejohn, "On the Decline of Competition in Congressional Elections," *American Political Science Review* 71 (1997): 166–177.

3. See Michael Krashinsky and William J. Milne, "Incumbency in U.S. Congressional Elections, 1950–1988," *Legislative Studies Quarterly* 18 (1993); also see the sources cited in chap. 1, nn. 41–43.

4. On the effect of candidate gender on voting behavior see Monika L. McDermott, "Voting Cues in Low-Information Elections," *American Journal of Political Science* 41 (1997): 270–283; Paul S. Herrnson, Celeste Lay, and Atiya Stokes, "Women Running 'as Women,' " *Journal of Politics* 65 (2003): 244–255.

5. The figures for candidate spending on campaign communications equal the sum of candidate expenditures on direct mail, television, radio, campaign literature, newspapers, mass telephone calls, the Internet, voter registration and get-out-the-vote drives, and other campaign communications. These funds exclude money spent on overhead and research and on contributions made to other candidates, party committees, and other political groups, which sometimes constitute considerable sums.

6. Tables 9-1, 9-2, and 9-3 were created using ordinary least squares regressions to analyze data from major-party contested House general elections conducted in 2002. The full regression for Table 9-1 is as follows: Percentage of vote $-$ 57.28 $-$ 1.96/(1.32) district is completely different or completely new $+$ .15/(.03) partisan bias $+$ .92/(.67) ideological strength $-$ 3.71/(2.62) incumbent implicated in scandal $-$ .84/(.21) opponent spending on campaign communications (per \$100,000) $+$ .13/(.20) incumbent spending on campaign communications (per \$100,000) $+$ 5.22/(2.31) incumbent received most media endorsements from local media $+$ 2.02/(1.25) national partisan tide; $F -$ 12.18, $p <$ .0001, Adj. R-square $-$ .48, $N -$ 97. The equations are the product of an extensive model-building process that tested the impact of numerous variables using a variety of statistical techniques. Because the hypotheses that were tested were pre-specified, one-tailed tests of significance were used. A .10 level was used to determine statistical significance because of the small sample sizes. Numerous regressions were tested prior to selecting the final equations. The final models were selected for reasons of statistical fit, parsimony, and ease of interpretation. They are statistically robust. The models replicated to the extent possible similar analyses for the 1992, 1994, 1996, and 1998 elections to verify that the basic relationships that are presented held across elections. More information about the equations and an overview of the survey and statistical methods used to conduct the study are presented at this book's web site (http://herrnson.cqpress.com).

7. Partisan bias was measured using the respondents' answers to question III.2 of the 2002 Congressional Campaign Study, Center for American Politics and Citizenship, University of Maryland.

8. John H. Aldrich and David W. Rohde, "The Logic of Conditional Party Government," in *Congress Reconsidered,* 7th ed., ed. Lawrence C. Dodd and Bruce I. Oppenheimer (Washington, D.C.: CQ Press, 2001), 269–292; Steven S. Smith and Gerald Gamm, "The Dynamics of Party Government in Congress," in *Congress Reconsidered,* 7th ed., ed. Dodd and Oppenheimer, 245–268.

9. A moderate incumbent would win 0 percent extra votes (0 multiplied by 0.92), and an extremely liberal or conservative incumbent would win 2.76 percent extra votes (3 multiplied by 0.92).

10. Shailagh Muray, "By Republicans' Counting 12 GOP House Seats Lost as a Result of Scandals," *Washington Post,* December 1, 2006.

11. Other studies of the impact of campaign spending on congressional elections use all candidate disbursements (including overhead, research, and contributions to candidates and other political organizations). See Gary C. Jacobson, *Money in Congressional Elections* (New Haven: Yale University Press, 1980); Gary C. Jacobson, "The Effects of Campaign Spending in House Elections," *American Journal of Political Science* 34 (1990): 334–362; Jonathan S. Krasno and Donald Philip Green, "Salvation for the Spendthrift Incumbent," *American Journal of Political Science* 32 (1988): 844–907; Donald Philip Green and Jonathan S. Krasno, "Rebuttal to Jacobson's 'New Evidence for Old Arguments,' " *American Journal of Political Science* 34 (1990): 363–372.

12. Jacobson, *Money in Congressional Elections,* 113–123; Jonathan S. Krasno, Donald Philip Green, and Jonathan A. Cowden, "The Dynamics of Fundraising in House Elections," *Journal of*

Politics 56 (1994): 459–474; Christopher Kenney and Michael McBurdett, "A Dynamic Model of Congressional Spending on Vote Choice," *American Journal of Political Science* 36 (1992): 923–937.

13. Figures for spending on campaign communications were not available for 2006. Based on previous editions of this book they were estimated to be 65 percent of a challenger's expenditures on campaigning, excluding contributions to other candidates and party committees.

14. Jacobson, *Money in Congressional Elections.*

15. Local media endorsements are measured using respondents' answers to question I.8 of the 2002 Congressional Campaign Study.

16. The regression equation for incumbents in races in which parties and groups sought to set the campaign agenda is as follows: Percentage of vote $- 59.89 - 4.95/(2.29)$ district is completely different or completely new $+ .10/(.05)$ partisan bias $+ 1.93/(1.27)$ ideological strength $- 9.03/(4.88)$ incumbent implicated in scandal $- 1.02/(.33)$ opponent spending on campaign communications (per \$100,000) $+ .13/(.26)$ incumbent spending on campaign communications (per \$100,000) $+ 4.38/ (3.33)$ incumbent received most endorsements from local media $+ 1.43/(2.25)$ national partisan tide; $F - 6.82, p < .0001$, Adj. R-square $- .54, N - 41$.

17. The full regression equation for Table 9-2 is as follows: Percentage of vote $- 25.29 + .13/(.03)$ partisan bias $+ 2.46/(1.03)$ contested primary $+ 2.50/(1.05)$ targeted own party members, independents, or both $+ 1.84/(1.09)$ advertising focused on challenger's or incumbent's issue positions $+ .31/(.15)$ challenger spending on campaign communications (per \$100,000) $+ .56/(.18)$ opponent spending on campaign communications (per \$100,000) $+ 5.50/(2.12)$ challenger received most endorsements from local media $+ 2.50/(1.17)$ national partisan tide; $F - 19.94, p < .0001$, Adj. R-square $- .52, N - 138$.

18. See, for example, Richard F. Fenno Jr., *Senators on the Campaign Trail* (Norman: University of Oklahoma Press, 1996), 100.

19. Ken Coriale, "How to Defeat an Incumbent," University of Maryland, unpublished paper, December 6, 2006.

20. Figures for spending on campaign communications were compiled from Political Money Line (www.tray.com).

21. Ibid.

22. The figures for each form of campaign communication expenditure (for radio, direct mail, and so on) are regression coefficients that were generated using separate equations. The equations used the same variables as those that appear in Table 9-2, except that they substituted the spending on the specific form of expenditure for overall spending on campaign communications. See the Appendix (http://herrnson.cqpress.com) for more details.

23. The regression equation for challengers in races in which parties and groups sought to set the campaign agenda is as follows: Percentage of vote $- 29.71 + .24/(.05)$ partisan bias $+ 2.54/(1.51)$ contested primary $+ .47/(1.94)$ targeted own party members, independents, or both $+ 1.75/(1.72)$ advertising focused on challenger's or incumbent's issue positions $+ .50/(.001)$ challenger spending on campaign communications (per \$100,000) $+ .20/(.001)$ opponent spending on campaign communications (per \$100,000) $+ 6.62/(2.84)$ challenger received most endorsements from local media $+ 2.22/(1.53)$ national partisan tide; $F - 13.86, p < .0001$, Adj. R-square $- .61, N - 66$.

24. The full regression equation for Table 9-3 is as follows: Percentage of vote $- 24.15 + .17/(.06)$ partisan bias $+ 4.68/(3.15)$ targeted own party members, independents, or both $+ 7.42/(3.84)$ Republican ran on Republican issues $+ 4.18/(3.48)$ Democrat ran on Democratic issues $+ 3.81/(.83)$ natural log of open-seat candidate spending on campaign communications $- 3.06/(.69)$ natural log of opponent spending on campaign communications $+ 6.70/(2.23)$ candidate received most endorsements from local media $+ 8.52/(3.46)$ national partisan tide; $F - 14.69, p < .0001$, Adj. R-square $- .69, N - 50$.

25. Figures for spending on campaign communications were compiled from Political Money Line (www.tray.com).

26. The Pearson correlations between the candidates' percentage of the vote and the communications techniques are as follows: campaign literature, $r - .27$ ($p < .01$); direct mail, $r - .26$ ($p < .01$); television $- .05$ ($p - .31$); radio, $r - .29$ ($p < .01$); campaign literature, $r - .27$ ($p < .01$); direct mail, $r - .26$ ($p < .01$); television $r - .05$ ($p - .31$).

27. Kyle L. Saunders and Robert J. Duffy, "Volatility and Volition," in *War Games*, ed. David B. Magleby and Kelly D. Patterson (Provo, Utah: Brigham Young University, Center for the Study of Elections and Democracy, 2007), 74–75.

28. The regression equation for open-seat candidates in races in which parties and groups sought to set the campaign agenda is as follows: Percentage of vote $- 21.15 - .18/(.08)$ partisan bias $+ 7.39/(4.48)$ targeted own party members, independents, or both $+ 11.21/(5.80)$ Republican ran on Republican issues $+ 1.81/(3.88)$ Democrat ran on Democratic issues $+ 4.35/(1.10)$ natural log of open-seat candidate spending on campaign communications $- 3.40/(1.02)$ natural log of opponent spending on campaign communications $+ 3.65/(2.97)$ candidate received most endorsements from local media $+ 6.39/(4.21)$ national partisan tide; $F - 9.60$, $p < .0001$, Adj. R-square $- .67$, $N - 35$.

29. Jonathan S. Krasno, *Challengers, Competition, and Reelection* (New Haven: Yale University Press, 1994), esp. chaps. 4–7; Peverill Squire and Eric R. A. N. Smith, "A Further Examination of Challenger Quality in Senate Elections," *Legislative Studies Quarterly* 21 (1996): 231–248.

30. Alan I. Abramowitz and Jeffrey A. Segal, *Senate Elections* (Ann Arbor: University of Michigan Press, 1992), 109–114; Kim Fridkin Kahn and Patrick J. Kenney, *The Spectacle of U.S. Senate Campaigns* (Princeton: Princeton University Press, 1999), 216–223; Ken Goldstein and Paul Freedman, "New Evidence for New Arguments," *Journal of Politics* 62 (2000): 1087–1108.

31. John R. Hibbing and John R. Alford, "Constituency Population and Representativeness in the United States Senate," *Legislative Studies Quarterly* 15 (1990): 581–598.

32. Kahn and Kenney, *The Spectacle of U.S. Senate Campaigns*, 12.

33. See Mark C. Westlye, *Senate Elections and Campaign Intensity* (Baltimore: Johns Hopkins University Press, 1992), chaps. 7 and 8; Abramowitz and Segal, *Senate Elections*, 109–115.

34. The coverage of the Brown-DeWine contest draws from Stephen Brooks, Michael John Burton, David B. Cohen, Daniel Coffey, Anne C. Hanson, Stephen T. Mockabee, and John C. Green, "The Battle for Ohio 2006," in *War Games*, ed. Magleby and Patterson, 162–178.

35. The first four items in Table 9-4, and items seven, eight, nine, and sixteen are from the 2002 Congressional Campaign Study (*N* for winners = 137; *N* for losers = 171); the rest are from the 1998 Congressional Campaign Study (*N* for winners = 154; *N* for losers = 159).

36. The figures also include a small number of independent expenditures by individuals and other groups. They exclude issue advocacy ads used in parallel campaigns and the voter mobilization activities comprising coordinated campaigns.

37. See John W. Kingdon, *Candidates for Office: Beliefs and Strategies* (New York: Random House, 1968), chap. 2.

38. See the sources listed in notes 36–40 and 42 of Chapter 1.

39. See Kingdon, *Candidates for Office*, chap. 2.

40. See the sources listed in notes 36–40 and 42 of Chapter 1.

10. ELECTIONS AND GOVERNANCE

1. See Roger H. Davidson and Walter J. Oleszek, *Congress and Its Members*, 8th ed. (Washington, D.C.: CQ Press, 2004), esp. chap. 1.

2. Richard F. Fenno Jr., *Home Style* (Boston: Little, Brown, 1978), 54–61.

3. Ibid., 153.

4. David R. Mayhew, *Congress: The Electoral Connection* (New Haven: Yale University Press, 1974), 49–68.

5. The distance of the member's district from Washington, the cost of local office space, and a few other factors also influence the funds members of the House and Senate receive. Congressional Management Foundation, *Setting Course* (Washington, D.C.: Congressional Management Foundation, 2006), chap. 3.

6. Ibid., chap. 5.

7. Scott Adler, Chariti E. Gent, and Cary B. Overmeyer, "The Home Style Homepage," *Legislative Studies Quarterly* 23 (1998): 585–596.

8. Timothy E. Cook, *Making Laws and Making News* (Washington, D.C.: Brookings Institution Press, 1989), 71.

9. See Adler, Gent, and Overmeyer, "The Home Style Homepage."

10. Laura Langbein, "Money and Access," *Journal of Politics* 48 (1986): 1052–1062; John Wright, "Contributions, Lobbying, and Committee Voting in the U.S. House of Representatives," *American Political Science Review* 84 (1990): 417–438.

11. Richard F. Fenno Jr., *Congressmen in Committees* (Boston: Little, Brown, 1973), 13.

12. Harrison W. Fox and Susan Webb Hammond, *Congressional Staffs* (New York: Free Press, 1977), 121–124.

13. Fenno, *Congressmen in Committees,* 1–14.

14. Kenneth J. Cooper, "The House Freshmen's First Choice," *Washington Post,* January 5, 1993.

15. Davidson and Oleszek, *Congress and Its Members,* 355–357; Susan Webb Hammond, "Congressional Caucuses in the 104th Congress," in *Congress Reconsidered,* 6th ed., ed. Lawrence C. Dodd and Bruce I. Oppenheimer (Washington, D.C.: CQ Press, 1996), 274–292.

16. Jeffrey H. Birnbaum, "The Road to Riches Is Called K Street," *Washington Post,* June 22, 2005.

17. Spending figures include soft money contributions to parties during the 1998 through 2006 elections. Figures compiled from the Center for Responsive Politics (www.opensecrets.org).

18. See, for example, Public Citizen, *The Medicare Drug War* (Washington, D.C.: Public Citizen, 2004), www.citizen.org.

19. Kay Lehman Schlozman and John T. Tierney, *Organized Interests and American Democracy* (New York: Harper and Row, 1986), 289–310.

20. Linda L. Fowler and Ronald D. Shaiko, "The Grass Roots Connection," *American Journal of Political Science* 31 (1987): 484–510; James G. Gimpel, "Grassroots Organizations and Equilibrium Cycles in Group Mobilization and Access," in *The Interest Group Connection,* ed. Paul S. Herrnson, Ronald G. Shaiko, and Clyde Wilcox (Chatham, N.J.: Chatham House, 1998), 100–115.

21. See Gordon Adams, *The Iron Triangle* (New York: Council on Economic Priorities, 1981), 175–180; Hugh Heclo, "Issue Networks and the Executive Establishment," in *The New American Political System,* ed. Anthony King (Washington, D.C.: American Enterprise Institute, 1978), 87–124.

22. See, for example, Sarah A. Binder, *Stalemate* (Washington, D.C.: Brookings Institution Press, 2003), chap. 4. For a different perspective, see David E. Mayhew, *Divided We Govern* (New Haven: Yale University Press, 1991).

23. Paul S. Herrnson and Kelly D. Patterson, "Toward a More Programmatic Democratic Party?" *Polity* 27 (1995): 607–628; Paul S. Herrnson and David M. Cantor, "Party Campaign Activity and Party Unity in the U.S. House of Representatives," *Legislative Studies Quarterly* 22 (1997): 393–415.

24. Kelly D. Patterson, *Political Parties and the Maintenance of Liberal Democracy* (New York: Columbia University Press, 1996), chap. 4.

25. See Leon D. Epstein, *Political Parties in Western Democracies* (New York: Praeger, 1967), 340–348.

26. Joseph Cooper and David W. Brady, "Institutional Context and Leadership Style," *American Political Science Review* 75 (1981): 411–425; David Rohde, *Parties and Leaders in the Postreform House* (Chicago: University of Chicago Press, 1991); Steven S. Smith and Gerald Gamm, "The Dynamics of Party Government in Congress," in *Congress Reconsidered,* 7th ed., ed. Lawrence C. Dodd and Bruce I. Oppenheimer (Washington, D.C.: CQ Press, 2001), 245–268.

27. John H. Aldrich and David W. Rohde, "The Logic of Conditional Party Government," in *Congress Reconsidered*, 7th ed., 269–292.

28. See, for example, David E Price, "Reflections on *Congressional Government* at 120 and Congress at 216," *PS: Political Science and Politics* 39 (2006): 231–235; and Donald R. Wolfensberger, "Can Party Governance Endure in the U.S. House of Representatives?" paper presented at the Conference on Woodrow Wilson's Congressional Government, Woodrow Wilson International Center for Scholars, Washington, D.C., November 14, 2005. See also Barbara Sinclair, *Unorthodox Lawmaking* (Washington, D.C.: CQ Press, 1997), esp. chaps. 1 and 6.

29. Hannah Pitkin, *The Concept of Representation* (Berkeley: University of California Press, 1967).

30. Bruce Cain, John Ferejohn, and Morris Fiorina, *The Personal Vote* (Cambridge: Harvard University Press, 1987).

31. David R. Jones, "Position Taking and Position Avoidance in the U.S. Senate," *Journal of Politics* 65 (August 2003): 851–863.

32. Quoted in Jonathan Weisman, "House Votes to Toughen Laws on Immigration," *Washington Post*, December 17, 2005.

33. See Alex Wayne, "Getting Tough on Illegal Immigration," *CQ Weekly*, December 26, 2005.

34. See, for example, Frances E. Lee, "Geographic Politics in the U.S. House of Representatives," *American Journal of Political Science* 47 (2003): 714–728.

35. Davidson and Oleszek, *Congress and Its Members*, 286–287.

36. John Ferejohn, "Logrolling in an Institutional Context," in *Congress and Policy and Change*, ed. Gerald C. Wright Jr., Leroy N. Rieselbach, and Lawrence C. Dodd (New York: Agathon Press, 1986), 223–253.

37. In recent Congresses, legislation was supposed to stay within a set of overall budgetary limits in order to limit growth of the federal deficit. This zero-sum process has frequently required legislators to cut spending in some areas if they wish to increase it in others.

38. John Solomon and Jeffrey H. Birnbaum, "In the Democratic Congress, Pork Still Gets Served," *Washington Post*, May 24, 2007, A1.

39. Herrnson and Patterson, "Toward a More Programmatic Democratic Party?"; Herrnson and Cantor, "Party Campaign Activity and Party Unity."

40. Paul S. Herrnson, Kelly D. Patterson, and John J. Pitney Jr., "From Ward Heelers to Public Relations Experts," in *Broken Contract?* ed. Stephen C. Craig (Boulder, Colo.: Westview Press, 1996), 251–267.

41. V. O. Key Jr., "A Theory of Critical Elections," *Journal of Politics* 17 (1955): 3–18; Walter Dean Burnham, *Critical Elections and the Mainsprings of American Politics* (New York: Norton, 1970); Everett Carll Ladd Jr. with Charles D. Hadley, *Transformations of the American Party System* (New York: Norton, 1978).

42. Alan I. Abramowitz, "The End of the Democratic Era?" *Political Research Quarterly* 48 (1995): 873–889; Gary C. Jacobson, *The Politics of Congressional Elections*, 4th ed. (New York: Longman, 1997), 219–224.

43. Committee on Political Parties, American Political Science Association, "Toward a More Responsible Two-Party System," *American Political Science Association Review* 44, no. 3, part 2 (1950): 21; Leon D. Epstein, *Political Parties in the American Mold* (Madison: University of Wisconsin Press, 1986), 30–38.

11. CAMPAIGN REFORM

1. See, for example, John R. Hibbing and Elizabeth Theiss-Morse, *Congress as Public Enemy* (Cambridge: Cambridge University Press, 1995), 63–71.

2. These generalizations are drawn from responses to questions V.1 and V.2 of the 2002 Congressional Campaign Study, Center for American Politics and Citizenship, University of Maryland.

3. The winners were somewhat more likely to state that campaign issues were occasionally important and somewhat less likely to state that they were never important. These generalizations are drawn from responses to question V.3 of the 2002 Congressional Campaign Study.

4. Peter L. Francia, John C. Green, Paul S. Herrnson, Lynda W. Powell, and Clyde Wilcox, *The Financiers of Congressional Elections* (New York: Columbia University Press, 2003); Peter L. Francia and Paul S. Herrnson, "The Thrill and the Agony," in *Campaign Battle Lines,* ed. Ronald A. Faucheux and Paul S. Herrnson (Washington: D.C.: Campaigns & Elections, 2002), 284–290; Kevin E. Greene and Paul S. Herrnson, "Running against a Stacked Deck," in *Campaign Battle Lines,* ed. Faucheux and Herrnson, 278–283.

5. These generalizations are drawn from responses to question VIII.3 of the 2002 Congressional Campaign Study.

6. On the passage of the Bipartisan Campaign Reform Act in the House, see Diana Dwyre and Victoria A. Farrar-Myers, *Legislative Labyrinth* (Washington, D.C.: CQ Press, 2001); on unorthodox lawmaking, see Barbara Sinclair, *Unorthodox Lawmaking* (Washington, D.C.: CQ Press, 1997).

7. Anthony Corrado, "Money and Politics," in *The New Campaign Finance Sourcebook,* ed. Anthony Corrado, Thomas Mann, Daniel Ortiz, and Trevor Potter (Washington, D.C.: Brookings Institution Press, 2003).

8. For a more detailed review of the BCRA, see Corrado et al., *The New Campaign Finance Sourcebook.*

9. Adam Clymer, "Foes of Campaign Finance Bill Plot Legal Attack," *New York Times,* February 17, 2002.

10. Helen Dewar, "Lawsuits Challenge New Campaign Law," *Washington Post,* May 8, 2003.

11. Amy Keller, "Debate Rocks FEC," *Roll Call,* March 4, 2002; Helen Dewar, "FEC Rules on 'Soft Money' Challenged," *Washington Post,* October 9, 2002.

12. Paul S. Herrnson, "The Bipartisan Campaign Reform Act and Congressional Elections," in *Congress Reconsidered,* 8th ed., ed. Lawrence C. Dodd and Bruce I. Oppenheimer (Washington, D.C.: CQ Press, 2005), 107–135.

13. The parties of the golden age, especially the political machines, also had shortcomings, including corruption, secrecy, and formal and informal barriers to the participation of women and various racial, ethnic, and religious groups. For some lively accounts, see William Riordan, *Plunkitt of Tammany Hall* (New York: E. P. Dutton, 1905); and Mike Royko, *Boss: Richard J. Daley* (New York: E. P. Dutton, 1971).

14. See Hibbing and Theiss-Morse, *Congress as Public Enemy,* esp. chap. 5.

15. L. Sandy Maisel, "Competition in Congressional Elections," in *Rethinking Political Reform,* ed. Ruy A. Teixeira, L. Sandy Maisel, and John J. Pitney Jr. (Washington, D.C.: Progressive Foundation, 1994), 29.

16. Gary W. Cox and Michael C. Munger, "Closeness, Expenditures, and Turnout in the 1982 U.S. House Elections," *American Political Science Review* 83 (1989): 217–231.

17. Free television and radio time is an idea that has been around for many years. See, for example, Twentieth Century Fund Commission on Campaign Costs, *Voters' Time* (New York: Twentieth Century Fund, 1969); and Campaign Study Group, "Increasing Access to Television for Political Candidates" (Cambridge: Institute of Politics, Harvard University, 1978).

18. Paul S. Herrnson, *Party Campaigning in the 1980s* (Cambridge: Harvard University Press, 1988), 127.

19. Doris A. Graber, *Mass Media and American Politics,* 4th ed. (Washington, D.C.: CQ Press, 1993), 53–55.

20. Larry J. Sabato, *Paying for Elections* (New York: Twentieth Century Fund, 1989), 31.

21. For more information on this bill, see "Summary of S. 3124, the Free Air Time Bill Introduced by Senators McCain, Feingold and Durbin," *The Political Standard,* Washington, D.C.: Alliance for Better Campaigns, October 2002.

22. See Ruth S. Jones and Warren E. Miller, "Financing Campaigns," *Western Political Quarterly* 38 (1985): 190, 192.

23. For countries and American states that offer citizens the opportunity to obtain tax credits for political contributions, see the case studies in Arthur B. Gunlicks, ed., *Campaign and Party Finance in North America and Western Europe* (Boulder, Colo.: Westview Press, 1993).

24. Francia et al., *The Financiers of Congressional Elections.*

25. Matthew Mosk, "Resignation of Lawyers at FEC Raises Concern," *Washington Post,* January 18, 2007.

26. Associated Press, "Voter Turnout a Tad Higher than Last Midterm," November 8, 2006 (www.msnbc.msn.com/id/15621554/).

27. Raymond E. Wolfinger and Stephen J. Rosenstone, *Who Votes?* (New Haven: Yale University Press, 1980), 61–88.

28. J. Eric Oliver, "The Effects of Eligibility Restrictions and Party Activity on Absentee Voting and Voter Turnout," *American Journal of Political Science* 40 (1996): 498–513; Peter L. Francia and Paul S. Herrnson, "The Effects of Campaign Effort and Election Reform on Voter Participation in State Legislative Elections," *State Politics and Policy Quarterly* 4 (2004): 74–93.

29. CalTech/MIT Voting Technology Report, "What Is; What Could Be," July 2002, 8–9, 21, 32 (www.vote.caltech.edu).

30. Paul S. Herrnson, "Improving Election Technology and Administration," *Stanford Law and Policy Review* 13 (2002): 147–159.

31. Paul S. Herrnson, Richard G. Niemi, Michael J. Hanmer, Benjamin B. Bederson, Frederick G. Conrad, Michael W. Traugott, *Voting Technology: The Not-So-Simple Act of Casting a Ballot* (Washington, D.C.: Brookings Institution Press, 2007).

Index

*References to figures and tables are denoted by "f" and "t" following the page numbers.
Alphabetization is letter-by-letter (e.g., "Freedom" precedes "Free media").
Names in the notes are in a separate index.*

Notes Name Index